REPORTING

REPORTING

Lillian Ross

DODD, MEAD & COMPANY
NEW YORK

Library of Congress Cataloging in Publication Data

Ross, Lillian.
  Reporting.

  Reprint of the ed. published by Simon and Schuster,
New York; with new introd.
  I. Title.
[AC8.R64 1981]   070.4'33   80-28929
ISBN 0-396-07948-2
ISBN 0-396-07949-0 (pbk.)

*Remembering my mother
and my father*

CONTENTS

INTRODUCTION

Every reporter must work in his own way, speak with his own voice, find his individual style. So there is no reason for one writer to lecture another on how to do his work. I have been asked repeatedly "how" I did the reporting pieces in this book. There is no "how" that can be passed along, because the "how" of each writer's work resides somewhere deep in the fabric of that writer's being. All I have to offer as answers to the question of "how" are some principles—some of them old, instinctive ones that guided me from the beginning, and others that I learned, and learned to define, along the way. They are right for *me*. They may be wrong for others, but, for better or worse, they are mine. Here they are, as I have formulated them for myself and incorporated them into my thinking:

1. Write as clearly and simply and straightforwardly as possible. In poetry and fiction there may be a place for ambiguity, but not in reporting.

2. Write about people, situations, events that attract you, for whatever reason. You may be attracted to an event that you do not approve of, but you must, for one reason or another, like *being* there.

3. Do not write about anyone who does not want to be written about.

4. Do not write about anyone you do not like.

5. Trust the way you react to a person in the first few moments of meeting him.

6. As soon as another human being permits you to write about him, he is opening his life to you, and you must be constantly aware that you have a responsibility in regard to that person. Even if that person encourages you to be careless about how you use your intimate knowledge of him, or if he is indiscreet about himself, or actually eager to invade his own privacy, it is up to you to use your own judgment in deciding what to write. Just because someone "said it" is no reason for you to use it in your writing. Your obligation to the people you write about does not end once your piece is in print. Anyone who trusts you enough to talk about himself to you is giving you a form of friendship. You are not "doing him a favor" by writing about him, even if he happens to be in a profession or business in which publicity of any kind is valued. If you spend weeks or months with someone, not only taking his time and energy but entering into his life, you naturally become his friend. A friend is not to be used and abandoned; the friendship established in writing about someone usually continues to grow after what has been written is published.

7. Do not permit yourself to be "persuaded" by a publisher or literary agent or a relative to write about anything or anyone in which you have no true, natural interest. Some agents may want you to take on a project for financial reasons. The money offered is often designated as the element that is supposed to "free you" to "do what you want." If you're going to "do what you want," you will do it now, not at some later date. One certain method of preventing yourself from doing what you want is to do something "for the money." (This principle, like some of the others, obviously does not apply to newspaper reporting, in which a reporter must cover the story he is assigned to cover.)

8. Do not use a tape recorder. The machine, surprisingly, distorts the truth. The tape recorder is a fast and easy and lazy way of getting a lot of talk down, but conversationalists are not necessarily writers. A lot of talk does not in itself make an interview, or an interesting interview. Not only are tape-recorded interviews mis-

leading; they are usually boring. (Even television interviews usually distort the truth. For one thing, the personality of the interviewer, whether it is pleasant or witty or intimidating, is intrusive and distracting, for he is focussing on his purpose: to put on a "show." Presenting an image of a person is not presenting the person.) When a tape recorder is used for an interview, the person who is supposed to be talking to you is self-consciously talking to a machine. That in itself tends to distort. In addition, *you* are not *listening*; the machine is listening for you. A writer must use his own ears to listen, must use his own eyes to look. That is the only way you are going to get your subject to react to you directly. And that is also the only way you are going to be able to take this raw material and fashion it into writing.

What about quoting? You shape *all* the writing, including whatever you quote. In the relationship you establish with the person you are writing about, it is up to you to find the quotations that get to the truth of what that person is. That does not mean that you make up quotations. Somewhere along the line, in the time you spend with your subject, you will find the quotations that are significant—that reveal the character of the person, that present as close an approximation of the truth as you can achieve.

9. Reporting is difficult, partly because the writer does not have the leeway to play around with the lives of people, as he does in fiction. There are many other restrictions, too. The soul and nature of any writer are invariably found in his writing. In reporting, he mush watch his own weaknesses. A reporter who has meanness or pettiness in his nature, or is superficial or sentimental, or is closely attached to other worlds—of wealth, glamour, academe, politics, gossip, show business, say—may not only impose those tendencies on what he sees and hears but try to reduce his subjects to what is within him. Actually, your attention at all times should be on your subject, not on you. Do not call attention to yourself. As a reporter, serve your subject, do not serve yourself. Do not, in effect, say, "Look at *me*. See what a great reporter I am!" Do not, if you want to reveal that the Emperor is not wearing any clothes, write, "I am showing that the Emperor is naked."

A few more admonitions: do not promote yourself; do not advertise yourself; do not sell yourself. If you have a tendency to do these things, you should go into some line of work that may benefit from your talents as a promoter, a salesman, or an actor. Too many extraneous considerations have been imposed on reporting in recent years, and it is time now to ask writers who would be reporters to report.

10. Avoid interpretation, analysis, passing judgment, telling readers what to think. Stick to what can be observed and reported. Come as close as you can to telling the truth, and let the reader make up his own mind. If you have an uncontrollable impulse to make your opinions explicit, write a polemic or an essay or a pamphlet or an editorial, but don't try to do reporting. Having a point of view is another matter: your point of view should be implicit in the facts you present.

11. If you are on the staff of a newspaper and if what you want is to become a writer, don't stay on the staff for more than two or three years. Do not stay on "news magazines" for more than a couple of years, either. Newspaper-reporting experience may be helpful in the following ways: in learning a kind of discipline, in getting a sense of the multitude of subjects you may want to write about, in developing self-control in the face of frustration. Occasionally, working on a newspaper may give someone of exceptional will power and talent an interlude for self-discovery. Staying for very long on a news magazine, however, may actually train you *not* to see, hear, or feel accurately and naturally and may also lead you to forget that you ever learned the meaning of the word "responsible." If you must choose between newspaper experience and news-magazine experience, I would recommend the former. Although newspapers have suffered in recent years from a self-imposed pressure to be "lively" in order to imitate the news magazines, they still offer an opportunity to learn to write with clarity and with speed, and, of course, they do teach you to meet deadlines. The rewrite system common to news magazines is ruinous to a writer. It leads to distortion and inaccuracy. The reporter loses control over his story. "Style" is the word that news magazines have invented for the result of their efforts to make things "jazzy," "snappy," and "lively." The word "interesting" on news magazines usually means "hopped-up" and "artificially heightened." "Eye-catching" leads are artificial. They have nothing to do with writing to get at the truth.

At this point, I might as well mention two other words and one phrase that have muddied the vocabulary of journalism. One of the words is "reportage." It is pretentious. A writer doesn't do "writage." A writer does writing. A reporter does reporting. The other word is "investigative." Every reporter investigates. That is what he does. The phrase is "in-depth reporting." All reporting should be as deep as it deserves to be.

12. Similarly, the length of a piece is not an arbitrary matter. Your piece should be as long as it needs to be for you to convey what you have to say about a situation, an event, a person.

13. Don't show your writing to other writers or ask their opinion of what you write. Keep it to yourself if you want it to be an expression of you and only you. The better and stronger the writer, the less reason there is for him to ask other writers for their opinion. What most writers need is not another writer but an editor—someone to talk to about their work, someone capable of giving guidance and help without getting in the writers' way. A helpful editor should have the following qualities: understanding of and sympathy for writers; the editorial talent to recognize and appreciate journalistic and literary talent; an openness to all kinds of such talent; confidence and strength in his own judgment; resistance to fads and fakery in publishing; resistance to corruption and opportunism, to exhortations from people, including writers and other editors, who are concerned with "popularity" and "the market"; moral and mental strength, and the physical strength to sustain these; energy and resourcefulness in helping writers discover what they should write about; literally unlimited patience with selfishness and egotism; the generosity and character required to give away his own creativity and pour it into a group of greedy and usually ungrateful writers. This kind of editor is a rarity. If you're lucky, you may find one. Avoid the following kind of editor: one who does not like writers.

14. Do not be afraid to acknowledge that you have learned from other writers. All good writers, somewhere along the line, learn from reading what others have written. I have had dozens of wonderful writers to learn from at *The New Yorker*—ranging over the years from Joseph Mitchell, Philip Hamburger, and Berton Roueché to George W. S. Trow, Mark Singer, and Jamaica Kincaid. Do not spend your time trying to kill off other writers and other reporters. The more talented you are, the more you can learn from

other writers, and the freer you are to admit that you have learned. The very young sometimes feel that unless *they* discovered something, it has no value. If what you want is to become a good writer, get out from under the deluge of propaganda about doing what is "new." Don't worry about the "new." Just find what is a natural expression of yourself.

15. Let your work speak for itself. Do not go on television to sell yourself or your books to as much of the public as you can reach. That is to play the role of a self-promoter, not of a reporter or a writer. It is a good idea to decide by the time you are twenty-two whether you have something within yourself pushing you to become either a writer or a promoter, because the two activities are mutually exclusive. Whatever you are as a writer that is special or different will be recognized by readers in their response to what you write. Writing is, after all, for readers. You must be strong in resisting the attempts of your publisher—if you move from newspapers or magazines to books—to enlist you in the cause of selling your book. That is not easy to do. Publishers are well-educated, friendly people who like writers, who like culture, who often smoke pipes and have good cooks, and who occasionally have their own private tennis courts. Many editors at publishing houses are very astute and helpful in matters of syntax, grammar, clarity, and organization. Many have good taste. A few have an eye for beauty in making a book or a dust jacket. All are very knowledgeable about paperback sales, about movie sales, about spin-offs into television series, about the mass market, about the scholastic market, about the market in general. But then they are in a business whose purpose is to sell books. They may say to you, "You want your book to *sell*, don't you?" You can't very well say, "No, I don't want my book to sell." Or they may say, "We want to put your picture on the dust jacket —a picture that makes you look interesting." It's difficult to reject the prospect of being shown, looking clever, at your desk, but you will find it resistible if you try. The moment—literally, the moment —you embark on exploiting yourself or anything that you love, you have spoiled what you loved, or what you wanted to impart of yourself in your writing.

16. Hold on to the quietness in your life. If you betray yourself, there may be a dreadful bitterness in your soul, and that bitterness will make it difficult for you to work. There are many ways to live,

of course, and I would not condemn the material things that selling a lot of books might bring. I would never condemn your having your own private tennis court with a lot of friendly tennis players to run around with on it. But there is a deeper longing in me, and a love of my work—small as its scale may be—that at the same time gives me a kind of contentment. I love having my say in reporting. But to go on a television talk show to sell myself and my books or to try to be a stand-up comic or a sit-down celebrity in order to interest people in reading what I *write* would be the ultimate foolishness. It would be a betrayal of the force within me that made me want to write in the first place.

17. Write to please yourself. That does not mean that you are not responsible to your readers. You are. But if you are going to carry out your responsibility you must not cater to them or condescend to them or regard them as a "market" and try to give them what you think they want. Rather, you will be showing them the ultimate respect if you assume that what they want from you is for you to be true to yourself and to do your best work.

REPORTING

1

THE YELLOW BUS

A FEW SUNDAYS AGO, in the late, still afternoon, a
bright-yellow school bus, bearing the white-on-blue license plate of
the State of Indiana and with the words "BEAN BLOSSOM TWP MON-
ROE COUNTY" painted in black letters under the windows on each
side, emerged into New York City from the Holland Tunnel. Inside the bus were eighteen members of the senior class of the Bean
Blossom Township High School, who were coming to the city for
their first visit. The windows of the bus, as it rolled out into Canal
Street, were open, and a few of the passengers leaned out, deadpan and silent, for a look at Manhattan. The rest sat, deadpan and
silent, looking at each other. In all, there were twenty-two people
in the bus: eleven girls and seven boys of the senior class; their
English teacher and her husband; and the driver (one of the regular bus drivers employed by the township for the school) and his
wife. When they arrived, hundreds of thousands of the city's eight
million inhabitants were out of town. Those who were here were
apparently minding their own business; certainly they were not
handing out any big hellos to the visitors. The little Bean Blossom
group, soon to be lost in the shuffle of New York's resident and
transient summer population, had no idea of how to elicit any

hellos—or, for that matter, any goodbyes or how-are-yous. Their plan for visiting New York City was divided into three parts: one, arriving; two, staying two days and three nights; three, departing.

Well, they had arrived. To get here, they had driven eight hundred and forty miles in thirty-nine and a half hours, bringing with them, in addition to spending money of about fifty dollars apiece, a fund of $957.41, which the class had saved up collectively over the past six years. The money represented the profits from such enterprises as candy and ice-cream concessions at school basketball games, amusement booths at the class (junior) carnival, and ticket sales for the class (senior) play, "Mumbo-Jumbo." For six years, the members of the class had talked about how they would spend the money to celebrate their graduation. Early this year, they voted on it. Some of the boys voted for a trip to New Orleans, but they were outvoted by the girls, all of whom wanted the class to visit New York. The class figured that the cost of motels and hotels—three rooms for the boys, three rooms for the girls, one room for each of the couples—would come to about four hundred dollars. The bus driver was to be paid three hundred and fifty dollars for driving and given thirty for road, bridge, and tunnel tolls. Six members of the class, who were unable to participate in the trip, stayed home. If there should be any money left over, it would be divided up among all the class members when the travellers returned to Bean Blossom Township. The names of the eighteen touring class members were: R. Jay Bowman, Shelda Bowman (cousin of R. Jay), Robert Britton, Mary Jane Carter, Lynn Dillon, Ina Hough, Thelma Keller, Wilma Keller (sister of Thelma), Becky Kiser, Jeanne Molnar, Nancy Prather, Mike Richardson, Dennis Smith, Donna Thacker, Albert Warthan, Connie Williams, Larry Williams (not related to Connie), and Lela Young.

It was also a first visit to New York for the English teacher, a lively young lady of twenty-eight named Polly Watts, and for her husband, Thomas, thirty-two, a graduate student in political science at Indiana University, in Bloomington, which is about twelve miles from the Bean Blossom Township school. The only people on the bus who had been to New York before were the driver, a husky, uncommunicative man of forty-nine named Ralph Walls, and his wife, Margaret, thirty-nine and the mother of his seven children, aged twenty-one to two, all of whom were left at home. Walls was the only adviser the others had on what to do in New York. His advice consisted of where to stay (the Hotel Woodstock, on West Forty-third Street, near Times Square) and where to eat (Hector's Cafeteria, around the corner from the hotel).

The Bean Blossom Township school is in the village of Stinesville, which has three hundred and fifty-five inhabitants and a town pump. A couple of the seniors who made the trip live in Stinesville; the others live within a radius of fifteen miles or so, on farms or in isolated houses with vegetable gardens and perhaps a cow or two. At the start of the trip, the travellers gathered in front of their school shortly after midnight, and by one in the morning, with every passenger occupying a double seat in the bus (fifty-four-passenger, 1959 model), and with luggage under the seats, and suits and dresses hung on a homemade clothes rack in the back of the bus, they were on their way.

The senior-class president, R. (for Reginald) Jay Bowman, was in charge of all the voting on the trip. A wiry, energetic eighteen-year-old with a crew haircut, he had been president of the class for the past five years, and is one of two members of the class who intend to go to college. He wants to work, eventually, for the United States Civil Service, because a job with the government is a steady job. Or, in a very vague way, he thinks he may go into politics. With the help of a hundred-and-two-dollar-a-year scholarship, he plans to pay all his own expenses at Indiana University. The other student who is going to college has also chosen Indiana University. She is Nancy Prather, an outdoorsy, freckle-faced girl whose father raises dairy and beef cattle on a two-hundred-and-fifty-acre farm and who is the class salutatorian. As for the valedictorian, a heavyset, firm-mouthed girl named Connie Williams, she was planning to get married a week after returning home from New York. The other class members expected, for the most part, to get to work at secretarial or clerical jobs, or in automobile or electronic-parts factories in Bloomington. The New York trip was in the nature of a first and last fling.

·　　·　　·

Ralph Walls dropped the passengers and their luggage at the Woodstock and then took the bus to a parking lot on Tenth Avenue, where he was going to leave it for the duration of the visit. His job, he had told his passengers, was to drive *to* New York, not *in* it. He had also told them that when he got back to the Woodstock he was going to sleep, but had explained how to get around the corner to Hector's Cafeteria. The boys and girls signed the register and went to their rooms to get cleaned up. They all felt let down. They had asked Walls whether the tall buildings they saw as they came uptown from the Holland Tunnel made up the skyline, and Walls had said he didn't know. Then they had asked him which was the Empire State Building, and he had said they would have to take a tour to find out. Thus put off, they more or less resigned themselves to saving any further questions for a tour. Jay Bowman said that he would see about tours before the following morning.

Mrs. Watts and her husband washed up quickly and then, notwithstanding the bus driver's advice, walked around the Times Square area to see if they could find a reasonably priced and attractive place to have supper. They checked Toffenetti's, almost across the street from the hotel, but decided it was too expensive (hamburger dinners at two dollars and ten cents, watermelon at forty cents) and too formidable. When they reconvened with the senior class in the lobby of the Woodstock, they recommended that everybody have this first meal at Hector's. The party set out— for some reason, in Indian file—for Hector's, and the first one inside was Mike Richardson, a husky, red-haired boy with large, swollen-looking hands and sunburned forearms. A stern-voiced manager near the door, shouting "Take your check! Take your check!" at all incomers, gave the Indiana group the same sightless once-over he gave everybody else. The Bean Blossom faces, which had been puzzled, fearful, and disheartened since Canal Street, now took on a look of resentment. Mike Richardson led the line to the counter. Under a sign reading "BAKED WHITEFISH," a white-aproned counterman looked at Mike and said, "Come on, fella!" Mike glumly took a plate of fish and then filled the rest of his tray with baked beans, a roll, iced tea, and strawberry shortcake (check—

$1.58). The others quickly and shakily filled their trays with fish, baked beans, a roll, iced tea, and strawberry shortcake. Sweating, bumping their trays and their elbows against other trays and other elbows, they found seats in twos and threes with strangers, at tables that still had other people's dirty dishes on them. Then, in a nervous clatter of desperate and noisy eating, they stuffed their food down.

"My ma cooks better than this," said Albert Warthan, who was sitting with Mike Richardson and Larry Williams. Albert, the eldest of seven children of a limestone-quarry worker, plans to join the Army and become a radar technician.

"I took this filet de sole? When I wanted somethin' else, I don't know what?" Mike said.

"I like the kind of place you just set there and decide what you want," said Larry, who is going to work on his grandfather's farm.

"My ma and pa told me to come home when it was time to come home, and not to mess around," Albert said. "I'm ready to chuck it and go home right now."

"The whole idea of it is just to see it and get it over with," Mike said.

"You got your money divided up in two places?" Albert asked. "So's you'll have some in one place if it gets stolen in t'other?"

The others nodded.

"Man, you can keep this New York," said Larry. "This place is too hustly, with everybody pushin' and no privacy. Man, I'll take the Big Boy any old day."

Frisch's Big Boy is the name of an Indiana drive-in chain, where a hamburger costs thirty cents. The general effect of Hector's Cafeteria was to give the Bean Blossom Class of 1960 a feeling of unhappiness about eating in New York and to strengthen its faith in the superiority of the Big Boys back home.

Jay Bowman went from table to table, polling his classmates on what they wanted to do that evening. At first, nobody wanted to do anything special. Then they decided that the only special thing they wanted to do was to go to Coney Island, but they wanted to save Coney Island for the wind-up night, their last night in New York. However, nobody could think of anything to do that first night, so Jay took a re-vote, and it turned out that almost all of them wanted to go to Coney Island right away. Everybody but three girls voted to go to Coney Island straight from Hector's. Mrs. Watts was mildly apprehensive about this project, but Mike Richardson assured her it was easy; somebody at the hotel had told him that all they had to do was go to the subway and ask the cashier in the booth which train to take, and that would be that. Mrs. Watts said she was going to walk around a bit with her husband. The three girls who didn't want to go to Coney Island explained that they firmly believed the class should "have fun" on its last night in the city, and not before. The three were Ina Hough, whose father works in an R.C.A.-television manufacturing plant in Indianapolis (about fifty miles from Stinesville); Lela Young, whose foster father works in a Chevrolet-parts warehouse in Indianapolis; and Jeanne Molnar, whose father is a draftsman at the Indiana Limestone Company, in Bloomington. All three already knew that they disliked New York. People in New York, they said, were all for themselves.

At nine o'clock, while most of their classmates were on the Brighton B.-M.T. express bound for Coney Island, the three girls walked to Sixth Avenue and Fiftieth Street with Mr. and Mrs. Watts, who left them at that point to take a walk along Fifth Avenue. The girls stood in a long line of people waiting to get into the Radio City Music Hall. After twenty minutes, they got out of the line and walked over to Rockefeller Plaza, where they admired the fountain, and to St. Patrick's Cathedral, which looked bigger to them than any church they had ever seen. The main church attended by the Bean Blossom group is the Nazarene Church. No one in the senior class had ever talked to a Jew or to more than one Catholic, or—with the exception of Mary Jane Carter, daughter of the Nazarene minister in Stinesville—had ever heard of an Episcopalian. At ten o'clock, the three girls returned to the Music Hall line, which had dwindled, but when they got to the box office they were told that they had missed the stage show, so they decided to skip the Music Hall and take a subway ride. They took an Independent subway train to the West Fourth Street station, which a subway guard had told them was where to go for

Greenwich Village. They decided against getting out and looking, and in favor of going uptown on the same fare and returning
to their hotel. Back at the Woodstock, where they shared a room,
they locked themselves in and started putting up their hair, telling
each other that everybody in New York was rude and all for himself.

At Coney Island, the Indiana travellers talked about how they
could not get over the experience of riding for forty-five minutes,
in a shaking, noisy train, to get there.

"The long ride was a shock to what I expected," said Albert
Warthan.

Nancy Prather said she didn't like the looks of the subway or
the people on it. "You see so many different people," she said.
"Dark-complected ones one minute, light-complected ones the
next."

"I hate New York, actually," Connie Williams said. "I'm satisfied with what we got back home."

"Back home, you can do anything you please in your own back
yard any time you feel like it, like hootin' and hollerin' or anything," said Larry Williams. "You don't ever get to feel all cooped
up."

"I sort of like it here in Coney Island," said Dennis Smith. "I
don't feel cooped up."

Dennis's buddies looked at him without saying anything. His
"sort of liking" Coney Island was the first sign of defection from
Indiana, and the others did not seem to know what to make of
it. Dennis is a broad-shouldered boy with large, beautiful, wistful
blue eyes and a gold front tooth.

"I hate it," Connie said.

Jay Bowman organized as many of the group as he could to take
a couple of rides on the Cyclone. Most of the boys followed these
up with a ride on the parachute jump, and then complained that
it wasn't what they had expected at all. Some of the boys and girls
went into the Spookorama. They all rode the bobsled, and to top
the evening off they rode the bumper cars. "The Spookorama was
too imitation to be frightening," Albert said. Before leaving Coney

Island, Jay got to work among his classmates, polling them on how much money they were prepared to spend on a tour of the city the next day. They stayed in Coney Island about an hour. Nobody went up to the boardwalk to take a look at the ocean, which none of the class had ever seen. They didn't feel they had to look at the ocean. "We knew the ocean was there, and anyway we aim to see the ocean on the tour tomorrow," Jay said later.

When Ina, Lela, and Jeanne got in line for the Music Hall, the Wattses took their stroll along Fifth Avenue and then joined a couple of friends, Mike and Ardis Cavin. Mike Cavin plays clarinet with the United States Navy Band, in Washington, D.C., and is studying clarinet—as a commuter—at the Juilliard School of Music. At Madison Avenue and Forty-second Street, the two couples boarded a bus heading downtown, and while talking about where to get off they were taken in hand by an elderly gentleman sitting near them, who got off the bus when they did and walked two blocks with them, escorting them to their destination—the Jazz Gallery, on St. Mark's Place. Mike Cavin wanted to hear the tenor-saxophone player John Coltrane. The Wattses stayed at the Jazz Gallery with the Cavins for three hours, listening, with patient interest, to modern jazz. They decided that they liked modern jazz, and especially Coltrane. Leaving the Jazz Gallery after one o'clock, the two couples took buses to Times Square, walked around for twenty minutes looking for a place where they could get a snack, and finally, because every other place seemed to be closed, went to Toffenetti's. Back at the hotel, the Wattses ran into one of the Coney Island adventurers, who told them that Ina, Lela, and Jeanne were missing, or at least were not answering their telephone or knocks on their door. Mr. Watts got the room clerk, unlocked the girls' door, and found them sitting on their beds, still putting up their hair. Everybody was, more or less unaccountably, angry—the three girls who hadn't gone to Coney Island, the girls who had, the boys who had, the Wattses, and the room clerk. The Wattses got to bed at 3:30 A.M.

At 6:30 A.M., Mrs. Watts was called on the telephone. Message: One of the anti-Coney Island trio was lying on the floor of the room weeping and hysterical. Mrs. Watts called the room clerk, who called a doctor practicing in the Times Square area, who rushed over to the hotel, talked with the weeping girl for twenty minutes, and left her with a tranquillizing pill, which she refused to take.

By the time everybody had settled down enough to eat breakfast in drugstores and get ready to start out, it was after nine in the morning, half an hour behind time for the scheduled (by unanimous vote) all-day tour of the city by chartered sightseeing bus, at six dollars per person. The tour was held up further while Mrs. Watts persuaded the weeper to take a shower, in an effort to encourage her to join the tour. After the shower, the unhappy girl stopped crying and declared that she would go along. By the time the group reached the Bowery, she felt fine, and in China-town, like the other boys and girls, she bought a pair of chopsticks, for thirty-five cents. The Cathedral of St. John the Divine was the highlight of the tour for many of the students, who were delighted to hear that some of the limestone used in the cathedral interior had very likely come from quarries near Stinesville. Mrs. Watts, on the other hand, who had studied art, had taught art for five years at Huntington College, in Huntington, Indiana, and had taken an accredited art tour of Europe before her marriage, indignantly considered the cathedral "an imitation of European marvels."

Mrs. Watts took the Bean Blossom teaching job, at thirty-six hundred dollars a year, last fall, when her husband decided to abandon a concrete-building-block business in Huntington in order to study for a Ph.D. in political science, a subject he wants to teach. Since he had decided that Indiana University was the place to do this, they moved from Huntington—where Mr. Watts had won the distinction of being the youngest man ever to hold the job of chairman of the Republican Party of Huntington County —to Bloomington. Mrs. Watts drives the twelve miles from Bloomington to Stinesville every day. She teaches English to the tenth, eleventh, and twelfth grades, and, because the school had no Spanish teacher when she signed up for the job, she teaches Spanish, too. She considers the Bean Blossom Township school the most democratic school she has ever seen. "They vote on everything," she says. "We have an average of two votes on something or other every day." Having thus been conditioned to voting as a way of life, Mrs. Watts left the voting on day-to-day plans for the group visit in the capable hands of Jay Bowman. He solved the problem of the tour's late start that morning by taking a vote on whether or not to leave out the Empire State Building. It was promptly voted out of the tour, and voted in for some later time as a separate undertaking.

The tour included a boat trip to the Statue of Liberty, where the group fell in with crushing mobs of people walking to the top of the torch. Mrs. Watts found the experience nightmarish, and quit at the base of the torch. Most of the boys and girls made it to the top. "There are a hundred and sixty-eight steps up the torch, and there were forty thousand people ahead of me, but I was determined to climb up it," Jay Bowman reported to Mrs. Watts. "It took me twenty minutes, and it was worthwhile. The thing of it was I had to do it."

For the tour, Jay, like the other boys, had put on dress-up clothes bought specially, at a cost of about twenty-five dollars an outfit, for the trip to New York—white beachcomber pants reaching to below the knee, white cotton-knit shirt with red and blue stripes and a pocket in one sleeve, white socks with red and blue stripes, and white sneakers. The girls wore cotton skirts, various kinds of blouses, white cardigan sweaters, and low-heeled shoes. Mrs. Watts wore high-heeled pumps, even for sightseeing. Everyone else on the tour was astonished at the way New York City people dressed. "They look peculiar," Nancy Prather said. "Girls wearing high heels in the daytime, and the boys here always got a regular suit on, even to go to work in."

"I wouldn't trade the girls back home for any of the girls here," Jay Bowman says. "New York girls wear too much makeup. Not that my interests are centered on any of the girls in the senior class. My interests are centered on Nancy Glidden. She's in the junior class. I take her to shows in Bloomington. We eat pizzas, listen to Elvis Presley—things of that nature—and I always get her home by twelve. Even though my interests are centered on the junior class, I'm proud to say my classmates are the finest bunch of people in the world."

Jay lives with his parents and two brothers in an old nine-room house on thirty acres of land owned by Jay's father, who works in the maintenance department of the Bridgeport Brass Company, in Indianapolis. His mother works in Bloomington, on the R.C.A. color-television-set assembly line. Jay's grandfather, who has worked in limestone quarries all his life, lives across the road, on five acres of his own land, where he has a couple of cows and raises beans and corn for the use of the family. The Bowman family had no plumbing in their house while Jay was a child, and took baths in a tub in the kitchen with water from a well, but a few years ago, with their own hands, they installed a bathroom and a plumbing system, and did other work on the house, including putting in a furnace. Jay's parents get up at four in the morning to go to work. Jay, who hasn't been sick one day since he had the mumps at the age of twelve, never sleeps later than seven. He is not in the least distressed at having to work his way through college. He plans to get to school in his own car. This is a 1950 Chevrolet four-door sedan, which he hopes to trade in, by paying an additional four hundred dollars, for a slightly younger model before the end of the year.

"The thing of it is I feel proud of myself," Jay says. "Not to be braggin' or anything. But I saved up better than a thousand dollars to send myself to college. That's the way it is. I scrubbed floors, put up hay, carried groceries, and this last winter I worked Saturdays and Sundays in a country store on the state highway and got paid a dollar an hour for runnin' it."

The Bowman family has, in addition to a kind of basic economic ambition, two main interests—basketball and politics. Jay, like most of the other boys on the trip, played basketball on the school basketball team, which won the first round in its section of the Wabash Valley tournament last season. Jay talks about basketball to his classmates but never about politics. Talk about the latter he saves for his family. His grandfather is a Democrat. "If it was up to my grandpa, he'd never want a single Republican in the whole country," he says. "And my Dad agrees with him. I agree with my Dad. My Dad thinks if Franklin D. Roosevelt was still President, this country wouldn't be in the trouble it finds itself in."

At 5 P.M. of this second day in the City of New York, the members of the Bean Blossom senior class returned to their hotel and stood in the lobby for a while, looking from some distance at a souvenir-and-gift stand across from the registration desk. The stand was stocked with thermometers in the form of the Statue of Liberty, in two sizes, priced at seventy-nine cents and ninety-eight cents; with silver-plated charm bracelets; with pins and compacts carrying representations of the Empire State Building; with scarves showing the R.C.A. Building and the U.N. Building; and with ashtrays showing the New York City skyline. Mike Richardson edged over to the stand and picked up a wooden plaque, costing ninety-eight cents, with the Statue of Liberty shown at the top, American flags at the sides, and, in the middle, a poem, inscribed "Mother," which read:

> To one who bears the sweetest name
> And adds a luster to the same
> Who shares my joys
> Who cheers when sad
> The greatest friend I ever had
> Long life to her, for there's no other
> Can take the place of my dear mother.

After reading the poem, Mike smiled.

"Where ya from?" the man behind the stand asked him.

"Indiana," Mike said, looking as though he were warming up. "We've been on this tour? The whole day?"

"Ya see everything?" the man asked.

"Everything except the Empire State Building," said Mike.

"Yeah," said the man, and looked away.

Mike was still holding the plaque. Carefully, he replaced it on the stand. "I'll come back for this later," he said.

Without looking at Mike, the man nodded.

Mike joined Dennis Smith and Larry Williams, who were standing with a tall, big-boned, handsome girl named Becky Kiser. Becky used to be a cheerleader for the Bean Blossom Township basketball team.

"We was talkin' about the way this place has people layin' in the streets on that Bowery sleepin'," Larry said. "You don't see people layin' in the streets back home."

"I seen that in Chicago," Dennis said. "I seen women layin' in the streets in Chicago. That's worse."

The others nodded. No argument.

Mike took a cigarette from his sleeve pocket and lit it with a match from the same pocket. He blew out a stream of smoke with strength and confidence. "I'll be glad when we light out of here," he said. "Nothin' here feels like the farm."

Becky Kiser, with an expression of terrible guilt on her attractive, wide-mouthed face, said, "I bet you'd never get bored here in New York. Back home, it's the same thing all the time. You go to the skating rink. You go to the Big Boy. In the winter, there's basketball. And that's all."

"When I was in Chicago, I seen a man who shot a man in a bar," Dennis said. "I stood right across the street while the man who was shot the people drug him out." He looked at Becky Kiser. The other boys were also looking at her, but with condemnation and contempt. Dennis gave Becky support. "In Stinesville, they see you on the streets after eleven, they run you home," he said. "Seems like here the city never closes."

"Man, you're just not lookin' ahead," Mike said to Dennis, ignoring Becky.

"You like it here?" Larry asked, in amazement. "Taxes on candy and on everything?"

The Nazarene minister's daughter, Mary Jane Carter, came over with Ina Hough.

"Dennis, here, likes New York," Mike announced.

"I don't," said Ina. "I like the sights, but I think they're almost ruined by the people."

"The food here is expensive, but I guess that's life," said Mary Jane, in a mood of forbearance.

"Oh, man!" said Mike.

"Oh, man!" said Larry. "Cooped up in New York."

Ina said stiffly, "Like the guide said today, you could always tell a New Yorker from a tourist because a New Yorker never smiles, and I agree with him."

"After a while, you'd kinda fit in," Dennis said mildly.

Before dinner that night, Mr. Watts walked through the Times Square area checking prices and menus at likely restaurants. He made tentative arrangements at The Californian for a five-course steak or chicken dinner, to cost $1.95 per person, and asked Jay Bowman to go around taking a vote on the proposition. Half an hour later, Jay reported to Mr. Watts that some of the boys didn't want to go to The Californian, because they thought they'd have to do their own ordering. So Mr. Watts talked to the boys in their rooms and explained that the ordering was taken care of; all they had to say was whether they wanted steak or chicken. On the next ballot, everybody was in favor of The Californian. The class walked over. When the fifth course was finished, it was agreed that the dinner was all right, but several of the boys said they thought the restaurant was too high-class.

After dinner, it started to rain, and it rained hard. The Wattses and seven of the girls decided that they wanted to see "The Music Man." The four other girls wanted to see "My Fair Lady." None of the boys wanted to see a musical show. In the driving rain, the Wattses and the girls ran to the theatres of their choice, all arriving soaked to the skin. By good luck, each group was able to buy seats. At "The Music Man," the Wattses and the seven girls with them sat in the balcony, in the direct path of an air-conditioning unit that blew icy blasts on their backs. At "My Fair Lady," the four girls sat in the balcony, where an air-conditioning unit blew icy blasts at their legs. The girls liked their shows. The "My Fair Lady" group was transported by the costumes. Ina Hough, who went to "The Music Man," thought that it was just like a movie, except for the way the scenes changed.

The boys split up, some of them taking the subway down to Greenwich Village, the others heading for the Empire State Building, where they paid a dollar-thirty for tickets to the observatory and, once up there, found that the fog and rain blotted out the view completely. "We stood there about an hour and a half messin' around, me and my buddies," Jay later told Mrs. Watts. "Wasn't no sense in leavin' at that price." In Greenwich Village, Mike Richardson, Dennis Smith, and Larry Williams walked along the narrow streets in a drizzling rain. All were still wearing their beachcomber outfits. Nobody talked to them. They didn't see anybody they wanted to talk to. They almost went into a small coffee-house; they changed their minds because the prices looked too high. They went into one shop, a bookstore, and looked at some abstract paintings, which appealed to them. "Sort of interestin', the way they don't look like nothin'," Mike said. Then they took the subway back to Times Square, where they walked around for a while in the rain. Toward midnight, Mike and Dennis told each other they were lonesome for the smell of grass and trees, and, the rain having stopped, they walked up to Central Park, where they stayed for about an hour and got lost.

The next morning, a meeting of the class was held in the hotel lobby to take a vote on when to leave New York. Jay Bowman reported that they had enough money to cover an extra day in the city, plus a side trip to Niagara Falls on the way home. Or, he said, they could leave New York when they had originally planned to and go to Washington, D.C., for a day before heading home. The bus driver had told Jay that it was all one to him which they chose. The class voted for the extra day in New York and Niagara Falls.

"I'm glad," Becky Kiser said, with a large, friendly smile, to Dennis Smith. Several of her classmates overheard her and regarded her with a uniformly deadpan look. "I like it here," she went on. "I'd like to live here. There's so much to see. There's so much to do."

Her classmates continued to study her impassively until Dennis took their eyes away from her by saying, "You get a feelin' here of goin' wherever you want to. Seems the city never closes. I'd like to live here, I believe. People from everyplace are here."

"Limousines all over the joint," Albert Warthan said.

"Seems like you can walk and walk and walk," Dennis went on

dreamily. "I like the way the big buildin's crowd you in. You want to walk and walk and never go to sleep."

"I hate it," Connie Williams said, with passion.

"Oh, man, you're just not lookin' ahead," Mike Richardson said to Dennis. "You got a romantic notion. You're not realistic about it."

"This place couldn't hold me," Larry Williams said. "I like the privacy of the farm."

"I want to go to new places," said Becky, who had started it. "I want to go to Europe."

"Only place I want to go is Texas," Larry said. "I got folks in Texas."

"There's no place like home," Mike said. "Home's good enough for me."

"I believe the reason of this is we've lived all of our lives around Stinesville," Dennis said. "If you took Stinesville out of the country, you wouldn't be hurt. But if you took New York out of the country, you'd be hurt. The way the guide said, all our clothes and everything comes from New York."

Becky said, "In Coney Island, I saw the most handsome man I ever saw in my whole life. I think he was a Puerto Rican or something, too."

Albert said, "When we get back, my pa will say, 'Well, how was it?' I'll say, 'It was fine.'"

"I'd like to come back, maybe stay a month," Jay Bowman said diplomatically. "One thing I'd like to do is come here when I can see a major-league baseball game."

"I'd like to see a major-league baseball game, but I wouldn't come back just to see *it*," Mike said.

"I hate New York," Connie said.

"Back home, everybody says 'Excuse me,'" Nancy Prather said.

"I like it here," Dennis said stubbornly.

This day was an open one, leaving the boys and girls free to do anything they liked, without prearranged plan or vote. Mike passed close by the souvenir-and-gift stand in the hotel lobby, and the proprietor urged him to take home the Statue of Liberty.

"I'd like to, but it won't fit in my suitcase," Mike said, with a loud laugh.

A group formed to visit the zoo in Central Park, got on the subway, had a loud discussion about where to get off, and were taken in hand by a stranger, who told them the zoo was in the Bronx. Only the boy named Lynn Dillon listened to the stranger. The others went to the zoo in Central Park. Lynn stayed on the subway till it reached the Bronx, and spent the entire day in the Bronx Zoo by himself. The rest of the zoo visitors, walking north after lunch in the cafeteria, ran into the Metropolitan Museum of Art and went in. "It was there, and it was free, so we did it," Nancy Prather said. "There were these suits of armor and stuff. Nothin' I go for myself."

That morning, the Wattses had tried to get some of the boys and girls to accompany them to the Guggenheim Museum or the Museum of Modern Art, but nobody had wanted to pay the price of admission. "Why pay fifty cents to see a museum when they got them free?" the class president asked. Mrs. Watts reported afterward that the Guggenheim was the most exciting museum she had ever seen, including all the museums she had seen in Europe on her accredited art tour. "There aren't big crowds in there, for one thing," she said. "And I don't think the building overpowers the paintings at all, as I'd heard." From the Guggenheim, the Wattses went to Georg Jensen's to look at silver, but didn't buy anything. Then they went to the Museum of Modern Art and had lunch in the garden. "Lovely lunch, fabulous garden, fabulous sculpture, but I'm disappointed in the museum itself," Mrs. Watts said. "Everything jammed into that small space! Impossible to get a good view of Picasso's 'Girl Before a Mirror.'"

By dinnertime, more than half of the Bean Blossomers had, to their relief, discovered the Automat. Jay Bowman had a dinner consisting of a ham sandwich (forty cents), a glass of milk (ten cents), and a dish of fresh strawberries (twenty cents). Then, with a couple of buddies, he bought some peanuts in their shells and some Cokes, and took them up to his room for the three of them to consume while talking about what to do that night. They decided, because they had not yet had a good view of the city from the Empire State observatory, that they would go back there. They were accompanied by most of the girls and the other boys, and this time the group got a cut rate of sixty-five cents apiece. Dennis went off wandering by himself. He walked up Fifth Avenue to Eighty-fifth Street, over to Park Avenue, down Park to Seventy-second Street, across to the West Side, down Central Park West to Sixty-sixth Street, over behind the Tavern-on-the-Green (where he watched people eating outdoors), and down Seventh Avenue to Times Square, where he stood around on corners looking at the people who bought papers at newsstands.

The Wattses had arranged to meet anybody who was interested under the Washington Arch at around nine-thirty for an evening in Greenwich Village. The boys had decided to take a walk up Broadway after leaving the Empire State Building, but the girls all showed up in Washington Square, along with two soldiers and three sailors they had met in the U.S.O. across the street from the Woodstock. The Wattses led the way to a coffeehouse, where everybody had coffee or lemonade. Then the girls and the servicemen left the Wattses, saying they were going to take a ride on the ferry to Staten Island. The Wattses went to the Five Spot, which their jazz friend had told them had good music.

After breakfast the following morning, the bus driver, Ralph Walls, showed up in the hotel lobby for the first time since the group's arrival in New York and told Jay Bowman to have everyone assembled at five-forty-five the following morning for departure at six o'clock on the dot. The driver said that he was spending most of his time sleeping, and that before they left he was going to do some more sleeping. He had taken his wife on a boat trip around Manhattan, though, he said, and he had taken a few walks on the streets. After reminding Jay again about the exact time planned for the departure, he went back upstairs to his room.

Mrs. Watts took nine of the girls (two stayed in the hotel to sleep) for a walk through Saks Fifth Avenue, just looking. Mr. Watts took three of the boys to Abercrombie & Fitch, just looking.

Everybody walked every aisle on every floor in each store, looking at everything on the counters and in the showcases. Nobody bought anything. The two groups met at noon under the clock in Grand Central; lunched at an Automat; walked over to the United Nations Buildings, where they decided not to take the regular tour; and took a crosstown bus to the Hudson River and went aboard the liner S.S. Independence, where they visited every deck and every lounge on the boat, and a good many of the staterooms. Then they took the bus back to Times Square and scattered to do some shopping.

Mike Richardson bought all his gifts—eleven dollars' worth—at the hotel stand, taking not only the plaque for his mother but a set of salt and pepper shakers, with the Statue of Liberty on the salt and the Empire State Building on the pepper, also for his mother; a Statue of Liberty ashtray for his father; a George Washington Bridge teapot for his sister-in-law; a mechanical dog for his niece; a City Hall teapot-cup-and-saucer set for his grandparents; and a cigarette lighter stamped with the Great White Way for himself. At Macy's, Becky Kiser bought a dress, a blouse, and an ankle chain for herself, and a necklace with matching bracelet and earrings for her mother, a cuff-link-and-tie-clasp set for her father, and a bracelet for her younger sister. Albert Warthan bought a miniature camera for himself and a telephone-pad-and-pencil set stamped with the George Washington Bridge and a Statue of Liberty thermometer, large-size, as general family gifts, at the hotel stand. Jay Bowman bought an unset cultured pearl at Macy's for his girl friend in the junior class, as well as silver-looking earrings for his married sister and for his mother, and at a store called King of Slims, around the corner from the hotel, he bought four ties—a red toreador tie (very narrow) for his older brother, a black toreador tie for his younger brother, a conservative silk foulard for his father, and a white toreador tie for himself. Dennis Smith bought a Statue of Liberty ashtray for his mother and a Statue of Liberty cigarette lighter for his father. Connie Williams bought two bracelets and a Statue of Liberty pen for herself. The bus driver and his wife spent sixty dollars on clothes for their children, six of whom are girls. Nancy Prather didn't buy anything. The Wattses spent about a hundred dollars in the course of the visit, most of it on meals and entertainment.

On their last evening in New York, all the boys and girls, accompanied by the Wattses, went to the Radio City Music Hall, making it in time to see the stage show. Then they packed and went to bed. The bus driver, after an early dinner with his wife at Hector's Cafeteria, brought the yellow school bus over from Tenth Avenue and parked it right in front of the hotel, so that it would be there for the early start.

Next morning at five-forty-five, the Bean Blossomers assembled in the lobby; for the first time since the trip had started, nobody was late. The bus pulled out at exactly 6 A.M., and twenty minutes after that, heading west over the George Washington Bridge, it disappeared from the city.

—1960

2

SYMBOL OF ALL WE POSSESS

THERE ARE THIRTEEN MILLION WOMEN in the United States between the ages of eighteen and twenty-eight. All of them were eligible to compete for the title of Miss America in the annual contest staged in Atlantic City last month if they were high-school graduates, were not and had never been married, and were not Negroes. Ten thousand of them participated in preliminary contests held in all but three of the forty-eight states. Then, one cool September day, a Miss from each of these states, together with a Miss New York City, a Miss Greater Philadelphia, a Miss Chicago, a Miss District of Columbia, a Miss Canada, a Miss Puerto Rico, and a Miss Hawaii, arrived in Atlantic City to display her beauty, poise, grace, physique, personality, and talent. The primary, and most obvious, stake in the contest was a twenty-five-thousand-dollar scholarship fund—a five-thousand-dollar scholarship for the winner and lesser ones for fourteen runners-up—which had been established by the makers of Nash automobiles, Catalina swimsuits, and a cotton fabric known as Everglaze. The winner would also get a new four-door Nash sedan, a dozen Catalina swimsuits, and a wardrobe of sixty Everglaze garments. The contest was called the Miss America Pageant. The fifty-two competitors went into it seeking, beyond the prizes, great decisions. Exactly what was decided, they are still trying to find out.

Miss New York State was a twenty-two-year-old registered nurse named Wanda Nalepa, who lives in the Bronx. She has honey-blond hair, green eyes, and a light complexion, and is five feet three. Some other statistics gathered by Miss America Pageant officials are: weight, 108; bust, 34; waist, 23; thigh, 19; hips, 34; calf, 12¼; ankle, 7½; shoe size, 5; dress size, 10. She was asked in an official questionnaire why she had entered the Atlantic City contest. She answered that her friends had urged her to. The day before the contest was to start, I telephoned Miss Nalepa at her home to ask when she was leaving for Atlantic City. She said that she was driving down the next morning, and invited me to go along.

Miss Nalepa lives in a second-floor walkup apartment in a building near 164th Street on Sherman Avenue, a couple of blocks from the Grand Concourse. At eight the following morning, I was greeted at the door of the Nalepa flat by a thin young man in his late twenties wearing rimless glasses. "Come right in, Miss," he said. "I'm Teddy, Wanda's brother. Wanda's getting dressed." He led me into a small, dim living room, and I sat down in a chair next to a table. On the table were two trophies—a silver loving cup saying "Miss Sullivan County 1949" and a plastic statuette saying "Miss New York State 1949"—and a two-panel picture folder showing, on one side, Miss Nalepa in a bathing suit and, on the other, Miss Nalepa in a nurse's uniform. Teddy sat on the edge of a couch and stared self-consciously at a crucifix and a holy picture on the wall across the room. I asked him if he was going to Atlantic City. He said that he was a tool-and-die maker and had to work. "Bob—that's Wanda's boy friend—he's driving you down," he said. "Bob can get more time off. He's assistant manager for a finance company."

One by one, the family wandered into the room: Mr. Nalepa, a short, tired-looking man who resembles Teddy and who works in a factory making rattan furniture; Mrs. Nalepa, a small, shy woman with gray hair; and Wanda's younger sister, Helen, a high-school senior. Each of them nodded to me or said hello, but nobody said anything much after that. Then a pair of French doors opened and Wanda came in and said hello to me. Everybody studied her. She wore an eggshell straw sailor hat set back on her head, a navy-blue dotted-swiss dress, blue stockings, and high-heeled navy-blue pumps. For jewelry, she wore only a sturdy wristwatch with a leather strap and her nursing-school graduation ring.

"I hope this looks all right," Miss Nalepa said in a thin, uncertain voice. "I didn't know what to wear."

"Looks all right," her father said.

The doorbell rang. Teddy said that it must be Bob. It was Bob —a tall, gaunt man of about thirty with a worried face. He nodded to everybody, picked up Miss Nalepa's luggage and threw several evening gowns over one arm, said that we ought to get going, and started downstairs.

"Well, goodbye," said Miss Nalepa.

"Don't forget to stand up straight," her sister said.

"What about breakfast?" her mother asked mildly.

"I don't feel like eating," Miss Nalepa said.

"Good luck, Wanda," said Teddy.

"Well, goodbye," Miss Nalepa said again, looking at her father.

"All right, all right, goodbye," her father said.

Miss Nalepa was about to walk out the door when her mother stepped up timidly and gave her a peck on the cheek. As we were going downstairs together, Miss Nalepa clutched at my wrist. Her hand was cold. "That's the second time I ever remember my mother kissed me," she said, with a nervous laugh. "The first time was when I graduated from high school. I looked around to see if anybody was watching us, I was so embarrassed."

We found Bob and a pudgy, bald-headed man named Frank stowing the bags in the luggage compartment of a 1948 Pontiac sedan. I learned that Frank, a friend of Bob's, was going along, too. Women neighbors in housecoats were leaning out of windows to watch the departure. Frank told Miss Nalepa that a photograph of her taken from the rear had come out fine. "Wanda has a perfect back," he said to me. "I'm getting this picture printed in the *National Chiropractic Journal*. I'm a chiropractor."

I got in front, with Bob and Miss Nalepa. Frank got in back. On our way downtown, Miss Nalepa told me that we were to stop at Grand Central to pick up her chaperone, a Miss Neville. Miss Neville represented WKBW, the radio station in Buffalo that, with the blessings of the Miss America Pageant people but without any official blessings from Albany, had sponsored the New York State contest. A couple of weeks before competing in that one, which was held at the Crystal Beach Amusement Park, near Buffalo, Miss Nalepa had won the title of Miss Sullivan County in a contest held in the town of Monticello, thus qualifying for the state contest, and a week or so before that she had won the title of Miss White Roe Inn, the inn being situated outside the town of Livingston Manor, in Sullivan County. She had gone to the inn for a short vacation at the insistence of a friend who thought she could win the beauty contest there. Miss Nalepa had heard of such contests and of others, held at local theatres, but hadn't ever entered one before. "I never had the nerve," she told me. "I always knew I was pretty, but it always made me feel uncomfortable. When I was six, I remember a little boy in the first grade who used to watch me. I was terrified. I used to run home from school every day. At parties, when I was older, the boys paid a lot of attention to me, and I didn't like it. I wanted the other girls to get attention, too." Miss Nalepa went to a vocational high school, to study dressmaking; worked in a five-and-ten-cent store for a while after graduation; considered taking singing lessons but dropped the idea after her two sisters told her she had no singing ability; and went to the Rhodes School, in New York City, for a pre-nursing course and then to Mount Sinai Hospital, where she got her R.N. degree in 1948. She didn't like to go out on dates with the hospital doctors. "Doctors are too forward," she said.

At Grand Central, Miss Neville, a pleasant, gray-haired lady, who said she had not been in Atlantic City in twenty years and was very enthusiastic about going there now, got in the back seat with Frank, and they began talking about chiropractic. As we headed for the Holland Tunnel, the three of us in the front seat discussed the contest. "Don't expect much and you won't be disappointed," Miss Nalepa said, clutching Bob's arm. She thought it would be nice to have some scholarship money, and said that if she won any, she might use it to learn to play some musical instrument. No money had come with the Miss White Roe Inn title. She had received seventy-five dollars from the Sullivan County Resort Association for becoming Miss Sullivan County, and a picture of her in a bathing suit had appeared in the New York *Daily News* captioned "Having Wandaful Time." When she was named Miss New York State, she was given three evening gowns and two pieces of luggage. She earned ten dollars a day nursing, but she hadn't worked in more than a month—not since she started entering beauty contests—and she had had to borrow three hundred dollars from members of her family for clothes, cosmetics, jewelry, a quick, $67.50 course in modelling, and other things designed to enhance beauty, poise, and personality. She was worried about being only five feet three. The Miss Americas of the preceding six years had all been five feet seven or more. The contestants would be judged on four counts: appearance in a bathing suit, appearance in an evening gown, personality, and talent. Miss Nalepa was wondering about her talent. Her act, as she planned it, was going to consist of getting up in her nurse's uniform and making a little speech about her nursing experience.

"I don't know what else I can do to show I've got talent," she said. "All I know how to do is give a good back rub."

"Listen, what you need right now is a good meal," Bob said.

Miss Nalepa said she wasn't hungry.

"You've got to eat," Bob said. "You're too skinny."

"You've got to eat," Frank repeated. "You're too skinny."

We stopped for breakfast at a roadside restaurant. Miss Nalepa had only half a cheeseburger and a few sips of tea.

In Atlantic City, Miss Nalepa and her chaperone headed for the hotel they had been assigned to, the Marlborough-Blenheim, where they were to share a double room. I said I was going to check in at the Claridge, across the street, and Bob offered to take my bag over. As the two of us walked over, he said that he and

Frank were going to hang around for a short while and then go back to New York. "She's not going to win," he said. "I told her she's not going to win. That nursing isn't the right kind of talent. They'll want singing or dancing, or something like that."

In the lobby there were large photographs of Miss America of 1948, and of the current Miss Arizona, Miss Florida, Miss Chicago, and Miss District of Columbia, all of whom, I learned from my bellhop, had been assigned to that hotel. "Big crowd comes down every year to see the crowning of Miss America," he said. "This is America's Bagdad-by-the-Sea. The only place on the ocean where you'll find a big crowd relaxing at recreations in the fall."

On my bureau was a small paper cutout doll labelled "Miss America, Be Be Shopp, in her official gown of Everglaze moire for the Miss America Pageant, September 6-11, 1949."

"You seen Be Be yet?" an elevator boy with round shoulders and watery eyes asked me as I was going back down. "Be Be's staying with us. Be Be looks real good. Better than last year. You seen Miss Florida yet?" I shook my head. "She's something!" he said.

I went out to the boardwalk, where booths for the sale of tickets to the Pageant had been set up in a line running down the middle, between two rows of Bingo Temples, billboard pictures of horses diving into the ocean from the Steel Pier, and places named Jewelry Riot, Ptomaine Tavern, and the Grecian Temple. The roller chairs were rolling in and out among the ticket booths. "Get your ticket now to see the beauties at the parade!" a middle-aged lady called to me from one of them. "Bleacher seats are twenty-five cents cheaper than last year!"

The contestants were registering for the Pageant at the Traymore, so I went over there. A couple of dozen policemen were standing outside the registration room. I asked one of them if Miss New York State had arrived. "Not yet, sister," he said. "Stick around. I got my eye on all of them."

A white-haired gentleman wearing a green-and-purple checked jacket asked him how the registration was going.

"You want to see the beauties, buy a ticket to the Pageant," the policeman said.

"They got any tall ones?" asked the gentleman.

"Yeah, they got some tall ones," the policeman said. "Utah is five ten. She comes from Bountiful—Bountiful, Utah."

"Hope it won't rain for the parade tomorrow," said the gentleman.

"It don't look too promising," said the policeman.

Miss Nalepa and her chaperone turned up, and I went inside with them. The contestants were standing in an uneven line, looking unhappily at each other, before a table presided over by a middle-aged woman with a Southern accent. She was Miss Lenora Slaughter, the executive director of the Pageant. The atmosphere was hushed and edgy, but Miss Slaughter was extravagantly cheerful as she handed out badges and ribbons to the contestants. When Miss Nalepa's turn came to register, Miss Slaughter gave her a vigorous hug, called her darling, handed her a ribbon reading "New York State," and told her to wear it on her bathing suit, from the right shoulder to the left hip. I introduced myself to Miss Slaughter, and she shook my hand fervently. "You'll want to follow our working schedule," she said, giving me a booklet. "All the girls are going upstairs now to be fitted with their Catalina bathing suits, and then they get their pictures taken, and tonight we're having a nice meeting with all the girls, to tell them what's what. The Queen—Miss America of 1948; we call Miss America the Queen—will be there. You're welcome to come. . . . Miss California!" she cried. I moved on and Miss California took my place. Miss New York State clutched at my arm again and nodded toward Miss California, who had a large, square face, long blond hair, and large blue eyes. (Height, 5′ 6¼; weight, 124; bust, 36; waist, 24¼; thigh, 20; hips, 36; shoe size, 6½-AA; dress size, 12; age, 19. Reason for entering the contest: "To gain poise and develop my personality.") Miss New York State stood still, staring at her. "Come on, Wanda," said her chaperone. "We've got to get you that bathing suit."

The bathing suits were being handed out and fitted in a two-room suite upstairs. The contestants put on their suits in one room while the chaperones waited in the other. The fitting room was very quiet; the other was filled with noisy, nervous chatter.

Miss Alabama's chaperone was saying, "I'm grooming one now. She'll be ready in two years. She's sure to be Miss America of 1951."

"Have you seen Nebraska? She's a definite threat," said Miss New Jersey's chaperone to Miss Arkansas's chaperone.

"What's her talent?" asked Miss Arkansas's chaperone.

"Dramatic recitation," said Miss N.J.'s.

"She'll never make the first fifteen," said Miss Ark.'s.

"Confidentially," said one chaperone to another, "confidentially, I wouldn't pick any of the girls I've seen to be Miss America."

"Some years you get a better-looking crop than others," her companion said. "At the moment, what I've got my mind on is how I can get me a good, stiff drink, and maybe two more after it."

I went into the other room, where Miss New York State was having trouble with her suit. She did not like Catalina suits, she told me; they didn't fit her, and she wished the Pageant officials would let her wear her own. Another contestant paused in her struggle with her suit and said it was very important to like the official Pageant suits. "There just wouldn't be a little old Pageant without Catalina," she said severely.

Outside, in an open patio, the contestants posed in their suits —all ribbons running from right shoulders to left hips—for a band of photographers. Miss Shopp, Miss America of 1948, of Hopkins, Minnesota (height, 5′ 9; weight, 140; bust, 37; waist, 27; hips, 36; age, 19), also in her Catalina suit and her "Miss America" ribbon, joined them. She had a dimpled smile on her face. A cool breeze blew in from the ocean and Miss New York State folded her arms and shivered.

"Be Be! Be Be! Wouldja mind waving?" a photographer called.

Miss America waved.

"She made fifty thousand dollars in her year as Miss America," said Miss New York State, without much enthusiasm. "I wouldn't mind making fifty thousand dollars. Maybe I could be a model or something." She looked at the other contestants and remarked, with surprise, that there were a lot of short ones. She said this made her feel better. Miss Arizona, she pointed out, was about her height. Miss Arizona looked worried. Her chaperone, a thin, freckle-faced woman, touched her arm, and Miss Arizona tried to smile. Miss New York State thought Miss Arizona was sort of pretty. She had brown hair, cut short, and dark-brown eyes. (Height, 5′ 3½; weight, 106; bust, 34; waist, 22; thigh, 20; hips, 34; shoe size, 6½-AA; dress size, 9; age, 18. Reason for entering the contest: "Because it would be a great honor to be Miss America.")

"The kid looks so *strained*," said Miss New York State, finally.

A photographer called to Miss Arizona and Miss New York State to sit on a railing with some other girls. They sat, shivering in the breeze but smiling broadly. On the first page of the booklet given to me by Miss Slaughter was a welcome to the contestants by the president of the Miss America Pageant, Park W. Haverstick, who is president of the Atlantic City Chamber of Commerce. "The hearts of the people of Atlantic City are open equally to the winners or to the losers," it began, and it ended with a quotation:

> For when the One Great Scorer comes
> To write against your name,
> He marks—not that you won or lost—
> BUT HOW YOU PLAYED THE GAME.

That night, Mr. Haverstick acted as chairman of the meeting of the contestants in Convention Hall, the world's largest auditorium. He is a solid elderly gentleman with a large, bald head. He introduced the first speaker of the evening, Miss Slaughter, describing her as a friend they all knew and loved, the friend who had been working for the Pageant since 1935. Miss New York State and most of the other contestants were wearing suits and hats. They sat attentively, their hands folded in their laps, as Miss Slaughter stood up and shook her head unbelievingly at them. "I see your faces and I see a dream of fifty-one weeks come true," she said. "Now, I want you all to listen to me. I'm going to ask you girls to keep one thought in mind during this great week. Think to yourself: There are fifty-one other talented, beautiful girls in this contest besides myself. Get out of your head the title of Miss America. You're already a winner, a queen in your own right."

She announced that a special prize—a thousand-dollar scholarship—would be awarded to the contestant elected Miss Congeniality by her competitors.

An elderly, heavyset woman with a high-pitched, martyred voice, Mrs. Malcolm Shermer, chairman of a group of local hostesses who would escort the contestants from their hotels to the Pageant activities and back again, stood up and said that she would personally watch over the girls in their dressing room. "When I wake up on Pageant morning, it's like another Christmas Day to me," she said, and went on to list some rules of decorum the contestants would have to follow. The girls were not to make dates with any man, or even have dinner with their fathers, because the public had no way of knowing whether or not a man was a contestant's father; they were not to enter a cocktail lounge or night club; they were to stick to their chaperones or their hostesses. "You have reached the top of the Miss America mountain," Mrs. Shermer said in a complaining tone, "so we're making you almost inaccessible, because all good businessmen put their most valuable belongings in a safe place." The contestants looked impressed. Miss New York State sighed. "They don't take any chances," she remarked to me. "This is just like school."

Miss America of 1948, clad in a suit of Everglaze (I later discovered that she had driven over faithfully in a Nash), then welcomed the fifty-two contestants. She smiled and told the contestants to keep smiling from the moment they woke up every day to the moment they fell asleep. Mr. Haverstick nodded solemnly. "Always have that smile on your face," she said. "Your smiles make people feel happy, and that's what we need—happier people in the world." The contestants all managed a smile. They continued to smile as Mr. Bob Russell was introduced as the master of ceremonies of the Pageant. He came forward with that lively skip characteristic of night-club m.c.s and said, "Girls, this week you're performers, you're actresses, you're models, you're singers and entertainers. Girls, show this great city that you're happy American girls, happy to be in Atlantic City, the city of beautiful girls!" Mr. Haverstick blushed and managed a small smile of his own. The contestants were instructed to wear evening gowns, but not their best ones, in the parade that was going to take place the next day. Still conscientiously smiling, they filed out of the hall. Miss New York State let go of her smile for a moment and told me that she was returning to her room. She would lie down and elevate her feet for twenty minutes, put pads soaked with witch hazel over her eyes, take two sleeping pills, and go to sleep.

On the way out, Miss Slaughter stopped me and said that I was going to see the best contest in the Pageant's history. It had come a long way, she said, from the first one, in 1921, when it was called the Bathers' Revue. The first winner, given the title of the Golden Mermaid, was Margaret Gorman, of Washington, D.C., who briefly considered a theatrical career and then went home and married a real-estate man. "In those years, we offered nothing but promises and a cup," Miss Slaughter said. "Now we get real big bookings for our girls, where they can get started on a real big career. This is not a leg show and we don't call the beauties bathing beauties any more. The bathing part went out in 1945, when we started giving big scholarships." Miss America of 1945 —Bess Myerson, of the Bronx—the first winner to be awarded much more than promises and a cup, won a five-thousand-dollar scholarship and bookings worth ten thousand dollars. "Bess went right out and capitalized," Miss Slaughter said. "She went to Columbia and studied music, got married, and had an adorable baby girl, and now she runs a music school and does modelling, too." The next winner—Marilyn Buferd, of Los Angeles— wanted to get into the movies. She got a two-hundred-and-fifty- dollar-a-week job as a starlet with Metro-Goldwyn-Mayer. She is now in Italy, under contract to Roberto Rossellini. Miss America of 1947—Barbara Jo Walker, of Memphis—caused the Pageant officials considerable worry. "She upped and announced she wanted to get married; she didn't want to go out and make money and get publicity," Miss Slaughter said. "Well, there was nothing we could do but let her get married to this medical student of hers, and now we've brought her back this year to be a judge." Be Be Shopp, whose term would run out in five days, had been the biggest money-maker as Miss America. "She just never stopped working at it," Miss Slaughter said. "She set a real good example for our girls." Miss Shopp travelled across three continents, appearing at conventions and similar gatherings with a vibraharp, the instrument with which she had demonstrated her talent at last year's contest by playing "Trees." Miss America of 1944 went back to her home in Kentucky and married a farmer. Miss America of 1943 is singing in a night club in Paris. Miss America of 1942 married Phil Silvers, the comedian. Most of the Miss Americas back to 1921 got married soon after winning their titles. Miss America of 1937, however, has neither married nor embarked on a career. "Miss America of 1937 got crowned, and the next morning she just vanished," Miss Slaughter said, looking pained. "Why, she ran right home, someplace in New Jersey, and when we found her, she refused to come out—no explanation or anything. Just the other day, she decided she wanted to be a model or actress or something, but maybe it's too late now."

The following morning, the contestants were photographed again in their Catalina swimsuits. After lunch, they were assembled in the ballroom of a hotel near one end of the boardwalk for the American Beauty Parade, which would wind up near the other end, a distance of four and a half miles. Roller chairs and beach chairs were lined up along the route; the supply had been sold out (at $6.15 and $2, respectively) three weeks before. State police had been brought in to help keep order. It was a fine day for a parade—clear, sunny, and brisk. The business streets back of the boardwalk were almost deserted. The boardwalk was packed. Every roller chair was occupied, occasionally by as many as six people. Along the parade route a shabby, eager, excited crowd of men, women, and children stood six and eight deep or sat in bleachers. Some carried small American flags, and others waved the paper-doll replicas of Be Be Shopp. Miss Arizona stood near the door of the ballroom. She would be one of the first to leave. She wore a long skirt of red suède, slit at one side, and a multi-colored blouse of Indian design. Miss New York State, looking rested and wearing an aquamarine-colored satin gown, was off in a corner, watching Miss America of 1948, who was wearing a slip and contemplating the original of the dress she was pictured in on the paper doll. The dress lay across the backs of two chairs. It had a large hoop skirt and was decorated on the front with the official flowers, appliquéd, of the forty-eight states. She announced that she had to wear the gown in the parade and every night of the Pageant. "It weighs thirty pounds," she said. "How am I ever going to play my vibraharp in it?"

Miss New York State shook her head in speechless marvel. "Will you play every night Miss Shopp?" she asked.

"Call me Be Be, please," Miss America said, showing a dimpled smile. "Everybody calls me Be Be. I play my vibraharp everyplace I go. I've made two hundred and sixty-one appearances with it, opening stores and things. The vibraharp weighs a hundred and fifty pounds, and a man usually carries it for me. They were the only men I got close to all year. I worked so hard I didn't have a chance to have any real dates."

Miss Florida, who was standing nearby, shook her head sadly. "Mah goodness, no dates!" she said.

Two women attendants climbed up on chairs and held the thirty-pound gown aloft while the Queen crawled under it. "Is it in the center of me?" she asked as her head and shoulders emerged. Everybody said that it was in the center of her and that she looked glorious. Miss America was now ready to lead the parade. I went outside and found a place on the boardwalk near a mobile radio-broadcasting unit, where Miss America's father, who is physical-education director at the Cream of Wheat Corporation in Minneapolis, was being interviewed. "I'm just as excited this year as last year," he was saying. "I'm just starting to realize she's Miss America."

The parade took two hours. Each contestant sat on a float pushed by a couple of men. Not one contestant let Atlantic City down by failing to keep a smile on her face. Miss New York State, preceded by Hap Brander's string band and a float proclaiming the merits of Fralinger's Salt Water Taffy, got a big hand from the audience. Most of the other contestants merely sat and smiled, but she stood and waved and laughed and shouted and seemed to be having the time of her life.

. . .

The contestants were to rehearse that night with Bob Russell in Convention Hall, and I decided to go over there. On my way through the lobby of my hotel, I ran into Miss Florida with her mother.

"Don't forget to smile, honey," her mother said, smiling.

"Ah don't have *any* trouble smilin', Mama," said Miss Florida.

"That's a good girl, honey," her mother said.

The statistics on Miss Florida showed that at eighteen she was already a veteran beauty. She was Citrus Queen of Florida in 1947, Railroad Exposition Queen in Chicago in 1948, Miss Holiday of Florida of 1949, and Miss Tampa of 1949. (Reason for entering the Atlantic City contest: "Because the Chamber of Commerce of Tampa asked me to compete.")

At Convention Hall, Mr. Russell, standing on the stage surrounded by weary-looking contestants, was outlining the procedure for the next three nights. A long ramp ran out into the auditorium at right angles to the stage, and a few of the contestants squatted on it, as though they were too exhausted to move back to the stage with the others. Miss New York State seemed fairly fresh. Her face was flushed, but she appeared to smile without effort. She wanted to know whether I had seen her in the parade. "That was *fun*," she said. "I was standing and yelling things, and people were yelling things to me. That was really a lot of *fun*. I never thought that people would be so *friendly*."

"Please, girls," said the m.c. "I need your attention."

"I'm used to a long, hard day from nursing," Miss New York State whispered. "Some of these girls look all done in." Smiling, she gave the m.c. her attention. He explained that the contestants would be divided into three groups. Each night, one group would compete for points on their appearance in evening dress, another in bathing suits, and the members of the third would demonstrate their talents. The girls would be judged on personality at two breakfasts, when the judges would meet and talk with them. Every girl would be scored in these four categories, and the fifteen girls with the highest total number of points would compete in the semifinals of the contest, at which time the judges would reappraise them and choose the queen and the four other finalists. Miss New York State was assigned to a group that included Miss Florida, Miss California, and Miss Arizona; they would appear the first night in bathing suits, the second in evening gowns, and on the third they would demonstrate their talents. The winners of the bathing-suit and talent competitions would be announced each night, but not the runners-up, and neither the winners nor the runners-up in the evening-gown competition. In this way, it would not be known who the semifinalists were until they were named on the fourth, and last, night of competition. Each day, Mr. Russell said, he would rehearse the girls in whatever they had prepared to do to show their talent that night. He then made the contestants line up in alphabetical order and parade together from the wings onto the stage and off it down the long ramp—the same ramp each would eventually be required to walk alone. The parade would wind up on each of the first three nights with the appearance of Miss America of 1948 in her thirty-pound gown. The other girls would raise empty water glasses in a toast to her while Mr. Russell sang the Miss America Pageant song, which goes:

> Let's drink a toast to Miss America,
> Let's raise our glasses on high
> From Coast to Coast in this America,
> As the Sweetheart of the U.S.A. is passing by.
> To a girl, to a girl,
> To a symbol of happiness.
> To the one, to the one
> Who's the symbol of all we possess.

Mr. Russell then asked each contestant to walk onstage by herself and onto the ramp, to model before the judges' enclosure, and to walk off the ramp. He started with Miss Alabama, giving her a briefing in walking and modelling. Miss Arizona, the second contestant, walked gracefully and modelled knowingly, obviously needing no instruction at all.

In the wings, where the contestants were waiting their turns and eight or nine policemen were standing guard, there was a lot of discussion about which one would win the title. "I been picking 'em for years," one cop was saying loudly to another. "It'll be California. You want to bet it won't be California?" A bet was made. Miss Montana asked if the policemen had seen her horse anywhere; she was going to show talent in horsemanship by riding her horse across the stage, but her father hadn't shown up with it. The police didn't know anything about the horse.

Miss Greater Philadelphia, a five-foot-seven girl with black hair, said she felt ill and was going to lie down. Miss New York State told a policeman she wanted to go back to the dressing room with her and see if she could help. "I'm a nurse. I might be able to do something for her," she said.

"You're a beauty, you're no nurse," said the policeman. "Now, you go on back in line and rehearse, like Bob Russell tells you."

Miss New York State returned to her place in line, and when her turn came to walk down the ramp, she walked with her arms hanging stiffly; she didn't seem to be familiar with the technique of modelling. "Do something with your hands, honey," Mr. Russell told her. "Remember—you're a model. Hold your hands together in front of you." As she went back to the line, she looked despairingly at me. After a while, she got out of line again and joined me in the wings. "West Virginia got six new suits from her state before she came here," she said after a silence, in an unenvious tone. "And she got six new dresses and six pairs of shoes and five hundred dollars in cash, besides a thousand dollars from her home town. Colorado got a silver-fox scarf—there's only two in the world of that particular shade—and a lot of the girls got things like silverware and automobiles and radios for winning their state contests. Nobody ever told me the girls got things like that."

Miss New York State took only an hour to get dressed for the opening night. I stopped by her room before dinner. She was studying herself in a mirror. She wore an ice-blue satin evening gown, her hair was shining, she had on very little makeup, and her face was smooth and pale. She put on a rhinestone necklace, looked hard at herself, wiped a bit of lipstick from a front tooth, and shrugged. "I'm so vain," she said.

"We'd better go down to dinner," Miss Neville said. "You're due at Convention Hall at eight."

The hotel dining room was filled, mostly with elderly ladies in high lace collars, canes hanging from the backs of their chairs. Several of them applauded as Miss New York State made her entrance, and one later sent her a note wishing her good luck. Miss New York State ordered onion soup, filet of sole, a caramel-nut sundae, and tea with lemon. After she had finished her fish, she waited placidly for her sundae, which was not served until almost eight.

I found a seat at the press table at Convention Hall, abreast of the ramp, as Mr. Russell, wearing a dinner jacket, skipped out and announced that the parade was going to begin. Miss Alabama and the fifty-one others came onto the ramp, smiling but shaking with nervousness. My seat was not far from where Miss New York State stood on the ramp, and I could see her trembling with a kind of sick, forced laughter. The judges, all in evening dress, were introduced: Vyvyan Donner, women's editor of the Twentieth Century-Fox Movietone News; Ceil Chapman, dress designer; Clifford D. Cooper, president of the United States Junior Chamber of Commerce; Guy E. Snavely, Jr., who was described as a husband, father, and executive secretary of Pickett & Hatcher, an educational foundation in Birmingham, Alabama; Paul R. Anderson, president of Pennsylvania College for Women, in Pittsburgh; Mrs. Barbara Walker Hummell, Miss America of 1947; Conrad Thibault, baritone; Vincent Trotta, art director of the National Screen Service, a company that makes posters and billboards for motion pictures; Coby Whitmore, commercial artist; Hal Phyfe, photographer; and Earl Wilson, columnist. Voting was by ballot, with two certified public accountants acting as tellers of the ballots. From the press table I picked up a brochure about Convention Hall, and read that it was 488 feet long, 288 feet wide, and 137 feet high, and that it could be transformed in a few hours into a full-size football field or into the world's largest indoor fight arena. "The place dwarfs," a gentleman seated next to me said with finality.

After the parade, the group competing in evening gowns that night came onstage one by one, modelled before the judges, and walked down the ramp. Then they came out in a group and lined up in front of the judges, who sat in their enclosure, which adjoined the ramp. Miss Illinois, a pert girl with green eyes and blond hair, fixed in a Maggie (Jiggs' Maggie) hair-do, winked saucily at the judges. She wore a strapless white gown with a rhinestone-trimmed bodice. (Height, 5′ 6¼; weight, 118; bust, 35; hips, 35½; age, 19. Reason for entering the Pageant: "I entered with the sincere hope of furthering my career.") Mr. Russell urged the girls to give big smiles and urged the judges to pay attention to coiffure, grooming, and symmetry of form. The contestants faced front, turned to show their profiles, turned to show their backs, turned to show their other profiles, then faced front again, and retired. The tellers collected the ballots. Next, a group in bathing suits came out, led by Miss Arizona. Miss California, the tall blonde, came next. Miss Florida followed, and, after a few other contestants, Miss New York State. As they stood before the judges, the m.c. asked them to examine the girls' figures carefully for any flaws. For example, he asked, did the thighs and the calves meet at the right places? Miss New York State stood rigidly, once grasping the hand of Miss North Dakota. The audience of nine thousand, who had paid from $1.25 to $6.15 for their tickets, sat patiently and stared. The bathing-suiters retired, and Mr. Russell announced that he would do impersonations of Al Jolson, Bing Crosby, Eddie Cantor, and Enrico Caruso. After this demonstration of versatility, he said that the curtains were about to open on "our beautiful old-fashioned Southern garden." The curtains parted. All the girls, in evening gowns, were seated in chairs on simulated grass. Here and there were potted palms. For some reason, Miss New York State sat behind one of them.

The talent competition began. Miss Alabama, a mezzo-soprano, led off by singing " 'Neath the Southern Moon," accompanied, more or less, by a pit orchestra. Miss Nevada's talent, it seemed, was raising purebred Herefords; she had wanted to bring one of her cows, she said in a brief speech, but the officials wouldn't let her. Miss Colorado gave a monologue from "Dinner at Eight."

Miss Hawaii danced a hula. Miss Indiana showed a movie demonstrating her talent in swimming. Miss New Jersey sang "Mighty Lak a Rose." Miss Minnesota, a small version of Be Be Shopp, played some gypsy airs on a violin. While the judges marked their ballots, Miss Shopp entertained by playing "Smoke Gets in Your Eyes" on her vibraharp, evidently not handicapped by the thirty-pound gown. Then the preliminary winners were announced: Bathing Suit, a tie between Miss Arizona and Miss California; Talent, Miss Minnesota.

The contestants got back to their hotels late, because Miss Michigan was given a party backstage in honor of her nineteenth birthday. This had come about because she had decided early in the evening that she wanted to drop out of the Pageant and go home at once. I had been advised of the circumstance by an official of the Pageant. "This little brat wants to run out on us," he had said, stuffing some chewing tobacco into his mouth. "We're taking a gamble and blowing a sawbuck on a cake for her. It better work." It worked. Miss Michigan decided to stay in Atlantic City. Everybody appeared to enjoy the party, and everybody made a determined effort to be Miss Congeniality. Miss New York State showed no disappointment at not having won first place in the swim-suit competition. "California is so *tall*," she said to me.

At my hotel the next afternoon, I ran into Miss Arizona's chaperone in the elevator. "I thought I would die last night before they announced that my girl had won," she said. "I've been with her ever since she won her first contest, three years ago, but I've never been through anything like *that* before." Three years ago, she told me, Miss Arizona had won a teen-age beauty contest sponsored by Aldens, a mail-order house in Chicago; she had then attended a modelling school and had modelled teen-age clothes for the Aldens catalogue. The business people of Arizona (Arizona has the largest man-made lake in North America and the largest open-pit copper mine in the world, and it is great to live in Arizona, a brochure entitled "Miss Arizona, 1949—Jacque Mercer," put out by the contestant's sponsor, the Phoenix Junior Chamber of Commerce, and handed to me by the contestant's chaperone, said) had given her twenty-five hundred dollars to prepare for the Atlantic City contest. The chaperone invited me to come up to her room to look at Miss Arizona's wardrobe. It was a spectacular wardrobe, put together with taste. Miss Arizona was an only child. Her mother had married at fifteen and had named her daughter Jacque after a doll she had had. "Jackie's parents are here, but I'm making them stay away from her," the chaperone said. "They're schoolteachers. Schoolteachers don't know what to do with children." Miss Arizona came into the room.

"The Pageant asked Jackie what kind of car she likes and I said to put down Nash," said the chaperone.

"I like Cadillacs," Miss Arizona said. She opened a shoe box and stared at a pair of high-heeled button-strap shoes.

"Your mother went right out and bought a pair just like them," the chaperone said to her.

I told Miss Arizona and her chaperone that I had to get along, in order to look in on Miss New York State. Miss Arizona immediately said she liked Miss New York State. "She doesn't giggle, the way some of the others do," she explained. "I don't care for girls who giggle." She flicked a speck of dust off one of her new shoes. "I'll be glad when this is over and I can frown at people if I feel like it," she said. "I sometimes feel as though my face is going to crack. But I keep that bi-ig smile on my face." She laughed.

When I joined Miss New York State, she was wearing her nurse's uniform—white dress, white stockings, and white shoes. She was going, she said, to the Atlantic City Hospital. Two photographers covering the Pageant had heard that she had no way of demonstrating her talent, and had arranged to make a movie short showing her in professional action. She looked crisp and efficient. She had had a busy morning, she said, having been examined for personality at the first of the two breakfasts with the judges. The contestants sat at small tables, with a couple of judges at each. After each course, a bell rang and the judges changed tables, which gave them an opportunity to talk with all the contestants. Miss New York State said that most of the girls had trouble getting their breakfast down but that she had had orange juice, bacon and eggs, toast, marmalade, and tea. "I wasn't going to sit there and let all that good food go," she said. She didn't know whether she had made a favorable impression on the judges. "I told Conrad Thibault I had never heard of him," she said. "He didn't seem to like that."

Before the Pageant's second-evening program began, some of the judges wandered about Convention Hall, presumably judging the new Nash waiting in the lobby for the winner and judging the audience, which was approximately the same size it had been the first night. Earl Wilson stopped at the press table and said he had been reading an essay on beauty by Edmund Burke. "He says that an object of beauty should be comparatively small and delicate, bright and clear, with one section melting neatly into the other," he said. "The essay didn't affect me any. I like 'em big." He was joined by a gentleman from Omaha, who listened to him impatiently for a while. "I tell you what you're gonna pick, Earl," he finally broke in. "You're gonna pick the kind of girl I would pick for my own wife or daughter. That's what we got this contest for." Mr. Wilson nodded respectfully and moved on.

In front of the dressing room, Miss Florida was taking leave of her mother.

"Smile, now, honey," said her mother.

"Ah am smilin', Mama," said Miss Florida.

Inside, Miss New York State was standing with her back right up against an ironing board while a lady attendant pressed the skirt of the gown she was wearing for the evening's competition. It had a white net skirt and a white satin bodice. She had bought it at a New York wholesale house for $29.75. She looked around admiringly and objectively at the dresses of the other girls. "What beautiful gowns," she said.

Miss Florida was smiling at no one in particular. The city of Tampa had given her her gown—ruffled champagne-colored lace (a hundred and fifty yards)—and matching elbow-length gloves. Miss California sat gravely before a mirror in a dress of blue satin trimmed with black lace on the bodice and a black lace bow at the waist. Miss Arizona stood in a corner, a tense smile on her face, in a gown with a hoop skirt of ruffles of white organdie eyelet (a hundred and sixty yards) with a bouquet of red carnations at one side.

Miss Missouri came in, and Miss New York State waved to her. "Missouri is going to dance tonight," she told me. "I like dancing. It always makes me feel good. You know," she went on rapidly, "I found out today I'm photogenic. One of those photographers told me I could be a model, and my picture is in all the papers. One of the papers said I was *outstanding*." She grabbed my arm. "Nobody ever called me *outstanding* before."

Mrs. Shermer, the chief hostess, called out that the girls were to line up in the wings, and that they should be careful not to step on each other's dresses. Miss New York State took her place in line and the contestants started to move onto the stage, big smiles on their faces.

"Mind my horse!" Miss Montana said cheerily to her hostess.

"I *would* get the one with the horse," the hostess said to me.

I went out front and again sat down at the press table, next to a man whose badge said he was Arthur K. Willi, of R.K.O. Radio Pictures. Throughout the evening-gown and bathing-suit parades, he held a pair of opera glasses to his eyes; then he put them down with a groan. "I look and I look and I look, and what do I see?" he said. "If Clark Gable walked out on that stage right now, he would fill it up, or Maggie Sullavan, or Dorothy Maguire. There's nothing here, nothing—not even when I look at these kids with the eyes of the masses."

The m.c. brought out two platinum blondes and introduced them as Miss Atlanta of 1947 and Miss Omaha of 1947. They did a tap dance to "I Got Rhythm." "Those poor kids," Willi said. "Those poor, poor kids. Look at them. They look as though they had been knocking around Broadway for fifteen years." When the talent session began, he put the glasses back to his eyes. Miss Kansas, who was twenty-two, sang "September Song" with a deliberately husky voice. Miss Canada sang "Sempre Libera" from "La Traviata." Miss Connecticut recited "Jackie, the Son of the Hard-Boiled Cop." Miss Montana, wearing a conventional riding coat and frontier pants, rode her horse, a nine-year-old mare named Victory Belle, out onto the stage. Miss Illinois grinned confidently

at the judges and, in a strong soprano, sang "Ouvre Ton Cœur" as
though she meant it. Miss Wisconsin wound up with a baton-
twirling act. The winners: Bathing Suit, Miss Colorado; Talent,
Miss Canada.

"The Pageant wants publicity in the Canadian papers," a news-
paperman near me said.

Willi put his opera glasses in his coat pocket. "They've all lost
their youth already," he said. "They come down here for what? To
lose their youth!"

Miss New York State's picture was in the New York, Philadelphia, and Atlantic City newspapers the next morning. She was
shown at the Atlantic City Hospital, wearing her uniform and
holding a two-year-old girl who had just had her tonsils out. Photographers from the wire services had accompanied the movie-
makers to the hospital, and pictures of her had been sent out
across the country. Miss Arizona had dark circles under her eyes
when I encountered her in our hotel lobby after lunch, and she
said that she was going to spend the afternoon thinking about
Shakespeare and listening to a recording of Tchaikovsky's "Romeo
and Juliet" overture, to get in the mood for her talent demonstration that night—Juliet's potion scene. She had stayed up all the
night before talking about it and other Pageant matters with her
chaperone. Miss Arizona had played Juliet at Phoenix Junior College, having been chosen from five hundred girls who had tried
out for the part. She wanted to be an actress; she wouldn't go to
Hollywood until she had attended drama school and spent several
years in the theatre. "Hollywood would try to make me be something *they* wanted me to be," she said. "I won't do that. My grandfather always said that you can have anything you want in the
world, any way you want it, if you want it enough to work hard
enough for it."

That night, Miss Arizona came out in a wispy white nightgown
and, in the auditorium that could be transformed in a few hours
into a full-size football field, called up the faint, cold fear thrilling
through her veins that almost freezes up the heat of life. The audience was restless and noisy as she expressed her fear that she

would die ere her Romeo came. She was followed by Miss Greater Philadelphia, playing "I'm in the Mood for Love" on an electric guitar. Miss Mississippi did Hagar berating Abraham, in a dramatic reading popular with elocution teachers. Miss California acted the part of a girl who had been wronged by a man, in a reading even more popular with elocution teachers. Miss Florida sang "Put Your Shoes On, Lucy," which was announced in a release to the press as "Put Your Shoes on Lucy." Miss New York State, wearing her ice-blue evening gown, gave a short talk on nursing. She spoke without any expression at all, as though she were reciting something she had memorized with difficulty. "Ever since I was a little girl, I was taught that people were here for the purpose of serving others," she said. The audience shifted unsympathetically in its seats. Somebody muttered that Miss Illinois ought to stop flirting with the judges. Miss New York State said she had decided to become a nurse when she visited a friend who was a patient in a veterans' hospital during the war. She had been shocked by the men's helplessness. She would now show a film of herself going about her usual duties. While the film was being run, she made flat, realistic comments on it. She was pictured in the children's ward, in the maternity ward, and assisting a surgeon at an operation. At the end of the picture, the audience applauded halfheartedly. The winners: Bathing Suit, Miss Illinois; Talent, Miss Arizona.

I met Miss New York State as she was going back to her hotel. She felt pretty good, she said. She had enjoyed standing before all those people and telling them about nursing, and she had liked watching the talent of the others. "Wasn't Miss Arizona good?" she said. "She got hysterical so easily."

I was awakened at seven by the sound of gunfire. Some former Seabees had arrived in the city for a convention, and the Navy was welcoming them with a mock assault landing on the beach. It was the last day of the Pageant, and the boardwalk seemed to sag with the crowds.

The auditorium that night had a capacity audience, including standees, of twenty thousand. The Seabees came en masse. Most of the police at the hall felt that Miss California would be the winner, but the captain in charge of the detail was indifferent. "All you can do is look, and you get tired looking," he said. "I been guarding the beauties since 1921. An old lady come up to me during the parade the other day and says hello. I must of looked at her strange, because she says she was Miss Maryland of 1924. She was a grandmother! That kind of thing don't make me feel no better."

The contestants arrived and were counted. No one was missing; no one had walked out on the Pageant. The girls had had breakfast that morning with the judges again and then had voted for Miss Congeniality; Miss Montana and Miss New Jersey had tied for the honor and split the thousand-dollar scholarship. An only fairly congenial Miss wanted to know what kind of education you could get with a five-hundred-dollar scholarship. "Why, same as you can do with a bigger one," said Miss New Jersey. "Take voice lessons, or go to tap-dance school, or even go to Europe and learn something." Miss Slaughter nodded staunchly in approval. Also at the breakfast, Miss America of 1948 had made all fifty-two Misses members of the Pageant sorority—Mu Alpha Sigma, whose letters stand for Modesty, Ambition, and Success—and each girl had been given a gold-filled pin. "The most thrilling thing a girl could have," Miss America had said. "It means that all of you are queens. Remember that when the fifteen semifinalists are named tonight, all of you are queens." Miss New York State had asked if the sorority high sign was a big smile, a remark that didn't get much of a laugh. "Well," said Miss New York State to me that evening, looking at her sorority pin, "I finally belong to a sorority." She had voted for Miss Montana as Miss Congeniality. "I knew that I would never be elected," she told me. "In nursing, I got to know too much about human nature to be able to act congenial."

Mrs. Shermer was looking very pleased. She told Earl Wilson she had a hot item for his column—she had discovered some contestants putting on false eyelashes. Mr. Wilson looked pleased, too. He had spent the afternoon autographing copies of his latest book at a department store in town. Miss Arizona had received a wire from her father (who was staying at a nearby hotel) saying that she had made first base, second base, and third base, and concluding, "Now slide into home!" Miss Arizona was excited, and so was her chaperone. Miss New York State was unusually high-spirited and talkative; another photographer had called her photogenic, she said.

Mr. Russell was in tails for the big night. The curtains opened on the "beautiful old-fashioned Southern garden" again. One by one, the fifteen semifinalists stood up as their names were called: Miss Arizona, Miss Arkansas, Miss California, Miss Canada, Miss Chicago, Miss Colorado, Miss Hawaii, Miss Illinois, Miss Kansas, Miss Michigan, Miss Minnesota, Miss Mississippi, Miss New Jersey, Miss New York City, and Miss Wisconsin. Each of them was now sure of at least a thousand-dollar scholarship. The losers sat motionless in the Southern garden, some smiling, some in tears, others trying unsuccessfully to look indifferent. Out front, Miss Florida's mother cried softly, but Miss Florida was still smiling. Miss New York State, this time only half hidden behind a potted plant, looked puzzled, but interested in what was going on.

The semifinalists paraded before the judges once again, then withdrew to change into bathing suits. Mr. Russell asked the losers to walk the ramp, one by one, for the last time. "Give the valiant losers a hand, folks," he said. "They've got what it takes. They are your future wives and mothers of the nation." The valiant losers got a big hand. Miss New York State walked very gracefully—better than she had walked in competition. She waved cheerfully as she passed me, and with her lips silently said, "Bob—is—here." She received more applause than any of the other losers and quite a few whistles from the gallery. Then Miss Omaha of 1947 and Miss Atlanta of 1947 did their tap dance. Miss New York State watched them with a look of resigned but genuine appreciation.

The semifinalists paraded in bathing suits, and then demonstrated their talent all over again. While the judges marked their ballots, a six-year-old girl named Zola May played Chopin's "Minute Waltz" on a piano. The m.c. then spoke glowingly of the three donors of the prizes, and introduced the president of the company that makes Everglaze, the president of Catalina, and a delegation of three stout men in white linen suits from Nash. They all took bows. Then the m.c. asked Eddie Cantor to come out of the audience and up on the stage. Cantor did, and said hoarsely and passionately, "Communism hasn't got a chance when twenty thousand people gather to applaud culture and beauty."

Then the five big-prize finalists were announced: Miss Arizona, Miss California, Miss Colorado, Miss Illinois, and Miss Mississippi. Mr. Russell interviewed them, and their manner in replying was supposed to help the judges measure them for poise and personality. Each girl was asked three questions: "How do you plan to use your scholarship?" "Do your future plans include marriage, a career, or what?" "What did you get out of the Pageant?" Miss New York State peeked attentively around the potted plant as Miss Arizona, leading off in alphabetical order, replied tersely but politely that she planned to study dramatics at Stanford University, that she wanted marriage first and a career second, and that the Pageant had given her a chance to test herself before a new audience in a new part of the country. Miss California wanted to study interior decorating at the University of California and then go into the furniture business with her father; she wanted a career, so that she could help whomever she married; she was grateful to the Pageant for giving her the opportunity to meet so many wonderful girls from all over the country. Miss Illinois said that music was her first ambition. Mr. Russell, breaking the routine, asked her if she had ever been in love. She replied that she was in love but that music was still her first ambition. Miss New York State watched and listened carefully. No entertainment was at hand while the judges were voting again, so Mr. Russell asked the audience to sing "Smiles" until the ballots were counted, and he waved at the valiant losers to join in.

The winners were announced in reverse order: fifth place, Miss California ($1,500); fourth place, Miss Colorado ($2,000); third place, Miss Illinois ($2,500); second place, Miss Mississippi ($3,000); first place, Miss Arizona ($5,000, plus the new four-door Nash sedan, the dozen Catalina swimsuits, and the wardrobe of sixty Everglaze garments), now Miss America of 1949. There were hoots and boos, as well as cheers, from the audience.

The Governor of New Jersey, who had arrived after Miss Arizona had done her Juliet scene, awarded her a gilt statue, half as high as she was, of a winged Miss and said, "The world needs the kind of beauty and talent you have." Most of the losers then straggled out of the Southern garden into the wings, and a number of chaperones, hostesses, parents, and press people crowded onto the stage. I went along. Miss New York State came forward to watch Miss America of 1948 crown her successor. Miss America of 1948 wept, and her mother, standing nearby, wept with her. The new Miss America, tremulous but happy, said, "I only hope you'll be half as proud of me as I am of the title Miss America." Her mother, who had suddenly been surrounded by a group of admiring strangers, was much too occupied with her own emotions to notice her daughter coming slowly down the ramp, crown on her head, purple robe over her shoulders, and sceptre in her hand. The orchestra (the violinist holding a cigar in a corner of his mouth) played "Pomp and Circumstance," and Miss America of 1949 walked the length of the ramp, smiling graciously.

"This is the beginning," a reporter said to me. "She's going to spend the rest of her life looking for something. They all are."

"She is now the most desirable girl in the United States," another said.

When the Queen got back to the stage, Miss New York State offered her her solemn congratulations. "I'm glad you won, kid," she said. "I was rooting for you."

Then the new Miss America was engulfed by still photographers, newsreel men, and interviewers. Miss New York State stood beside me on the fringe of the crowd and watched.

"Everybody wants my autograph because I'm her father," Miss America's father was saying.

Her mother wanted to know whether the parents were to get a badge or ribbon, too.

"We rehearsed what she would say for hours," Miss America's chaperone was saying.

"We got to get her in the Nash!" one of the Nash triumvirate in white suits was saying.

A group of people were asking Miss Slaughter about the new

Queen's plans. "She's going to have breakfast with all the newspaper people in New York," Miss Slaughter said. "Then she gets outfitted with a whole new wardrobe by Everglaze, and she wears Everglaze whenever she goes out in public—it's in her contract. She's got to fly to California to preside at the Catalina swimsuit show, and after that she's got to make a couple of screen tests in Hollywood. I've been going mad arranging for those screen tests." A perspiring gentleman said that the winner of the recent Mrs. America contest at Asbury Park had invited the new Miss America to compete in a contest with her and he wanted to know how the Queen felt about this. "She says no comment because I say she says no comment," the head of the Pageant public relations said firmly.

Miss New York State shook her head at the wonder of it all. "Going to Hollywood!" she said. "She'll probably be in the movies."

The two of us walked back to the dressing room, where we found Miss Missouri tearfully folding up her Catalina swimsuit. Miss New York State looked puzzled at her tears and said that she hadn't cried, because when you don't expect very much, you're never disappointed. She was returning to New York with Bob the next morning. She had the name of a photographer who wanted to take a lot of pictures of her to sell to magazines, and another man wanted to talk to her about becoming a model. She was not going back to nursing if she could help it. "You get more when you're a model," she said.

—1949

3

THE BIG STONE

Harry Winston, a short, round, bushy-haired man of fifty-four, who owns the jewelry establishment of Harry Winston, Inc., at 7 East Fifty-first Street, and who is regarded by his rivals and his associates alike as the world's most daring dealer in precious stones, has for forty years been making his way to the top of his hotly competitive profession, inspired principally by a passionate devotion to diamonds. It has been estimated that he sells twenty-five million dollars' worth of jewels a year, and it is generally conceded by those in a position to know that he does a greater dollar volume of business, and has a bigger and more varied stock of diamonds on hand at any given time, than any other independent diamond dealer in the world. His stock is insured with Lloyd's of London for twenty-five million dollars—the largest jewel-insurance policy that the company has underwritten in its two-and-a-half-century history. His staff—executives, buyers, salesmen, cutters, designers, sorters, accountants, secretaries, and so on—numbers two hundred and fifty. Among big-time diamond dealers, who constitute a small, intimate, and not always charitable group, Winston, a cool-eyed man who is nevertheless tense and given to high-powered histrionics, is sometimes referred to as "our little

Napoleon," but even those who use the term most disparagingly do not deny having a certain admiration for him. And as for the several thousand small-time dealers in New York City who eliminate overhead by carrying their wares in their pockets, they look upon Winston, who started out from scratch himself, as the outstanding example of how far a man can go, given luck, intelligence, and sure instinct, in just the right proportions. "Harry Winston is *the* genius of our time," one of these sidewalk salesmen often says. "Genius" is a word that is subjected to a good deal of kicking around when diamond men get to talking about Winston. "Harry Winston started with nothing and became the biggest man in the business," a man working for a rival firm said not long ago. "He copies no one. He goes on his own. He's a gambler and he's got the guts to gamble. Why, he's got *salesmen* making twenty, forty thousand a year. He's a genius." One such fortunate salesman recently recalled an occasion when he told his employer that he thought a certain diamond Winston owned was worth seven hundred thousand dollars. "And what was his answer?" the salesman said. "He turned to me and he said, 'Why not a million?' And why *not?* Only a genius can think like that." Walter Lehman, the secretary and treasurer of Eichberg & Co., which was founded in 1867 and is one of the oldest New York importers and cutters of rough diamonds, says, "Harry Winston is a brilliant man. He has the nerve to buy in tremendous quantities, and his courage and foresight help the entire industry. He's a true genius." An official of I. Hennig & Co., Ltd., a London firm of diamond brokers, says, "He's the only man in the diamond business who has no fear of spending a million dollars in cash at a time. Clearly, an authentic genius." And a Belgian diamond salesman who has operated in Cairo, Rome, Paris, and Madrid as well as in New York puts it this way: "In life, if you are fifty-one per cent right, you are ahead. If you are more than fifty-one per cent right, you are a genius. Harry Winston is always more than fifty-one per cent right."

The chorus is, however, by no means unanimous. Among retailers of diamonds who are in competition with Winston, the word "genius" is seldom, if ever, applied to him. Indeed, at some of the big houses even the word "Winston" is taboo. "Tiffany is interested in Tiffany," an official of that firm said not long ago, in a five-word summary of what it thought of Winston. A Cartier man sized Winston up similarly by saying, "Once you know Cartier style, you want Cartier style and you don't want anything else." A Van Cleef & Arpels man was equally pithy. "Van Cleef is tops in the retail field," he said, referring to Winston. Back in the days when Winston was a struggling wholesaler of jewels, both Tiffany and Cartier occasionally bought from him, and more recently Van Cleef & Arpels, which is a French firm that has had a branch here only since 1938, did some business with him, but nowadays all three are competitors of his, and each goes its own individualistic way.

Another voice that seldom joins in the chorus of praise is that of Lazare Kaplan, who learned the art of cutting diamonds as a child in Antwerp and has been a wholesale diamond dealer here since 1914. Nineteen years ago, Kaplan cut up the famous 726-carat Jonker diamond for Winston, who owned it, and, while the press of the nation reported his every move, converted it into twelve smaller diamonds, ranging in weight from five to a hundred and forty carats. Kaplan isn't so sure there would be a Harry Winston, Inc., today if Winston had not commissioned him to cut the diamond. "I saved Winston a fortune," Kaplan said a while back. "In 1935, when he brought the Jonker to me, I agreed to cut it for him, but only if he took the entire responsibility. In cutting diamonds, you must know the grain, in order to determine the softest direction to cut in. Winston brought the stone to me with a cutting plan that someone in Europe had given him, and it would have meant disaster. He had invested a fortune in the Jonker, and if it had been cut according to his plan, he would have lost it. Instead, my staff and I spent a year making a new cutting plan and then cutting the Jonker. That stone was worth seven hundred thousand dollars when we started and two million when we finished." Kaplan paused and sighed. "And what did Winston do?" he went on. "A few years later he advertised that *he* was the one who had cut the Jonker diamond." Kaplan sighed again, and said, "But

Winston is fabulous. He is a remarkable gambler and a brilliant salesman, and he is the only real showman we have in the diamond business."

Winston has a rather different version of the cutting of the Jonker. "I didn't give Kaplan a plan for cutting it," he says. "Afterward, following a plan of my own, I recut ten of the diamonds Kaplan had cut. I paid him thirty thousand dollars to cut the stone, right in the middle of the depression. I even put his picture in the paper." Winston also resents being referred to as a gambler—by Kaplan or anybody else. "When the other man doesn't know what you're doing, he calls you a gambler," he says. "I'm no gambler, because I know what I'm doing. It's because they know so damn little about me and what I do that they call me a gambler."

After Winston had recut the big 140-carat stone from the Jonker, it weighed a hundred and twenty-five carats. "Keeping one even that large was risky," he has since said. "I priced it at a million dollars and it took me fourteen years to sell it. In the end, it took a king—Farouk of Egypt—to buy it. That's why I wanted the Jonker cut up in the first place. If I'd kept it as a single stone, it would have turned out to be a four-hundred-carat one, impossible to sell at its true value. A million dollars is about as high a price as you can ask for a diamond."

The Jonker was one of the six largest high-grade diamonds in the world; the five others, which have also been cut into a number of smaller stones, and their weights when found, were the Cullinan, 3,106 carats; the Excelsior, 995.5 carats; the Vargas (which Winston has also owned), 726.6 carats; the Jubilee, 650.8 carats; and the Victoria, 469 carats. Four smaller but almost equally famous stones that Winston owns or has owned, together with their weights after polishing (no record of their original weights exists), are the Star of the East, 94.8 carats, and the Hope, 44.5 carats, both of which were owned by Mrs. Evalyn Walsh MacLean; the Idol's Eye, 72 carats; and the Nassak, 43 carats. (The diamond in the average thousand-dollar engagement ring weighs from one to three carats, depending on its quality.)

Although Winston derives his greatest aesthetic pleasure from the company of large, expensive, perfect stones, he takes a kindly paternal interest in diamonds both good and bad, all the way— to use the idiom of the trade—from top blue-white diamonds, through fine white diamonds, white diamonds, top silver Cape, top light-brown, light brown, and silver Cape, to Cape, or yellow. Unlike the ancient Hindus, who believed that flawed diamonds brought on jaundice, pleurisy, leprosy, lameness, and similar misfortunes, Winston is also tolerant of diamonds that contain imperfections, such as bubbles, clouds, cracks, carbon spots, and the white, cracklike markings known as feathers. "Diamonds are like your children," he says. "No matter how bad they are, if they're yours, you can't help being fond of them. Once you get them, you don't want to give them up." Winston's relationship to his diamonds is as nearly like that of a parent to a child as he can make it; he tries to superintend every stage of their development. He buys diamonds in the rough, imports them, cuts them, polishes them, designs their settings, sells them, and, whenever possible, follows their careers after they leave his hands. And he does this not with just a few stones but, insofar as it is practicable, with thousands of them every year. He also exports diamonds wholesale and buys diamonds from the heirs of estates. Nor is Harry Winston, Inc., by any means his only outlet in this country; department stores, other retail jewellers, and installment houses sell Winston diamonds, and readers of the Montgomery Ward catalogue may buy them through its pages. While other diamond men are content to specialize in one—or, at most, two or three—of these many and varied activities, Winston thinks that his parental relationship is still not quite all it should be; as matters stand, he feels he is in the position of a foster parent, for he doesn't so much as hear about a new diamond until weeks, or even months, after it has left the mine. This is because ninety-five per cent of the world's diamond supply is controlled by De Beers Consolidated Mines, Ltd., a closemouthed British-owned company, commonly known as the Syndicate, which has held a monopoly on the mining of diamonds in South Africa since 1889. The Portuguese colony of Angola, in southwest Africa, produces about a million carats of rough diamonds—or fifteen million dollars' worth— a year from mines that are owned jointly by the Angola Diamond

Corporation and the Portuguese government. The Angola Diamond Corporation—which is owned by American, British, and Portuguese interests—has been selling its output to De Beers, under a contract that was signed in 1950, without the sanction of the Portuguese government, and that expires in 1955. Winston is currently negotiating with the Portuguese government to purchase the total Angola diamond output over the next ten years—a bid for independence that the Syndicate considers so presumptuous that it has tried, without much success, to cut him off from obtaining any diamonds at all. "De Beers might make me a preferred client if I'd pass up the Portuguese deal," Winston said the other day. "But I'd rather have an independent diamond supply, and I'm going to try to get it." Winston's ambitious scheme has been received with admiration and without surprise—and also without support—by the rest of the diamond men in this country. "Let's face it. Harry Winston is the most impressive man in the business today," one of his bitterest rivals said recently. "I wouldn't lift a finger to help him in this deal, but if he comes out a winner again, he'll not only be a genius, he'll be more so."

At noon on Tuesday, January 13, 1953, Winston was sitting alone in his office on the second floor of the six-story granite building that his firm occupies, a building that was the town house of the late Mrs. Marius de Brabant, a daughter of Senator William A. Clark, the mining millionaire. Seated at a Louis XV desk, Winston looked bleakly through his window at the people filing steadily in and out of St. Patrick's Cathedral, directly opposite. He was wearing, as usual, a neat, dark, impeccably tailored double-breasted suit and no jewelry at all. Before him on the desk was a large square of black velvet, on which lay a gauge for estimating the weight of stones in settings, a pair of tweezers for picking up small stones, a couple of yellow pencils with sharp points, a silver pillbox, a jeweller's loupe, a pad of white paper, on which he had been doodling, and a couple of his diamonds—a blue-white 60-carat stone set in a ring and the 44½-carat Hope, a deep-blue, oval stone set in a pendant. Also on the desk was a telephone, connected with the house switchboard; on a stand behind him was a second telephone, this one a private wire. Several framed photographs of Winston's wife and their two sons—Ronald, thirteen, and Bruce, ten—stood on a small desk in a corner, and an oil painting of the trio hung on the wall. A couple of love seats faced each other before a fireplace, and several chests, tables, and chairs of the same period were scattered about the room.

The door to Winston's office opened, and his secretary, a young, pleasant blonde named Polly Rowe, came in, carrying a delicately flowered china cup and saucer. "Your coffee, Mr. Winston," she said.

Winston sighed deeply and nodded. "Why everybody goes out to lunch, I'll never understand," he said. "All that eating. Why?"

"I really don't know, but everybody does it," Miss Rowe said respectfully.

Winston took a saccharin pill from the silver box. He sighed again as he dropped the pill into the cup. While sipping his coffee, he put his forefinger through the 60-carat diamond ring and looked thoughtfully at its stone. Then he wrenched the ring off, tossed it impatiently toward Miss Rowe, and told her to put it away. "And the Hope, too," he said. "I don't feel very well. I think I'm coming down with one of those virus things."

Winston's private telephone rang, and as he answered it he suddenly became alert. He lowered his voice to a tone of confidential intimacy, and spoke more and more softly as the conversation went on. After he hung up, he motioned to Miss Rowe to hand the Hope diamond and the ring back to him. "I'll play with them awhile," he said. "And would you ask Ludel to come down as soon as possible?" As Miss Rowe left the room, he put the ring on his forefinger again and looked at it with admiration.

"You have to go to London," Winston said a few minutes later to Bernard Ludel, a bald, square-faced, amiable man, who has been Winston's buyer of rough diamonds for the past seven years, during which time he has enthusiastically spent thirty million Winston dollars. Ludel has been in the diamond business for forty years. Born in Amsterdam, he was trained there by his father to be a diamond cleaver. He came to the United States in 1916, at the age of twenty, and in the ten years that followed he cleaved approximately fourteen thousand diamonds, ranging in size from six carats to eighty. Then he became an independent buyer and seller of diamonds. After some twenty years of that, he gave up his own business to join Winston.

"I am ready," Ludel replied now. The previous week, he had returned from his forty-sixth trip to Europe, his eighth in six months. He and his wife were living in a small hotel on the West Side, where they were expecting a visit any day from a married daughter living in Panama. "I am always ready," Ludel added.

"I just got a call from London," Winston said sharply. "Prins tells me he's got a one-hundred-and-fifty-four-and-a-half-carat stone. Just arrived from Jagersfontein. Prins says it's perfect. A perfect stone."

Ludel smiled and said nothing.

"Take a look at it," Winston said, his voice soft and low again. "See if it's perfect."

"I can take the plane tomorrow," Ludel told him.

"Good luck," said Winston. He put his head in his hands and closed his eyes. "I think you're coming down with something, Harry," he said aloud to himself. "You'd better go home and go to bed." He put on a black cashmere overcoat and a black homburg, and as he was leaving his office, his secretary handed him, as she does every day, a crisp new dollar bill—he hates to carry money around with him—for his taxi fare to his apartment, on upper Fifth Avenue.

As soon as Ludel's plane landed in London, on Thursday, he took a taxi directly from the airport to the diamond-brokerage offices of I. Hennig, on the third floor of Audrey House, a gray stone Edwardian building on Ely Place, in the city's jewelry district. It was late afternoon when he arrived. George F. Prins, a thoughtful, scholarly gentleman, who is one of the two directors of the firm and the man who sold Winston the Jonker diamond, told Ludel that the light wasn't right for looking at the stone then, and suggested that he come back in the morning. Ludel drove to a hotel, where, after an early dinner, he went to bed and lay awake all night thinking about the 154½-carat diamond. At nine-thirty, he was back at the Hennig establishment. Prins told him that the vault in which the diamond was kept could not be opened until ten. Ludel stood around waiting and smoking one cigarette after another. At three minutes after ten, Prins took the diamond out of the vault. It was in a small folder of heavy white paper lined with a sheet of thin waxed paper. Prins handed the folder to Ludel, who smiled slightly as he unwrapped the stone. It was a little more than an inch and a half long and an inch thick at one end, tapering to about a third that thickness at the other, and, like most rough diamonds, it had a frosted coating that made it look rather like a wad of frozen absorbent cotten. Its avoirdupois weight was a bit over an ounce. Ludel held the stone between his thumb and forefinger, and continued to smile. Prins left the room, and returned in a few minutes with a cup of lukewarm coffee, with milk, which he handed to Ludel. Then, without saying anything, he left the room again. Ludel sat down at a table near a window facing north over the roofs of several fine old Georgian houses. He put a jeweller's loupe to his eye and looked at the diamond through it. Despite its coating, he could tell with reasonable certainty that there were no imperfections in the interior. Ludel sat there silently studying the diamond through the loupe for two hours. Then he returned the stone to Prins, went back to his hotel room, and, sitting on his bed, put in a call to his employer on East Fifty-first Street.

"Ludel!" Winston said.

"The biggest sensation of my life," Ludel said, without preliminaries. "The stone is absolutely perfect, I feel sure. I could never dream of a stone like that—it's the finest I have ever seen. So magnificent in color. Blue-white."

"Ludel, is it clean?" Winston asked impatiently. "Is it absolutely clean?"

"I am convinced that it is absolutely clean," said Ludel. "Also, it is an ideal shape for a pear-shaped diamond. You should own this stone."

"Is it perfect, Ludel?" Winston asked.

"Perfect, perfect," Ludel assured him.

Winston and Ludel went on to discuss the price Hennig was asking—a quarter of a million dollars—and ways of persuading Hennig to knock twenty-five thousand dollars off that figure. They talked for thirty-eight minutes, and the cost of the call came to a hundred and ninety dollars. It was the first of thirteen transatlantic telephone calls Ludel made to Winston during ten days of intensive negotiations. Then Ludel told Winston that there was nothing further he could do in the way of bargaining and that he would wait in London until he received orders, one way or the other, from New York. On the evening of February 3rd, Winston went to bed early with a virus infection and a high fever. At midnight, he suddenly made up his mind about the 154½-carat diamond. He picked up the telephone at his bedside and sent a cable to Ludel, via Western Union. The cable consisted of one word—"BUY." Winston thereupon fell into a deep sleep, and when he awoke in the morning, his fever was gone.

As soon as Ludel received the cable, he notified Prins that Winston was going to buy the big diamond and that Winston's bank in New York would make arrangements with a London bank to pay I. Hennig, Ltd., $230,807—the price agreed upon, plus the broker's commission. The next day, Ludel left London for Amsterdam, to see about buying some other diamonds for Winston. On February 6th, Winston received the following cable:

LONDON VIA WU CABLES FEB 6 316P

HARWINSTON

NYK

154-½ CARATS AIRMAILED TODAY

HENNIG

1108A

The 154½ carats were fully insured on their flight. Winston regards the mails as the safest way of moving diamonds from one place to another. He does not like to have his employees carry valuable jewels on long journeys alone, because of the obvious risks involved.

• • •

Embedded in a fragment of blue ground, or kimberlite—the volcanic-rock formation in which most diamonds are found—the 154½-carat stone was brought up out of a De Beers mine at Jagersfontein, in the Orange Free State, during the latter part of 1952. The African natives who were working the mine were then drilling and blasting in a vein of blue ground located at a depth of about thirteen hundred feet. It is doubtful whether any of the miners who were responsible for getting the big stone to the surface were aware that they had done a particularly valuable day's work, for diamonds are rarely visible in the pieces of shattered blue ground that are hauled up—ten tons at a time—in huge skips, or steel buckets. These buckets are raised and lowered in the mine shafts at a speed greater than man can endure, and there is good reason for speed, since it takes ten thousand tons of blue ground from the average South African mine to produce one pound of diamonds. Each skipful, as it comes up out of the earth, is dumped into a bin, from which a conveyor belt hauls it to a mill. There the blue ground is crushed, screened, and washed to cull out all but the very heaviest particles, known as the diamondiferous concentrate. The concentrate is then placed on an oblong table that has been coated with petroleum jelly. The table is flooded with water and made to shake violently from side to side, and as it shakes, all the remaining waste rock is washed away, and the diamonds, which have the peculiar property of shedding water, remain stuck in the jelly. Finally, the jelly is scraped off the table and boiled, setting the diamonds free.

The 154½-carat stone was found in the normal course of mining operations, and recovered on the grease table like any run-of-mine stone. Despite its large size, no special record was made of its discovery. It was simply listed in De Beers' record of all stones over ten carats, in accordance with the diamond laws of the Union of South Africa. De Beers, through its distributing organization called the Diamond Trading Company, sold the diamond in London to Diamond Realisations, Ltd., wholesalers of rough diamonds. Diamond Realisations placed it with Hennig for resale.

• • •

In New York, the afternoon of February 11th was gray, damp, and bone-chilling. At four-thirty that afternoon, a large, white-haired man, hatless and wearing rimless spectacles, got out of a taxi in front of 7 East Fifty-first Street. He wore a dark overcoat belted in the back, and he was chewing gum. The taximeter registered a dollar and ninety cents. The white-haired man gave the driver three dollars. "Take it easy, Mac," he said.

"Same to you, Mr. Siegel," said the driver.

Sam Siegel, an employee of Meadows Wye & Co., which acts as Custom House brokers for Winston, touched a forefinger to his temple in farewell. When he has valuable packages to deliver, he makes a point of taking taxis whose drivers he knows and trusts. On this occasion, the package he was delivering was a small one that he had enclosed in a Manila envelope. As the taxi drove off, Siegel went up to the iron-grilled door leading to the foyer of the Winston establishment, a door that is kept locked at all times. He rang the doorbell and was recognized by a broad-shouldered, prematurely gray man, wearing a gray business suit and an automatic pistol in a holster, who was standing just inside, and who guards the house of Harry Winston, Inc., against all comers. The guard nodded to a receptionist seated at a desk on the left side of the foyer, and she pushed a button that unlocked the door.

"Hello, Mr. Chaplin," Siegel said to the guard upon entering, and then he nodded to the receptionist and said, "Miss Shaw, how are you?"

Just beyond the receptionist's desk was a circular marble staircase, leading to Winston's office. Siegel glanced into a mirror on the wall opposite, and straightened his tie.

"You're looking well, Mr. Siegel," the receptionist said.

Siegel smiled, glanced into the main salon, beyond the foyer, and then, escorted by Chaplin, entered a small elevator next to the staircase. The two men rode up to the third floor, where they made their way to the comptroller's office through a series of doors, which were unlocked for them by clerks and secretaries. There Siegel handed the Manila envelope to the comptroller, Bertram Barr, a thin, worried-looking man, who removed the package from it. It was wrapped in blue paper, tied with brown string, and sealed with red wax, which had been stamped by a customs inspector with the words "U.S. Appraiser of Mdse." It was addressed, in long-hand, to Winston, and had three British stamps on it, totalling one pound five shillings and sixpence—a mailing cost of three dollars and sixty-one cents.

Siegel remarked to Barr that the weather was rotten, and offered him a stick of chewing gum. The comptroller unwrapped the gum and put it in his mouth. A secretary came forward and handed Siegel a receipt specifying that he had delivered one parcel, with the United States customs seal intact, containing one rough diamond weighing 154½ carats and costing $230,807. She also handed him a check for twenty-eight dollars and seventy-five cents, to cover the brokerage fee; because the diamond was in its rough state, it had been admitted to this country duty-free. Siegel folded the check, slipped it into an inside coat pocket, and left. Barr placed the blue package, still unopened, in a huge, electrically con-trolled safe, and hurried away to attend a meeting of the Federal Government Accountants Association of New York, of which he is a director.

The next morning, Winston saw the 154½-carat diamond for the first time. He arrived at his office at eight-fifty-five and im-mediately asked Miss Rowe to tell Barr to bring the diamond in. Before he had time to do more than glance through a few of the letters in his morning mail, the comptroller came in and put the package on the desk in front of him. It was just nine o'clock.

"Turn out the light, so I can see the color," Winston said as he cut the string. Barr flicked the switch. There was a happy and ex-pectant smile on Winston's face. Quickly, he broke the seal, un-wrapped a plain white cardboard box, and opened it. Inside the box, on a bed of cotton, lay the diamond, done up in white tissue paper. Winston held his breath, and his smile grew numb. Then he drew back the edges of the tissue paper. His smile vanished. He took the stone out of the wrapping and looked at it, and his face froze. Without saying a word, he held the stone up to the light, grasping it between thumb and forefinger. Then he stood up, kicked his chair back, and took the stone over to the window. Put-ting his loupe to his eye, he studied the stone for some time. "I suppose I've got to take Ludel's word for it," he said at last, in a flat, cold voice. "He should know what he's talking about. Otherwise he'd be getting twenty dollars a week instead of what he's getting. But a piece is missing from this stone. An important piece. A third of the stone is missing. Maybe a million years ago some sort of volcanic disturbance broke it off. It might be fifty miles away from where this was found." Turning the diamond slowly in his fingers, he went on, talking to himself, "It's a fine stone, all right. It's a great stone, Harry. But I'm not sure I agree with Ludel that it's the finest color." He was silent for a few moments. Then he said abruptly, "Perhaps we're being unfair to the stone. The light is bad here. I want to look at it upstairs."

Leaving Barr standing in the office, Winston went out and waited briefly for the elevator, and then turned impatiently and ran up four flights of stairs to the sixth floor, where loose diamonds are sorted according to color, size, and quality. He walked over to one of a row of desks standing under several windows that faced north, and sat down at it. "Now we see the purity of it," he said, looking at his diamond again. With a faint smile, he tossed the stone on a piece of white tissue paper. "It does look a little bluer on the paper," he said, without spirit.

A young man, one of the sorters, came up and saw the diamond lying on the paper. "Oh, my!" he said, leaning over to get a closer look at the diamond but not touching it. "Oh, my!" he repeated. "Beautiful!"

"Do you like it?" Winston asked crossly.

"Oh, it's beautiful!" said the sorter.

"A piece is missing," Winston said. "Isn't that criminal?"

"But it's a glorious stone," said the sorter. "There aren't many like that one."

Winston said, "Let me have some of the silver Capes." The sorter brought over a paper folder full of rough diamonds. "Do you see the contrast?" Winston said. "This stone looks so superior now. But that's just because of these silver Capes. A small jeweller would rate them as first-class, of course, but they're fourth-class by our standards." Talking as much to himself as to the sorter, he went on, "Ludel says it's the finest he's ever seen. Well, I think it's a fine stone, all right, but we'll wait and see how fine. Ludel says the yield will be sixty-five carats after it's been cut. That's a big diamond. The average broker says you've got to have a prospective client when you spend a quarter of a million on a stone. I don't know whether I'm crazy or not, but at the present time I haven't even a *dream* of a client." He picked up the diamond, and it slipped from his fingers and fell to the floor. He stooped quickly and retrieved it.

"Mr. Winston, that means good luck, dropping a diamond," the sorter said.

"Maybe, maybe not," Winston said, with a dry laugh.

"It's got the beauty of a miniature Jonker," the sorter said.

"Maybe by the time it's finished it'll be much more brilliant," Winston said. "The more I look at it, the better I like it. I'm beginning to feel closer to it. Yes, I do believe it's going to be a beautiful stone after all."

Still clutching the diamond, Winston headed back downstairs. The sorter accompanied him. "I kept asking Ludel over the phone, 'If it's so perfect, why is the yield going to be so low?'" Winston said in the elevator. "He didn't tell me anything about the missing piece, and I think he should have, but I suppose he had so much confidence in the stone that he didn't feel it was necessary." He shrugged.

At the second floor, the sorter complimented Winston again on his new acquisition, and went on downstairs. Back in his office, Winston sat down at his desk and tossed the diamond on the velvet pad. Miss Rowe came in and said that Daniel Frey, the general manager of the company, wanted to see him, and Winston told her to send him in. "And get a cable off to Ludel in Amsterdam," he added. "Say, 'Stone beautiful.' That's all." He looked at the diamond again. "It *is* going to be beautiful," he said, almost in a whisper. "Nature produces so few perfect stones. I hope this stone will turn out to be perfect."

When Frey came in, he looked first at the diamond, and whistled. Then he looked at Winston. "That's quite a piece," Frey said. He is a friendly, hard-working man of forty-six, who, twenty-eight years ago, while a student at City College, took a summer job with Winston as an errand boy. After he graduated, in 1928, he was given a full-time job with the firm, and he has been with Winston ever since. Now he picked up the diamond and studied it against the light from the window. "Spectacular," he said, and handed it to Winston, who held it up, turning it this way and that. "Here will be the table, and this will be the culet, and this the girdle," he said, indicating in succession where he thought the diamond's large, flat upper facet should be cut, and its small lower facet, and the edge that would be grasped by the setting. "We'll tilt it just like that."

"Beautiful," said Frey.

"It may turn out to be perfect," Winston said softly, looking at the diamond through his loupe. "If it does, maybe we'll sacrifice a little of it to get a better slope. It looks to me as if the heart of this stone is clean." He put aside the loupe, held the diamond at arm's length, and looked at it thoughtfully. "No two diamonds are alike," he said. "Each diamond has a different nature. Each diamond has different problems. Each diamond must be handled as you handle a person."

At nine-thirty the next morning, right after arriving at his office, Winston called in Frey and Bernard De Haan, who is the head of Winston's diamond-cutting-and-polishing department. De Haan, a good-natured, steady, solid-looking man, is a cousin of Ludel's, and their careers have for the most part followed parallel lines. He was born fifty-six years ago in Amsterdam, where he started learning to be a diamond cutter and polisher at the age of fourteen. His father and one of his great-grandfathers were diamond polishers, and one of his grandfathers was a diamond setter. De Haan came to this country at eighteen and had had a business of his own for some years when Winston asked him to take over the cutting department, in 1952. This morning, De Haan was wearing Army suntans and a pair of shell-rimmed spectacles with large, round, steamy lenses. De Haan and Frey entered the office together, and Winston immediately handed the 154½-carat diamond to De Haan.

De Haan's spectacles grew even steamier as he stood facing the light and studying the stone. "You certainly got something special with this one," he said.

"As you can see, there's a piece missing," Winston said. "What a stone it would have been if that piece hadn't shot off! Isn't it criminal?" The telephone on his desk rang. It was a salesman calling from downstairs. "Yes," Winston said. "I remember the man. He's looking for a pair of earrings. Let Joe work with him on it." He hung up and took the diamond from De Haan. "There isn't any question of trying to get more than one stone out of it, and the loss shouldn't be over fifty-five per cent," he said. "Or do you think we might go through here and make two stones?" He pointed to what looked like a ridge in the stone.

"Oh, no," De Haan said. "This should be one stone. One pear-shaped stone."

"That's what I thought," Winston said, looking satisfied.

"This is going to be your stone," said De Haan. "A stone like this comes once in a lifetime." He held his hand out for the diamond, but Winston did not give it to him. He was busy rubbing it with his thumb and rolling it around in the palm of his hand.

The door opened and a young salesman came in with a black velvet jewel box containing a diamond necklace. "You wanted to see this," he said to Winston.

Winston handed the diamond to De Haan and, turning his attention to the necklace, sighed, put his fingertips to his temples, and said wearily, "When we designed this necklace, she said she wanted to be able to wear it as a bracelet, too. So Eddie delivered it to her yesterday, and she said it was too long to wear as a bracelet. She asked Eddie if he'd make it shorter. Eddie said no, he couldn't, and she became hysterical. It was hardly discreet of him to say no."

"You want to take out a few stones?" the salesman asked.

"Yes," Winston said. "And you'll have to air-mail it to her in Palm Beach. She wants to wear it to a party there Wednesday night."

The salesman picked up the box with the necklace and left.

"My God!" Winston said. "What we go through to adorn women! What we have to do in this business! The talking I have to do! I'm constantly hoarse from the talking. These people take everything out of you. For two hours yesterday afternoon, I pleaded with a woman to choose a forty-thousand-dollar necklace of round diamonds instead of a marquise-diamond one for sixty-five thousand dollars. She's fifty years old, and she's had a mean life. The round diamonds would have softened her, but she insisted on the long, tapered ones. No matter how successful you are, you still must bow to the whims of these people." He took the big diamond from De Haan and put it on the velvet pad. After looking at it for a few moments, he said hopefully, "You know, I wouldn't be surprised if we get a seventy-three-carat stone out of it."

"It's easier to visualize the stone than the customer," Frey remarked.

"Well, seventy-three-carat diamonds aren't sold every day," Winston said, holding his loupe to his lips.

"This will be much more brilliant than the Jonker," said De Haan.

"Prins claimed it was bluer," Winston said.

"The Jonker had more of an icy color," De Haan said. "When I first saw it, I was really a little let down. It didn't have as much life as I'd expected. Now I look at this and I don't feel a bit let down. I never liked the Jonker. It was a colder color."

"I'll be satisfied if this is the same color," Winston said. He rang for Miss Rowe and asked her to get him a photograph of the Star of the East, the diamond he had sold to Farouk eighteen months earlier and had not yet been paid for.

"Don't get me wrong," Frey said while they were waiting. "You'll sell this stone. It'll just be a matter of time."

"I'll sell it, all right," Winston said. "No matter what it costs us by the time we're through. Some people want the finest."

Miss Rowe brought in the photograph. After studying it intently, he said that when the new diamond was finished, it would be smaller than the Star of the East but it would also be a finer stone. With that, he rewrapped the diamond in its original tissue paper, gave it to De Haan, and asked him to take it upstairs and register it in stock.

De Haan went upstairs with Frey to the accounting department, where he turned the stone over to a girl clerk, who weighed it. It weighed exactly 154½ carats. It was then registered as No. 20118. "Anyone superstitious?" the girl said. "It's Friday the thirteenth." Pointing to a page in a loose-leaf folder, she turned to De Haan and said, "Sign here." De Haan signed for the diamond, and the girl rewrapped it in the tissue paper and handed it back to him. Then he went upstairs to the polishing room, where rough diamonds are ground to give them the facets, or windows, that admit and reflect light and produce the characteristic sparkle. The polishing room was dominated by a couple of long tables on which stood perhaps a dozen machines somewhat resembling record-players. On each machine a cast-iron disc, coated with a paste of diamond dust and olive oil, was spinning at the rate of twenty-two hundred revolutions a minute, and pressed against each disc was a diamond, held in a dop, or metal cup, that was supported by a wood-and-metal arm. Four men—dressed, like De Haan, in suntans—were watching the machines; from time to time they made tiny adjustments in the dops as the discs gradually ground the diamonds to the desired shape.

De Haan stood silently in the doorway for a while. Then he coughed ostentatiously. His colleagues looked up and immediately gathered around him. Still without speaking, he unwrapped the diamond and showed it to them.

"What a terrific piece," said one.

"Nice color," said another.

"Beautiful stuff," said a third.

A fourth nodded and said, "That *is* a diamond."

"Now I get to work," De Haan said. "I make a little window or two in the stone, so we can look inside to be sure there is no blemish."

One of the cutters asked De Haan how long he expected to have to work on the diamond.

"What's the rush?" De Haan said. "It took millions of years to make this diamond. Why hurry now?"

• • •

One morning a few weeks later, Frey stopped in at the polishing room to ask De Haan how the big stone was coming along. De Haan showed it to him. The skin had been removed from the table of the diamond, revealing the interior, and lines had been inked on the exposed surface as a guide in polishing. "No grave internal problems?" Frey asked. De Haan said no—none. As a matter of fact, he went on, he was about to take the diamond down and show it to Winston. He removed the stone from the dop and held it up to Frey, tantalizingly waving it this way and that just out of his reach. Then both men took the elevator to Winston's office, and De Haan placed the diamond before Winston, who was seated at his desk. The diamond was beginning to show a blue-white brilliance.

Winston smiled as he looked at it. "There's your diamond, Harry," he said. "No pin-point marks. No little white flaws. We've seen the heart, and the heart is pure. This diamond is going to be like a glorious woman. It's going to have everything—form, grace, beauty, and perfect health." He told Frey and De Haan that he had been afraid that an imperfection would be found in the diamond, and it was a relief that none had been. There had been no accidents so far during the polishing of the stone, either, and that was a relief, too. Winston is generally philosophical about accidents. Only the week before, there had been a slip while an eighty-carat stone was being cleaved, and ten carats had been lost. It was, as he had remarked at the time, fifty thousand dollars down the drain.

Frey asked Winston whether he would soon be showing the diamond to a prospective buyer. Winston looked horrified. "You can make a great thing common by showing it at this stage," he said. "That's the last thing I want to do. I'm going to keep this stone quiet. I want to keep it to myself. I'll put it in the safe for a while after it's finished. I may play with it for a while"— he rolled the stone across his desk like a marble—"or I may just look at it. This stone is like a great painting. You want to keep on looking at it." He put his loupe to his eye and scrutinized the diamond. "This is one of the finest stones in the world," he said, with a catch in his voice. Then he handed the stone back to De Haan, saying, "I want to look at the stone again when this little flaw in the skin here has been removed." De Haan nodded and left. "Fastest man in the world—De Haan," Winston said to Frey. "Yet he's like a first-class chess player. He works slowly on the dangerous moves."

Winston turned to a black jewel box on his desk, opened it, and took out a necklace set with fourteen marquise diamonds, and a matching bracelet. "What beautiful eyes!" he said, admiring the elliptical stones. "This is that bracelet I sold the Princess a few years ago," he went on. "Later, I made the necklace to match it. She's calling me this morning about it. She and I are thinking of taking this necklace and combining it with the bracelet to make two bracelets. Then she'll have twenty-eight beautiful eyes as well as her own two." He added, with a short, low laugh, "She'll have a bracelet on each arm, and she'll be continually raising her arms—first one, then the other—as she smokes cigarettes." He raised his arms to show what he meant. "Twenty-eight marquises like that!" he said softly to himself. "All the same color! It's a dream! Where else could you get such stones? You could sort your way through fifty million dollars' worth of diamonds and never find anything like them. I can tell you—" His private telephone rang.

"Your Highness, good morning!" Winston said into the phone, his voice coaxing and gentle. "How are you, Your Highness? . . . Did you have a good sleep? . . . Am I going to have the pleasure of seeing you today, Your Highness? . . . You'll have a pair of bangles, each with fourteen beautiful eyes. Wait till you see the designs." The conversation ambled along for ten minutes or so. After hanging up, Winston called Miss Rowe and told her that the Princess would be around late that afternoon and that she should be shown up to his office as soon as she arrived. "She'll have two of the most elegant bangles in the world," he said to Frey. "*Fit* for a princess!"

At ten o'clock on the morning of April 16th, Winston went upstairs to the polishing room with Frey to check on the progress of his big diamond. De Haan, smiling but silent, took the diamond out of the dop, where it had been running on the wheel, and handed it to Winston. Then, folding his arms, he cast a significant glance at a couple of his polishers. Winston held up the diamond and gave a long, low hum of pleasure. He quickly fished his loupe from his coat pocket and examined the stone more closely. Then he looked unbelievingly at De Haan, who grinned at him but still said nothing. The two polishers grinned at each other. Winston, his hands trembling as he started to take another look at the diamond, dropped his loupe. The polishers laughed as it rolled across the floor.

"I told you it was better than the Jonker," De Haan said.

When Winston finally spoke, he spoke to himself. "The softness!" he said, his voice tremulous. "Harry, the brilliance!" He handed the diamond back to De Haan.

Winston and Frey returned to Winston's office. "When that diamond first arrived, I really did think it was wonderful, but you can never be sure until a stone is finished," Winston said. "I have seen rough diamonds that seemed full of promise, but when they were finished they looked yellow. I thought this stone was beautiful in the rough. But now the coating is off and— Well, I've seen some great stones, but this one looks to me as though it will be the finest diamond in the world." He suddenly groaned and covered his eyes with his hands. "I'm so tired," he said. "Last night, my wife and I went to Barney Balaban's daughter's wedding. The tension! The women parading to show off their jewels! The gowns! The drinking and the smoking! I can't do it. It kills you. If it weren't for my wife, I'd never go to a party. When you're with people, they take everything out of you." He rubbed his eyes for a moment or two, and then started to talk about the diamond again. "De Haan has been saying all along that this stone is the finest diamond he's ever worked on. I thought it was because he was new here and hadn't seen some of our diamonds in the past. Now I see he was right. It's turning out to be a perfect pear shape. This stone will go down in history."

Miss Rowe came in and announced that he had a visitor, a woman from Fort Worth. Winston said, "Bring her in," and the secretary retired.

Almost at once, the door burst open and in strode a smartly dressed middle-aged woman wearing a mink stole and carrying a violet umbrella. "Harry, you rascal, you had a beautiful girl in here yesterday!" she said, in a loud, hoarse voice. Winston stood up, smiling, and held out his hand. The woman shook his hand, laughing, and the laugh turned into a brief fit of coughing. "I've just come from Saint Patrick's," she went on, tapping him on the shoulder with her umbrella. "Here's what I do, Harry. I go in to see the Blessed Mother and I come out the side door and look right up into your office, and that way I know whether you're here and what you're doing."

Winston laughed dutifully, and they both sat down.

"I'm having lunch with Cardinal Spellman tomorrow," the woman said.

"And how is His Eminence?" Winston asked.

"He's just as busy as can be," said the woman. "But every time I'm in town, he makes it a point to have lunch with me."

"You're such good friends," said Winston. "And did you see Bishop Sheen?"

"No, not this trip. Harry, I've decided to take the big sapphire."

"It's a glorious stone," Winston said, lowering his voice. "You'll look glorious with it."

"You don't think it's too big for me, Harry? You think I can wear it?"

"You certainly can wear it," said Winston. "It's glorious on you."

"Harry, here's what I think. Nobody would ever think it's just a piece of costume jewelry—not seeing it on me—so I guess I can get away with wearing it."

Winston leaned across the desk and, in a still lower voice, said, "I've got a new stone—a diamond."

"What you going to call it?" the woman asked.

Winston said he didn't know yet.

"What's this heart-shaped diamond they're all yelling and screaming about?" the woman asked. "And comparing it with the Hope, only it's not as blue?"

Winston waved a hand disparagingly. "Oh, that's a good diamond, all right," he said. "But wait till you see this diamond. It will be one of the great stones of the world."

The woman's eyes gleamed.

"And how are your poodles?" Winston asked.

The woman laughed. "We've got a new one we call Lover Boy," she said. "He makes love to everybody who crosses his path. Harry, I want you to promise me you'll show that diamond to me before anybody else."

Winston gave her a knowing smile, and she smiled back.

"I'm counting on you, Harry," she said.

The next day, while Winston was conferring in his office with one of his polishers about several diamonds that had been partly cut, De Haan came in with the 154½-carat stone. Winston was holding a diamond about a tenth its size up to the window. "Lengthen your culet a little," he told the polisher. "The stone should have more brilliance. The color is magnificent, but it lacks a kick. With that color, it should live! It should talk to you!" The polisher nodded, took the stone, and left.

"I don't like this business of expecting to get fifteen carats out of a stone and getting ten," Winston said to De Haan when the polisher was out of earshot. "We took a terrific beating on that stone, Bernard." On his desk lay a ring set with a large marquise diamond. Winston picked it up and tried it on his forefinger. He held the finger out and looked at the ring blankly. Then he put it aside and reached for the big stone. After studying it through his loupe for a while, he held it up to the window, turning it around and around between his fingers. "It's beginning to talk," he said, finally, with a sigh of pleasure.

"That stone is in a class all by itself," said De Haan.

"I visualized the brilliance, but I didn't visualize the color," said Winston. "It shows there's no limit to beauty. It's more beautiful than the Star of the East."

De Haan said that the stone now weighed 126 carats. Polishing had already taken off 28½ carats.

"And to think it's absolutely perfect!" Winston said, looking at it fondly. "The delicacy and softness of the blue! You feel like diving right into it! This is no hard, cold blue. I see the Jonker blue but much more brilliant. God, this is glorious!" Then the light caught the stone at a new angle, and he grew tense. "I think the bottom lacks brilliance," he said in a sharp, angry voice.

"That's not the fault of the bottom," De Haan said indulgently. "It's the top. There's still some work to be done on top."

Winston's face relaxed. "Hmm," he said, and now he gave the diamond a friendly, affectionate look. Then he abruptly handed it back to De Haan. "I don't even know the value of the stone you're holding," he said. "I don't know how to put a price on it. All right, Papa, go to work."

As De Haan started for the door, Winston said, "You know, I'm beginning to feel elated."

Early one afternoon in May, Winston was sitting in his office discussing with Frey the prospects of the 154½-carat diamond. Winston, who had been checking with De Haan on its progress two or three times a week, was gradually reaching the conclusion that he had come into possession of a truly remarkable stone; in his more buoyant moments he was beginning to feel that in its color and purity it was equal, if not superior, to the Jonker diamond, and he had come to have a deep attachment for it. Now, talking with Frey about the diamond, Winston impulsively picked up the telephone on his desk to ask De Haan to bring it down from his workshop on the sixth floor. He was told that De Haan was at lunch but should be back any minute.

"How the Dutch do love to eat!" Winston said peevishly.

Frey smiled placatingly. "He'll be back soon," he said. "Most people like to eat."

Winston appeared mollified. "Every time I look at that diamond now, I get excited," he said.

"The thrill you'll get when somebody buys that stone!" Frey said.

Winston looked gloomy. "I hate to think of parting with it," he said.

Frey did not seem to have heard him. "The thrill I get every time I sell an engagement ring!" he said. "Just from looking at a kid who's getting married and is seeing his diamond for the first time!"

"I hate to think of that stone going to some of the women I know," Winston said. In front of him, on a black velvet pad, lay a number of round diamonds that had been set in wax on a square of cardboard to indicate the way they were going to be mounted for a necklace, which he planned to price at fifty thousand dollars. "These round stones are good for women over forty or fifty," he said idly to Frey. "When women get that hard look from all the smoking and the drinking, they need the softness and roundness of these stones." Suddenly angry, he gave the cardboard square a shove. "Adornment!" he said. "They'd wear diamonds on their ankles if it was stylish! They'd wear them in their noses! They have no real feeling for diamonds."

"Some of these women don't appreciate half the stuff they're given," Frey said. "But I must say most of the people I sell diamonds to really get the thrill of a lifetime."

Winston's anger subsided. "What can you do?" he said philosophically. "You can't control them." A faraway look came into his eyes. "I have no worries about our big stone," he said. "The child is healthy. It has ten toes." He smiled faintly.

"You've got more than toes in that stone," Frey said. "You've got a great stone."

"It is great—that is beyond question," said Winston. "How great is the only question. The color is breathtaking. That stone talks to you." He became irritable again. "Where's De Haan?" he demanded. "He can't still be at lunch." He picked up the telephone, and this time De Haan answered. After a brief conversation, Winston hung up. "He's got Ludel with him," he told Frey.

"Ludel just got back this morning," Frey said. "I guess he can't tear himself away from the diamond."

A moment later, De Haan and Ludel came in. De Haan held out the diamond, and Winston took it with his left hand while rising and holding out his right to Ludel, who shook it heartily.

"Well, Ludel, how do you like our baby?" Winston said, holding the diamond up.

"I never dreamed of a stone like that," Ludel said, grinning broadly.

De Haan stood by with a proud smile. "I was bringing it along so nicely," he said. "Now maybe it'll be days before I get it back. Mr. Winston likes to hold on to it."

"Yes, yes," Ludel said, still grinning.

Winston sat down and looked at the stone through his loupe. "The child is healthy," he said. "Healthy and pure."

"Pure," said Ludel. "I was saying as we came down in the elevator that in forty years I never dreamed of a stone like it. The moment I saw it, I knew I was going to buy it for you."

"The stone was not misrepresented," Winston said, turning the diamond around and around on his fingertips. "But I might as well tell you, Ludel, that for a while I was worried. That piece that cracked off. You should have mentioned it to me."

"I felt as confident as anyone can feel with a rough diamond that in itself it was a perfect stone," Ludel said. "I didn't want to raise doubts in your mind. Doubts can be very upsetting when there is an ocean between us. And I wanted you to have that stone. When you finally decided to buy it, I was the happiest man in the world. It's the biggest stone I've ever bought. And the highest in price. When I went to Antwerp from London, and walked into the Diamond Club on Pelikaanstraat, every diamond man in town came up and wanted to know what the stone looked like. Everybody asked me, 'Is it really so magnificent, Ludel?' And I said to everybody, 'Don't ask so many questions.'" Ludel slapped his thigh and laughed long and loud.

"It's coming along," Winston said, studying the diamond. By this time, De Haan, after removing most of the stone's skin, had started to rough out sixteen basic facets that would give the stone a pear-shaped contour; later on, the basic facets would be broken up into smaller facets, to provide greater brilliance—a process known as brillianteering. "We're centering it up," Winston went on. "Getting the girdle a little thinner. There's a slight surface defect—just like a little scab—on the side here. But it's going to come off and everything will be beautiful. Just now our diamond looks a trifle clumsy. It looks too short and round and fat and thick and heavy in the belly—it looks a little bit like me." He gave a quick, hoarse laugh, and went on, "And the girdle's too heavy on the bottom. There's too much of a behind. So we'll just take the fat off the hips. And we'll make the table larger, Bernard. There's still a lot to be done, but there aren't any major problems left. I want to see this stone have grace and form and beauty. I'd rather lose ten carats and have a perfectly proportioned stone. This isn't the kind of diamond that should be sold by the carat. It's too great for that." Winston put the diamond on a sheet of white paper and pushed it roughly back and forth.

Ludel asked Winston if he had shown the diamond to any prospective buyers. Winston curtly said that he hadn't, and picked up the stone again. "I may keep it to play with for a few months," he added. "I don't want to show it for a while yet."

"In the meantime, I'd like to take it back upstairs and go to work on it," De Haan said, holding out his hand.

Winston made no move to give it to him.

Ludel turned to his cousin and asked who was working on the stone with him. Frey laughed. "If his job was at stake, he wouldn't let anyone else touch that stone," he said.

"As long as I have two hands, I'll do it all myself," De Haan said. Again he asked for the stone, but Winston shook his head. "I want to keep it close to me," he said.

The following week, Winston surprised De Haan by not calling for the big diamond for his usual Monday-morning inspection. The entire week passed, and Winston spent each day in his office and did not ask to see the stone. Most of the time, he had been busy with Ludel buying up some large diamonds that had just become available, in an effort to protect what he calls "the big-stone market." He had been made apprehensive by talk in the diamond business that the prices of large diamonds might drop.

"We've been offering fair prices for them," Winston said to Ludel on Friday afternoon. "I want to treat everybody fairly. I don't want to cut any throats."

"You never cut throats," Ludel assured him.

"I don't want to see great things cheapened," Winston said.

"That new big stone of ours! My God, a thing like that! We've got to protect it!"

Ludel nodded.

"Of course, buying this way is extremely speculative," Winston said. "I've already spent a million dollars today on rough diamonds. If things work out right, we'll do fine. But you can get hurt very badly doing what I'm doing if you don't know the market. The risks I've taken! Look at King Farouk. Last July, when Farouk already owed me more than a million dollars for the Star of the East and some other jewels, he heard I had a certain emerald that he wanted. Worth a quarter of a million dollars. I sent him the stone and then I told my son Ronnie about it. My little fella is only thirteen, but I talk everything over with him. Ronnie is like a sponge. He soaks up everything about the business. The conversations I have with him! He talks like a jewel merchant. Anyway, I said to Ronnie, 'I sent His Majesty the emerald even though he owes me more than a million.' My little fella listened, and finally he said, 'Daddy, if he still owed you the money, I wouldn't have sent him the emerald.' The stone arrived in Alexandria two days before His Majesty abdicated. Just before he went aboard ship to flee from Egypt, he handed the emerald to an American Embassy man, and it came back to me. With all his problems, he took the time when he arrived in Naples to send me a cable saying, 'Article you are interested in given to your embassy.' I told Ronnie about it, and I said, 'When dealing with royalty, you must remember you're dealing with people who are brought up with honor. And a king, of course, is above the law anyway.' "

Ludel asked Winston if he had heard anything from Farouk about the million dollars still due on the Star of the East, and Winston replied that he hadn't. "Most of the time I don't try to fathom the people in that part of the world," he said. "Once, I made a deal to sell an Indian prince five hundred thousand dollars' worth of jewels, to be paid for over a period of a year. A few days later, he called me and said he wanted to sell me some other jewels, for two hundred and fifty thousand dollars—cash. He said he wanted the money to bet on the horses. Well, I bought the jewels, and he bet on three horses. The first two came in. The third ran out of the money, and he lost the entire quarter of a million. I had to comfort him through his ordeal. *His* ordeal! But I must say he paid the five hundred thousand on schedule."

Miss Rowe came in with some papers, and he asked her whether she had heard from a woman who had called earlier to say she'd be in to see him. Miss Rowe said she hadn't, and left.

"She's a good customer, if she ever gets here," Winston said to Ludel. "She went to the hairdresser's four hours ago. Said she'd be over as soon as she was finished there. I'm selling her a pair of earrings for a hundred and fifty thousand." After a moment, he added, "She has unusually small ear lobes. I've been trying for months to get her a pair of earrings that will do something for her lobes."

The telephone rang. Winston answered it and talked to someone for a few minutes about an oil well, remarking that forty barrels a day seemed rather low. After he had hung up, he grimaced and said, "Dull business, Ludel. So you drill a hole and you strike oil. I don't know why I let myself be talked into buying an oil well. I'm not even interested." He sighed, and picked up his telephone and asked to speak to De Haan. "Bernard!" he said. "Before you go home, bring down the big stone. You can go home, but I want the baby."

All the next week, up in the polishing room, De Haan happily kept the big diamond running on the polishing wheel that was taking the fat off, making the table wider and the girdle leaner. On Friday afternoon, an industrial-diamond man named Daniel S. de Rimini dropped in for a visit, and De Haan took the diamond out of the dop at the end of the metal arm holding the diamond on the wheel, and showed it to him. De Rimini whistled. "That's really something!" he said. At the time, he was the general manager of a tool corporation in Tuckahoe, which uses diamonds in precision-tool work. "If I had a wife, I wouldn't let her wear that stone," de Rimini said. "Somebody might steal it—and her, too."

De Haan looked flattered.

"I once held the Cullinan in my hands," de Rimini went on. "I was a little boy at the time. My father worked for Asscher's Diamond Works, in Amsterdam, and they were cutting the Cullinan. My father let me hold it. I'll never forget how I felt. If you'd let me hold this stone, I'd feel the same way—I know it."

A slow grin spread over De Haan's face. "You'll remember to give it back?" he said. Then he laughed loudly and handed the diamond to de Rimini.

De Rimini hefted the stone in the palm of his hand. "I'm telling you the truth, Bernard," he said. "I feel more impressed than I did when I held the Cullinan."

De Haan took the diamond back and put it in the dop. "The Cullinan was all cut up," he said. "Our stone will never be cut up."

A few days later, Winston had the big diamond in his office again. It was lunchtime, and his customary cup of coffee, with its milk and saccharin tablet, was in front of him on the desk. Beside it lay three pairs of platinum earrings; each earring was set with ten diamonds, weighing from five to twenty carats. Winston had been rolling the big diamond between his fingers, and now he laid it down on the other side of his coffee cup. Its girdle had been slimmed and its table had been made larger. The sun was shining that day, and its rays, coming through the window, were reflected with more intensity and emphasis by the big stone than by the diamonds in the earrings. In a few moments, Miss Rowe came in and asked what jewels Winston wanted to lend Mrs. William K. Carpenter, who was about to be photographed with some Winston jewels for an advertisement of the annual flower show in Wilmington. Winston put his hands to his head for a moment. Then he got up and took a large black leather box from his safe, and from among the jewels in it he selected a long diamond necklace, which he handed to his secretary. "We want Mrs. Carpenter to look beautiful, don't we?" he said.

"What about a bracelet, Mr. Winston?" Miss Rowe asked.

Winston gave her a diamond bracelet, and then a pair of diamond ear clips. He told her he thought that would be enough. "What ads are we in this week?" he asked.

"Cadillac, Parliament, Tabu, Maximilian Furs, Lucky Strike, and Revlon Nail Enamel," the secretary told him.

"Good," Winston said. "Don't keep Mrs. Carpenter waiting for her jewels," he said. As Miss Rowe was putting the box back in the safe, he picked up the big diamond and smiled at it, and then, with his other hand, picked up the cup and took a sip of coffee. "There, now, Harry," he said to himself. "There we are."

Miss Rowe went out, closing the door. It opened again almost immediately, and Richard Winston, a handsome, soft-spoken man of twenty-seven, who is Harry Winston's nephew and works for his uncle as a salesman, came in, carrying a large black suède-covered jewel box.

"Did you get the necklace, Dick?" Harry Winston asked, closing his hand over the big diamond.

Dick opened the jewel box and showed his uncle a diamond necklace. Winston gave it a quick glance, still holding on to the big stone. "Who's going to take it over to her?" he asked. A prospective customer—a woman—had asked to have the necklace brought to her hotel, so she could make her final decision.

Dick said that he would take it over himself, and that he hoped to return with a check for seventy-five thousand dollars. "She was in this morning with her husband," he said.

"What happened?" Winston asked.

"I'm not sure how we stand," Dick told him earnestly. "Her husband said to her, 'What occasion would you have to wear a necklace like that? We don't go anywhere.' So she said, 'Don't worry. First buy the necklace, and then we'll make the occasion.' "

Winston smiled. "Those two need to be educated," he said. "We'll educate them."

"Suppose she changes her mind again?" Dick asked.

"Leave the necklace with her overnight," Winston said casually.

"Leave it?"

Winston laughed. "Sure," he said. "She ought to get used to having important jewels around. She ought to get used to living with them. It's all part of her education."

Just then, Winston's wife, Edna, came in. A slim, attractive woman, she was wearing a smart black suit that had large round buttons, each set with twenty tiny round diamonds. The Winstons were married in 1933. They had met on a train to Atlantic City four years earlier, when Winston was taking some diamonds there to sell; his bride-to-be had just had her tonsils out, and was on her way to the resort to recuperate, accompanied by her father, a physician and sociologist who was head of a settlement house on the Lower East Side called the Educational Alliance.

Mrs. Winston greeted Winston and Dick warmly and sat down across the desk from her husband. Winston asked Dick to tell her what the woman customer had said in the salesroom that morning. Dick told the story again, and Mrs. Winston laughed. "Oh, Dick, that's a funny story," she said.

"I hope she buys the necklace," Dick said.

"She'll buy it," Winston said. "I've told Dick to leave it with her overnight. She'll buy it."

"The way you handle jewels!" Mrs. Winston said. "It seems so careless."

"I never lose one," Winston said.

"Only because you're lucky," his wife said. "You weren't so sure about that the time you lost the hundred-thousand-dollar diamond when the Windsors were here."

"I never heard about that," said Dick.

"That was before you were with me," Winston said, still keeping his hand closed over the big diamond. "I never even mentioned it to the Duke and Duchess. About seven years ago, they were in here one day and I was showing them some things. This whole desk was covered with jewels—diamonds, rubies, emeralds, pearls, everything. After they left, my secretary came in and cleared the stuff away. Well, I went home to dinner, and about nine o'clock that night I got a call from Frey. He was in a terrible state. Said the nightly inventory had shown a fifty-five-carat diamond was missing. We called the Holmes company to arrange for reopening the safe in my office. Not a sign of it. What we went through! The next day, the insurance people wanted to go ask the Duke and Duchess if they remembered seeing the diamond, but I said no—they could talk to anybody else they wanted to but not to the Duke and Duchess. I told them I'd take the responsibility for the loss—if it was lost—and the insurance company wouldn't have to make good. Anything, so long as they didn't bother the Windsors. We searched the entire building. We went through all our wastepaper. Fifty-five carats! It couldn't be missing! It was big enough to trip over! We all went through agony for weeks. It was a reflection on everyone in the building. My secretary, of course, was a nervous wreck. Three months later, a customer came in here and bought a pearl necklace, and I asked my secretary to bring in an empty jewel case to put it in. She brought the case in, and when I opened it, there was the diamond. It had fallen in there by mistake while I was showing all those things to the Duke and Duchess. So you see I was right. It would have been a dreadful thing if we'd let the insurance investigators go around and bother the Duke and Duchess of Windsor."

With his free hand, Winston held up the three pairs of diamond earrings. "Which do you like, Edna?" he asked. "For a woman with very small ear lobes?"

Mrs. Winston tried the various earrings on, and her husband watched her with admiration. "I hate to see the woman get any of them," he said.

Mrs. Winston laughed. "Oh, Harry!" she said. "Always complaining about selling your babies. Dick, did I ever tell you about the time Harry sold two million dollars' worth of diamonds all at once? When he came home that night, I said to him, 'Harry, you must be awfully happy.' You know what he said? 'I'm *miserable*,' he said, and, what's more, he looked it. He's always been that way. He never could stand to see anything get away from him, even before we were married. There never really was anyone else for me, but Harry was in love with his diamonds, so I got engaged to another man. Two days before I was supposed to marry this other man, I got a call from Palm Beach. It was Harry. He'd been selling jewels down there. We hadn't seen each other for a year, but after we'd talked for a minute or two he said, 'Why don't you marry me instead?' I told him I would if he'd come back to New York and marry me right away. He came up the next day and we got married. Then he took me to Palm Beach and he went straight back to selling jewels. He spent most of our honeymoon talking

about the big diamonds he hoped to buy. We've been chasing diamonds ever since." Mrs. Winston laughed again, and went on,
"Harry just can't forget about a diamond once he's made up his
mind he wants it. A few years ago, while we were in Paris, he
saw a diamond he liked, and decided to buy it. But it was awfully
hot, and before he got around to it, I persuaded him to take me to
Deauville for the weekend. By the time we got back, the diamond
had been sold to someone else. Six months later, in New York,
Harry saw the same stone and paid sixty thousand dollars more for
it than he could have got it for in Paris. He just had to have that
diamond."

"It was an expensive weekend," Winston said. Smiling, he
slowly unclenched the hand that held the big diamond.

"Oh, Harry!" Mrs. Winston said as her husband began rubbing the stone against his coat sleeve. "Is that *it?*"

Winston held the stone away from her.

"My mouth is watering," Mrs. Winston said. "Do you know
what you're going to do with it?"

Winston did not reply, and his wife asked the question again.

"I may sell it in two weeks," Winston said. "Or I may sell it in
ten years."

Late in May, Ludel had to go to Europe on another buying trip.
The day before he left, he met his brother, a diamond broker, in
front of the Winston establishment at noon and walked with him
to the Diamond Dealers Club, at 36 West Forty-seventh Street,
which is one of the local centers for buying, selling, and talking
about diamonds. On the way down Fifth Avenue, Ludel's brother
asked him if he had seen the big diamond recently.

"Of course," said Ludel.

"I hear it is a perfect stone," his brother said.

Ludel grinned. "Don't ask so many questions," he said.

As the two men turned west on Forty-seventh Street, Ludel nodded to an elderly gentleman who was hurrying in the opposite direction. "I saw that man in Antwerp a few weeks ago," he said.
"Did you notice his pockets? They're bulging with diamonds."

The block between Fifth and Sixth Avenues was lined with one jewelry shop or exchange after another. Since it was the lunch hour, the sidewalks were packed with small groups of men who were standing around and showing one another diamonds. Uniformed police were patrolling the street, and in almost every second doorway stood a plainclothes detective. Here and there among the people entering and leaving the shops and exchanges were men with long beards and earlocks, who were wearing the black, round-brimmed hat and the long black frock coat often worn by Hasidic Jews. As businessmen, they attracted no particular attention from the others, who had long taken their dress for granted.

Ludel and his brother entered the building where the club had its quarters, and took an elevator to the ninth floor, where, after being waved on by a receptionist, sitting in a small glass cage, who knows every one of the club's fifteen hundred members by sight, they were admitted to a long room whose north wall consisted almost entirely of large windows. At the windows were rows of long tables, on which paper packets of diamonds were spread out. Dealers and brokers were sitting at the tables and bargaining in several languages—English, Dutch, French, Flemish, German, and Yiddish. Against the opposite wall was a small lunch counter, and between the tables and the counter stood groups of members who were waiting their turn at the tables.

Ludel strolled past the tables, smiling and nodding at the men seated there. He seemed to be enjoying himself. Looking around the crowded room, he said to his brother, "Diamond clubs all over the world are alike. Some people making peanuts on a sale, others making millions. It is hard to realize that Harry Winston used to work this way, too."

A small man with a Vandyke beard and bright-blue eyes elbowed his way through the crowd to Ludel and, without saying anything, opened a small packet of diamonds and showed them to him. Ludel looked at the stones without interest, but picked one up and examined it politely. "Very nice," he said, and returned it.

Apparently satisfied, the small man rewrapped his packet and beamed at Ludel. "How's the big stone you bought?" he asked.

Ludel looked pleased. "Don't ask so many questions," he said.

• • •

Late the following month, Winston sat at his desk with the big stone in the palm of his hand. The diamond had three new basic facets. As Winston stared thoughtfully at it, De Haan walked in. "When am I going to get it back?" De Haan asked, nodding toward the diamond. "I haven't been able to get any work done on it for almost two weeks."

"I like to keep it down here with me," Winston said, almost timidly. "You've got other stones to work on, Bernard. You don't really need it."

De Haan looked helplessly at Winston. Then he said, "At this rate, the stone won't be finished before you go to Europe."

"There's no rush," Winston said.

"I thought you wanted to take it with you," De Haan said.

"Well, I'll give it to you tomorrow morning," Winston said. At that moment, Frey entered, and Winston looked relieved.

"I just had a letter from another one of those nuts," Frey said. "This time, it's someone who says he's found a twenty-two-hundred-carat diamond in his back yard in Nashville. The letters we get! Last week, somebody thought he'd found the treasure of the Incas. In Brooklyn!"

Neither De Haan nor Winston seemed to be listening. De Haan looked around reproachfully and left the office. Frey looked at the diamond in Winston's hand. "It's shaping up," he said.

Winston smiled sadly at the diamond. "I started in this business when I was fourteen years old," he said. "My father was always afraid that jewels would someday possess me. He was satisfied with just a small neighborhood jewelry business uptown, but I was always interested in large stones. He used to say to me, 'Harry, you're the master of your jewels now, but if you keep on buying such big stones, someday your jewels will master you.' Sometimes I think he was right."

In the main salesroom, on the ground floor, where clients who do not see Winston personally are waited on, a salesman was displaying some jewelry to a young lady and her mother. "I'm going to show you the heart that practically beats," the salesman said, and brought out a platinum-mounted diamond clip in the shape of a heart.

"Mother, it *does* look as if it might beat at any moment, doesn't it?" the young lady said.

The price, said the salesman, was forty thousand dollars.

It was quiet in the room. The two women were the only customers. Two other salesmen stood in a corner talking about Winston.

"I saw him with that big stone of his," one of the salesmen said. "Why is he taking such a long time finishing it, I wonder."

"The way he looks at that stone!" said the second. "I doubt if he's thought about anything else around here since it came in."

Winston planned to go to Europe about the middle of the summer. He was sitting at his desk late one afternoon studying a schedule of transatlantic sailings when Frey came in and asked how soon he was leaving. Winston said he wasn't sure exactly when he would go. He called Miss Rowe in and asked her to have De Haan come down with the big diamond.

"You're not taking it with you, are you?" Frey inquired anxiously. "It's not finished."

"I'm not taking it with me," Winston said.

Frey asked Winston if he was going to Portugal, and Winston said yes. He hoped that he might then sign the contract with the Portuguese government enabling him to buy the production of the diamond mines in Angola. "Our government wants an independent source of industrial diamonds, and I've been talking to Portugal about it on the telephone all day," Winston said. "England is against it. I'm fighting the whole British government—not just De Beers."

The door opened and De Haan came in. As he handed the diamond to Winston, he remarked that he was just about to start brillianteering it. "And then you'll mount it?" he asked Winston.

Winston examined the diamond, and the two other men watched him gravely. "Beautiful," he said, in a low, hoarse voice. "It's beautiful."

"Wait till you see it after we've brillianteered it," said De Haan.

"I hate to see it finished," Winston said.

"You're not taking it to Europe?" De Haan asked. He seemed worried.

Winston said no, he wasn't, and De Haan's face brightened. He held out his hand for the stone, but Winston did not give it to him. He looked embarrassed and apologetic. "I can't bear to see it finished," he said.

Winston returned from his European trip early in October, and on his first morning back in the office De Haan came down and presented him with the diamond. It was finished, and it had been mounted in a simple temporary setting of platinum wire. The diamond weighed 62.05 carats. More than half of the original stone had been lost. What remained was a pear-shaped diamond an inch and a half long and about an inch across at its widest point. Glass replicas of the diamond—in both its rough and its finished form— had been made, and sets of them were going to be sent to the Smithsonian Institution and to the American Museum of Natural History to be added to their collections of replicas of great diamonds. Winston held the stone in the palm of his hand and for more than a minute looked at it tenderly, without speaking. De Haan waited, his arms crossed over his chest.

"It's like a soft, beautiful day in June," Winston said, finally. "It's like a June day when the sky is absolutely clear and the color of the sky is that delicate blue, that brilliant— And pure, absolutely pure." His voice broke, and he cleared his throat. "So soft, so blue," he said.

"It's a greater stone than the Jonker," De Haan said.

"It isn't cold like the Jonker," said Winston. "It lives. It talks to you. In fact, now it *sings* to you."

"A perfect pear shape," De Haan said. "Fifty-eight facets, and every facet perfect."

Winston was not listening. "Isn't it beautiful, Harry?" he said as he stared at the diamond. "Harry, it's a mass of brilliance."

Frey came into the office, and whistled when he saw the diamond. "What a lovely piece!" he said.

"That's what man has done to perfect nature," Winston said.

"Do you know yet what you're going to call the baby?" Frey asked.

"We don't need a name," Winston said. "We'll probably leave that up to whoever buys it." Then he added, with a smile, "But it's great enough to be called the Winston diamond."

One morning early in November, Winston called Frey into his office and handed him a small case made of smooth black leather. Frey opened the case. In it, on a white doeskin lining, lay the big diamond, still in its temporary setting. Winston, obviously dispirited, told Frey that a European count wanted to see the stone, and that he had agreed to send it to him in Zurich. Frey asked what price Winston had set on it, and Winston said he was asking six hundred thousand dollars. Frey nodded, lifted the diamond from the case, and took it upstairs to the shipping room. There the stone was wrapped in tissue paper, placed in a cardboard box with four gummed flaps, and sent off to Zurich that same day—by registered air mail, fully insured. Within a few hours, Winston instructed one of his salesmen, a man named Oberlander, to fly to Zurich to answer any questions the count might have. Eighteen days later, the diamond was returned by registered air mail, beating Oberlander back by twenty-four hours. When Oberlander reported to Winston, he found his employer holding the black leather case that contained the big stone.

"The little fella has done some travelling," Winston said, looking fondly at the diamond. He shook hands with Oberlander, a neat, gray-haired man of fifty who wears tortoise-shell spectacles and speaks with a Viennese accent.

"If he had had the money, he would have written a check on the spot," Oberlander said. "He wants the stone. He goes around Europe talking about 'my diamond.'"

Winston grunted.

"Now he's getting divorced," Oberlander said. "His divorce is costing him a great deal—I believe he just gave his wife a couple of million dollars—so he's a bit short of cash right now. But he's got a new girl and he wants to give the diamond to her."

"I know the girl," Winston said angrily. "One of those Continental glamour girls." He snapped the lid shut over the diamond. "We can wait until he raises the money," he said. "We'll keep the little fella right here."

One afternoon about two weeks later, Winston showed the diamond to another prospective buyer—a middle-aged businessman from Texas, who had recently made quite a bit of money in oil, and whose wife, a client of Winston's, had asked him to stop in and take a look at the diamond. The businessman sat in Winston's office for an hour and a half, staring at the big stone. Neither he nor Winston spoke very much. The businessman asked an occasional question about such matters as the quality of the stone, how long Winston had worked on it, and how it might be worn. Winston answered the questions briefly, making no attempt to influence his client's decision. The businessman held the open case in his hand most of the time, looking at the diamond without touching it. Finally, he snapped the case shut, handed it back to Winston, and stood up. "I'll let you know," he said.

Winston nodded and went to the door with the man. A few minutes later, Frey came in and found Winston with his fingers pressed against his temples.

"You look exhausted," Frey said.

Winston told him that he had been showing the big diamond to a possible customer. "I sat here for an hour and a half while he looked at it," he said. "I was afraid he was going to take it."

"*Is* he going to take it?" Frey asked.

Winston opened the jewel case and snapped it shut with a gesture of finality. "He closed the case this way and said, 'I'll let you know,' which means he's interested," he told Frey glumly.

A few days before Christmas, at seven-thirty in the evening, Winston, in his apartment on upper Fifth Avenue, was having dinner with his wife and their two sons when he was summoned to the telephone. After a few minutes, he returned to the dining room and told his wife that a client had called him and that he was going down to the office. He telephoned his nephew Dick, and then he took a taxi to his office, where he found two Holmes detectives waiting on the sidewalk; they had been sent around after Dick had informed their headquarters that one of the Winston safes was about to be opened. Winston identified himself, went in, and opened the safe in his office, setting off an alarm at the Holmes headquarters. While one of the detectives called in and reported that all was well, Winston removed from the safe the leather case containing the big diamond. A few minutes later, Dick arrived, breathless and looking excited. He was, as always, carefully dressed, washed, and brushed, and his face had the perpetual glow that comes from enthusiasm and good circulation. Winston handed him the case and told him to take it up to the Hotel Pierre, where the wife of a Detroit industrialist was waiting to see the diamond.

It was half past eight when Dick hailed a cab and headed for the Pierre. He was wearing a light overcoat, and he carried the jewel case in the right-hand pocket, keeping his hand on it the whole way. Upon reaching the Pierre, he took an elevator to the thirty-ninth floor, where he rang a bell and was admitted by a maid to the foyer of a suite. In the middle of the living room, just beyond, stood his client, a slender woman in her late sixties, with a pale, thin face and soft gray hair. She was wearing a housecoat, and as Dick stepped out of the foyer, she disappeared into an inner room. The maid left, and a moment later a young woman in a tailored suit, who was evidently the older woman's secretary, came in and offered to take Dick's coat. Dick took off his coat but said he'd just as soon hold it. She asked him if he'd care to sit down, and he said he didn't mind standing. She said the weather was unusually warm for December, and he agreed that it was. Then she, too, left. Half an hour later, the maid came back and ushered Dick into the inner room, where the woman from Detroit was waiting for him. Dick noticed that the window shades had been drawn. The woman had changed from her housecoat into a purple satin evening gown with a high neckline and wrist-length sleeves, and she had put on a diamond necklace, diamond ear clips, and a diamond-and-ruby pin at her shoulder. She was standing in front of a full-length mirror, and as Dick entered, she said, "Good evening, Mr. Winston. Where are your detectives?"

Dick smiled, produced the jewel case, opened it, and held it toward her. There lay the big stone, in its temporary platinum setting. Without speaking, she picked up the diamond with her thumb and forefinger, carefully touching only the sides, so as not to blur the facets with fingerprints. She held the diamond to her neck and asked Dick how he thought she could attach it to her dress to get its full effect. He suggested sewing it on. The maid brought a needle and some blue silk thread, and Dick, gently refusing her offer of help, threaded the needle with steady hands and sewed the platinum wire holding the diamond to the neckline of his client's dress. The woman then turned back to the mirror and looked at the reflected diamond, in a way that Dick later told his uncle he considered the typical look of people who really know what they are looking at. A bit of color came to her face, but otherwise there was no change in her cool, gracious, confident manner.

The woman stood in front of the mirror for fifteen minutes, turning this way and that. Then she said she was going into the next room to show it to her husband, and asked Dick to wait in the living room. She was gone nearly another quarter of an hour. At nine-forty-five, she came into the living room, and Dick, who had been sitting in an armchair, stood up, and remained standing while she walked about pulling down window shades. Then, for an hour and a half, he stood there while she paced the room and they talked about great jewels.

Back on East Fifty-first Street, Harry Winston sat at his desk waiting for his nephew to return. Across the room from him sat the two Holmes detectives, with their hats on. No one said anything. Winston lighted a cigarette, smoked it a quarter of the way down, and crushed it out. He picked up some sketches he had been working on earlier in the day—designs for jewelry to go with strapless evening gowns—and puttered over them for an hour or so. Then he put them aside.

"Nice quiet building, Harry," he said. "I love it this way."

The detectives said nothing.

· · ·

At eleven-fifteen, at the Pierre, the woman from Detroit looked at her watch and said to Dick, "Oh, my goodness, you must want to get back!"

Dick said it was perfectly all right; as far as he was concerned, he wouldn't mind staying and talking about diamonds all night, but his uncle was waiting for him at the office. The woman agreed that he should go, so he telephoned Winston and said he'd be back in about ten minutes. Then he offered to help the woman take off the big diamond. She gave him a pair of scissors, and he cut the blue silk thread. But after the diamond was off, she held it lovingly in her hand and talked on and on about the histories of great stones. It was nearly an hour before she said, "Thank your uncle for being kind enough to send the diamond over."

"It was a privilege," said Dick.

Shortly after midnight, Dick had not returned to the office, and Winston was beginning to worry. He telephoned the woman at the Pierre and was told that his nephew had just left. Then Winston and the detectives went downstairs and out onto the sidewalk, and looked up and down the street. Just as they were starting back inside, a cab drew up and Dick stepped out. The detectives accompanied Winston and his nephew up to the office, and they put the diamond back in the safe. Then the detectives saw them into a cab and left.

"She appreciated what a great jewel it is," Dick said as they rode toward his uncle's apartment. "She understands great jewels."

The next morning, the Detroit industrialist called on Winston at his office and looked at the diamond again. The man said his wife liked the stone very much, and Winston smiled faintly. The stone had looked very beautiful on his wife, the man said. Again Winston smiled faintly. The man thanked Winston for sending the diamond over, so that his wife could try wearing it with an evening dress and her other jewels. Winston replied that he had been happy to send it over. The man said he would let Winston know his decision. As he was leaving, he paused and, after a moment's hesitation, said, "Isn't it a shame she couldn't have had that diamond when she was younger?"

Later that day, Winston's son Ronald paid a Christmas-holiday visit to his father at the office. He marched in announcing in a matter-of-fact tone that his dog had eaten a Christmas-tree bulb right after breakfast and hadn't been hurt at all. Winston said he was glad to hear that. He seemed happy to see Ronald, and pulled up a chair facing his desk. Ronald was wearing a dark-blue suit with long pants, and a blue-and-gray striped tie. He sat on the edge of the chair, his toes just touching the floor, and waited politely and seriously for his father to begin the conversation. Winston smiled at his son and plunged into an account of how he had spent part of the morning showing the big diamond to a very wealthy gentleman from Detroit.

"Get the stone, Ronnie," said Winston. "You know where to find it."

Ronald went to the safe, pulled open the door, and took out the jewel case, which he handed to Winston. "You consider it your best diamond?" he asked earnestly.

Winston said he did. He took the diamond from the case and held it up before the boy. "The little fella has travelled," he said. "Our baby has been to Switzerland and back."

"Is it better than the Jonker diamond?" Ronald asked.

"The Jonker was much harder in color, Ronnie," said Winston. "This diamond is softer. The brilliance didn't come through in the Jonker. I couldn't want a finer stone than this."

"Is it better than the Idol's Eye?" Ronald asked.

"That Golconda stone?" said Winston. "Ronnie, you have the natural reaction of a diamond merchant—the natural reaction of comparing one stone with all other stones. I showed you the Idol's Eye six years ago, and it was an old stone even then. This stone has been cut with a lot more knowledge of the art and science of diamond cutting."

"It took millions of years to make that diamond," Ronald said, solemnly contemplating the stone. "And you cut it and polished it in a few months. Did you get another diamond out of the rough stone?"

"No, Ronnie," Winston said. "The stone weighed a hundred and fifty-four and a half carats originally, and we've got a sixty-two-carat stone now."

Ronald was silent while he did some mental arithmetic. "Then you lost ninety-two and a half carats, just blown into the air," he said presently. "What are you going to call this diamond, Daddy?"

"We may call it the Winston diamond," said Winston.

"Good idea," said Ronald.

"Of course, we may sell the diamond to someone who will want to choose his own name for it," Winston said.

"I think you ought to name it the Winston diamond before you sell it," Ronald said.

Winston looked hard at the diamond. "You may be right, Ronnie," he said.

Ronald asked his father whether he knew of anybody besides the man from Detroit who wanted to buy the diamond, and how much it would cost. Winston said that he had shown it to three people, and that the price was six hundred thousand dollars. "All three want the diamond, Ronnie," he went on. "One is a Texas oilman. Another is a European count, and he would have bought the diamond last month, but he was a little short of cash at the time. And the third is the man I saw this morning. His wife's getting quite old, and it may be the last diamond he'll be buying for her."

Ronald asked whether Winston cared which of the three bought the diamond.

"That's very difficult to say," Winston replied. "You know, I like the diamond very much myself."

"Yes, Daddy," said Ronald. "I know. And I like it very much, too."

"Whoever buys the diamond now will buy it over the telephone," Winston said, suddenly assuming a palpably false air of heartiness. "They've all seen it. The preliminaries are over. I'll get a telephone call, and I'll hear that one of the three will take it—and that will be that, Ronnie." Winston's voice trailed off on a note of misery.

"Yes, Daddy," Ronald said, his own voice loyally miserable.

One morning shortly after the New Year, Ludel, who had just returned from another European trip, was on his way down to

Winston's office with De Haan to see the diamond for the first time since it had been finished. In the elevator, he told his cousin about a plane crash he had been in while taking off from Amsterdam for Paris, where Winston had asked him to look at some diamonds. Ludel had suffered six broken ribs and a broken chest bone.

"I called Mr. Winston and told him I was sorry but I was going to be late getting to Paris," Ludel said. "You know what he said? 'The *hell* with Paris,' he said. 'How are you?' You don't find that sort of consideration among rich men in Europe."

The two cousins entered Winston's office, and he greeted them with a smile. On the black velvet pad on his desk lay the big stone. Ludel stared at it for a long time while Winston waited expectantly for his reaction.

"Such a wonderful color!" Ludel said, at last.

"You were right on the weight, Ludel," said Winston. "I was influenced by De Haan, here. He thought it would be bigger."

"I happen to be an optimist," De Haan said.

Apparently, Ludel's response was not all Winston had hoped it would be, for he said a bit sharply, "Ludel, you'd always rather see a stone in the rough, wouldn't you?"

Ludel blushed slightly. "Absolutely right," he said.

Winston's annoyance was soon gone. "Within a period of about a month, I paid over a million dollars for four stones, and I haven't sold any of them yet," he said cheerfully. "This is just one of them. I'm a patient man."

The door opened, and Dick Winston came in, carrying a box that contained necklaces and bracelets that were being set with diamonds. He put the box down on his uncle's desk and told him that the diamond setters were asking for smaller stones that would match the others in color. Winston sighed in mock despair. He had thousands and thousands of diamonds, he said, but he always seemed to be short of the diamonds the setters wanted.

"Still, you can get thousands and thousands of the diamonds they want," Dick said comfortingly. Then he pointed to the big diamond. "But *this* you get only once in a thousand years."

"What nature and man have combined to make!" Winston said in an awed voice.

"We certainly have the finest diamond nature ever produced," Ludel said.

"And yet you can never be sure," Winston said. "You're always wondering. It's like seeing a beautiful girl and asking yourself, 'Is she as beautiful as *that* girl?' You're always comparing. You always feel you may be missing something. You're never sure."

Miss Rowe came into the office and said that the count was calling from Zurich. Winston looked flustered as he picked up the telephone. While he waited for the call to be put through to him, he said, in a weak, dazed voice, "Well, Harry, it's all over now."

—*1954*

4

TERRIFIC

THE JUNIOR LEAGUE OF THE CITY OF NEW YORK, Inc., a fifty-three-year-old club for women under forty, gave its third annual Mardi Gras Ball—"a brilliant assemblage of those prominent in society, stage, screen, and television," the *Herald Tribune* called it—on Tuesday evening, March 2, 1954, in the Grand Ballroom of the Hotel Astor. About eight hundred Junior League members and husbands, and friends of members and friends of husbands, attended, paying fifteen dollars a head for the privilege, and one and all agreed that it was quite a do. Emil Coleman's twenty-four-piece, two-piano orchestra played for dancing, and the highlights of the evening were the crowning of a Queen of the Mardi Gras by Mayor Robert F. Wagner, Jr., and a parade of fifteen Junior Leaguers and two professional models who wore costumes more or less expressing the spirit of seventeen commercial firms (including Pepsi-Cola and United States Steel) that had sponsored the ball by donating fifteen hundred dollars each to the New York Junior League's Welfare Trust Fund. The New York League has fifteen hundred members (it is one of a hundred and eighty-three chapters, with a total membership of sixty-three thousand), who dedicate themselves, upon joining, to serving the social, economic, educational, cultural, and civic interests of the community, and the League spends the money in its Welfare Trust Fund for the operation of volunteer services it carries on in hospitals, settlement houses, and similar worthy centers. A week after Mardi Gras night, the treasurer of the Junior League Mardi Gras committee reported to her forty-five glinting-eyed co-members that by the time the books were balanced the ball would net a profit for the Welfare Trust Fund of something over eighteen thousand dollars.

Preparations for the ball began more than a year before it was held. At eleven-fifteen on the morning of February 18, 1953, the day after the second annual Mardi Gras Ball, which was also held at the Astor, and which, sponsored by only fourteen commercial firms (including Flamingo Orange Juice and Pepperidge Farm Bread), netted $11,517.02, the chairman of the second Mardi Gras committee, Mrs. Thomas D. Luckenbill, turned up at the League's headquarters and clubhouse—a five-story building, at 130 East Eightieth Street, that was formerly the town house of Vincent Astor. Mrs. Luckenbill immediately set to work writing thank-you notes to sponsors, celebrities, and others who had helped with the second Mardi Gras Ball. She was joined a few minutes later by Mrs. Stirling S. Adams, one of the four vice-chairmen of the committee. Mrs. Adams, looking cool and satisfied with everything around her, said she had got to bed at five that morning and had got up again at eight, to go down to the Astor and pick up the Queen's throne and some trumpets, and return them to a rental company. By noon, more than half the members of Mrs. Luckenbill's committee were on hand to help write the thank-you notes, many of them coming in after laboring all the morning at volunteer jobs in clinics or day nurseries. Everybody was already enthusiastically looking ahead to the 1954 ball. They rehashed the previous night's ball and determined to improve on it in certain ways the third time around. There was the problem of the Astor's public-address system, for example (it had conked out just as the Queen was being crowned), and the problem of guarding the dressing room of the models (newspaper photographers had wandered in while the girls were putting on their costumes). Mrs. Adams said that Mrs.

Henry I. Stimson, the committeewoman in charge of costumes, had done a terrific job, and that the costume she herself had admired the most was the one worn by Mrs. Wickliffe W. Crider, who had appeared as a chicken sandwich, to represent Pepperidge Farm Bread. Mrs. Crider had worn two giant slices of bread and had been carried in by four gentlemen dressed to look like toothpicks. "Next year, we might have someone dressed up as an olive if we have the sandwich again," Mrs. Adams said. "But then I suppose Pepperidge will want something different costumewise."

Mrs. Luckenbill told Mrs. Kevin McLoughlin, the liaison member between the Mardi Gras committee and the League's board of managers, that she was recommending Mrs. Stimson for the job of Mardi Gras chairman for the next year. Mrs. McLoughlin looked delighted. "Louise Stimson is a nifty gal," she said. "That pink-clown drawing she made for the program could be our permanent motif for all future Mardi Gras." Mrs. Luckenbill agreed, and suggested that someone should make a motion endorsing the clown drawing at the next meeting of the League's board of managers. "I'm sure everyone will be for it policywise," Mrs. McLoughlin said.

Mrs. Albert C. Santy, who had been in charge of reservations for the ball, said that everyone was happy about the selection of Mrs. Oliver Rea as Queen the night before. There had been five candidates, known as Maids, for the crown, and the Queen had been chosen by three civic-minded men in public office, on the basis of her personality and the work she had done for the Junior League and for the community at large. Mrs. Rea had served as chairman of the League's Volunteer Social Work Aides, chairman of its placement committee, and chairman of a rehabilitation project it set up at Bellevue Hospital. As Queen of the Mardi Gras the night before, she had sat on her throne on a stage and reigned over the ball. Now, with no further regal duties, she was up at Riverside Hospital, an institution for adolescent narcotics users, on North Brother Island, in the East River, doing her regular volunteer work with the patients there. "Betty Rea is a nifty gal," Mrs. McLoughlin said. "All five Maids were nifty, but *somebody* had to be Queen."

Mrs. John C. Carrington, who is vice-president of the New York Junior League, joined the group. "Wasn't Betty Rea a doll as Queen!" she said. "My only suggestion for improvement next year is to get escorts and Maids to match. Tall for tall. Short for short."

Mrs. W. Mahlon Dickerson, a tall, broad-shouldered woman, who had been one of the four Maids not chosen for the throne, remarked good-naturedly that her escort had been short but very charming. Her only complaint was that the room upstairs reserved for the Maids had been so well guarded that she herself had had a good deal of trouble getting admitted. "Next year, we ought to have smoother functioning of who gets in and who stays out," she said. "Next year, we ought to do a really bang-up job."

Mrs. Paul H. Raymer, another committee member, observed that the models had been left stranded on the stage after the show and that no one had seemed to know what to do with them. "My husband grabbed Flamingo Orange Juice and danced with her," she said, and everybody laughed. "Next year, we ought to have more of a proper conclusion to things."

Everybody agreed that for the third Mardi Gras Ball there would be smoother functioning of who got in and who stayed out, as well as more of a proper conclusion to things.

During the following month, in accordance with Mrs. Luckenbill's suggestion, the New York Junior League's board of managers, presided over by Mrs. Samuel Wilson Moore, the New York president, voted unanimously to appoint Mrs. Stimson chairman of the third Mardi Gras Ball. In addition, it voted unanimously to make Mrs. Stimson's pink-clown drawing a permanent fixture on the program. In April, Mrs. Stimson, a serious and efficient woman who has belonged to the League for six years and is a past president, and present member, of the board of the Manhattanville Day Nursery, began organizing her committee to prepare for the ball. She named Mrs. Adams chairman of the subcommittee in charge of the pageant, Mrs. Crider chairman in charge of costumes, and Mrs. Santy chairman in charge of hotel arrangements and reservations, and put Mrs. Raymer and Mrs. McLoughlin in charge of special invitations and publicity, respectively. At 10:30 A.M. on

May 6th, these members, along with two others—Mrs. Dickerson and Mrs. Robert Cooke, who were as yet unassigned—were
called to order by their chairman at a preliminary meeting of the
1954 Mardi Gras committee.

The women assembled in the board room, on the third floor of
the League building, walking to it through a corridor whose walls
are hung with photographs of the twenty-five past presidents of
the New York League—a new one is elected every second year—
beginning with Mrs. Charles C. Rumsey, the former Mary Harri-
man, who in 1901 conceived the idea of founding an organization
to be called the Junior League for the Promotion of Settlement
Work. (The name was shortened in 1912.) At the outset of the
meeting, everybody agreed that the coming ball should be a dinner
affair. The previous ball had been a supper dance, and the general
feeling was that it had made Mardi Gras night too expensive for
the individual members of the League, because so many of them
had felt it mandatory to give dinner parties at home before going
to the Astor. Everybody also agreed that the charge for the next
Mardi Gras should again be fifteen dollars a head, eight of which,
it was hoped, would cover the cost of the dinner and the other expenses, so that the remaining seven could be turned over to the
Welfare Trust Fund. There was some discussion about the date of
the ball. The two previous ones had been held on the night of
Shrove Tuesday, the actual Mardi Gras. Some of the committee members thought that a weekend might be better, but the
majority insisted that the traditional night was the best, and that
this was one time when people would simply have to stay up late
in the middle of the week. Once that had been settled, Mrs.
Stimson explained that she was going to delay awhile before naming someone to the critical post of chairman of sponsors, because
she wanted to be sure of finding a woman with some understanding of the problems of the business world. "Let's not be afraid to
face facts, girls," said Mrs. Dickerson. "We're out to make money.
We want sponsors who will fork over money." Her fellow-members
nodded in agreement that she had a sound point there. Mrs.
Adams said that she thought the Astor had the best ballroom for
the purposes of the Mardi Gras, and she proposed that, provided

the hotel had fixed up the public-address system, the ball be held there again. Then she looked at her wristwatch, gave a little cry, and asked to be excused from the meeting, because a quartet of Junior League members, in which she sang second soprano, was scheduled to sing in one of the wards at St. Luke's Hospital in half an hour. She went on to explain breathlessly that the quartet wanted to have at least one run-through of "Tulip," "Daisy," and "Easter Parade" before singing for the patients. Mrs. Stimson adjourned the meeting.

The first official meeting of Mrs. Stimson's committee was held at ten-thirty on the morning of June 3rd, at the Junior League clubhouse. Mrs. Santy and Mrs. Raymer had visited the Astor's banquet department a few days before, and Mrs. Santy reported that a roast-sirloin-of-beef dinner would cost the League seven dollars a person, plus a fifteen-per-cent service charge—a total of eight dollars and five cents. It was a good dinner, Mrs. Santy said, and it didn't have what she called "that hotel-chicken-dinner personality." Mrs. Raymer put in hastily that the dinner started with clear green-turtle soup, instead of what she called "that hotel-chicken watery stuff." She looked around at her fellow-members and went on, "The soup is more important than you might think. If we're going to have a dinner, we must keep in mind the discouragement everybody feels if the soup is cold and dishpanny. If they get that discouraged feeling at the outset, the party is sunk moralewise." Mrs. Stimson said all that was true, but the price of the dinner was about two dollars more than the price of the supper at the last ball. In a rather weak voice, Mrs. Adams pointed out that the extra cost of the meal might mean a loss of as much as sixteen hundred dollars to the Welfare Trust Fund.

After a few moments' silence, Mrs. Santy said loudly, "Let me read you the entire menu for the roast-sirloin-of-beef dinner." She cleared her throat and read, " 'Clear green-turtle soup, celery, paillettes of corn, olives, roast sirloin of beef Chevreuse, mushroom sauce, potatoes dauphine, new peas, salad chiffonade, peach Melba, petits fours, demitasse.' " Mrs. Santy stopped reading and sighed.

"It does sound so good," said Mrs. Stimson. She looked around encouragingly at her committee members.

"Well," Mrs. Adams said, "it would be nice to have roast beef, and all that, but I do think we ought to pause and consider the fundamental objective of Mardi Gras. I move that we postpone our decision until Mrs. Santy and Mrs. Raymer have an opportunity to obtain other menus at lower prices."

"Second the motion," said Mrs. Santy.

A low moan rose in the committee room, but everybody voted to postpone the decision on the menu.

Mrs. Stimson said that this year there ought to be more emphasis in the *Observer*, the League's monthly magazine, and, if possible, in general publications, on how the five Maids who are candidates for Queen are chosen, and a lot more about how their service to the League and to the community qualifies them for that honor. Mrs. McLoughlin, in her capacity as publicity director, agreed. The point ought to be driven home once and for all to the whole membership, she said, that the Maids are picked from among twenty candidates who are selected by the League's placement committee on the basis of the time and energy they have devoted to worthwhile services. "They're chosen by sensible, serious-minded gals," she went on. "Those gals do a terrific job studying the records of all the active members except the board of managers, and the membership ought to know that everybody's record gets examined seriously."

"And that only active members are eligible," said Mrs. Stimson.

Mrs. Santy wanted to know whether the provisional members—those newly elected to the League—wouldn't feel left out.

"You can't be provisional forever, dear girl," Mrs. Stimson said, with a little laugh. She added that she hoped Mrs. McLoughlin would make it clear that the placement committee submits the names of all its candidates to the board of managers. "We're counting on you to point up the fact that if the board feels some deserving member has been overlooked, it can say, 'Heavens, why isn't So-and-So a candidate?'" she continued, and Mrs. McLoughlin replied that she would and that she would also try to impress upon the membership the fact that five judges not connected with the League make the final selection of the Maids, on the basis of interviews with the twenty candidates and a study of their service records. This year, she said, the judges were to be James F. Macandrew, director of broadcasting at the Board of Education's radio station; Miss Helen M. Harris, the executive director of United Neighborhood Houses of New York; Mrs. Joseph P. Lash, the executive director of the Citizens' Committee on Children of New York City; Stanley P. Davies, the general director of the Community Service Society of New York; and Clyde E. Murray, executive director of Manhattanville Neighborhood Center.

"Very good," Mrs. Stimson said. "Now—costumes?" She turned to Mrs. Crider, who, after consulting a sheaf of papers, announced that her preliminary investigation of the matter of the models' costumes had been very encouraging. She thought that instead of having each costume made in a different place, as in the past, it might be feasible to have them all made at the Brooks Costume Company. She said she had spoken with James Stroock, the head of that company, and he had estimated that each costume would cost about seventy-five dollars, or nearly twenty dollars less than the average cost of the costumes for the previous ball. Furthermore, Mrs. Crider said, she thought it would be a fine idea to ask Gunther Jaeckel, which had placed an advertisement in the most recent issue of the Observer, to contribute gowns for the five Maids. The other members applauded Mrs. Crider, and the committee then turned to a general discussion of a number of questions: Could the Astor provide the master of ceremonies with two microphones, so that all the guests could hear the program? Could the Astor take the hum, whistles, and squeaks out of the public-address system? Could the Astor be enlisted as a sponsor of the ball, and perhaps be represented by a Miss Astor, who might hold a large numeral "50," to commemorate the fiftieth anniversary of the hotel, which was coming up the following year? Could Jo Mielziner, the theatrical designer, be persuaded to do the staging for the Mardi Gras show? Could Rodgers and Hammerstein be enlisted to contribute a score written specially for the Mardi Gras? Or, failing that, could Rodgers and Hammerstein do at least one special song for the Mardi Gras? Mrs. Stimson said the committee now had some meaty questions to work on before its first meeting in the fall.

· · ·

The first fall meeting of the committee was held on November 4th at 10:30 A.M. The members looked authoritative and eager. To start things off, Mrs. Stimson asked Mrs. Santy to give her report on the question of the menu. Mrs. Santy asked if the committee wanted to hear the eight-dollar-and-five-cent roast-sirloin-of-beef menu again, and said that if so, she would read it first and then read the menus of two less expensive dinners. Everybody wanted to hear the roast-sirloin-of-beef menu again, so Mrs. Santy started with the clear green-turtle soup and went right on through to the *petits fours* and demitasse. Everybody sighed, and then Mrs. Santy read the menu of a six-dollar roast-turkey dinner. This one was greeted with cold silence. Mrs. Santy went on to read a third menu: fruit cocktail, celery, olives, broiled breast of chicken Virginie, Virginia ham, broiled mushrooms, candied yams, asparagus tips, hearts of lettuce with Roquefort dressing, baked Alaska, Bing cherries *flambées*, demitasse. This dinner would cost six-fifty, plus the fifteen-per-cent service charge, which would bring the cost to seven-forty-eight. Mrs. Adams said that the menu sounded pretty good, even if it did include chicken, and the other members agreed without enthusiasm that when you came right down to it a chicken-and-ham dinner was better than a turkey one. Mrs. Dickerson wanted to know if the fruit cup would be made of canned fruit or fresh fruit. Fresh, Mrs. Santy said, and pointed out that the chicken was *breast* of chicken and that this automatically raised it above the level of many hotel dinners.

Mrs. Dickerson's expression was that of a person who has reached a decision. "If it's *breast* of chicken, I'd say it's a darn nice dinner and we needn't worry about the word chicken," she said cheerfully. "We might aim for seafood cocktail, though—or anything but fruit cup. Fresh or canned, fruit cup is rather down-beat, partywise."

"I move we axe the fruit cup and take the third menu," Mrs. McLoughlin said. The motion was seconded and carried. Everybody applauded.

"All right, then," Mrs. Stimson said sternly. "Now we must buckle down and get those sponsors. Mrs. Correa will be chairman of sponsors. Mrs. Correa?"

Mrs. Henry A. Correa stood up and asked all the committee members to get after everybody they knew in big business who might be influential in producing a sponsor. There were three sponsors so far, she said—WNBC, WNBT, and Liggett & Myers. "Caroline Burke spoke to Pepsi-Cola, and she thinks they will be a sponsor," she went on. "But so far only the other three are absolutely definite."

Mrs. Luckenbill suggested that it wasn't a bit too early to put the heat on everybody to get sponsors.

"Sponsors are basic," Mrs. Adams said.

Mrs. Crider said that she was having a bit of a problem with Liggett & Myers over its model's costume.

"Liggett & Myers apparently wasn't too happy at the last Mardi Gras," she said. The Liggett & Myers costume at the 1953 ball had been a tube of white felt, mounted on a wire frame, that glowed at the tip.

"Liggett & Myers was unhappy about the way the girl was hidden inside the tube, instead of looking glamorous or something," said Mrs. Stimson. "We did the best we could with a limited budget."

"Liggett & Myers wants a Parade of Quality," Mrs. Crider said. "They want their four cigarettes—Chesterfield, king-size Chesterfield, Fatima, and L & M—represented by four models, with perhaps a man lighting their cigarettes."

Mrs. Adams, looking alarmed, said that to go along with this request might raise problems in dealing with other sponsors who made more than one product. After a half-hour discussion, it was decided that if any sponsor wanted to pay the cost of additional costumes, and if it didn't require more parade time than any other sponsor got, it could have additional models.

Mrs. Stimson then said that she had met a number of gentlemen from the National Broadcasting Company, and they had all agreed that Faye Emerson and Skitch Henderson would be ideal for mistress and master of ceremonies. A motion to try to get Faye and Skitch to lend their services was made, seconded, and carried, and everybody applauded again.

Mrs. Stimson blushed slightly at this tribute to her enterprise and frowned at her agenda. "Since the last Mardi Gras, a new Mayor has been elected," she said. "Would someone make a motion to the effect that Betsy Carrington, who knows Mayor Wagner, contact him and invite him to crown the Queen at the next Mardi Gras?" A motion to that effect was then made, seconded, and carried.

Mrs. Adams rose and said that everybody ought to set to work getting famous people to submit sketches for costumes. Mrs. Dickerson added that everybody also ought to be thinking of somebody famous to serve as King.

"Let's have some famous names suggested now," said Mrs. Stimson.

The members decided to ask Fannie Hurst, Irving Berlin, Hedda Hopper, Red Barber, and Dale Carnegie to submit sketches for costumes. Then, as possible Kings, they nominated Adolphe Menjou, Robert Montgomery, Conrad Thibault, Charles Boyer, John Cameron Swayze, James Stewart, Fredric March, Douglas Fairbanks, Jr., and Lawrence Tibbett. Mrs. Stimson looked satisfied. "Kingwise we don't have anything to worry about," she said.

At the beginning of December, Mrs. Stimson stood before her committee with a budget—drawn up by Mrs. John R. Stevenson, the treasurer of the committee, and approved by the New York Junior League board of managers—that, based on a thousand paying guests and fifteen paying sponsors and an expenditure of $16,500, showed a profit of $17,535 for the Welfare Trust Fund. Mrs. Stimson was prepared to place an order for sixty-five hundred invitations, to be printed at a cost of $438. She had already worked out one design for these and had brought it along for the members to look at. On the outside of the invitation, a folded affair, were two gay faces—one of a clown and the other of a devil—smiling down at the words "You Are Invited to the New York Junior League Mardi Gras." On the inside, the invitation read, "GLAMOUR," "FUN," "GAYETY," "FROLIC," "MELODY," and "PAGEANTRY." Beneath these words was inscribed "A PAGEANT WITH

COSTUMES OF FANTASY—A Glamorous Parade of Junior League Models in Fabulous Costumes." To the left of this boast were a large pink star with a blue question mark in its center and the words "QUEEN OF THE MARDI GRAS." All Mrs. Stimson's committee members thought that her design was terrific, and it was swiftly adopted.

By mid-December, the committee had signed up five more sponsors—T.W.A., the Moore-McCormack Lines, Fuller Brush, Philco, and the Astor Hotel. Shortly thereafter, consternation set in, for Mrs. Correa had to accompany her husband on a business trip to South America and would not be back until after the ball. An emergency meeting of the committee was called, and Mrs. Stimson named Mrs. Dickerson, who had just nabbed not only Moore-McCormack but the Packard Motor Car Company, to carry on as chairman of sponsors. Mrs. Dickerson got to work at once. At a brief committee meeting shortly before Christmas, she announced, "I want to put up a poster on the main floor of the clubhouse with a thermometer on it showing that we have nine sponsors, and then as the list grows the thermometer will be filled in. And we've got to make it grow. I knew some of the Moore-McCormack people and that helped me get them as sponsors. But, on the other hand, I sold Packard cold. Just went in there and said I had something that might interest them, and that was *that*." There was a prolonged hum of approval from the other committee members, and Mrs. Dickerson acknowledged it with a nod. "Pepsi-Cola looks good," she said. "Miss Burke is still after them. The only other thing I want to ask is whether there is any objection to approaching None Such Mince Meat in addition to Borden's, since None Such Mince Meat is a Borden product." The committee unanimously sanctioned going after anybody and everybody who might be a sponsor, instead of worrying about who owned what.

On January 7th, the five judges interviewed twenty Junior Leaguers whose names had been put up by the placement committee as potential Maids of the Mardi Gras Ball, and, after conferring among themselves for more than three hours, submitted the following list of the five indefatigable winners:

NANCY ANNE BARTON. Born 1927. Years in League—eight.
Schools: Dana Hall, Smith, Radio Advertising, Speedwriting
Institute, University of Wisconsin. League: Library Bureau.
Children's Arts. Follies, Singer (chorus). Evening Group:
Plan Pine Room Program, Hostess, Dinner Chairman.
Library-by-Mail. Community: Red Cross staff assistant, Pel-
ham. Red Cross, Hampshire County Chapter (Special Re-
port). Manor Club, Jr. Section, Recording Secretary, Pro-
gram Chairman.

ENA GARVIN. Born 1918. Years in League—seventeen.
Schools: Miss Spence, Barnard, Parsons School of Design.
League: Children's Arts, Docent. Evening Program: Surgical Dressings. Pine Room Program, Hostess, Opening Dinner. Follies, Page Girl. Placement Interviewer (evening).
U.N. Evening Parties. Volunteer Social Work Aide, Riverside Hospital Out-Clinic. Community: Metropolitan Museum of Art. Catholic Charities.

JOAN GRAY. Born 1921. Years in League—eight. Schools:
Branson, Sarah Lawrence. League: Observer, Article. Fur-
lough Recreation. Membership Survey. Children's Arts,
Vice-Chairman. New Members. Education: Vice-Chairman,
Chairman, Member. Training Courses, Chairman. Place-
ment, Chairman. N.Y.J.L. Board. Admissions Study, Chair-
man. Case Work Aide, Co-Chairman. Program Planning,
Member-at-Large. N.Y.J.L. Vice-President. Community Re-
lations, Chairman. Evaluation, Vice-Chairman. Commu-
nity: Children's Center. Library. Home for Young Girls,
Board, Secretary. Girls' Service League: Board, Chairman,
Education Committee. Federation of Protestant Welfare
Agencies: Board Members' Education Committee, Child
Care. Yorkville Civic Council, Executive Committee. State
Charities Aid Association: Committee on Mental Health,
Executive Committee. UNESCO Conference, Hospitality.
Women's City Club, Board.

MRS. N. EDWARD MITCHELL. Born 1915. Years in League
—seven. Number of Children—one. Schools: Weston, University of Toronto, Parsons School of Design Paris Scholar-

ship, New York Advertising Club Course in advertising, radio. League: Training Course, Provisional Chairman. Provisional Interviewing. Toy Shop: Vice-Chairman, Chairman. Community Services. Membership Activities, Chairman. House Committee. Follies: Vice-Chairman, Skit. Placement: Vice-Chairman, Chairman. N.Y.J.L. Board. Community Relations: Community Services, Poster for Professional Tea. Volunteer Social Work Aide Project, Vice-Chairman. Program, Vice-Chairman. *Observer:* "Volunteer Help Wanted" column, Articles. Public Relations. N.Y.J.L. American Red Cross Bloodmobile. Mardi Gras, Placement Liaison. Placement, Interviewer. Community: Brick Church Fair, Committee Chairman. Chairman Christmas Card, Decorating, and Fashion Committees. Greater New York Council for Foreign Students: Hostess, Trip to Ford Plant. Blue Ridge Auxiliary, Dance Committee. Protestant Federation, Advisory Board. Jury Duty. Brick Church: Chancel Committee, Fashion Show, Ticket Committee. V.S.W.A. Project, Trustee Rockefeller Fund.

MRS. GEORGE E. MURPHY. Born 1918. Years in League— five. Schools: Notre Dame de Sion, Mount Vernon Junior College, Scripps College, California. League: Hospitality. Public Relations, Secretary. Placement, Interviewer. Provisional Training, Fall Course. Community Services: Professional Tea, Mailing List. Provisional Committee, Chairman. American Red Cross Junior League Blood Bank, Spot Job. *Observer*, Article. Community: Kansas City League: Art Gallery, Docent. Junior League Thrift Shop, Selling. N.Y.J.L.: Metropolitan Museum, Heart Fund Drive.

The February issue of the *Observer* carried a tribute to all the candidates for Maids from the president of the New York Junior League, Mrs. Moore. "I wish each and every one could have been a 'Maid' and I know, because they told me so, that the judges had a terrible time choosing five Maids from among them," Mrs. Moore wrote.

·   ·   ·

Three weeks before the date of the ball, Mrs. Stimson held a meeting of the executive committee of the Mardi Gras committee —Mrs. Adams, Mrs. McLoughlin, Mrs. Dickerson, Mrs. Santy, Mrs. Raymer, Mrs. Crider, and Mrs. Stevenson—at which she regretfully announced that it didn't look as if any of the Kings who had been nominated would ever reach the throne: Adolphe Menjou was in Hollywood, James Stewart was in Hollywood, Robert Montgomery would be on his way to Washington, and the others were too busy. Everyone looked downcast. Then Mrs. Stimson said, "But Henry Fonda is in town now, with a new play. I think Henry Fonda would make a charming King." The committee responded with energetic approval and voted to ask Mrs. Douglas Leigh, a committee member who knew Fonda, to invite him to serve as King.

"I regret to say that Rodgers and Hammerstein can't do a special score for us," Mrs. Stimson next announced. "But I'm sure that Emile Coleman will provide whatever we need in the way of music." The board expressed understanding and agreement.

Mrs. Santy reported that applications for tickets to the ball were pouring in. "Martha Wadsworth sent out over six thousand invitations on January 25th," she said. "She stamped, stuffed, addressed, and mailed them practically all by herself. There's no beating Martha when it comes to that hideous job."

Two weeks before the date of the ball, a clipping from the World-Telegram & Sun was posted on a bulletin board beside the elevator at League headquarters. It was a photograph showing the five Maids grouped around Fonda, who, with a royal smile, was holding a diamond tiara that Napoleon had once given to the Empress Josephine and that the jewelry firm of Van Cleef & Arpels was going to lend to the League for the crowning of its Queen.

On the afternoon the clipping was posted, Mrs. Cooke, the chairman of models, and her assistants, Mrs. Frederick R. Hanson and Mrs. Kilner Husted, were seated in a corner of the Pine Room —a large lounge on the second floor of the clubhouse, with a fireplace, and comfortable armchairs arranged around several small cocktail tables. With them were two of the League members who were going to serve as models at the ball—Miss Polly Ann

Bryant and Mrs. David Drew Zingg. "We want our sponsors to be happy," Mrs. Cooke was saying to Miss Bryant, a pretty, dark-haired girl with large blue eyes, who had agreed only a few hours before to be the Philco model. "It was very nice of you to come on such short notice, Miss Bryant."

"Mardi Gras is two weeks from tonight," Mrs. Hanson said. "I'm exhausted. I hope somebody reminds all the models and Maids to get enough sleep."

Mrs. Cooke asked Miss Bryant to stand up, so that she could show her how to move when she had the Philco costume on. "You're a refrigerator and you're all filled with stuff," Mrs. Cooke said. "Now, you're all in white as you walk in, and your white robe comes to a kind of V in front. You fling one arm out"— Miss Bryant flung one arm out—"and inside there's the tomato juice and soft drinks and oranges. Then you open the other side" —Miss Bryant flung out her other arm—"and there's the eggs and butter and milk and cream. Do you think you get the idea?"

Miss Bryant nodded eagerly. "Oh, yes," she said. "All I do is open the doors and I have all the stuff inside the costume."

"Right," Mrs. Cooke said crisply. "Now Mrs. Zingg." The other model stood up. She was tall and very slim, with long, slender legs. Mrs. Cooke explained that she would model for the American Express Company, a newcomer. "You're just terrific," Mrs. Cooke said. "You simply wear the company's uniform—jacket and cap, that is—and tights."

"Just tights?" Mrs. Zingg said, rather proudly. "Not trousers?"

"American Express prefers tights, and thank goodness you have the figure for them," Mrs. Cooke said. "Do you think you've got the idea, Mrs. Zingg?"

Mrs. Zingg said it sounded like a cinch. Then Mrs. Cooke told the two models that Mrs. Hanson would make an appointment for each of them for a costume fitting and would telephone them in a day or so, and Miss Bryant and Mrs. Zingg left. Mrs. Cooke told Mrs. Husted that Fannie Hurst, Irving Berlin, Hedda Hopper, Red Barber, and Dale Carnegie had not come across with designs for costumes. An auxiliary list of celebrities had been got up, and as a result of it Bing Crosby had agreed to let his name be used as the designer of the American Express Company's costume—coat, cap, tights, and all; Rosalind Russell had suggested that the American Viscose Corporation, another newcomer, have Queen Guinevere escorted by a white knight in shining armor, just like its trademark; Perry Como had suggested that the Liggett & Myers girl wear a slinky evening gown and a necklace of Liggett & Myers cigarettes; and Charles Boyer had authorized the use of his name as the designer of a costume that included a spool hat and a dressmaker's dummy, for Singer Sewing Machine, which had recently signed up. "Groucho Marx gave us a peach for Fuller Brush," Mrs. Cooke said. "He came up with something real dreamy. One of our girls will be dressed as Groucho and smoking a long cigar with gold ashes that she'll drop as she walks down the aisle, and she'll be followed by a tall blonde who'll sweep up the ashes with a Fuller brush. Jo-Jeanne Barton is going to be Groucho. All she does all day, she says, is practice her walk. And she just had a baby two weeks ago, too."

Mrs. Husted asked if Pepperidge Farm Bread was a sponsor again this year, and Mrs. Cooke said no, adding that Pepperidge somehow felt last year's sandwich had said everything and there just wasn't anything else to say. But among the new sponsors the League did have were Pepsi-Cola, United States Steel, Cities Service, and Rheingold Beer, which was going to send its own Miss Rheingold to represent it.

"That Pepperidge sandwich last year was a dream," Mrs. Husted said wistfully.

"Wait'll you see Moore-McCormack's fruit salad," said Mrs. Cooke.

That same afternoon, on the fifth floor of the clubhouse, in a small office shared by the editor of the Observer and Mrs. Mc-Loughlin, the latter was having a conference with Miss Margaret Roberts, a serious, quiet-spoken young lady, who had been engaged by the League as the professional producer of the Mardi Gras show and whose job included, among many other things, keeping the pageant within the time limit set by the television people. Miss Roberts told Mrs. McLoughlin that the television people were giving the League only forty minutes. "They've pre-empted our time, but it will really be a much better show that way," she said. Mrs. McLoughlin did not question the point, and Miss Roberts continued, "This is what we call the rundown—the sequence of events as they will be filmed by the cameras. We open with balloons falling from the ceiling and everybody dancing. Then we go to Faye and Skitch sitting at a small ringside table, and they say, 'The Junior League—' "

"The New York Junior League," Mrs. McLoughlin said.

Miss Roberts accepted the correction and went on to tell her that, after saying hello, Faye and Skitch would explain the purpose of the ball. "Then Faye and Skitch go over to the Mayor's table," Miss Roberts said, "and there we meet Mayor and Mrs. Wagner, and Mrs. Moore and her husband, Dr. Moore, and they talk about the history of the Junior League."

"The New York Junior League," said Mrs. McLoughlin.

Miss Roberts nodded. "And the New York Junior League's accomplishments of the past year," she said. "Now, what should Faye and Skitch say about the volunteer work?"

Mrs. McLoughlin said Faye and Skitch ought to mention the work of the Volunteer Social Work Aide Project, which was set up by the League to pay tuition at the New York School of Social Work not only for League members but for members of other welfare agencies, and to place the League volunteers trained there at Riverside Hospital. Miss Roberts assured Mrs. McLoughlin that she would pass this information along to Faye and Skitch. They were leaving for Europe that evening, she said, but they would be back a day or two before the Mardi Gras. She then outlined the rest of the television program—the costume parade, the introduction of the five Maids, the announcement by the Mayor of the name of the Maid chosen as Queen, and the march through the ballroom by the King and Queen. "With only forty minutes, it's going to be very tight," Miss Roberts said.

"Well," said Mrs. McLoughlin, "it's the New York Junior League. Let's be sure to get that in, anyway."

At ten the next morning, there was a meeting of the executive committee of the Mardi Gras committee, presided over by Mrs. Stimson, who started out briskly by announcing that this year there would be about eight hundred people at the ball—a hundred more than had come the year before; this would probably mean turning some people down, but it had been decided that the one thousand originally figured on would make things too crowded. The members of the executive committee were beginning to wear a look of combined worry, distraction, and great expectation. One after another, problems were disposed of: Had the Astor been advised that the hum, whistles, and squeaks from the mikes last year had made it difficult to hear and that the public-address system ought to be fixed? (Mrs. Adams said that the Astor had promised to have all the mikes in good working order.) Did all the sponsors know that each sponsor would be given only a few seconds for commercials, to be delivered by Faye and Skitch? (Mrs. Dickerson said she had personally informed them all of this fact.) Had tables been allocated to all the sponsors? (Mrs. Santy said American Express had had no table until a quarter of an hour ago, but now an entire table was reserved for American Express and it was ringside.) Where was Pepsi-Cola sitting? (Mrs. Santy said with Miss Burke, who had nabbed Pepsi-Cola.) Three commercial photographers had telephoned to ask whether they might take the official photographs, and what should Mrs. Stimson tell them?

"Mr. Dahlheim has done it every year for us, bless his heart," said Mrs. Adams.

"Mr. Dahlheim doesn't get in anybody's hair, either," Mrs. Dickerson added. "He would never bother one of the Maids just going onstage, or something."

Mrs. Adams—tall, cool, and self-possessed—reported on the matter of prices. "We'll just skimp by under the budget," she said. "I told the Astor they've simply got to come down on some of the prices, and they may, but the fact remains that in order to make the ballroom look right, you've got to do certain things that cost money." The rest of the committee looked glum. "It isn't the things that are so expensive," Mrs. Adams continued. "It's all in the labor." The pageant designer, Lester Gaba, had all sorts of wonderful ideas for decorating the ballroom, she said, but they would cost money. The rest of the committee looked glummer.

Mrs. Adams picked up a sheet of paper and rattled it. "Lester thinks we should have an underwater theme," she said. "Lester wants to do the stage up in sea-blue satin drapes and have it all sort of bubbly-looking, with balloons held up by mermaids."

"Mmm, yummy!" said Mrs. Stimson, and then blushed and looked apologetically at the rest of the committee.

Mrs. Adams went on to explain that Gaba also wanted to extend the undersea theme of the stage all through the ballroom, which would mean an additional $375 for labor. She read off a list of other costs, including $55 for robes and sceptres for the King and Queen, $5 for a page's trumpet, $150 for balloons, $50 for hoops (wooden frames with canvas spread loosely across them to hold balloons near the ceiling until the time for their release), $150 apiece for two papier-mâché mermaids, and $100 for a pink-and-blue papier-mâché shell, ten feet high, to hold the throne chairs. The mermaids, she explained, would be faceless and silvery-looking.

"Oh, let's have them flicker," said Mrs. Dickerson.

"Well, the light to make them flicker costs twenty-five dollars extra," said Mrs. Adams.

"Oh dear!" said Mrs. Dickerson.

"We must be strong, girls," said Mrs. Stimson. "Of course, we're ahead of last year on sponsors. We just got Forstmann Woolens today. And with the eight hundred people we expect—"

"I'd rather see that money go into the Welfare Trust Fund," said Mrs. McLoughlin.

"Of course," said Mrs. Adams. "And if we drape just one tier of the ballroom, instead of both, we'll save a hundred and fifty dollars."

"Rosie, take one more crack at seeing if you can get the Astor to shave the price," Mrs. Dickerson said to Mrs. Adams. "We're not getting anywhere with None Such Mince Meat."

Mrs. Adams nodded. "Another thing," she said. "Lester Gaba wants these long candles for the tables. That's fifty dollars."

"I tried to talk him out of it," Mrs. Stimson said. "Last year, we spent a hundred and fifty for extra-long candles—long pink candles.

The Astor wanted to give us those little beaded mushroom things, and if we have those this year, Lester is just going to be sick."

"I'm afraid we'll have to axe the long candles this year," said Mrs. Adams.

"See what you can do, Rosie," said Mrs. Dickerson.

A couple of mornings later, with the ball hardly a week away, Mrs. Santy called on Robert Howard, the Astor's banquet director, in his office at the hotel. Howard is a patient, hoarse-voiced man with a round, pink face and a small mustache. Mrs. Santy was accompanied by three other members of the Mardi Gras committee —Mrs. Dickerson, Mrs. J. Calhoun Harris, and Mrs. Edmund Johnstone—and by Miss Eva M. Scism, assistant to the Junior League treasurer. All five women had on little hats with little veils, and three-strand chokers of pearls, and they sat around Howard's desk in a semicircle.

"Well, ladies," Howard said, somewhat nervously, "are you all set for the big night?"

"You're never really set until it's all over," Mrs. Santy said.

Howard laughed wanly.

"If you'll take some notes on what I tell you . . ." Mrs. Santy began. Howard drew up a pad and seized a pencil. Mrs. Santy asked him to have the models' room properly guarded, and the Maids' room, too, because the year before, Mrs. Dickerson, a Maid herself, had had trouble getting in; to have a waiter on hand to take food to the models, who hadn't been able to get anything to eat the last time until after the show was over, and had starved; and to bear in mind the names of the judges who would choose the Queen—Mrs. Oswald B. Lord, the United States representative to the United Nations Commission on Human Rights; Dr. Howard A. Rusk, the chairman of the Department of Physical Medicine and Rehabilitation at the New York University College of Medicine; and Russel Crouse, the playwright—because they would have to be passed by the guards and admitted to the Maids' room.

"Everything will be taken care of, ladies," Howard said.

Mrs. Santy brought up the question of cocktails before dinner, and Howard told her that the Coral Room was very good for cocktails. "It's really green," he said, and laughed.

Mrs. Johnstone wanted to know if there would be peanuts on the tables there.

Howard made a note. "Now I'd like to ask you some questions," he said.

"Yes, sir," said Mrs. Santy.

"What about cigarettes?" Howard asked.

Mrs. Dickerson started. "Nothing but Chesterfields," she said. "Liggett & Myers is one of our sponsors. And there must be Pepsi-Cola. If Mr. Steele, the Pepsi-Cola man, asks for Pepsi-Cola, he mustn't get Coca-Cola."

Howard made another note. "You want pink tablecloths, ladies?" he asked.

"What did Mrs. Adams say?" asked Mrs. Santy.

"She said to use as many as we have but not to buy any," Howard replied. He shrugged wearily. "As soon as I get through with one committee, another comes in," he said. "I don't think we'll be able to cover more than half the tables with pink cloths."

Mrs. Santy nodded and looked worried. "There was something else, but I've forgotten it," she said.

"I write everything down," said Mrs. Dickerson.

"Well, ladies," Howard said cheerfully, "shall we go in and take a look at the tables?"

Everybody rose and walked into the ballroom. The floor was bare, and the tables, their brown wooden tops exposed, looked dark and dreary in the dimly lit room. The stage was deserted. The balconies were undraped. There were no blue satin draperies and no sign of an underwater theme. Mrs. Santy took a list of table reservations out of her pocketbook and Howard produced a chart, and they went to work on the problem of who was going to sit where.

The last general meeting of the 1954 Mardi Gras committee was held the following morning, five days before the ball. It was a tense session. Miss Roberts outlined the parts that would be played by the producer, the director, the cameramen, the electricians, and all the others who would be on hand for the televising of the show. After her report, everybody looked both pleased and apprehensive.

"I think it's going to be a very good party," Miss Roberts said.

Mrs. Stimson wanted to know whether the television people were coming in dinner clothes.

Miss Roberts looked apologetic and said it was unlikely.

"I guess we can't be too horrified if a man running a spotlight isn't in dinner clothes," said Mrs. Adams.

"Would you suggest that they wear dark suits and black bow ties?" Mrs. Stimson asked hopefully.

Miss Roberts promised that she would.

Mrs. Adams read off the names of the men who had volunteered to escort the Maids to the stage—John Cameron Swayze, Shepperd Strudwick, and three League members' husbands, Robert Cooke, Russell Nype, and Thomas D. Luckenbill.

"On models, are our ladies all squared away?" Mrs. Stimson asked.

Mrs. Cooke reported that they were squared away.

Mrs. Dickerson said that she hoped someone would be sure to see that Pepsi-Cola was on hand, in case the Pepsi-Cola people ordered it. "It seems Mr. Steele went to a party and ordered Pepsi-Cola and got Coca-Cola," she said. The other committee members shuddered, and there were murmurs of "Oh, oh, oh!"

Mrs. Santy announced that the League stood to profit by the serving of drinks. To make things simple, she said, they had decided to charge a flat dollar for all drinks. "The Astor charges fifty-five cents for a Manhattan, and if we sell it for a dollar, we make forty-five cents," she said. "Isn't that nice?" The committee indicated that it was indeed nice.

Mrs. Adams said that she had bargained with Mr. Howard over the price of hanging blue satin draperies and gold fish net that would produce a bubbly, undersea effect, and had succeeded in getting him to knock fifty dollars off the price, but that, even so, she had decided they might better do without the draperies entirely and just use balloons or some other less expensive bubbly device. "So I cancelled the drapes, at least for the time being, and left Mr. Howard feeling a bit angry," she said. "I'm meeting with

Lester Gaba and a balloon man this afternoon. And if you feel you can leave it up to me, I'll decide between the drapes and the balloons, or possibly some cellophane fringe we just heard about. Anyway, we're going to have a ballroom that looks pretty." The committee members decided to leave it to Mrs. Adams.

After lunch that day, Mrs. Adams went to a room behind the Astor ballroom for a meeting with Gaba and P. Raymonde Warny, a bald, mournful balloon salesman, who was wearing heavy shell-rimmed glasses. As she joined them, Warny pulled a fistful of balloons from a briefcase and blew up a silver one.

"Doesn't it look like a pearl?" Gaba asked Mrs. Adams.

"Well . . ." said Mrs. Adams.

Warny held the balloon up to the light.

"You certainly get the biggest effect for the least money with balloons," Gaba said. "Now, remember, we want them to look like bubbles and pearls."

Warny lugubriously blew up a green balloon.

"Pretty," said Gaba. "But we don't want to get off the track."

Mrs. Adams asked how much it would cost to drape the balconies with balloons. Warny replied that at least three thousand balloons would be needed for the balconies and, at twelve dollars a hundred, the price would come to three hundred and sixty dollars, in addition to the hundred and ninety-eight dollars for the balloons he had already planned to use for the ceiling and tables.

"Pretty expensive," Mrs. Adams said thoughtfully.

"The draped tiers got kicked out because they were too expensive," said Gaba irritably.

Just then, a young man came in carrying a large suitcase and introduced himself as the cellophane-fringe salesman. He opened his suitcase and displayed the fringe—gleaming, transparent stuff. He could drape the balconies with it for a hundred and eighty dollars and twenty cents, he said.

"We can't afford it," said Gaba. "Unless we kick out the balloons."

Warny looked unhappy.

"The fringe has that watery, bubbly look," Gaba said.

Mrs. Adams agreed that it looked pretty.

"If we have just balloons, it ends up looking like a high-school dance," Gaba said.

Gaba told the cellophane-fringe salesman that he would let him know their decision, and the salesman packed up his fringe. Mrs. Adams said that the League had some giant harlequin masks left over from the previous year's ball, and suggested using them again, to cover the second tier of balconies.

"I'm not mad about those masks," said Gaba.

"It's just that we have them," said Mrs. Adams.

"I really think we need the balloons if we're going to have a truly bubbly and watery effect," said Gaba.

Warny nodded, and started blowing up a pink balloon.

"Do a clear one," Gaba said. "I think we'll stick to clear, watery-looking ones only."

Warny dropped the pink balloon and blew up a clear one. Gaba stared moodily at it. "Without the blue satin draperies, the theme is neat but it certainly isn't the spirit of Mardi Gras," he remarked.

Mrs. Adams looked dismayed. "Oh, Lester!" she said. "Come on, now!"

"There was no reason for picking the undersea motif except that we were counting on the blue satin draperies and stuff," Gaba said. "Now that that's all kicked out, what's the point? We might just as well have another theme."

Mrs. Adams reminded him that anyway the King and Queen would have a large sea shell for their throne.

"But what's the point?" Gaba asked.

Then Mrs. Adams made up her mind. They would decorate the ballroom, stage, and balconies with blue satin draperies, she said firmly, and give the ball an undersea motif. And they would have some bubbly-looking balloons, too.

As the evening of the ball approached, the members of the committee took to having sandwiches sent in at lunchtime and munching them while they conferred. The five Maids were fitted for gowns at Gunther Jaeckel, and tried to get to bed early each night. It was found that by scrimping here and there it would be possible to have blue satin draperies on both tiers of balconies in the ballroom for three hundred dollars, and there would be balloons there, too, and the stage not only would be draped but would sport gold fish net and two blank-faced mermaids, and everything would look lovely after all. Mrs. Stimson and the other members of her committee backed Mrs. Adams up solidly. At three o'clock on the afternoon of March 1st, the day before Mardi Gras, most of the committee members, together with the five Maids and all the models, gathered in the ballroom for a dress rehearsal. The ballroom did look lovely. The stage and both tiers were draped with sequinned blue satin, and interspersed here and there along the tiers were branches of coral made of sparkling papier-mâché. Gaba stood on the stage surveying the scene. Everybody looked dazed. Mrs. Barton, wearing striped pants and a long coat, after the fashion of Groucho Marx, was practicing her walk. The Singer Sewing Machine model, with a gold spool on her head, was urging her to bend her knees more, with more of a side-to-side waddle. Mrs. Zingg, wearing black tights, high-heeled shoes, and an American Express Company coat and cap, joined them just as Anita Colby, who appears on television for Pepsi-Cola, walked onstage wearing an old-fashioned pink tulle gown and carrying a fan with "Pepsi-Cola" written on it.

"Professional competition," said Mrs. Zingg. "Pepsi-Cola is so particular."

"I can't sleep at night," said one of the Maids to nobody in particular. "I have a steady feeling of being sick to my stomach."

Mrs. Adams arrived, and asked if anybody had seen her husband. "Stirling is supposed to be here to try on his knight's armor," she said. "He's escorting Guinevere for American Viscose."

Mrs. Dickerson came up to her and said she had reserved three tables for a total of fifty-six people and she was sure she'd never have a chance to get her place cards properly distributed. "I've got forty people coming to my house for cocktails earlier in the evening," she said, sitting down on a table. "I've hired a bus to bring them over." They were joined by Mrs. McLoughlin, who said she was late because she had tried on her ball gown that morning and found she had lost so much weight working on the Mardi Gras that she had had to have it taken in two inches at the waist.

Mrs. McLoughlin then wandered off again, and, a minute later, shouted to Mrs. Adams, "Here's Stirling!"

"Bless you!" cried Mrs. Adams, and hustled her husband backstage to try on his armor.

Half an hour later, Mr. Adams, who is assistant vice-president of Commercial Investment Trust, Inc., had succeeded in putting it all on, even to long, pointed sollerets, or flexible steel shoes, and a helmet with a visor. "This darn thing can cut your darn head off!" he roared to his wife from the recesses of the helmet. "Now, don't go off and leave me here!"

"Stick your chin in, Stirling," Mrs. Adams said soothingly.

"You're convinced you want it worn?" Mr. Adams said. "You're convinced the party won't come off unless it's worn?"

"We'll stop by Brooks on the way home and get it fixed," Mrs. Adams said. "Now try to walk."

"I wish you'd stick your hands in and put my ears where they belong," said Mr. Adams. "And I can't see a darn thing. Holy cow! Now I'm stuck to the floor! Heck! Get a pair of pliers!" he shouted wildly. "Somebody bend up my toes!"

"Walk sideways, Stirling," Mrs. Adams said gently. "Like we do going uphill skiing."

On the morning of the day of the ball, the first person to show up at the ballroom, around nine o'clock, was Warny, the balloon man, who had brought along an assistant named Leroy Williams and a machine for blowing up balloons. Soon handymen and League members began to arrive, and at noon some truckmen hauled in the blank-faced mermaids, the pink-and-blue shell for the thrones, and quite a bit of gold fish net. Gaba appeared and began arranging the stage set. The Astor keeps a Bahama sea grotto on hand for just such occasions as Mardi Gras balls, and he ordered it installed on the stage. After it was in position, he ordered it taken down. "Too corny," he said. "We don't want it. It gives the scene a gooked-up character. I'd rather keep it simple."

"Lunch," Warny said suddenly. Williams dropped a half-filled balloon, and as it sputtered into a state of collapse, the two hurried out.

Mrs. McLoughlin came over to Gaba and said the mermaids looked just dreamy. Mrs. Adams came over and said the balloons looked just divine. Mrs. Stimson came over and said everything looked just peachy.

Faye Emerson and Skitch Henderson arrived, and were soon joined by a number of television men, one of whom handed them a sheaf of papers outlining the roles of master and mistress of ceremonies.

"What's all this—*commercials?*" Henderson said, leafing through the script.

"This is a *commercial* show?" Miss Emerson said incredulously.

"Kids, this is very important," one of the television men said. "If we get messed up here, we're dead."

"Who's going to be the Queen?" one of the television men asked Mrs. Stimson.

"Nobody knows," said Mrs. Stimson.

"G'wan!" said the television man.

"Oh dear!" said Mrs. Stimson.

"Faye, you grab the Mayor, and you say, 'Look who I found!' " the television man said. "Then he gives the official ad-lib rehearsed greeting to the throng."

"Go, man! Go!" said Miss Emerson.

Henry Fonda arrived and tried on the King's robes. "Lord, these are warm!" he said.

"Hank's costume looks tacky," said a television cameraman.

Emil Coleman, a heavyset, distraught-looking man wearing thick eyeglasses, turned up with his twenty-three musicians and tried out one of the pianos. "This is awful!" he cried. "Out of tune! No pitch! Where are my pianos?"

Miss Roberts began alerting everybody to prepare for a television-time dress rehearsal. "Play 'Everywhere You Go'!" she called to Coleman.

"Lady, please get me a piano tuner!" Coleman shouted back, clasping his hands in supplication.

"Everything looks so lovely," Mrs. Luckenbill said to Mrs. Stimson.

"Everybody *couldn't* be nicer," Mrs. Stimson replied.

By seven-thirty that night, the tables had been set in the ball-room. Two-thirds of them glowed with pink cloths; the others had white cloths. There were no tall pink candles on any of the tables; instead, there were small candle lamps like mushrooms, with fringed shades. An aquamarine program, with Mrs. Stimson's pink clown on the cover, lay at each guest's place. Helium-filled clear balloons floated above the tables, held fast to them by strings. Clusters of clear balloons were held in their hoops close to the ceiling, ready to drop. The blue satin draperies on the stage and hanging from the ballroom's two tiers of balconies sparkled with sequins in the rays of multicolored spotlights. The pink-and-blue shell, with two thrones in it, stood in the center of the stage, and the two faceless mermaids, almost swamped in bubbly balloons, clutched at gold fish net. Everything looked soft and gleaming and quiet. The only people in the ballroom were Coleman and the members of his orchestra. Coleman was wearing white tie and tails, and he had exchanged his glasses for a monocle in his right eye. He sat at the piano, gloomy and silent, his elbows on the key-board and his fingertips at his temples. All at once, he looked at his watch and came to life. He took his elbows off the keyboard, sighed loudly, adjusted his monocle, and started to play "Young at Heart," and the members of his orchestra joined in. At the end of the number, Coleman struck a loud chord and stood up. "Why can't they get me a tuner?" he said plaintively.

The green Coral Room was doing a lively business in mixed drinks at a dollar apiece.

"So nice to see you," Mrs. Adams said to Mrs. Stimson.

"So nice to see you," Mrs. Stimson said to Mrs. Adams.

Mr. Adams was at the bar buying drinks for a party of five. Mrs. Cooke asked him why he wasn't wearing his suit of armor.

"I get into it at ten," he said heartily. "I've been repairing the goldarn thing. You might say I'm getting canned tonight! Ha!"

In the hotel florist shop, a young man asked for a white camellia, and the clerk had to turn him down. The young man was the clerk's twenty-first disappointed white-camellia customer that evening. "You going to that thing, too?" the clerk said. "Well, they're all gone. They were all gone at six o'clock."

Mrs. Adams dashed into the main ballroom for a quick look at the décor. She waved gaily to Coleman, who struck up "Stranger in Paradise." Then she turned around and around, looking at the room. "Goodness, isn't it the prettiest decoration ever?" she said as a few of the guests strolled in.

"Heavenly," one of them said.

"Terrific," said another.

Mrs. Dickerson came in and began putting place cards at her tables. "They just handed me the Philco people," she said. "That means I've got three sponsors at my tables. Oh, what a hassle!"

"I bet we'll never have another dinner dance," Mrs. McLoughlin said. "It's just too rough getting everybody to sit down to the table at the same time."

The ballroom was filling up. A couple of television technicians wearing tweeds and limp bow ties wandered in and appraised the scene. Most of the male guests were wearing black tie, even though white tie was preferred.

Upstairs, in a well-guarded private room, the five Maids were putting on their ball gowns.

"My shoes actually fit!" one of them cried joyfully.

"Are you relaxed?" asked another. "Or do you wish it was to-morrow?"

Downstairs, a uniformed guard stood at the entrance to the models' dressing room backstage. A waiter was on hand to take orders for food if any of the models wanted food. None did. At nine, waitresses in the ballroom started serving dinner to the guests. Instead of fruit cup, there was seafood cocktail, and it looked up-beat, partywise, Mrs. Dickerson said.

Just before coffee was served, Mrs. Moore, as the League's president, corralled the three judges preparatory to escorting them up to the Maids' room to pick the Queen. "Did you get a chance for any coffee?" Russel Crouse asked Dr. Rusk, who replied that he had not. Crouse sighed. "I'm not too good before coffee," he said. "I live for coffee."

Dr. Rusk cleared his throat. "We'll do our best," he said.

"It's a difficult assignment," Mrs. Lord said.

On the way to the elevators, Mrs. Moore and the judges ran

into a small woman who was wearing a flowered hat and carrying a brown paper bag.

"Where's the Queen?" the woman in the flowered hat asked.

Mrs. Moore told her the Queen had not yet been chosen.

"Well, I've got the crown," said the woman in the flowered hat. "I'm Van Cleef & Arpels."

"Backstage," said Mrs. Moore.

"After the Queen is crowned, have them take her picture fast, and then give me back the crown," said Van Cleef & Arpels. "You get about one hour with the crown, that's all."

Mayor Wagner arrived late and was ushered to a ringside table. People were already dancing. "I got up to the good seats the hard way," he said.

"O.K., let's get on with the show!" one of the television men called out.

The lights dimmed and a spotlight played on the dance floor. Someone shouted for balloons, and a few of them floated down from the ceiling.

"The hoops aren't working right," Gaba said nervously.

At Miss Burke's table, a Pepsi-Cola man asked for Pepsi-Cola and got it. Miss Emerson and her husband sat at a ringside table and talked into microphones about the work of the New York Junior League. Everything went off the way Miss Roberts, the professional producer, had said it would. Miss Emerson went over to the Mayor's table and said into a microphone, "Look who I found in the audience!" The Mayor made a speech thanking the League on behalf of the City of New York for giving help to those who needed help so badly. He referred to the League members as "wonderful young ladies," and told them that "with the help of you young ladies we'll leave a better heritage to our children." Then a page blew a trumpet, accompanied by a fanfare from the orchestra, and unfurled a banner that read, "Parade of Fabulous Costumes." The parade started with Mrs. Zingg, who made her way from the stage down an aisle cleared through the center of the ballroom, to the strains of "Everywhere You Go," for the American Express Company. The people at the American Express Company table applauded fervently. Miss Emerson and her husband read off the commercial for each sponsor. Mrs. Dickerson observed that the Liggett & Myers people looked happier this year than they had the year before, and Mrs. Stimson observed that the Liggett & Myers girl, wearing the slinky gown and a necklace of Liggett & Myers cigarettes, looked glamorous. Mrs. Barton got quite a laugh as Groucho Marx, and the blonde following her swept up her cigar ashes with a brush labelled "Fuller." Miss Bryant opened up as a refrigerator on cue, and all the fruit and dairy products were clearly displayed. Mr. Adams stepped lightly along in his shining armor beside Guinevere. Then Henderson introduced each of the five Maids. The judges handed a scroll bearing their decision to a page, who handed it to the Mayor, and the Mayor announced that the Maid who had been chosen for Queen of the 1954 Mardi Gras was Miss Joan Gray. Everybody applauded.

"How dreamy!" Mrs. McLoughlin said. "Joan's a nifty gal."

Henry Fonda and Miss Gray paraded in the royal robes and took their places on the thrones in the pink-and-blue shell. The Mayor placed the tiara on Miss Gray's head, saying it was a privilege to crown her Queen on behalf of the Junior League and the people of the City of New York. "I know you'll carry on this work even after this—the ultimate in honor—tonight," he concluded.

All the Maids and models gathered around the King and Queen and were photographed, and then Van Cleef & Arpels stepped forward and took back the crown.

The guests got up to dance, and a few more balloons floated down on their heads. On the stage, several of the models looked as if they felt stranded. Mr. Raymer went up and grabbed the model representing Moore-McCormack Lines, took a basket of fruit off her head, and led her gallantly onto the dance floor.

Coleman looked at his watch. "One hour and thirty-five minutes to go," he said. "There's *still* time to get me a tuner."

Early the next morning, Mrs. Stimson turned up at the League's headquarters and immediately started writing thank-you notes to sponsors. She had already read with delight several lengthy accounts of the ball in the newspapers. She was presently joined by Mrs. Adams, who said she had got to bed at five that morning and had got up again at eight, to arrange to have the costumes returned to the Brooks company. By noon, about half of Mrs. Stimson's committee had turned up to help with the thank-you notes. Mrs. Stimson said she was recommending Mrs. Dickerson for chairman of the 1955 Mardi Gras, and everybody said that that was wonderful. The committee members were full of enthusiasm for plans for the 1955 Mardi Gras Ball, and they talked about improvements that should be made. Next year, they would make sure the hoops released all the balloons at the right time. Next year, they ought to have the Astor get the hum, squeaks, and whistles out of the microphones of its public-address system, because some of the guests hadn't been able to hear the program. Next year, they ought to have a supper dance instead of a dinner dance, so that people wouldn't feel so rushed. Next year, they would again try to get Rodgers and Hammerstein to write a special score for the show. Next year, they would make a determined effort to let no one get left stranded on the stage and to have more of the proper conclusion to things. Next year, they would do a really bang-up job.

—1954

5

EL ÚNICO MATADOR

THE BEST BULLFIGHTERS IN THE WORLD have come, traditionally, from Spain or Mexico. The old Spanish province of Andalusia has contributed more bulls and more bullfighters to the bull ring than all the rest of Spain. Manolete, probably history's top-ranking matador, who was fatally gored, at the age of thirty, in the summer of 1947, was an Andalusian. Carlos Arruza, who retired last year, at twenty-eight, with a two-million-dollar fortune and the reputation of fighting closer to the bull than any other matador had ever done, was born in Mexico, of Spanish-born parents. Belmonte, an Andalusian, and Joselito, a Spanish gypsy, were the leading figures in what is known in bullfight countries as the Golden Age of Bullfighting, which ended with Belmonte's retirement to breed bulls, in 1921, a year after Joselito's death in the arena. The only Mexican who ranked close to Belmonte and Joselito in their time was Rodolfo Gaona, an Indian, who, in 1925, retired a millionaire with large real-estate interests in Mexico City. Some years ago a Chinese bullfighter named Wong, who wore a natural pigtail, turned up in Mexico as El Torero Chino, and a Peruvian lady bullfighter, Conchita Cintrón, is active today. Only one citizen of the United States has ever been recognized as a full-fledged matador. He is Sidney Franklin, who was born and raised in the Park Slope section of Brooklyn.

Some years ago, at the age of forty-five, he estimated that he had already killed two thousand bulls. He was then much older than the usual bullfighter is at his peak. "Age has nothing to do with art," he says. "It's all a matter of what's in your mind." He hopes someday to introduce bullfighting into this country, and, if he succeeds, expects it to become more popular than baseball. Ernest Hemingway, who became an authority on bullfighting, and on Franklin as well, while preparing to write "Death in the Afternoon," maintained that to take to bullfighting a country must have an interest in the breeding of fighting bulls and an interest in death, both of which Hemingway felt were lacking in the United States. "Death, shmeath, so long as I keep healthy," Franklin says. When aficionados, or bullfight fans, charge that Americans born north of the border are incapable of the passion necessary for bullfighting, Franklin replies passionately that coldness in the presence of danger is the loftiest aspect of his art. "If you've got guts, you can do anything," he says. "Anglo-Saxons can become the greatest bullfighters, the greatest ballet dancers, the greatest anything." When, in 1929, Franklin made his Spanish début, in Seville, the aficionados were impressed by the coldness of his art. "Franklin is neither an improviser nor an accident nor a joker," wrote the bullfight critic for La Unión, a Seville newspaper. "He is a born bullfighter, with plenty of ambition, which he has had since birth, and for the bulls he has an ultimate quality—serene valor. Coldness, borrowed from the English, if you please. . . . He parries and holds back with a serene magnificence that grandly masks the danger, and he doesn't lose his head before the fierce onslaughts of the enemy." "Franklin fought as though born in Spain; the others fought as though born in Chicago," another critic observed a year later, in comparing Franklin's manner of dispatching two bulls with the work of the Spanish matadors who appeared on the same bill in a Madrid bull ring. One day early in his career, Franklin killed the two bulls that had been allotted to him, then, taking the place of two other matadors, who had been gored, killed four more. This set off such an emotional chain reaction in the ring that another bullfighter dropped dead of excitement. Today, many aficionados, both Spanish and Mexican, disparage Franklin's artistry. "Manolete made you feel inside like crying, but Franklin does not engrave anything on your soul," a Spanish aficionado of thirty years' standing complained not long ago. "Franklin has no class," another Spaniard has said. "He is to a matador of Spanish blood what a Mexican baseball player is to Ba-bee Ruth." "I am A Number One," Franklin says. "I am the best in the business, bar none."

Franklin was nineteen when he saw his first bullfight. He was in Mexico, having recently run away from home after a quarrel with his father. As he recalls this particular bullfight, he was bored. In Brooklyn, he had belonged, as a charter member, to the *Eagle's* Aunt Jean's Humane Club and to the old New York *Globe's* Bedtime Stories Club, which devoted itself to the glorification of Peter Rabbit. "At that time, the life to me of both man and beast was the most precious thing on this planet," he says. "I failed to grasp the point." The following year, he fought his first bull—a twelve-hundred-pound, four-year-old beast with horns a foot and a half long—and was on his way to becoming a professional. In the quarter of a century since then, Franklin has come to feel that the act of dominating and killing a bull is the most important and satisfying act a human being can perform. "It gives me a feeling of sensual well-being," he has said. "It's so deep it catches my breath. It fills me so completely I tingle all over. It's something I want to do morning, noon, and night. It's something food can't give me. It's something rest can't give me. It's something money can't buy." He is certain that bullfighting is the noblest and most rewarding of all pursuits. He often delivers eloquent discourses on his art to men who are more interested in power, money, love, sex, marriage, dollar diplomacy, atomic energy, animal breeding, religion, Marxism, capitalism, or the Marshall Plan. When his listener has been reduced to acquiescence, or at least bewilderment, Franklin will smile tolerantly and give him a pat on the back. "It's all a matter of first things first," he will say. "I was destined to taste the first, and the best, on the list of walks of life." The triumph of man over bull is not just the first walk on

Franklin's own list; it is the only one. There are no other walks to clutter him up. "I was destined to shine," he adds. "It was a matter of noblesse oblige."

The expression "noblesse oblige" is one that Franklin is fond of using to describe his attitude toward most of his activities in and out of the bull ring, including the giving of advice to people. He is an unbridled advice-giver. He likes to counsel friends, acquaintances, and even strangers to live in a sensible, homespun, conventional, well-tested manner, in line with the principles of saving nine by a stitch in time, of finding life great if one does not weaken, of gathering moss by not rolling, of trying and trying again if success is slow in arriving, and of distinguishing between what is gold and what merely glitters. He is convinced that he thought up all these adages himself. In order to show how seriously he takes them, he often pitches in and helps a friend follow them. He takes credit for having helped at least a half-dozen other bullfighters make hay while the sun shone; for having proved to habitués of saloons and night clubs that there is no place like home; for having taught a number of ladies how to drive automobiles, after telling them emphatically that anything a man can do, a woman can do; for having encouraged young lovers to get married, because the longer they waited, the more difficult their adjustment to each other would be; and for having persuaded couples to have babies while they were still young, so that they might be pals with their children while they were growing up. "I was destined to lead," Franklin states. "It was always noblesse oblige with me." Some Americans who have watched Franklin dispose of bulls on hot Sunday afternoons in Spain believe that he is right. "Sidney is part of a race of strange, fated men," says Gerald Murphy, head of Mark Cross and a lover of the arts. Franklin has a special category of advice for himself. "I never let myself get obese or slow," he says. "I make it a point never to imbibe before a fight. I never take more than a snifter, even when socializing with the select of all the professions. I am always able to explain to myself the whys and wherefores. I believe in earning a penny by saving it. By following the straight and narrow path, I became the toast of two continents. My horizon is my own creation."

Franklin is tall—five feet eleven and a half inches—thin, fair-skinned, and bald except for a few wavy bits of sandy-colored hair at the base of his skull. The backs of his hands and the top of his head are spotted with large tan freckles. His eyebrows are heavy and the color of straw. His ears are long. His eyes are brown, narrow, and lacking in depth, and there are a good many lines around them. There is a small scar at the tip of his nose. His build is considered good for bullfighting, because a tall bull-fighter can more easily reach over a bull's horns with his sword for the kill. Franklin's only physical handicap is his posterior, which sticks out. "Sidney has no grace because he has a terrific behind," Hemingway once said. "I used to make him do special exercises to reduce his behind." When Franklin walks down a street, he seems to dance along on his toes, and he has a harsh, fast way of talking. He sounds like a boxing promoter or a cop, but he has many of the gestures and mannerisms of the Spanish bullfighter. "Americans are taught to speak with their mouths," he likes to say. "We speak with our bodies." When the parade preceding the bullfight comes to a halt, he stands, as do the Mexicans and Spaniards, with the waist pushed forward and the shoulders back. When he becomes angry, he rages, but he can transform himself in a moment into a jolly companion again. In the company of other bullfighters or of aficionados, he glows and bubbles. Last winter, at a hotel in Acapulco, he discovered that the head-waiter, D'Amaso Lopez, had been a matador in Seville between 1905 and 1910. "Ah, Maestro!" cried Franklin, embracing Lopez, who grabbed a tablecloth and started doing verónicas. "He is overjoyed to see me," Franklin told his host at dinner. "I'm a kindred spirit." At parties, he likes to replace small talk or other pastimes with parlor bullfighting, using a guest as the bull. (Rita Hayworth is considered by some experts to make his best bull.) Claude Bowers, former United States Ambassador to Spain, used to invite Franklin to his soirées in Madrid. "Sidney loved to perform," an Embassy man who was usually Franklin's onrushing bull has said. "He'd give the most fascinating running commentary as he demonstrated with the cape, and then he'd spend hours answering the silliest questions, as long as they were about bullfighting. He was like a preacher spreading the gospel."

Franklin gets along well with Mexicans and Spaniards. "On the streets of Seville, everybody talks to him," a friend who has seen a good deal of him there says. "He knows all the taxi drivers and lottery venders, and even the mayor bows to him." Franklin claims that he has made himself over into an entirely Spanish bullfighter. "I know Spain like I know the palm of my hand," he says. "I happen to be much more lucid in Spanish than in English. I even *think* in Spanish." Franklin's lucidity in Spanish has been a help to other Americans. Rex Smith, former chief of the Associated Press bureau in Madrid, occasionally used him as a reporter. During a rebellion in 1932, he commissioned Franklin to look into a riot near his office. "Suddenly, I heard a great hullabaloo outside my window," Smith says in describing the incident. "I looked out, and there was Sidney telling the crowd, in Spanish, where to get off." "Sidney is fabulous on language," Hemingway said. "He speaks Spanish so grammatically good and so classically perfect and so complete, with all the slang and damn accents and twenty-seven dialects, nobody would believe he is an American. He is as good in Spanish as T. E. Lawrence was in Arabic." Franklin speaks Castilian, caló (or gypsy talk), and Andalusian. The favorite conversational medium of bullfighters in Spain is a mixture of caló and Andalusian. Instead of saying "nada" for "nothing" to other bullfighters, he says "na', na', na'," and he says "leña," which is bullfight slang, instead of the classical "cuerno," in talking of an especially large horn of a bull. In conversing with a lisping Spanish duke, Franklin assumes a lisp that is far better than his companion's, and he is equally at home in the earthy language of the cafés frequented by bullfighters. The Spanish maintain that Franklin never makes a mistake in their tongue. One day, he went sailing in a two-masted schooner. A Spanish companion called a sail yard a palo."You ought to know better than that," Franklin told him, and went on to explain that the sail yard he had spoken of was a verga, that palo meant mast, and that there were three terms for mast—one used by fishermen, another by yachtsmen, and the third by landlubbers.

When Franklin first went to Mexico, in 1922, he did not know any Spanish. A few years later, while he was training for bull-fighting on a ranch north of Mexico City, he started a class in reading and writing for forty illiterate peons, of all ages. After three months, sixteen of Franklin's pupils could read and write. "They idolized me for it," he says. In any restaurant—even a Schrafft's, back home—he follows the Spanish custom of calling a waiter by saying "Psst!" or clapping the hands. His Christmas cards say, "*Feliz Navidad y Próspero Año Nuevo.*" Conversation with bulls being customary during a fight, he speaks to them in Spanish. "*Toma, toro! Toma, toro!*" he says when urging a bull to charge. "*Ah-ah, toro! Ah-ah-ah, toro!*" he mutters, telling a bull to come closer.

In putting on his coat, Franklin handles it as though it were a bullfighter's cape, and his entire wardrobe is designed to express his idea of a bullfighter's personality. "Sidney always took a long time to dress in the morning," said Hemingway, who often slept in his underwear and took a half minute to put on his trousers and shirt. "I always had to wait for him. I don't like a man who takes a long time to dress in the morning." Most of Franklin's suits were tailored in Seville. "Genuine English stuff—nothing but the best," he tells people. His wardrobe includes a transparent white raincoat, several turtleneck sweaters, some Basque berets, a number of sombreros, and a purple gabardine jacket without lapels. His bullfighting costumes are more elegant and more expensive than those of any other matador in the business. He has three wigs—two parted on the left side, one parted on the right—which are the envy of bald bullfighters who have never been to Hollywood or heard of Max Factor. A bullfighter's looks have a lot to do with his popularity, especially in Mexico, where a bald bullfighter is not esteemed. A Spanish matador named Cayetano Ordóñez, professionally called Niño de la Palma, who was the prototype of Hemingway's young bullfighter in "The Sun Also Rises," lost a good part of his Mexican public when he lost his hair. In 1927, when he appeared in Mexico City and dedicated one of the bulls he was about to kill to Charles A. Lindbergh, he was young, slender, and graceful, with dark, curly hair. "An Adonis," Franklin says. "Niño had a marvellous figure. All the sexes were wild about him." Eight years later, Niño, who had been fighting in Spain, returned to Mexico heavier and partly bald. The moment he took off his matador's hat in the ring, the ladies in the audience transferred their affections to a slimmer and handsomer matador, and the men turned to the bulls. One day, Franklin showed his wigs to Niño. "Poor Niño was flabbergasted," says a witness. "He put on a wig and stood in front of the mirror for an hour, tears in his eyes. My God, what a scene when Sidney tried to take the wig away from him!" Franklin used to wear one of his wigs whenever he appeared in public, but lately he has worn a wig only in the bull ring, at the theatre, and when having his picture taken. He says that someday, if the action in the ring gets dull, he is going to hang his wig on a horn of the bull.

In accordance with his belief in noblesse oblige, Franklin feels that he can afford to be generous toward his fellow-man. "Sidney doesn't envy his neighbors a thing," says a friend. "He is the extreme of what most men like to think of themselves, so much so that he never thinks about it. He doesn't want things. He thinks he has everything." Although Franklin does not carry noblesse oblige so far as to forgive enemies, he is tolerant of those whose friendship for him has cooled. He has rarely seen Hemingway, whom he came to know in 1929, since leaving him in Madrid in 1937, in the middle of the civil war. Franklin had been doing odd jobs for Hemingway, then a war correspondent.

"I weighed Ernest in the balance and found him wanting," Franklin once remarked. "When he began coloring his dispatches about the war, I felt it was time for me to back out on the deal."

"Obscenity!" said Hemingway in reply.

"Ernest got to the point where I knew his mind better than he did himself. It began to annoy him," Franklin said.

"Obscenity!" said Hemingway.

"I may disagree with Ernest, but I'll always give him the benefit of the doubt, because he is a genius," Franklin said.

"Obscenity obscenity!" said Hemingway.

Franklin, asked what makes a good matador, has said, "Knowledge of the business, plus inventive artistry. I'd rather see a good artist do poor work than the most perfect mechanic do the best work. I am the artist, plus the possessor of the most extensive repertoire in the business. I do personal interpretation—spur-of-the-moment stuff." Franklin is highly critical of most of his confrères, but there are a few he praises when he feels they deserve it. After a bullfight in Mexico City a year ago, a friend commented to him that one of the matadors looked good only because he had been given a good bull to kill—a good bull being one that has perfect vision and is aggressive, high-spirited, and, from a human point of view, brave. Franklin said no—that the bull was a bad bull. "The fellow had the guts to stand there and take it and make a good bull out of a lemon," he said. "You can't understand that, because you have no grasp of noblesse oblige." Because of his own grasp of noblesse oblige, Franklin is determined to go on fighting bulls as long as his legs hold out, and he would like to see Brooklyn continue to be represented in the bull ring after he retires. To this end, he took under his wing for a while a twenty-six-year-old Brooklyn neighbor of his named Julian Faria, nick-named Chaval, meaning "the Kid." Chaval, whose parents are of English, Spanish, and Portuguese descent and whose face resembles a gentle, sad-eyed calf's, made his début as a matador in Mexico in the fall of 1947, fighting with Franklin in some of the smaller rings. On the posters announcing the fights, Chaval's name appeared in letters an inch high, beneath Franklin's name in letters two inches high, along with the proclamation that Franklin was "El Único Matador Norteamericano."

When Franklin has visited New York, he has lived with his mother, an unmarried brother, and a sister and her husband in a one-family house on East Twenty-ninth Street in Flatbush. It has been a point of noblesse oblige with him to help his neighbors during his visits. "They depend on me," he says. "They're always running in and out when I'm home. It's a regular merry-go-round fixing their stoves and radiators and answering to 'Hey, Sid, the faucet in my house don't work!' I feel duty-bound to lend a

helping hand." Some years ago, the Broad Street Hospital invited
Franklin to clock the rodeo events at a Madison Square Garden
benefit, and he helped it out, too. He turned up in a matador costume of apple-green silk embroidered in gold. "I was obligated to
let the audience know who and what I was," he said. During the
postwar shortage of men's shirts, a casual New York acquaintance
remarked that he needed one. Franklin spent three days looking
for what he thought was a proper shirt. "He came back from
Fourteenth Street with this goddam pongee silk thing and gave
me a bill for fourteen dollars," the beneficiary has since said. "He
thought he was doing me a goddam favor." When Franklin meets
Americans in Spain or Mexico, he always volunteers to take them
shopping. A lady who with his help bought some silver plates in
Madrid several years ago claims that he argued the shopkeeper into
letting them go for one-fifth of the original price. "He just reduced the man to pulp," she says.

In his efforts to help his fellow-men, Franklin occasionally
offers to make bullfighters out of them. He gave Hemingway's
eldest son, John, known as Bumby, a cape cut to his size and a
small sword, when Bumby was ten, and taught him how to execute
passes with the cape. He once thought he had succeeded in making a bullfighter out of Franklin D. Roosevelt, Jr. In 1933, young
Roosevelt, then nineteen, visited Spain and told Ambassador
Bowers that he'd like to learn something about the country's
favorite sport. Franklin was invited to dine at the Embassy. "He
hadn't been there more than ten minutes when I found myself
agreeing to go off with him on a two-week tour of Spain," Roosevelt recalls. They attended bullfights all over Spain, and after
each fight Franklin introduced Roosevelt to the matadors. Then
he sent Roosevelt to a friend's ranch to learn bullfighting. "He had
a high old time fooling around with calves," Franklin says. "He
got a wire from Washington, D.C., saying, 'What your father is
doing isn't bad enough, you've got to associate with bullfighters.'
He didn't pay any attention to it. I had pulled up the shade for
Frankie and the sun was streaming in."

"There are two kinds of people," Franklin repeatedly says.
"Those who live for themselves and those who live for others. I'm

the kind that likes to serve mankind." He believes that he would have made a wonderful doctor, and he acts as a general practitioner whenever he gets a chance. One afternoon, a bull ripped open one of his ankles. "I took a tea saucer and put some sand in it and mixed it up with tea leaves and manure and applied it to the injured member," Franklin says, with a look of sublime satisfaction. "I was then ready to get right back in the ring, functioning perfectly to a T." Once, when he was working on the ranch in Mexico, a peon accidentally chopped off two of his own toes. Franklin claims that he sewed them back on with an ordinary needle and thread. "I put a splint underneath the foot, bandaged it, and told him to stay off it for a few days," he says. "In no time at all, the man was as good as new." In Mexico a few years ago, Franklin stood by as an appendectomy was performed upon his protégé, Chaval, advising Chaval, who had been given a local anesthetic, not to show any fear or sign of pain, not even to grunt, because other bullfighters would hear about it. Chaval didn't make a sound. "I saw to it that the appendectomy was performed according to Hoyle," Franklin says.

Franklin considers himself an expert on mental as well as physical health. At a bullfight in Mexico City last winter, he sat next to a British psychiatrist, a mannerly fellow who was attending the UNESCO conference. While a dead bull was being dragged out of the ring, Franklin turned to the psychiatrist. "Say, Doc, did you ever go into the immortality of the crab?" he asked. The psychiatrist admitted that he had not, and Franklin said that nobody knew the answer to that one. He then asked the psychiatrist what kind of doctor he was. Mental and physiological, the psychiatrist said.

"I say the brain directs everything in the body," Franklin said. "It's all a matter of what's in your mind."

"You're something of a psychosomaticist," said the psychiatrist.

"Nah, all I say is if you control your brain, your brain controls the whole works," said Franklin.

The psychiatrist asked if the theory applied to bullfighting.

"You've got something there, Doc," said Franklin. "Bullfighting is basic. It's a matter of life and death. People come to see you take long chances. It's life's biggest gambling game. Tragedy and comedy are so close together they're part of each other. It's all a matter of noblesse oblige."

The psychiatrist looked solemn. Another bull came into the ring, and a matador executed a verónica. It was not a good one. The matador should hold the cape directly before the bull's face, one hand close to his own body, the other away from his body, stretching the cape, then pull it away from the bull's face in such a manner that when the animal follows it, he passes directly in front of him. This matador held both hands far away from his body, and the bull passed at some distance from him. The crowd whistled and shouted insults. "Look at that, Doc," said Franklin. "There's a guy who doesn't have the faintest grasp of noblesse oblige."

The psychiatrist cleared his throat. The bullfight, he said, might be looked upon as a plastic model of Freud's concept of the mind and its three divisions: the id, the uncivilized brute in man; the ego, a combination of environment, which has tamed the id, and of the id itself; and the super-ego, the conscience, often represented by the father or the mother, who approves or disapproves. He suggested that the id might be represented by the bull, the ego by the bullfighter, and the super-ego by the whistling and hooting crowd. "Many things you do in life," he added, "are a projection, or model, of what is going on in your mind. For instance, you might be fighting bulls because internally you have a conflict between your id and ego, id and super-ego, or ego and super-ego, or possibly a conflict between your combined id and ego and your super-ego. The bullfight, then, might be a good model of your state of mind."

"Nah," said Franklin. "If I had my life to live all over again, I'd do exactly the same thing. Do you grasp my point?"

The psychiatrist thought it over for a while, then said yes, he believed he did.

After the bullfight, Franklin, in saying goodbye to the British psychiatrist, advised him to take care of himself. "If you can't be good, be careful, Doc," he said.

Franklin maintains that he learned a lot about life from Hemingway. "Ernest taught me how to put people into two categories," he says. "One, the good guys, and, two, the bastards. If you're a good guy, anything goes. If not, I don't want to be around you. At first, I used to think, How can this person help me further my career? Now I think, How can this person help me to enjoy life? I've had my pick of the select of all the professions. I've picked those who could help me to enjoy life. It's this never being able to sit down, never knowing what I'll be doing next, that gives me my greatest enjoyment. When I take a trip down a highway anyplace in the world, I can drop in on this one or that one. Not everybody can do that."

One night in Charlottesville, after Franklin D. Roosevelt, Jr., had elected to go to law school in Virginia instead of becoming a bullfighter, he received an unexpected visit. "This guy just knocks on the door and says, 'Remember me?'" Roosevelt has recalled. "It was Sidney. He insisted on spending the rest of the night chewing the fat. He wanted to give me a lot of advice, kind of like an older brother checking up on me." In Paris, some years before that, Sidney dropped in on Roosevelt, then just out of Groton, and asked why he didn't get married. "He told me he knew this Ethel du Pont but was afraid to ask her," Sidney has said. "I got on my high horse and gave him a good talking to. 'Frankie, you're the son of the President, and you can have your choice of any girl in the world,' I told him. I insisted that he ask for Ethel's hand in marriage." Roosevelt says that he doesn't remember ever taking any advice that Franklin gave him. "After all, I had a father who was pretty good at it," he adds.

The reason he himself has never married, Franklin says, is that he has never found a woman who understood noblesse oblige. "Also, I've been around animal breeding too much, and that has affected my viewpoint," he explains. "Anyway, there's no real love other than a mother's love for her child."

Franklin shows no discrimination in practicing noblesse oblige. "Humanity is humanity," he says. "I serve without fear or favor." A few years ago, he tried singlehanded to prevent a hoof-and-mouth epidemic that had broken out among the cattle in Spain from spreading to other countries. He took it upon himself to deliver lengthy reports to officials in Washington and Mexico City on ships sailing for North America with animals he thought had the disease, and on where the cattle came from, and on the buyers and sellers of infected cattle. "I sent one report by diplomatic pouch from Madrid," he says. "One year later, there was a terrific outbreak of the disease in Mexico, all because those diplomats had been too busy to listen to me." In Washington, a while back, Franklin lunched with several senators, including Barkley, Tydings, Chavez, and Magnuson, ostensibly to tell them how the prevalence of hoof-and-mouth disease in Mexico was affecting the price of beef in this country. An onlooker says that the luncheon topic suddenly became United States domestic and foreign policy, and that Franklin did all the talking. After lunch, the onlooker took Franklin aside and suggested that he might have allowed the senators to get a word in. "What do you mean?" Franklin asked. "How often do senators have the chance to lunch with a bullfighter?"

Franklin's noblesse oblige was extended during the last war to include an offer to the United States government to make himself expendable. The offer was accepted, and he was assigned to some mysterious work in North Africa. "If I had told Sidney to walk barefoot across some high mountains, he would have done it," his superior in the war work recalls. "But it had to be a big thing. When you want to get credit for doing something big in war, you often get killed. Fortunately, I didn't have anything big for Sidney to do."

Some of Franklin's intimates say that he is one of the small percentage of men to whom friendship really means something. One day, he called at the home of a friend named Grant Mason, in Washington, and was told by Mason's wife that Mason, who had just got out of the Army, was resting for a few months. "Tell Grant to go back to work," said Franklin, and insisted that it would be bad for him to hang around the house all day. "You might say that Sidney is a kind of mother hen," Mrs. Mason has remarked in telling of this. Franklin mothers not only his friends but strangers. When he was in Spain during the Second World War, an American bomber was shot down by German planes over the Bay of Vigo. One injured flier was interned in a hospital at La Coruña, near Vigo. At Christmastime, Franklin, who had heard about the American's internment, spent three days with him. "I didn't want the kid to be alone over the holidays," he explained.

Franklin is always trying to prove that there is nothing man can do with his hands that he can't do. "He goes all over your house, getting half a dozen projects started," a New York friend recently recalled. "Then he goes home, and no one around the place knows how to finish them." Once, Franklin decided that a friend who lived in the country needed a doghouse. He went off into the woods, chopped down a tree, and made a rather large doghouse of hewn logs. His friend's dog refused to sleep in it. Another country-dwelling friend says that Franklin is always trying to get him to build a wing on his house, or to put up a garage, or to have a tile floor laid. "He took one look at a rock garden I was breaking my back to build, and told me to let it go," the friend says. "He said what I needed was a large circular stone seat, to hold a lot of people. 'But we don't have a lot of people coming to our house,' I told him. 'You can never tell when you will have,' he said. I built the seat."

Franklin likes to cook, and he has delighted fellow-bullfighters in Spain with his dinners. His specialties are lobster and home-made doughnuts. Gerald Murphy, the Mark Cross man, is an admirer of Franklin's cooking. "Sidney is an amazing gourmet, with a remarkably sensuous appreciation of foods," he says. Murphy's wife once let Franklin sample her special hors d'oeuvres— slivers of the skin of baked potatoes simmered in butter until brown, a delicacy no guest had ever been able to identify. "Sidney knew immediately what it was," Mrs. Murphy recalls. Another time, Franklin presented the Murphys with some delectable smoked fish. The Murphys went all over Brooklyn trying to get more of it. "Only Sidney knows where to get that smoked fish, and it's his secret," Mrs. Murphy says. "He knows the people who smoke the fish, and I think he knows the fish."

In general, Franklin says, he likes the life of a bullfighter because of the number of things he can pack into it. "You come into a town, and the moment you arrive, be it by plane, ship, train, or car, everybody is there to receive you," he says. "You barely have time to change your clothes before it's a high old round of banquets and dinners. You don't pay for a thing; others consider it a privilege to pay for you. You're yanked out to go swimming, hunting, fishing, and riding, and if you don't know how to do those things, others consider it a privilege to teach you, to satisfy your every whim and desire. The select of all the professions like to be seen with you." "They're never alone," Hemingway says morosely of bullfighters. "What Ernest has in mind when he says that is that all the sexes throw themselves at you," Franklin explains. "I never went in for that night-owl stuff. I never let myself become detoured. Many of them allow themselves to become so detoured they never get back on the main highway."

Chaval's attitude toward the bullfighter's life is rather different. "I just like to scare girls," he says. "Boy, I bring the bull so close to me, the girls, they scream. Boy, I get a kick out of making girls scream."

Franklin used to lecture Chaval on the significance of noblesse oblige in bullfighting to help the young man stay on the main highway. "I am alive today only because I was in perfect condition when I had my accidents in the ring," he sternly told Chaval, who had night-owl inclinations.

"Jeez, Sidney, all you gotta do in the ring is show you're brave," said Chaval. "That's what girls like, when you're brave."

Most bullfighters agree with Chaval, but they state their case with more dignity. A young woman who once met Carlos Arruza at a party in Mexico City complimented him on his bravery in fighting so close to a bull. "You think I am going to be killed, but for you I am courageous in the face of death," Arruza replied gallantly. "This is manliness. I fight to make money, but I like very much to bring the bull to his knees before me." The fearlessness of Manolete is legendary. He specialized in the most difficult and dangerous maneuver in bullfighting—the pase natural, which, properly executed, requires the bull to pass perilously close to the body. He had no worthy competitors, but he always tried to outdo himself. "Manolete was a tremendous personality," a Mexican aficionado said recently. "He never smiled." He was gored several times before he received his fatal wound. On more than one occasion, he might have saved himself by moving an inch or two. "Why didn't you move, Manolo?" he was asked after suffering a leg wound one afternoon. "Because I am Manolete," he replied sombrely. Lack of fear has been attributed by some people simply to lack of imagination. Franklin disagrees with this theory. "I believe in facing facts," he says. "If you're a superman, you're a superman, and that's all there is to it." Few of the critics who hold to the opinion that Franklin lacks artistry believe that he lacks valentía, or bravery. "Nobody ever lives his life all the way up except bullfighters," Franklin says, quoting from "The Sun Also Rises."

In giving advice to Chaval on how to live his life all the way up, Franklin once said, "You've got to be the sun, moon, and stars to yourself, and results will follow as logically as night follows day."

"Jeez, Sidney! I don't get it," Chaval replied. "All I know is I gotta kill the bull or the bull kills me."

"Bullfighting taught me how to be the master of myself," Franklin said. "It taught me how to discard all that was unimportant."

"Jeez, Sidney!" said Chaval.

Franklin began to make history in the bull ring at his Spanish début, on June 9, 1929, in Seville. Aficionados who saw him fight that day wept and shouted, and talked about it for weeks afterward. "On that day, I declared, 'Bullfighting will never again be the same,' " Manuel Mejías, the bullfighting father of five bullfighting sons, has said. "Sidney Franklin introduced a revolutionary style into the bull ring." "Sidney was a glowing Golden Boy," recalls an American lady who was at the fight. "He was absolutely without fear. He was absolutely beautiful."

The art of bullfighting is generally divided into two styles: the classical and the fancy. In the classical style, the matador's mastery of the bull and his purity of form with the muleta and sword in the killing are the most important aspects of the bullfight. In the fancy style, the grace and color of the matador's work with his capote de brega, or fighting cape, and with the muleta are more

important. In Spain, the classical style is favored, and there a bullfight audience esteems a good bull as highly as a good matador.
What counts most in Mexico, where the fancy style is preferred,
is the matador's grace, personality, and looks, and the public does
not pay a great deal of attention to the bull. A Spanish gypsy
named Cagancho, a graceful, green-eyed bullfighter, made a tremendous hit when he appeared in Mexico City in the season of
1936-37, and was in such demand that he fought in the same
ring on thirteen consecutive Sundays, setting a record. "In Mexico, it is all a question of smile-to-the-ladies-with-your-green-eyes,"
a Mexican observer has remarked.

Next to Franklin, Cagancho is the matador whose work Franklin admires most. Cagancho, he claims, is, like him, a creative
artist. "Sidney is not creative at all, he's classical," one knowledgeable American bullfight fan has said. "If he hadn't damn near got
himself killed when he was gored in 1930, he would have become
one of the great classical killers of the ring." There are three
schools of thought on Franklin. The first holds that he was both a
brave and an artistic fighter before he was gored, the second that
he is not artistic but is very brave, the third that he is both the
most artistic and the most courageous bullfighter in the business.
Some aficionados in Spain belong to the first school, and Hemingway belongs to it, too. Most Mexican aficionados belong to the
second. The third school is Franklin. It rarely engages in arguments with the others. "I am the sun, moon, and stars to myself,"
Franklin declares. "That's all I know or need to know." The other
schools, though, occasionally quarrel. "You should ask José Pérez
Gómez—Nili—who was Belmonte's confidential banderillero for
many years, whether or not Sidney was a fine performer and inno-
vator with the cape, and a facile killer. He saw Sidney fight in
Seville in 1929 and many other times," Hemingway once told a
member of the second school. "You ought to ask Marcial Lalanda,
who is now retired and living in Spain and who fought with Sidney several times and saw him many times. You ought to look at
the photographs of Sidney in 'Death in the Afternoon' and see
what the hell it is all about. Many of the people who would agree
with me are dead. I loved bullfighting very much. At one time I

took it seriously. I still take parts of it seriously. I remember the good things about Sidney and I will never forget them. Sidney was the first matador I saw drop his hands as low as all good matadors do now when manipulating the cape in verónicas. I know many fighters who have fought with him and what they have told me. I have much in common with them and therefore I speak for them, as they would authorize me to speak for them if we were together. I know how Sidney was in 1929 in Madrid, and it was a marvel and a miracle that an American should be able to fill the Madrid ring three times in that year and do splendid cape work and good work with the *muleta*, and kill excellently." "Death in the Afternoon," the only book written in English on the subject of bullfighting which is considered authoritative in bullfighting countries, also contains an appreciation of Franklin: "Franklin is brave with a cold, serene, and intelligent valor, but instead of being awkward and ignorant he is one of the most skillful, graceful, and slow manipulators of a cape fighting today. His repertoire with the cape is enormous, but he does not attempt by a varied repertoire to escape from the performance of the *verónica* as the base of his cape work and his *verónicas* are classical, very emotional, and beautifully timed and executed. You will find no Spaniard who ever saw him fight who will deny his artistry and excellence with the cape."

Most bullfight critics, both in Mexico and in Spain, accept bribes from bullfighters, and most matadors make use of their services. Franklin has the reputation of never having done this. Many Spanish critics wrote favorably about his early perform- ances in Spain, possibly in the hope that he might come across, but in general his work in Spain deserved praise anyway, and often enthusiastic praise. The Spanish papers took to calling him the Yanqui Flamenco (a Yankee real McCoy) and said that he was a natural bullfighter. "Sidney fought only twelve major *corridas* in 1929, but they were in the biggest and most important rings," Hemingway once said. "In Seville he was repeated twice and in Madrid the same, in spite of his big financial demands. If he had only been a curiosity or had not aroused the public and been a big drawing card, he would never have fought more than once in each of these, the two most important rings in Spain." Hemingway told an aficionado several years ago that one of Spain's leading matadors of the day, Domingo Ortega, saw Franklin fight in Madrid in 1929 and patterned his cape work after Franklin's. "Naturally, Ortega would deny this," Hemingway said. Even before Franklin's first fight in Spain, the Brooklyn *Eagle*, presumably not on his payroll, wrote, "Let us say a word for the good-will mission of Sidney Franklin, now in Madrid. He isn't a Lindbergh. But he is a Brooklyn lad, a graduate of our public schools, and without influence to back him, he has persisted in his task. Conceivably he has got closer to the idea of good will that prevails in Latin lands than Lindbergh ever did. For Sidney Franklin took to bullfighting, and that is getting down close to the masses, a lot closer than anyone can get by flying a few thousand feet above their heads." Newspapers over here were nearly as enthusiastic as the Spanish papers. When a bull put a horn through Franklin's sash and dragged him thirty feet across the ring in Madrid before he recovered his footing, the Providence *Journal* remarked in an editorial, "He expertly dispatched the animal with his sword in the impetuous manner of an American who has been grossly affronted. Now he has touched the apex of his meteoric career in this strangely un-American field by conquering the hero-worshipping public of Madrid."

At times, some of the Mexican papers have been unenthusiastic, and somewhat patronizing. *El Redondel*, a weekly blend of *Variety* and the *Morning Telegraph*, and an employer of supposedly incorruptible critics, said of a fight in the town of Villa Acuña, "Sidney fought his first bull without pain and without glory. He just defended himself with the *muleta* and got his job done, killing the bull promptly and neatly. Applause. Later he had a very brave and maneuverable bull, which he challenged with the cape, producing two *verónicas* and one *media*. Applause. The *muleta* work was done to the right of the bull. He used his arms a great deal, and stood quite close to the bull and was very valiant. He ended his job by a very able sword thrust, which gave all the desired results. Ovation." Of another fight, *El Redondel* reported, "Sidney limited himself to accomplishing his job decorously, and he had some fortunate moments. The best of his work was done with the sword, his two bulls being killed each with just one sword thrust. On the second bull he was able and brave, and did some of his fancy work by giving in to the bull, and this was applauded immensely. No more could be demanded of a fighter who is already past his prime."

The center of critical opinion on bullfighting in Mexico City is a café called the Tupinamba, a kind of Mermaid Tavern for aficionados, which has tables with white porcelain tops, useful for diagramming bullfights on. One Tupinamba table, called the *mesa de los Sabios*, is reserved for seven elderly men, known as the Seven Wise Men of Bullfighting, who have been aficionados for fifty years or more. The Seven Wise Men argue constantly about all bullfighters except Franklin, who is, they unanimously agree, very brave but not artistic in the bull ring. One of the seven sages, a former matador named Ignacio Monzón, who is now a mattress-maker, is noted at the Tupinamba for starting an argument and then defending whichever side nobody else will defend; it is constitutionally difficult for him to agree with anyone. Even Monzón, however, refuses to oppose the opinion of his colleagues on Franklin's artistry. When Franklin is in Mexico, he is a frequent visitor at the Tupinamba, where he is well liked. Everyone there calls him Sidney. He does not accept the judgment of his bull-fighting made by the *Sabios*, but he takes their comments good-naturedly. "They just don't understand that my coldness in the face of danger is the greatest art of all," he says.

Franklin has made two contributions to the art of bullfighting. ("Every artist likes to put his mark on history," he says. "I put oomph into the business.") He was the first matador to have white embroidery, rather than the traditional gold or silver, on his bullfight suit, and he was the first matador to add to the *verónica* the trick of dragging the cape on the ground. He invented this addition in Seville, during the excitement of his Spanish dé-but, by forgetting to hold his hands at the customary height. He is also believed to have made an innovation that day when he stood flat-footed instead of going up on his toes, in this way achieving the most stationary, and thus most arrogant, effect possible as the bull rushed past. He was twenty-five then, and nervous, though he had been fighting bulls off and on in Mexico for nearly six years. Today, Franklin often says that his novel cape work was deliberate. "I just figured, 'Hell, the bull has more energy than me, so let the bull do all the cavorting,' " he says.

Franklin is especially proud of his sartorial contribution to the ring. "It was the first time on earth that anyone dared to appear in a suit embroidered in white," he says. He wore the epochal suit—salmon pink under the embroidery—in the Madrid bull ring, on August 18, 1930, and the Brooklyn *Eagle*, after reporting that the bullfight crowd had booed and whistled at it, said knowingly, "The well-dressed matador always has a scarlet cape and gold braid, the colors of the Spanish flag." (Well-dressed matadors then had, as they still have, capes and suits in various colors.) Today, Franklin's wardrobe is still something special. "What Sidney lacks in art he makes up in his dress," one Mexican aficionado said recently. An average matador's outfit costs a thousand dollars. Franklin's outfits run from fifteen hundred to two thousand apiece. The matador's suit is called a *traje de luces*—literally, "suit of lights." Franklin has nine suits of lights, all made to order in Spain; five of them he has never worn and will not wear until he believes that the crowd, the bull, and the weather are worthy of them.

Most matadors employ helpers to sharpen their swords, wet down their capes if the afternoon is windy, and help them get dressed, a process that usually takes an hour. Franklin takes two hours. For his Mexican fights last year, he was assisted in his dressing by Chaval, who then dressed himself, in a rented suit, for his appearance on the same bill. Franklin dresses, from the inside out, in linen or chambray drawers, tied three inches below the knee; silk or cotton undershirt; elastic stockings, white cotton stockings, and pink silk stockings; black leather slippers, called *zapatillas*; starched dress shirt, with low collar and lace across the front; narrow tie, contrasting in color with his suit; embroidered silk knee breeches, called *taleguilla*, which fit very tightly, so that bulls cannot catch their horns in a fold; suspenders; silk sash, matching his tie; short jacket of silk and embroidery, called a *casaquilla* (this matches the *taleguilla;* no respectable bullfighter wears two-tone suits); and hat of black silk chenille, called a *montera.* The matador attaches a cork-based pigtail to his hair—a symbol of a similar device used in early bullfighting to protect the matador's head when he was tossed by a bull. Before Franklin became partly bald, he had a natural pigtail, to which he affixed the cork base. To-day, he attaches an artificial one to what hair he still has in back. During the parade called the *paseo de cuadrillos,* when the matadors and their helpers march into the ring before the bullfight, Franklin carries a long, colorfully embroidered parade cape, or *capote de paseo,* which he usually gives to a friend or patron in the audience to hold during the fight. His silk parade capes are beautiful. One is embroidered with butterflies and morning glories. Another is white embroidered with gold. Franklin claims that the collar of this cape has as much embroidery on it as the entire costume of any other bullfighter. A lady once told Franklin that his capes would make lovely evening wraps. "You don't pay six hundred dollars for an evening wrap!" he said coldly.

In the course of each engagement with a bull, Franklin uses one or two fighting capes, one or more *muletas,* and one *estoque,* or sword. He owns ten fighting capes, all of silk and linen, and two sets of swords, of four swords each. His hats, hand-sewn, are made to order, at a hundred and twenty-five dollars each. His slippers are of the finest glove leather. His favorite suit is of light coffee color embroidered in silver and gold. He considers it the most elegant one in the profession. He wore it in 1945 in the ring in Madrid when he received his matador's degree, or *alternativa,* there. (The *alternativa* qualifies a man as a full-fledged matador, who may fight in regular turn, or alternating, with other full-fledged matadors.) "It was the first time in history that a suit embroidered in both gold and silver was worn in the ring in Spain," he says. "I believe in keeping on my toes." His most expensive suit is of royal embroidered in silver and gold. He considers it the most elegant sunny day, to show off the color. It cost six hundred dollars. He has one of apple green and another of Spanish red, both embroidered in gold. Franklin loves to show visitors his suits, and he doesn't mind all the time and trouble it takes to unpack them from their protective covers. "You won't see the suits of the other fellows as heavily embroidered as these," he says. "I believe in having the things embroidered." A suit of lights weighs from twenty-five to thirty-seven pounds, depending on the amount of embroidery.

In Mexico, English-speaking customers can buy programs explaining the corrida in a semblance of English. One explanation begins by calling bullfighting a tragedy. "That is the best description of a bullfight," it says. "For all of those who enter the ring for a bullfight are risking their lives every minute. And all of them are in imminent risk of being killed, and death is lurking in every corner of the ring, and some one dies there, the bull for sure, and may be a horse or two, when Fate not choose one of the fighters themselves." Lovers of the bullfight must, according to Hemingway, have a sense of tragedy—in the death of the bull and the danger that the matador exposes himself to—and of the ritual of the fight. "Either you have this or you have not," he says, in "Death in the Afternoon," "just as, without implying any comparisons, you have or have not an ear for music." Franklin dismisses the idea that an interest in death is a requisite of bullfighting. Nevertheless, death is important to the majority of aficionados. The most popular poem in Spain for several years was "Lament for Ignacio Sanchez Mejías," by Federico García Lorca, the well-known Spanish poet, who was assassinated by Franco supporters at the outbreak of the civil war. Sanchez Mejías was killed in the ring. In the sort of lines that poets usually reserve for elegies to fellow-minnesingers, García Lorca wrote:

> There was no prince in Seville
> Who could compare with him,
> No sword like his sword,
> Nor heart so true.
> Like a river of lions
> Was his marvellous strength,
> And like a marble torso
> His delineated moderation.

The air of Andalusian Rome
Gilded his head,
Where his smile was a spikenard
Of wit and intelligence.
What a great *torero* in the ring!

It will be a long time, if ever, before there is born
An Andalusian so true, so rich in adventure.

In the poem, García Lorca described Sanchez Mejías' death as "the bull alone with a high heart," and said that he sang of the matador's "appetite for death and the taste of its mouth." "The matador, from living every day with death, becomes very detached," Hemingway has written. "The measure of his detachment of course is the measure of his imagination and always on the day of the fight and finally during the whole end of the season, there is a detached something in their minds that you can almost see. What is there is death and you cannot deal in it each day and know each day there is a chance of receiving it without having it make a very plain mark." A while ago, somebody asked Franklin whether he had a detached something in his mind that represented the thought of death. "I've got more important things on my mind," said Franklin. "I made myself over completely in the bull ring, mentally and physically. By killing bulls, I learned how to be interested in *life*."

Franklin likes to say that his most unusual accomplishment was getting himself born. He gives some credit to his mother but none at all to his father. "I'm afraid I was a *fait accompli*," he says. Looking at his origin another way, one of his friends has said, "Sidney was born to have the thing happen to him." Whatever the other natal circumstances were, he arrived upon this earth on July 11, 1903, at 14 Jackson Place, Brooklyn. He was once asked whether he would have preferred another birthplace. "Yes," he said. "A lonely island." Sidney was the fifth of ten children born to Abram and Lübba Frumkin, both of whom were natives of Russia. Abram Frumkin came to this country from Minsk in

1888, and his future wife came from Kazan the same year. For a while, Frumkin was a newsdealer in Brooklyn, and in 1896 he joined the Police Department as a patrolman. He was on the force twenty-five years, attached most of the time to what is now called the Seventy-eighth Precinct, in Brooklyn. He took his job very seriously and not once in his career asked for an extra day off. In 1921, he was retired on a pension, and until his death, in 1942, he worked at odd jobs in the wholesale dress industry. Various psychologists, both amateur and professional, have enjoyed pointing to the fact that Franklin's father, when he was a policeman, would have been referred to, as is customary in slangy circles, as a "bull," and that it is quite clear to *them* what Franklin is doing in the bull ring. Franklin good-naturedly dismisses such observations as being beside the point. "Once I stepped into a ring, I never even *thought* of my father," he says.

The Frumkins had five sons and five daughters. Sidney and most of the others attended Public School 10, in Brooklyn. Those of Sidney's teachers who are still about may not remember him as a pupil, but they clearly remember Patrolman Frumkin. "He'd come down here and make a big row any time one of his little girls was scolded," one teacher has recalled. "He acted rather like a policeman." "My father was a great big husky brute of a man," Franklin has stated. "He always bellowed. Neighbors a block away could hear him. He was dark, with a long walrus mustache. He never liked me. My mother was fair-skinned. I took after my mother. My father couldn't stand that." Sidney, though he has never married, is fond of advising his friends on the raising of their children, and claims that he learned a lot about it from the way he was brought up. "My father was of the old school that did not spare the rod to spoil the child," he says. "I was a very cranky baby, and he didn't like that. He was cold—on a pedestal. He never showed any affection for his children. Today, dads are pals with their children, but he didn't see it that way. I had brain fever when I was six. The doctor said I was dead. After three days, my father wanted to have me buried right away. My mother said, 'No, wait.' Her insistence saved me. Twelve days later, I was alive again."

In 1930, Frumkin bought a one-family house at 1538 East Twenty-ninth Street, in Flatbush, in which his widow still lives. It is one of a row of brick houses, on a maple-lined block. Sidney's oldest sister, Bella, who is married to a doctor, is a high-school teacher and was studying pedagogy when Sidney was a small boy. "Bella used to practice all her theories on me," Franklin says. "I never recovered from it." Sidney was smaller than the other boys in his class. "I didn't fit in," he says. "I was never allowed to participate in their athletics. It was because I was ahead of myself." The elder Frumkins were Orthodox Jews, and all their children had a strict religious upbringing. Franklin often speaks of the theatre as his first love. "To my father, the theatre was sacrilege. He detested it. But my mother encouraged every bit of artistic expression in me," he says. At the age of twelve, Sidney, with his mother's tacit approval, got himself a part-time job, through the New York *Globe*'s Bedtime Stories Club, at a neighborhood theatre. "I did between-the-acts entertainment with two girls," he explains. "Dramatic interpretation of the 'Marseillaise' and all that stuff." He used the name Sidney Franklin to keep his father from learning of his activities. Sidney had been reading a biography of Benjamin Franklin. " 'Frumkin,' in a way, means 'religious person,' " he says. " 'Franklin' can mean the same thing." After two years of singing and dancing here and there after school, he decided to give up the theatre. "It was too feministic," he says. "Of course, it's up to a man to assert himself, but that I had to learn later on."

The other Frumkin children have led quiet lives. Sidney's eldest living brother, Henry, is a policeman in Bensonhurst. Robert and Milton are certified public accountants. Samuel, a physician, died at the age of twenty-seven, of tuberculosis. Before Sidney was a song-and-dance man, he worked in a laboratory Samuel had in his office. "I used to help Sam cut up stiffs," he recalls. "We'd go to the morgue and get arms or legs and dissect them." Franklin believes that he would have become a surgeon as well as a bullfighter if his parents had not given his brother's equipment away after his death. "I had a natural feel for it," he says. Charlotte, a sister, is married to a Brooklyn fireman; her twin, Rosalind, is married to a

Brooklyn food-products salesman; Helen is the wife of a tobacco jobber in Jersey City. The fifth sister died at the age of two.

The other members of Franklin's family are not enthusiastic about the profession that has made him famous. They consider him a strange and mysterious man and are a bit afraid of him. A year ago last fall, Charlotte and Helen, their husbands, and Milton drove down to Mexico for a holiday, and Franklin took over all the arrangements for how their holiday should be spent. They remember especially a visit to a ranch north of Mexico City, where Franklin gave them a demonstration of a matador's cape work. "All we did was stand around in a big cloud of dust while Sidney fought cows," Charlotte says. "The dust was so thick we couldn't see him. And we couldn't get a bath for five days." In Mexico City, Franklin took his family to a bullfight, which they had never seen before. After the first two bulls of the afternoon had been killed, Helen, looking rather pale, said, "What's so special about this? They keep doing the same thing over and over again. What's the pleasure in it?" "Here you have the Spanish and the Anglo-American viewpoints in one family," Franklin remarked to a friend in the party. After the bullfight, Franklin's relatives adjourned to an ice-cream parlor and refreshed themselves with banana splits.

Franklin enjoys doing things for his family. An American named Spratling, who owns a fishing yacht, which he keeps at Acapulco, in Mexico, once invited Franklin to go fishing with him. Franklin turned up for the trip with six relatives in tow. "They caught a lot of fish," Spratling recalls genially. In his early years as a matador, however, Franklin did not keep in close touch with his family. "I guess he's forgotten us, with all his success," one of his sisters once complained to a reporter from the Brooklyn Eagle. "Sidney isn't the kind of boy you can tell what he must do," Patrolman Frumkin told the press around the same time. "When he was in Mexico, fighting bulls there, his mother wrote him asking him to stop. And after a while he wrote back and said he would. But he didn't." When a Madrid bullfight critic remarked that Franklin fought one afternoon as though he had been born in Spain, he declared that he had been born there. Back in

Brooklyn, in a newspaper interview, his father indignantly denied the truth of the statement. Another critic called Franklin a born bullfighter, possessed of the paramount British qualities of serene coldness and valor, and Franklin thereupon proclaimed that one of his parents was English. Again Frumkin pointed out to the press that Sidney was born in Brooklyn and that both his parents were Russian Jews. Franklin is not ashamed of having been born in Brooklyn or of being the son of Russian Jews. He simply believes in adapting himself to his environment. He is convinced that he has actually made himself over into a Spaniard. Because bullfighting is his specialty, he feels it was necessary for him to become Spanish—in everything but citizenship—and to familiarize himself thoroughly with Catholicism. "I intone all their chants better than they do," Franklin insists. Some years ago, a bullfight promoter in Mexico City was shot and killed in his office by a disappointed bullfighter. "Everyone was surprised to see me leading the funeral procession," Franklin says. "Then, when the recitation of the litanies began, they lagged so badly I had to jump up and raise my voice to quicken their pace." Catholic bullfighters usually spend an hour before each fight praying to their special saints, but Franklin doesn't bother with a prayer of any kind. "All I ask is to be left alone with my thoughts," he has remarked. "I live with religion, not for it. Over in Spain, if my friends go to a Catholic church, I'll go with them, kneel with them, and pray with them. When I'm with Protestants, I'm a Protestant. When I'm home, I go to the synagogue. When you reach a point where you belong to the whole world, you do when in Rome as the Romans do. It's the obligation you face in becoming the toast of two continents."

Franklin graduated from P.S. 10 shortly after this country entered the First World War, and spent the next three years at the Commercial High School, in Brooklyn. For the first year or so, he got average grades, and then he began to play hooky. He was particularly resistant to bookkeeping and stenography. The only course he liked and was good in was drawing. He wanted to be an artist, but his father wouldn't hear of it. In the fall of 1920, he left Commercial High and went to work stencilling silk screens.

One Friday night in the spring of 1922, Franklin and another young man went down to Asbury Park for a weekend with two chorus girls. "Nothing improper," Franklin says. "Just a social excursion." On Saturday, he telephoned his family to let them know where he was, but the line was busy. He forgot to try again until Sunday. His mother told him he'd better come home right away, because his father was in a rage. He returned late that afternoon. "I was sitting on my bed, minding my own business, when my father came in," Franklin says. "He didn't utter a word. He just took one swing at me and connected. I didn't know anything until I woke up in bed the next day. Then he came in and said, 'When you're in my house, I give the orders. If you don't like it, there's the door.' The next day, I shipped a trunk home from Gimbel's. I had six hundred dollars saved up. I took my savings and went out to find the first boat leaving New York." The first boat was bound for Mexico. Franklin decided to use the name Sidney Franklin full-time, bought a ticket in that name, and made plans to stay in Mexico for three weeks and then return home. He stayed six and a half years.

Franklin arrived in Veracruz in June of 1922, shortly before his nineteenth birthday. "The minute I hit Mexico, I knew it was for me," he says. "It was gorgeous. The sky was a lazy blue and the air was filled with perfume. It was God's own country." He went to Mexico City, where he rented a first-floor apartment-studio in the heart of the old business district, and there he lived and worked. He took out a patent on a stencilling process he had devised, and went around Mexico City getting orders for theatre and soda-pop posters and streetcar cards. He had no trouble drumming up business. "Sidney was such a nice boy—so slim, so correct, so respectful, with very pretty hair the color of a carrot," a Mexican restaurateur remembers. "Everybody said he was a good boy, and we gave him work to do." A bullfight promoter gave him an order to make some corrida-de-toros posters and offered him some free tickets to the show, but Franklin refused to go to the bullfight. For almost a year, he turned down all opportunities to see one. "I had been a charter member of Aunt

Jean's Humane Club," he says. "In my ignorance, I thought that bullfighting was a cruel sport." He got into the habit of sitting around evenings in the Fenix Café, a hangout for bullfighters and aficionados. He came to know a number of them and finally went with a friend to see a fight. "It left me cold," he says.

Franklin's friends at the time were what he calls "young Spanish society bloods." One night, when he was dining at the Fenix Café with some of the young bloods, one of them told him that Americans were scared to fight bulls. "They razzed me, but I said there was nothing to it—that Man was superior to Animal," Franklin recalls. "And eventually I said, 'Well, hell! I'll try it.'" He wrote to Rodolfo Gaona, then Mexico's leading matador, asking for an interview. "Having been told by the crowd that Gaona was superstitious, I bought some stationery decorated with the head of a black cat—a cat with golden whiskers and green eyes," he says. "When I did not receive an answer, I allowed myself to be pushed into calling him up on the telephone. Gaona's manager answered and suggested that I come to dinner immediately. Gaona then lived in a swanky house on Liverpool Street. The whole gang of society bloods went with me to see that I went in. Gaona at that time was God. The mere fact that you had spoken to him was something." Gaona's manager answered the door and introduced him to the maestro, who was wearing fastidiously tailored English sports clothes. Franklin was so terrified, he remembers, that he could hardly talk. "I was bowled over by his greatness and wealth," he says, "but I told him I wanted to learn the art of bullfighting. 'I know you're the greatest in the business,' I said. 'If you can't teach me, will you suggest someone who can teach me how to become as great a fighter as you are?' He asked me to stand away from him and turn around. He was silent for a while. Then he called for his sword handler and asked him to let me select one of his capes and one of his *muletas*. I selected the best."

Gaona told Franklin that he might come along to his morning practice sessions, at a small bull ring on the outskirts of the city. "Every morning, we went out with six or eight young society bloods," Franklin says. "I rode with Gaona in his car, as though I

were his own son. I had two weeks of shadowboxing. He taught
me the routine and the basic maneuvers. When I asked him to
give me some indication of what it was all going to cost me, he
said, 'I should be paying you for the entertainment you are giving
me.' I didn't know Spanish well enough at the time, or human
psychology well enough, to understand what he meant." At the
end of the two weeks, Gaona had to go on a bullfighting tour, and
he suggested that his pupil continue his studies with a bullfighter
who, as Franklin describes him, "knew the business but was
washed up in the ring." He started taking lessons with him. This
matador, he says, coached him for three days, borrowed some
money from him, and disappeared. Then a bullfight promoter, a
man of vision who thought that an American matador would be a
big draw with the American tourist trade, gave Franklin a letter
of introduction to Julio Herrera, a bull-breeder, who owned the
Xajay Ranch, a few hours by car north of Mexico City, and advised Franklin to go up there and learn some more about bulls
and the art of fighting them.

Franklin arrived at Xajay in September of 1923. The ranch, over
three hundred years old and with a ranchhouse that is surrounded
by a stone wall eighteen feet high, is in rolling, mountainous
country six thousand feet above sea level. "Xajay will always be
home to me in Mexico," Franklin says. "The place is mostly popu-
lated by Indians, who speak Otomian. I took pains to learn their
language. I would have done anything to please Herrera. He was
like a father to me. He was strictly on the level. He was the real
thing—no ifs, buts, or maybes. He taught me all the principles I
live by today. He was many times a millionaire, and made no
pretense. He always said he was not wealthy enough to buy
cheap things. He accepted me instantly, without question. We'd
sit around some nights till three or four, just talking. He tried to
forewarn me of the dangers of bullfighting, but he let me play
around with the animals." Franklin practiced cape work for a
week with some heifers. Then, to his astonishment, he discovered
that his public début—in the Chapultepec ring, in Mexico City
—had been arranged for by the forward-looking promoter, and

had already been announced for the following Sunday. "I was to be paid nothing and to receive nothing but the glory of letting the bull try to kill me," Franklin says. "I couldn't talk myself out of it. It was too late." He borrowed a bullfight suit of pearl-gray silk embroidered in gold. He put on the suit and sat in front of a mirror for a half hour. "It fit perfectly," he says. "I looked like a Christmas tree, but I felt so grand I wouldn't let anybody talk to me." Up to that time, Franklin had practiced only cape maneuvers, but he was expected to take on the bull not only with the cape but with the *muleta*, and to kill the animal with the sword, and he had had no education in either of these arts.

Franklin appeared, as advertised, on September 19, 1923. He was tossed twice by his bull, but it only knocked the wind out of him. "One of the fellows had to come out into the ring and show me how to use the *muleta*," he now recalls jauntily. "I don't know how I did it, but I went through the motions. It was a case of God taking care of drunks and little children. Then I was expected to kill the bull. The bull was as big as a cathedral, and I didn't have the faintest notion of how to get the sword in. At first, I refused to do the sword part. My friends came over to me at the *barrera* and warned me that the mob in the stands would do more damage to me if I kept on refusing than the bull could do. So the fellows showed me how to aim the sword and then gave me a push. My ignorance must have saved me. It flabbergasts me that I had the ignorant gall to do what I did. On my first try with the sword, I got it in. I killed the bull and gave the crowd a run for their money. I was carried out of the ring in triumph on the shoulders of the crowd."

People who saw Franklin make his début remember him as an appealing young man of twenty, tall and slender, with sandy-colored hair and an attractive grin. One witness has said, "Everybody came away surprised. Everybody said, 'This boy can be a bullfighter. He is not artistic, but he is very brave.' Everybody liked Sidney." As Franklin was carried out of the ring, he kept thinking, he says, This is so easy. Where have I been all my life? At the Fenix Café that night, he and his friends talked over the bullfight. "I thought, They're going to solve all my problems, and all I have to do is take a bumping," Franklin says. "I decided to make bull-fighting my profession."

That fall and winter, Franklin visited a number of ranches, where he watched two-year-old bulls being tested for bravery, and practiced cape work with heifers. "Being a novelty, I got invita-tions carte blanche from all the ranchers," he says. "I learned more about animals than I had ever known about human beings." In March, 1924, Franklin earned his first money in the ring—two hundred and fifty pesos, then the equivalent of a hundred and twenty-five dollars—at Ciudad Juárez, across the Rio Grande from El Paso. He did so well that he immediately received a con-tract for an appearance in Tampico the following month, again for two hundred and fifty pesos. There were flourishing oil de-velopments nearby, and the town was full of Americans. Frank-lin was being presented for their benefit. "The animals were poor, so my performance was poor," Franklin remembers. There fol-lowed two fights in Chihuahua, and although the judges had not yet awarded him the ears or the tails of any of the bulls he had killed, he believed that he was making progress. At the start of the bullfighting season for *novilleros*, which runs from May to Oc-tober, Franklin made his début in El Toreo, then Mexico City's biggest bull ring. After the *corrida*, his picture, in costume, ap-peared in the bullfight magazines and the newspapers, but the critics and aficionados had not been impressed by his perform-ance. He killed his bulls well, they said, but he did not handle them with the requisite grace. Franklin didn't mind the criticisms, because he was being booked for numerous appearances around the country.

Back home, Franklin's family had no idea of what was going on until he sent them some of the bullfight magazines. Not know-ing Spanish, they thought that Sidney had been photographed at a costume ball. Milton went out and showed the magazines to a Spaniard who lived in the neighborhood, and asked him what it was all about. "This fellow threw his arms around me," Milton says. "He pounded me on the back and yelled, 'He's a matador! You have a matador in the family!'" When Milton told Mrs. Frumkin what the Spaniard had said, she asked, "What's a matador?" "A bullfighter," Milton said. "Sidney is fighting bulls. In Mexico, it's a good profession." The rest of the family were pessimistic, and Father Frumkin wrote Sidney ordering him home and threatening to go down after him if he didn't come. "I told him to come ahead—that I had a twenty-five-hundred-mile head start and could run faster than he could," Franklin recollects. "I had had plenty of practice running from bulls. His opposition to the course I had chosen spurred me on to even greater heights."

One of the heights was Villahermosa, the capital of Tabasco, in southern Mexico, where he was booked to appear every other Sunday for three months. That engagement completed, he was invited to fight on Washington's Birthday, 1925, in Nuevo Laredo, a big town on the United States border. Instead of asking for five hundred pesos, which by then was Franklin's usual fee, he requested, and got, seven hundred and fifty. He killed his bulls so neatly that the crowd again carried him out of the ring on its shoulders. With the proceeds of the fight, the promoter was able to buy the Nuevo Laredo ring, and he booked Franklin in this and other rings throughout the country for the next six months. American newspapers began calling him the Brooklyn boy who had conquered the hearts of the Mexican fans. "Brooklyn Boy Wins Fame as Mexican Bullfighter, Acclaimed One of the Most Popular of Mexican Matadors," read a Brooklyn *Eagle* picture caption, and the text beneath it said, "He is the idol of the Mexican sport devotees and has been drawing record crowds for the last twelve months."

In 1926, Franklin decided that his technique with bulls needed polishing, so he returned to Herrera's ranch. This visit lasted two years. "Herrera convinced me that I was wasting my time piddling around in semiprofessional fights," he remembers. "I set out to prepare myself for big-time stuff in big-time rings in Spain. I acquired a thorough and subconscious knowledge of the animals and an anatomical understanding of their physical aspects." Late in 1928, he gave four performances on the border, which went off so well that he was awarded the ears and tails of all the bulls he killed. One fight, in Nuevo Laredo, was put on for American Legionnaires gathered for a convention in San Antonio, a hundred fifty miles away. The Legionnaires carried Franklin from the ring on their shoulders. Franklin thereupon announced that he was going to Spain, the home of bullfighting. In February, 1929, visiting Brooklyn on the way to Spain, he told the *Eagle*, "You see, they had the idea that only Latins are ever born with the feeling for bullfighting, as they put it. So I went into it to prove that anyone can have the feeling." In Brooklyn, Franklin found that he felt completely foreign. "I was speaking in English and thinking in Spanish," he says. "Nothing seemed right." Mrs. Frumkin was delighted to see her son again. Patrolman Frumkin refused to have anything to do with him. "It was only hello and goodbye with him," Franklin says.

In March, Franklin reached Madrid, and there he looked up some Spanish matadors he had met in Mexico. It was the beginning of the happiest year of his life. Every morning, he went out to practice cape work with other bullfighters. These practice sessions, called *toreo de salón*, were held in an outdoor restaurant, cleared of tables and chairs. A friend took movies of Franklin practicing and ran them off for him at night. "I studied myself with an eye to the effect I wanted to create," he says. One day, he was introduced to two girls who worked at the American Embassy. They suggested that he make his Spanish début during American Week at the International Exposition, in Seville. Franklin telephoned Seville and reached Thomas Campbell, the American representative at the Exposition whom he had met in Mexico City. Campbell, an ardent follower of bullfighting, told Franklin to catch the next plane for Seville, which he did. On his arrival, he and Campbell learned that there were no open dates in the bull ring for months to come.

Seville is the spiritual center of bullfighting. Bullfighters say they dream of fighting in Madrid, Barcelona, and Valencia but they dream of just *appearing* in Seville. The sand in the bull ring is a brilliant gold. Seville sand has been shipped to other parts of Spain, but the aficionados insist that it becomes dull as soon as it leaves Seville. "Seville is to bullfighting what Milan is to opera," Franklin says. "The bulls there are wonderful. The salt marshes around Seville impart something to them that makes them different from any other bulls." To make up for his disappointment over not being able to appear in Seville immediately, Franklin spent a few days seeing the Exposition, at which he met a young American engineer, Ross Denison, who was working on a reclamation project in Spain. "Ross came to the rescue," Franklin now says. "He went around to a hundred Americans and got a thousand pesetas from each one—about fifteen thousand dollars in all. Then he took the money to the promoters of the bullfights and said, 'Here's a hundred thousand pesetas to see that Franklin fights.' That kind of money would have covered three fights. Ross told the promoters he would provide the bulls, book the troupe, and charge no admission. The promoters said O.K. Then Ross played his trump card. He said, 'Nobody will be permitted in the stands except holders of American passports.' That was like saying nobody but Luxembourgians could go to Coney Island on the Fourth of July. This in Seville, the crème de la crème of bullfighting! The promoters, naturally, said they had to sell seats, and to sell them to anyone who wanted to buy them." Franklin was offered only a thousand pesetas, which was far below the local scale. "I took it," he says. "I could not afford to be particular at this moment in history."

Franklin made his Spanish début on June 9, 1929, seven years to the day after he had run away from home. Many spectators agree with his own evaluation of the performance he gave that day. "I was letter perfect," he said. "Artistically, dramatically, and technically, I made history in the bull ring. I startled everyone in the business, including myself. When the first bull came out, I had a momentary impulse to flee from the ring. The bull was enormous. Through my mind flashed the question: Should I take a taxi back to Madrid or should I kill the bull before he kills me? My decision is history." Matadors and aficionados who saw the fight were quoted afterward as saying that Franklin had introduced a revolutionary style of doing the verónica and that bullfighting would never be the same again. Moreover, he had killed his bulls expertly and courageously, using a single stroke of his sword to dispatch each one, and giving the bull, in the final moment of the killing, an honorable chance to kill him. Then he was carried out of the ring, as he had been carried in Mexico, on the shoulders of the crowd.

Denison took Franklin to a country house to recover from all the excitement, but the rest cure turned into a three-day party celebrating the launching of his career in Spain. "When I reappeared in the city, I found that the whole country had gone screwball over my fighting," Franklin says. "I put two and two together and realized that nobody could really believe it had happened. The only way to make them believe it was to get the most outlandishly impossible contract in the ring." Though still a *novillero*, Franklin asked the promoters of the Seville ring to book him for the next two Sundays and demanded the right to name the bulls, as well as the bullfighters, who would appear with him. He further demanded five thousand pesetas for each fight, a figure unheard of for a *novillero* and fifteen hundred more than the top semiprofessionals in Spain were being paid. (Top fee for full professionals at that time was twelve thousand pesetas.) "I was afraid of not being able to duplicate my performance," he says, "so I asked for terms so steep that if I got them, I would not be able to afford to turn them down. I'd be *obliged* to duplicate my performance." The promoters accepted his terms, which necessitated the cancellation of contracts with several other bullfighters. In the next four months, he fought in forty-two *corridas*, all over Spain, Portugal, and Spanish Morocco.

Shortly after his Spanish début, Franklin announced to a group of American correspondents in Seville, "I shall not return to my home town, Brooklyn, until I have gained fame throughout Spain. It is my intention to demonstrate to my countrymen that bullfighting is an art. I am sure that as soon as Americans are able to understand the beauty of this art, they will take to it, the same as they have taken to other sports." The Brooklyn branch of the American Society for the Prevention of Cruelty to Animals quickly stated, in a release to the press, "We are ready to take every legal measure to prevent such a thing. We are strongly against bullfighting." Franklin retorted that it was America's loss, not his, and that there were a couple of dozen countries that liked bullfighting. "It's a fine sport and a fine way to make a living," he said. (Franklin still has hopes of getting this country to take to bullfighting.) His success in Spain was responsible for some golden prose in the press back home. "Brooklyn Bullfighter Wins Great Ovation in Brilliant Spanish Début," a Brooklyn *Eagle* headline read. "Ten Thousand in Seville Arena Cheer Him As He Dispatches Bovine Foe with Single Stroke." "Sports now make the whole world kin," the *World* declared. " '*El Americano!* Viva *el Americano!*' Boxes and bleachers flung the cry across the golden sand of Seville's bull ring. The most critical audience in Spain was cheering the footwork, the cape play, and the final deadly thrust of a boy from Brooklyn. They awarded him the bullfighter's *Croix de guerre,* a hairy ear of the bull he had just killed. Then they poured down over the benches, and lifting his slender, gold-encrusted figure high in the air, they carried him in triumph from the ring." From the Spanish town of Andújar, a *Times* correspondent reported, "Two thousand wildly cheering people crowding the bull ring today saw Sidney Franklin, Brooklyn bullfighter, pick himself up out of the dust and, with rare courage, kill an infuriated bull after the animal's horns had pierced his thigh. Staggering to his feet, Franklin waved aside the attendants, and, as the bull, of the largest horned and most dangerous breed in Spain, returned to the charge, plunged his sword twice between the animal's shoulders." If Franklin had had to plunge the sword only once between the animal's shoulders, the two thousand wildly cheering people, if not the *Times* correspondent, would have liked it better.

During this successful period in Spain, by crowding as many as three *corridas* in different bull rings into one day, Franklin made up to fifteen thousand dollars a week. He kept two hundred and fifty dollars a week for living expenses and sent the rest to Milton, who put it in the bank. When Franklin came home again, in October, 1930, he set up a trust fund, which today gives him an income of nearly eighteen thousand dollars a year.

. . .

The meeting of Sidney Franklin and Ernest Hemingway, an important event in the lives of both men, took place in August, 1929. Franklin, in Spain, received a wire from Guy Hickok, the manager of the Paris bureau of the Brooklyn *Eagle*, saying that Hemingway wanted to meet him. "Who the hell is Hemingway?" Franklin asked aficionados. No one knew, so Franklin forgot about the matter. Hemingway, who had been going to bullfights for ten years, had heard reports that Franklin was good. Franklin's and Hemingway's recollections of the early days of their friendship do not completely coincide. "I met Sidney by speaking to him over the *barrera*, after he had killed his second bull on August 15, 1929, in the old ring at Madrid," Hemingway recalled on one occasion. "I made an appointment to meet him at a café the next day."

"This big hulk of a brute, unshaven and unkempt, with dirty pants and bedroom slippers, comes over to me in a café one day and asks if I'm Sidney Franklin," Franklin later said, commenting on Hemingway's recollection. "Automatically, I reached into my pocket, thinking the poor devil wanted a handout. But he sits down and orders Pernod. I had forgotten all about Hickok's wire. I didn't find out till months later that Hemingway was this famous writer everybody back home was nuts about."

"I saw no reason to tell him I had written any books," Hemingway said. "I was with him at many of his fights and during much of his training, and we passed many weeks in different parts of Spain together. Someone finally told him that I was a novelist, and he found it very hard to believe. This I took as a compliment."

"He was the first American who spoke to me intelligently about bullfighting," Franklin said. "Other Americans tried to tell me they knew more about the business than I did. Ernest let me do the talking. I found we both thought the same. Our minds ran along the same track. He wanted to go along with me on my tours. He used to stand behind the *barrera* and watch me fight. I would fight for Ernest, to solve the problems for his bullfight book—'Death in the Afternoon.' When I was on tour, he doubled up in a room with me, and we'd spend the whole night talking about fights, techniques, styles, and bulls. He'd tell me things I didn't know myself. For example, years ago bullfighters showed utter disregard of danger. They had such precision in their movements they'd let a handkerchief stick out of their breast pocket, then let the bull's horn pass so close that the bull would take the handkerchief out of the pocket on its horn. If you misjudged this trick by a fraction of an inch, you'd get your side torn out. Ernest showed me how to do it."

"Do I look like the kind of guy who would make that suggestion?" Hemingway asked indignantly. "The only thing I told Sidney was to dramatize his killing. He made it look too easy. He'd just go in, and wham! I told him not to make it look too easy."

"I didn't know what I was doing," Franklin said. "I just followed advice that Ernest gave me. We developed a set of signals. Apparently I'd be looking into the stands, but really I'd be spotting him, and he'd give me the high sign, to show me how to work the animal. It was his guidance, his knowledge of the business, that got me to do the impossible without my knowing what I was doing."

"Obscenity!" said Hemingway. "Sidney was a good killer and a good friend, and all I told him was not to make it look too easy."

Franklin has been badly gored twice. Hemingway believes that his first injury, which was the more serious one, prevented him from reaching the top in the bull ring. The goring—a goring is known in bullfighting as a *cornada*—took place on March 16, 1930, in Madrid. "After the horn wound, it was bad for him," Hemingway says. "Before the horn wound, he had the real completely. Because of his bad wound, he lost the real in bullfighting." A week before he was hurt, Franklin had given a brilliant performance in the Valencia bull ring, at the opening of the bullfight season. That was when he killed his own two bulls and then killed four more, replacing two matadors who had been gored. The following Sunday, in Madrid, Franklin marched confidently out into the ring to face his first bull of the afternoon. He went through the routine of the fight with grace and valor, and got the sword masterfully into the bull on his first try. Then he turned his back on the animal and walked over to the *barrera* to wipe his face. He woke up three and a half hours later in the hospital. "I was gored by a dead bull," he frequently says.

The beast's left horn caught Franklin at the base of his spine, penetrated the peritoneal cavity, and entered his intestines. Hemingway accompanied him to the hospital. "Sidney was absolutely brave," he said. Franklin says, "The doctors didn't expect me to pull through the night. I lay in the hospital for seventy-two hours with the drainage tubes in me. Finally, the doctors began to believe I would live. They warned me I would have to stay in bed for eight months. That would have meant an average loss of two or three thousand dollars a day, so two weeks after they brought me in, I amazed everyone by leaving the hospital, and a month later I was back at work." In the next thirteen years, Franklin underwent eight more operations because of this cornada. He loves to describe them all in detail, particularly to physicians, who are usually surprised at his familiarity with his intestines. The ninth operation, which finally repaired the damage, was performed in Washington, D.C., in 1943, by Dr. Eugene de Savitsch, a White Russian who had written a book called "In Search of Complications." He and Franklin were brought together at a dinner given by a mutual friend, a Washington party-giver named Grant Mason. "Sidney insisted on being examined while cocktails were being served," says Dr. de Savitsch. "It took all my persuasion to convince him I couldn't do it in front of the guests." "My God, what an uproar!" a witness recalls. "We spent the entire night talking about Sidney's intestines, with Sidney and de Savitsch trying to outshout each other about how to fix them up."

The operation, which was performed under a local anesthetic, took thirteen minutes. All through it, Franklin talked incessantly. By the time the operation was over, every doctor, interne, nurse, and orderly in the operating room had learned that sometimes it takes only one-fifth of a second to size up an onrushing bull. Franklin was considered a bold and charming patient in the hospital. He didn't complain so long as he had an audience. After two days, when everyone had heard the story of his life, he left the hospital.

Franklin maintains that unless a bullfighter understands just why he got hooked by a bull, he will lose his nerve when facing the possibility again. "In the beginning, in my astounding ignorance, I thought you got hooked only if you wanted to," he says. "I found out after I was hooked that I did not want to be." The scars of the Madrid cornada are not visible, but he still has a scar on one leg from a wound received at Nuevo Laredo in February of 1931. The Nuevo Laredo ring had been moved, and the beach sand of the surfacing had not been mixed and packed, as is customary, with powdered granite and ash to make it firm. "The minute the animals moved, the ring was full of holes," Franklin has explained. "I selected the only spot in the arena that was smooth. My first bull was on wheels—he was that good. I fought in a standstill position and gave him six verónicas. Then I moved, and my right leg sank into the sand, making me lose my balance. As I was falling, the bull caught me just below the knee, in the middle of the calf. The bull lifted his head, with me on his horn. I spun on the horn, head downward. Then I was tossed over the bull's shoulder, and as I was being tossed, the horn ripped upward from the knee to the ankle. Everybody insisted I should get out of the ring, but I saw the fight through."

Throughout the summer of 1930, after his goring in Madrid, Franklin was in and out of hospitals. In the fall, he decided to return to the United States and take it easy. At home in Brooklyn, he showed his family films of himself in action; they laughed at some scenes showing his best cape play with the bull, and he felt that they had no understanding of what he had been doing. This failure to understand the thing that meant most in life to him saddened him. He was further saddened when he picked up the Eagle one day and read a letter, signed "A Son of Brooklyn," saying, "Those of us old enough to remember conditions existing in the Philippines and Cuba before the United States went in and took charge must know what a bullfighting civilization has done for humanity. The best anyone could do for Sidney Franklin would be to induce him to give up his profession of cruelty to animals. . . . If so anxious to kill, why does he not apply for a job in the stockyards?" The city administration was more gracious.

Preceded by a band and an entourage in ten-gallon hats and cowboy boots, Franklin marched up Broadway to City Hall and was presented by his brother Milton to Acting Mayor McKee as "the idol of Spain."

The day was a great one for Franklin, and he wound it up by telling the Acting Mayor about that other great day, in Seville, when he made his Spanish début in the bull ring. "Your Honor," he said, "I was carried out on the shoulders of the crowd through the gates reserved for royalty. The history of the ring was then a hundred and ninety-nine years old. All that time, only four fellows had ever been carried out of the ring on the shoulders of the crowd. I was the fifth. Traffic in the streets of Seville was wrecked. The next day, they passed a law prohibiting the carrying of bullfighters through the public streets. I was taken out of the ring at seven and deposited at my hotel at twelve-twenty that night. I didn't know what I was doing or what had happened to me. I was so excited I took all my money out of a dresser drawer and threw it to the crowds on the street. The die was cast that day. I was riding on the highest cloud in this or any other world. I felt so far above anything mundane that nothing mattered. I didn't hear anything. I didn't see anything. I looked, but I didn't see. I heard, but nothing registered. I didn't care about food. I didn't care about drink. I was perfectly satisfied to lay my head on the pillow and pass out."

—1949

6

PORTRAIT
OF HEMINGWAY

Preface

I FIRST MET ERNEST HEMINGWAY on the day before
Christmas in 1947, in Ketchum, Idaho. I was on my way back to
New York from Mexico, where I had gone to see Sidney Franklin, the American bullfighter from Brooklyn, about whom I was
trying to write my first Profile for The New Yorker. Hemingway
had known Franklin as a bullfighter in Spain in the late twenties
and early thirties. I had gone to some corridas in Mexico with
Franklin, and had been appalled and scared to death when I got
my first look at what goes on in a bull ring. Although I appreciated the matador's cape work with the bulls, and the colorful, cere-
monial atmosphere, I wasn't fond of bullfighting as such. I guess
what interested me was just how Franklin, son of a hard-working

policeman in Flatbush, had become a bullfighter. When Franklin told me that Hemingway was the first American who had ever spoken to him intelligently about bullfighting, I telephoned Hemingway in Ketchum. Hemingway liked spending vacations there, skiing and hunting, away from his home in San Francisco de Paula, near Havana, Cuba, and later on he bought a house in Ketchum. When I called, Hemingway was staying in a tourist cabin with his wife, Mary, his sons—John, Patrick, and Gregory— and some fishing friends from Cuba, and he hospitably invited me to drop in and see him on my way back East.

The first time I saw Hemingway was about seven o'clock in the morning, in front of his tourist cabin, shortly after my train got in. He was standing on hard-packed snow, in dry cold of ten degrees below zero, wearing bedroom slippers, no socks, Western trousers with an Indian belt that had a silver buckle, and a lightweight Western-style sports shirt open at the collar and with button-down pockets. He had a graying mustache but had not yet started to wear the patriarchal-looking beard that was eventually to give him an air of saintliness and innocence—an air that somehow or other never seemed to be at odds with his ruggedness. That morning, he looked rugged and burly and eager and friendly and kind. I was wearing a heavy coat, but I was absolutely freezing in the cold. However, Hemingway, when I asked him, said he wasn't a bit cold. He seemed to have tremendous built-in warmth. I spent a wonderful day of talk and Christmas shopping with the Hemingways and their friends. Mary Hemingway, like her husband, was warm and gracious and knowledgeable, as well as capable of brilliantly filling the difficult role of famous writer's wife. She enjoyed the same things he did, and seemed to me to be the perfect partner for him.

Shortly after my Ketchum visit, Hemingway wrote to me from Cuba that he thought I was the person least suited in the world to do an article on bullfighting. Nevertheless, I went ahead, and eventually did finish the Profile of Franklin. After the magazine's editors had accepted it, I sent Hemingway some queries about it, and he replied most helpfully in a letter winding up with the statement that he looked forward with horror to reading it. In the meantime, though, The New Yorker published a couple of shorter pieces of mine, and Hemingway and his wife, both regular readers of the magazine (he once wrote me that my mob was his mob, too), seemed to like them. When the Franklin Profile was published, I had a letter from Hemingway, scrawled in pencil, from Villa Aprile, Cortina d'Ampezzo, Italy, in which he said that what he called the Sidney pieces were fine. In his crowded life, he did his best to remember exactly what he had said to you before, and he made a point, generously, of correcting himself when he felt that it was necessary. His compliments were straight and honest, and they were designed to make people feel good. He might call you reliable and compare you to Joe Page and Hugh Casey, and you wouldn't have to be an archivist of baseball to realize you were being praised. The way he wrote in his letters, the way he talked, in itself made me feel good—it was so fresh and wonderful. He was generous in his conversation. He didn't hoard his ideas or his thoughts or his humor or his opinions. He was so inventive that he probably had the feeling there was plenty more where that came from. But whatever his feeling might have been, he would have talked as he did out of sheer generosity. He offered so much in what he said, and always with fun and with sharp understanding and compassion and sensitivity. When he talked, he was free. The sound and the content were marvellously alive.

In the spring of 1950, I wrote a Profile of Hemingway for The New Yorker. It was a sympathetic piece, covering two days Hemingway spent in New York, in which I tried to describe as precisely as possible how Hemingway, who had the nerve to be like nobody else on earth, looked and sounded when he was in action, talking, between work periods—to give a picture of the man as he was, in his uniqueness and with his vitality and his enormous spirit of fun intact. Before it was published, I sent a galley proof of it to the Hemingways, and they returned it marked with corrections. In an accompanying letter, Hemingway said that he had found the Profile funny and good, and that he had suggested only one deletion. Then a strange and mysterious thing happened. Nothing like it had ever happened before in my writing experience, or has happened since. To the complete surprise of Hemingway and the editors of *The New Yorker* and myself, it turned out, when the Profile appeared, that what I had written was extremely controversial. Most readers took the piece for just what it was, and I trust that they enjoyed it in an uncomplicated fashion. However, a certain number of readers reacted violently, and in a very complicated fashion. Among these were people who objected strongly to Hemingway's personality, assumed I did the same, and admired the piece for the wrong reasons; that is, they thought that in describing that personality accurately I was ridiculing or attacking it. Other people simply didn't like the way Hemingway talked (they even objected to the playful way he sometimes dropped his articles and spoke a kind of joke Indian language); they didn't like his freedom; they didn't like his not taking himself seriously; they didn't like his wasting his time on going to boxing matches, going to the zoo, talking to friends, going fishing, enjoying people, celebrating his approach to the finish of a book by splurging on caviar and champagne; they didn't like this and they didn't like that. In fact, they didn't like Hemingway to be Hemingway. They wanted him to be somebody else—probably themselves. So they came to the conclusion that either Hemingway had not been portrayed as he was or, if he was that way, I shouldn't have written about him at all. Either they had dreary, small-minded preconceptions about how a great writer should behave and preferred their preconceptions to the facts or they attributed to me their own pious disapproval of Hemingway and then berated me for it. Some of the more devastation-minded among them called the Profile "devastating." When Hemingway heard about all this, he wrote to reassure me. On June 16, 1950, he wrote that I shouldn't worry about the piece and that it was just that people got things all mixed up. A number of times he wrote about the attitude of people he called the devastate people. Some people, he said, couldn't understand his enjoying himself and his not being really spooky; they couldn't understand his being a serious writer without being pompous.

Death puts certain things in perspective. No doubt if some of the people who misunderstood the Profile were to read it now, they would see it for what it is. When I wrote the Profile, I attempted to set down only what I had seen and heard, and not to comment on the facts or express any opinions or pass any judgments. However, I believe that today—with the advantage gained by distance —almost any reader would see that although I did not reveal my viewpoint directly, implicit in my choice and arrangement of detail, and in the total atmosphere created, was my feeling of affection and admiration. I liked Hemingway exactly as he was, and I'm content if my Profile caught him exactly as he was during those two days in New York.

While I'm at it, as somebody who has never been concerned with "rating" Hemingway's works but has simply been grateful for whatever joy his writing has offered, I might as well throw in a word about those critics who took an injured, censorious tone when discussing the life that Hemingway led in later years and what they considered a decline in his work. They sometimes sounded as if they thought that Hemingway made a point of letting them, specifically, down, in order to disport himself as a public figure, whereas, as I saw it, he was heroically and uncorruptedly and uncompromisingly occupied day after day with writing as hard as he could and as well as he could until the day he died. And when he was unable to write or was between books, he still did what he could, which was to live life to the full and then, with that limitless generosity of his, make his private experience public, so that everybody else could also have a wonderful time.

Hemingway was generous in so many different ways. In his letters and in his conversations with friends, Hemingway gave away the very substance out of which another man might have created an entire body of work. The style of Hemingway's letters was a separate style, free and loose and (since he knew that time was short) full of his own shorthand—much freer, as one might expect, than his formal writing. He was a tireless correspondent. I went out to Hollywood for a year and a half after the Profile appeared, to write a series of articles about the making of a movie, and I received scores of letters from Hemingway out there, giving me his views on movies and movie-making and life on the Coast, and also keeping me informed, and entertained, with accounts of his fishing and other adventures in Cuba. When he went to Africa to hunt in 1953, he wrote about the wonders of life there. Africa, he told me, was in many ways the best life of all, and I ought to come there and try it. He usually ended his letters by asking you to write soon. He didn't like to stop writing letters, he once told me, because then he wouldn't receive any, and that would make it lonely. Occasionally, Mary would write a letter, and it would have Hemingway's own kind of enthusiasm and humor. She would write from Kenya that it was the greatest place in the world for waking up in the morning, and that you had to encounter a live, two-ton rhinoceros before dawn, on your way to wash your face, to appreciate what living could be. A lot of other people the Hemingways knew—people who knew them better than I did—probably also got invitations to come there and try it. The Hemingways were always hospitable and friendly. They were always inviting you to visit them in Kenya or in Paris or at their farm in Cuba. I'm sorry that I was never able to do it.

Nobody could fool Hemingway about writing or about writers. He knew both, and he knew them deeply. He knew when a writer was worthless or a fraud, no matter how great the writer's reputation or his sales or his advances from movie companies. About himself he wrote, on August 8, 1950, that all his life he had tried to learn to write better and to know and understand. People, he said, imitated his defects, stole his cadences and rhythms, and called the result the Hemingway school of writing, and nobody wished him well. Then he had an afterthought, and wrote that that was wrong, that a lot of people wished him well but just didn't, he guessed, tell him about it. Writing and literature he took seriously. And whatever he was asked for he always tried to give. He was quick to respond to younger writers. Once, I asked him to give me a list of reading that he would recommend. He composed the following list:

"Boule de Suif" and "La Maison Tellier"—de Maupassant
"The Red and the Black"—Stendhal
"Les Fleurs du Mal"—Baudelaire

"Madame Bovary"—Flaubert
"Remembrance of Things Past"—Proust
"Buddenbrooks"—Mann
"Taras Bulba"—Gogol
"The Brothers Karamazov"—Dostoevski
"Anna Karenina" and "War and Peace"—Tolstoy
"Huckleberry Finn"—Twain
"Moby Dick"—Melville
"The Scarlet Letter"—Hawthorne
"The Red Badge of Courage"—Crane
"Madame de Mauves"—James

Whatever you brought up with Hemingway, he always tried—or so I found—to give you a response that would be helpful. At one point, after finishing a long piece of work, I told him that I wanted to write shorter and easier pieces from then on. His answer was that I would have to write harder ones and better ones until I died. Only, don't die, he added, explaining that that was the only thing he knew that was really worthless. He was helpful with minor matters, too. When I was in California, trying to learn to ride a horse, Hemingway advised me not to ride any big or fat horses but to get the smallest, smartest, and least mean horse there was. About Hollywood his advice was succinct. He told me not to stay too long.

Hemingway has been called romantic, as distinguished from realistic, about life, especially by some of the heavy thinkers. It always seemed to me that Hemingway was a sound observer and understander of the realities. Once, I passed along some pleasant remarks I had heard about his son John, and Hemingway wrote back that he loved his son very much and then went on to say that in his lifetime he had also loved three continents, several airplanes and ships, the oceans, his sisters, his wives, life and death, morning, noon, evening, and night, honor, bed, boxing, swimming, baseball, shooting, fishing, and reading and writing and all good pictures.

Not long before he died, when he was at the Mayo Clinic, in Rochester, Minnesota, Hemingway wrote to me that he had his blood-pressure "nonsense" licked again but that he was behind in his work, and that he and Mary were taking off soon for some place where people would leave them alone and "let me write."

—1961

How Do You Like It Now, Gentlemen?

ERNEST HEMINGWAY, who may well be the greatest American novelist and short-story writer of our day, rarely comes to New York. For many years, he has spent most of his time on a farm, the Finca Vigia, nine miles outside Havana, with his wife, a domestic staff of nine, fifty-two cats, sixteen dogs, a couple of hundred pigeons, and three cows. When he does come to New York, it is only because he has to pass through it on his way somewhere else. Late in 1949, on his way to Europe, he stopped in New York for a few days. I had written to him asking if I might see him when he came to town, and he had sent me a typewritten letter saying that would be fine and suggesting that I meet his plane at the airport. "I don't want to see anybody I don't like, nor have publicity, nor be tied up all the time," he went on. "Want to go to the Bronx Zoo, Metropolitan Museum, Museum of Modern Art, ditto of Natural History, and see a fight. Want to see the good Breughel at the Met, the one, no two, fine Goyas and Mr. El Greco's Toledo. Don't want to go to Toots Shor's. Am going to try to get into town and out without having to shoot my mouth off. I want to give the joints a miss. Not seeing news people is not a pose. It is only to have time to see your friends." In pencil, he added, "Time is the least thing we have of."

Time did not seem to be pressing Hemingway the day he flew in from Havana. He was to arrive at Idlewild late in the afternoon, and I went out to meet him. His plane had landed by the time I got there, and I found him standing at a gate waiting for his luggage and for his wife, who had gone to attend to it. He had one arm around a scuffed, dilapidated briefcase pasted up with travel stickers. He had the other around a wiry little man whose forehead was covered with enormous beads of perspiration. Hemingway had on a red plaid wool shirt, a figured wool necktie, a tan wool sweater-vest, a brown tweed jacket tight across the back and with sleeves too short for his arms, gray flannel slacks, Argyle socks, and loafers, and he looked bearish, cordial, and constricted. His hair, which was very long in back, was gray, except at the temples, where it was white; his mustache was white, and he had a ragged, half-inch, full white beard. There was a bump about the size of a walnut over his left eye. He had on steel-rimmed spectacles, with a piece of paper under the nosepiece. He was in no hurry to get into Manhattan. He crooked the arm around the briefcase into a tight hug and said that inside was the unfinished manuscript of his new book, "Across the River and Into the Trees." He crooked the arm around the wiry little man into a tight hug and said the man had been his seat companion on the flight. The man's name, as I got it in a mumbled introduction, was Myers, and he was returning from a business trip to Cuba. Myers made a slight attempt to dislodge himself from the embrace, but Hemingway held on to him affectionately.

"He read book all way up on plane," Hemingway said. He spoke with a perceptible Midwestern accent, despite the Indian talk. "He liked book, I think," he added, giving Myers a little shake and beaming down at him.

"Whew!" said Myers.

"Book too much for him," Hemingway said. "Book start slow, then increase in pace till it becomes impossible to stand. I bring emotion up to where you can't stand it, then we level off, so we won't have to provide oxygen tents for the readers. Book is like engine. We have to slack off gradually."

"Whew!" said Myers.

Hemingway released him. "Not trying for no-hit game in book," he said. "Going to win maybe twelve to nothing or maybe twelve to eleven."

Myers looked puzzled.

"She's better book than 'Farewell,'" Hemingway said. "I think this is best one, but you are always prejudiced, I guess. Especially if you want to be champion." He shook Myers' hand. "Thanks for reading book," he said.

"Pleasure," Myers said, and walked off unsteadily.

Hemingway watched him go, and then turned to me. "After you finish a book, you know, you're dead," he said moodily. "But no one knows you're dead. All they see is the irresponsibility that comes in after the terrible responsibility of writing." He said he felt tired but was in good shape physically; he had brought his weight down to two hundred and eight, and his blood pressure was down, too. He had considerable rewriting to do on his book, and he was determined to keep at it until he was absolutely satisfied. "They can't yank novelist like they can pitcher," he said. "Novelist has to go the full nine, even if it kills him."

We were joined by Hemingway's wife, Mary, a small, energetic, cheerful woman with close-cropped blond hair, who was wearing a long, belted mink coat. A porter pushing a cart heaped with luggage followed her. "Papa, everything is here," she said to Hemingway. "Now we ought to get going, Papa." He assumed the air of a man who is not going to be rushed. Slowly, he counted the pieces of luggage. There were fourteen, half of them, Mrs. Hemingway told me, extra-large Valpaks designed by her husband and bearing their hierro, also designed by him. When Hemingway had finished counting, his wife suggested that he tell the porter where to put the luggage. Hemingway told the porter to stay right there and watch it; then he turned to his wife and said, "Let's not crowd, honey. Order of the day is to have a drink first."

We went into the airport cocktail lounge and stood at the bar. Hemingway put his briefcase down on a chromium stool and pulled the stool close to him. He ordered bourbon and water. Mrs. Hemingway said she would have the same, and I ordered a cup of coffee. Hemingway told the bartender to bring double bourbons. He waited for the drinks with impatience, holding on to the bar with both hands and humming an unrecognizable tune. Mrs. Hemingway said she hoped it wouldn't be dark by the time they got to New York. Hemingway said it wouldn't make any difference to him, because New York was a rough town, a phony town, a town that was the same in the dark as it was in the light, and he was not exactly overjoyed to be going there anyway. What he was looking forward to, he said, was Venice. "Where I like it is out West in Wyoming, Montana, and Idaho, and I like Cuba and Paris and around Venice," he said. "Westport gives me the horrors." Mrs. Hemingway lit a cigarette and handed me the pack. I passed it along to him, but he said he didn't smoke. Smoking ruined his sense of smell, a sense he found completely indispensable for hunting. "Cigarettes smell so awful to you when you have a nose that can truly smell," he said, and laughed, hunching his shoulders and raising the back of his fist to his face, as though he expected somebody to hit him. Then he enumerated elk, deer, possum, and coon as some of the things he could truly smell.

The bartender brought the drinks. Hemingway took several large swallows and said he got along fine with animals, sometimes better than with human beings. In Montana, once, he lived with a bear, and the bear slept with him, got drunk with him, and was a close friend. He asked me whether there were still bears at the Bronx Zoo, and I said I didn't know but I was pretty sure there were bears at the Central Park Zoo. "I always used to go to the Bronx Zoo with Granny Rice," he said. "I love to go to the zoo. But not on Sunday. I don't like to see the people making fun of the animals, when it should be the other way around." Mrs. Hemingway took a small notebook out of her purse and opened it; she told me she had made a list of chores she and her husband had to do before their boat sailed. They included buying a hot-water-bottle cover, an elementary Italian grammar, a short history of Italy, and, for Hemingway, four woollen undershirts, four pairs of cotton underpants, two pairs of woollen underpants, bedroom slippers, a belt, and a coat. "Papa has never had a coat," she said. "We've got to buy Papa a coat." Hemingway grunted and leaned against the bar. "A nice, rainproof coat," Mrs. Hemingway said. "And he's got to get his glasses fixed. He needs some good, soft padding for the nosepiece. It cuts him up brutally. He's had that same piece of paper under the nosepiece for weeks. When he really wants to get cleaned up, he changes the paper." Hemingway grunted again.

The bartender came up, and Hemingway asked him to bring another round of drinks. Then he said, "First thing we do, Mary, as soon as we hit hotel, is call up the Kraut." "The Kraut," he told me, with that same fist-to-the-face laugh, was his affectionate term for Marlene Dietrich, an old friend, and was part of a large vocabulary of special code terms and speech mannerisms indigenous to the Finca Vigia. "We have a lot of fun talking a sort of joke language," he said.

"First we call Marlene, and then we order caviar and champagne, Papa," Mrs. Hemingway said. "I've been waiting months for that caviar and champagne."

"The Kraut, caviar, and champagne," Hemingway said slowly, as though he were memorizing a difficult set of military orders. He finished his drink and gave the bartender a repeat nod, and then he turned to me. "You want to go with me to buy coat?" he asked.

"Buy coat and get glasses fixed," Mrs. Hemingway said.

I said I would be happy to help him do both, and then I reminded him that he had said he wanted to see a fight. The only fight that week, I had learned from a friend who knows all about fights, was at the St. Nicholas Arena that night. I said that my friend had four tickets and would like to take all of us. Hemingway wanted to know who was fighting. When I told him, he said they were bums. Bums, Mrs. Hemingway repeated, and added that they had better fighters in Cuba. Hemingway gave me a long, reproachful look. "Daughter, you've got to learn that a bad fight is worse than no fight," he said. We would all go to a fight when he got back from Europe, he said, because it was absolutely necessary to go to several good fights a year. "If you quit going for too long a time, then you never go near them," he said. "That would be very dangerous." He was interrupted by a brief fit of coughing. "Finally," he concluded, "you end up in one room and won't move."

After dallying at the bar a while longer, the Hemingways asked me to go with them to their hotel. Hemingway ordered the luggage loaded into a taxi, and the three of us got into another. It was dark now. As we drove along the boulevard, Hemingway watched the road carefully. Mrs. Hemingway told me that he always watched the road, usually from the front seat. It was a habit he had got into during the First World War. I asked them what they planned to do in Europe. They said they were going to stay a week or so in Paris and then drive to Venice.

"I love to go back to Paris," Hemingway said, his eyes still fixed on the road. "Am going in the back door and have no interviews and no publicity and never get a haircut, like in the old days. Want to go to cafés where I know no one but one waiter and his replacement, see all the new pictures and the old ones, go to the bike races and the fights, and see the new riders and fighters. Find good, cheap restaurants where you can keep your own napkin. Walk all over the town and see where we made our mistakes and where we had our few bright ideas. And learn the form and try and pick winners in the blue, smoky afternoons, and then go out the next day to play them at Auteuil and Enghien."

"Papa is a good handicapper," Mrs. Hemingway said.

"When I know the form," he said.

We were crossing the Queensboro Bridge, and we had a clear view of the Manhattan skyline. The lights were on in the tall office buildings. Hemingway did not seem to be impressed. "This ain't my town," he said. "It's a town you come to for a short time. It's murder." Paris was like another home to him, he said. "I am as lonesome and as happy as I can be in that town we lived in and worked and learned and grew up in, and then fought our way back into." Venice was another of his home towns. The last time he and his wife were in Italy, they had lived for four months in Venice and the Cortina Valley, and he had gone hunting, and now he had put the locale and some of the people in the book he was writing. "Italy was so damned wonderful," he said. "It was sort of like having died and gone to Heaven, a place you'd figured never to see."

Mrs. Hemingway said that she had broken her right ankle skiing there but that she planned to go skiing there again. Hemingway had been hospitalized in Padua with an eye infection, which developed into erysipelas, but he wanted to go back to Italy and wanted to see his many good friends there. He was looking forward to seeing the gondoliers on a windy day, the Gritti Palace Hotel, where they stayed during their last visit, and the Locanda Cipriani, which was an old inn on Torcello, an island in the lagoon northeast of Venice where some of the original Venetians lived before they built Venice. Now about seventy people lived on Torcello, and the men were professional duckhunters. While there, Hemingway had gone duckhunting a lot with the gardener of the old inn. "We'd go around through the canals and jumpshoot, and I'd walk the prairies at low tide for snipe," he said. "It was a big fly route for ducks that came all the way down from the Pripet Marshes. I shot good and thus became a respected local character. They have some sort of little bird that comes through, after eating grapes in the north, on his way to eat grapes in the south. The local characters sometimes shot them sitting, and I occasionally shot them flying. Once, I shot two high doubles, rights and lefts, in a row, and the gardener cried with emotion. Coming home, I shot a high duck against the rising moon and dropped him in the canal. That precipitated an emotional crisis I thought I would never get him out of but did, with about a pint of Chianti. We each took a pint out with us. I drank mine to keep warm coming home. He drank his when overcome by emotion." We were silent for a while, and then Hemingway said, "Venice was lovely."

The Hemingways were stopping at the Sherry-Netherland. Hemingway registered and told the room clerk that he did not want any announcement made of his arrival and did not want any visitors, or any telephone calls, either, except from Miss Dietrich. Then we went up to the suite—living room, bedroom, and serving pantry—that had been reserved for them. Hemingway paused at the entrance and scouted the living room. It was large, decorated in garish colors, and furnished with imitation-Chippendale furniture and an imitation fireplace containing imitation coals.

"Joint looks O.K.," he said. "Guess they call this the Chinese Gothic Room." He moved in and took the room.

Mrs. Hemingway went over to a bookcase and examined its contents. "Look, Papa," she said. "They're phony. They're pasteboard backs, Papa. They're not real books."

Hemingway put his briefcase down on a bright-red couch and advanced on the bookcase, then slowly, with expression, read the titles aloud—"Elementary Economics," "Government of the United States," "Sweden, the Land and the People," and "Sleep in Peace," by Phyllis Bentley. "I think we are an outfit headed for extinction," he said, starting to take off his necktie.

After getting his necktie off, and then his jacket, Hemingway handed them to his wife, who went into the bedroom, saying she was going to unpack. He unbuttoned his collar and went over to the telephone. "Got to call the Kraut," he said. He telephoned the Plaza and asked for Miss Dietrich. She was out, and he left word for her to come over for supper. Then he called room service and ordered caviar and a couple of bottles of Perrier-Jouët, brut.

Hemingway went back to the bookcase and stood there stiffly, as though he could not decide what to do with himself. He looked at the pasteboard backs again and said, "Phony, just like the town." I said that there was a tremendous amount of talk about him these days in literary circles—that the critics seemed to be talking and writing definitively not only about the work he had done but about the work he was going to do. He said that, of all the people he did not wish to see in New York, the people he wished least to see were the critics. "They are like those people who go to ball games and can't tell the players without a score card," he said. "I am not worried about what anybody I do not like might do. What the hell! If they can do you harm, let them do it. It is like being a third baseman and protesting because they hit line drives to you. Line drives are regrettable, but to be expected." The closest competitors of the critics among those he wished least to see, he said, were certain writers who wrote books about the war when they had not seen anything of war at first hand. "They are just like an outfielder who will drop a fly on you when you have pitched to have the batter hit a high fly to that outfielder, or when they're pitching they try to strike everybody out." When he pitched, he said, he never struck anybody out, except under extreme necessity. "I knew I had only so many fast balls in that arm," he said. "Would make them pop to short instead, or fly out, or hit it on the ground, bouncing."

A waiter arrived with the caviar and champagne, and Hemingway told him to open one of the bottles. Mrs. Hemingway came in from the bedroom and said she couldn't find his toothbrush. He said that he didn't know where it was but that he could easily buy another. Mrs. Hemingway said all right, and went back into the bedroom. Hemingway poured two glasses of champagne, gave one to me, and picked up the other one and took a sip. The waiter watched him anxiously. Hemingway hunched his shoulders and said something in Spanish to the waiter. They both laughed, and the waiter left. Hemingway took his glass over to the red couch and sat down, and I sat in a chair opposite him.

"I can remember feeling so awful about the first war that I couldn't write about it for ten years," he said, suddenly very angry. "The wound combat makes in you, as a writer, is a very slow-healing one. I wrote three stories about it in the old days—'In Another Country,' 'A Way You'll Never Be,' and 'Now I Lay Me.'" He mentioned a war writer who, he said, was apparently thinking of himself as Tolstoy, but who'd be able to play Tolstoy only on the Bryn Mawr field-hockey team. "He never hears a shot fired in anger, and he sets out to beat who? Tolstoy, an artillery officer who fought at Sevastopol, who knew his stuff, who was a hell of a man anywhere you put him—bed, bar, in an empty room where he had to think. I started out very quiet and I beat Mr. Turgenev. Then I trained hard and I beat Mr. de Maupassant. I've fought two draws with Mr. Stendhal, and I think I had an edge in the last one. But nobody's going to get me in any ring with Mr. Tolstoy unless I'm crazy or I keep getting better."

He had begun his new book as a short story. "Then I couldn't stop it. It went straight on into a novel," he said. "That's the way all my novels got started. When I was twenty-five, I read novels by Somersault Maugham and Stephen St. Vixen Benét." He laughed hoarsely. "They had written novels, and I was ashamed because I had not written any novels. So I wrote 'The Sun' when I was twenty-seven, and I wrote it in six weeks, starting on my birthday, July 21st, in Valencia, and finishing it September 6th, in Paris. But it was really lousy and the rewriting took nearly five months. Maybe that will encourage young writers so they won't have to go get advice from their psychoanalysts. Analyst once wrote me, What did I learn from psychoanalysts? I answered, Very little but hope they had learned as much as they were able to understand from my published works. You never saw a counter-puncher who was punchy. Never lead against a hitter unless you can outhit him. Crowd a boxer, and take everything he has, to get inside. Duck a swing. Block a hook. And counter a jab with everything you own. Papa's delivery of hard-learned facts of life."

Hemingway poured himself another glass of champagne. He liked to write in longhand, he said, but he had recently bought a tape recorder and was trying to get up the courage to use it. "I'd like to learn talk machine," he said. "You just tell talk machine anything you want and get secretary to type it out." He wrote without facility, except for dialogue. "When the people are talking, I can hardly write it fast enough or keep up with it, but with an almost unbearable high manifold pleasure. I put more inches on than she will take, and then fly her as near as I know to how she should be flown, only flying as crazy as really good pilots fly crazy sometimes. Most of the time flying conservatively but with an awfully fast airplane that makes up for the conservatism. That way, you live longer. I mean your writing lives longer. How do you like it now, gentlemen?" The question seemed to have some special significance for him, but he did not bother to explain it.

I wanted to know whether, in his opinion, the new book was different from his others, and he gave me another long, reproachful look. "What do you think?" he said after a moment. "You don't expect me to write 'The Farewell to Arms Boys in Addis Ababa,' do you? Or 'The Farewell to Arms Boys Take a Gunboat'?" The book was about the command level in the Second World War. "I am not interested in the G.I. who wasn't one," he said, suddenly angry again. "Or the injustices done to me, with a capital 'M.' I am interested in the goddam sad science of war." The new novel had a good deal of profanity in it. "That's because in war they talk profane, although I always try to talk gently," he said. "I think I've got 'Farewell' beat in this one," he went on. He touched his briefcase. "It hasn't got the youth and the ignorance." Then he asked wearily, "How do you like it now, gentlemen?"

.   .   .

There was a knock at the door, and Hemingway got up quickly and opened it. It was Miss Dietrich. Their reunion was a happy one. Mrs. Hemingway came out of the bedroom and greeted the guest enthusiastically. Miss Dietrich stood back from Hemingway and looked at him with approval. "Papa, you look wonderful," she said slowly.

"I sure missed you, daughter," said Hemingway. He raised his fist to his face, and his shoulders shook as he laughed silently.

Miss Dietrich was wearing a mink coat. She sighed loudly, took off the coat, and handed it to Mrs. Hemingway. Then she sighed again and sat down in an overstuffed chair. Hemingway poured a glass of champagne, took it to her, and refilled the other glasses.

"The Kraut's the best that ever came into the ring," he said as he handed me my glass. Then he pulled a chair up beside Miss Dietrich's, and they compared notes on friends and on themselves. They talked about theatre and motion-picture people, one of whom, a man, Hemingway referred to as a "sea heel."

Miss Dietrich wanted to know what a sea heel was.

"The sea is bigger than the land," he told her.

Mrs. Hemingway went into the serving pantry and came out in a few minutes with caviar spread on toast.

"Mary, I am telling Papa how I have to behave because I am a grandmother," Miss Dietrich said, taking a piece of toast. "I have to think always of the children. You know, Papa?"

Hemingway gave a sympathetic grunt, and Miss Dietrich took from her purse some snapshots of her grandson and passed them around. He was eighteen months old, she told us. Hemingway said that he looked like a winner, and that he would be proud to own a piece of him if he ever got into the ring.

Miss Dietrich said that her daughter was going to have another child soon. "I'll be a grandmother again, Papa," she said.

Hemingway gave her a bleak look. "I'm going to be a grand-father in a few months," he said. "My son Bumby's wife."

Mrs. Hemingway told me that Bumby was the nickname of her husband's eldest son, John, an Army captain stationed in Berlin. His two other sons, she said, were Patrick, known as Mouse, who was a twenty-one-year-old sophomore at Harvard, and was planning to get married in June, and Gregory, known as Gigi, who was eighteen and a freshman at St. John's, at Annapolis. In addition to the present Mrs. Hemingway, Patrick was going to invite to his wedding his and Gigi's mother, Pauline Pfeiffer, who was Hemingway's second wife. Bumby's mother and Hemingway's first wife was Hadley Richardson, now Mrs. Paul Scott Mowrer, and Hemingway's third wife was Martha Gellhorn.

"Everything you do, you do for the sake of the children," Miss Dietrich said.

"Everything for the children," Hemingway said. He refilled Miss Dietrich's glass.

"Thank you, Papa," she said, and sighed. She lived at the Plaza, she told him, but spent a good deal of her time at the apartment of her daughter, who lived on Third Avenue. "Papa, you should see me when they go out," she said, and took a sip of champagne. "I'm the baby-sitter. As soon as they leave the house, I go around and look in all the corners and straighten the drawers and clean up. I can't stand a house that isn't neat and clean. I go around in all the corners with towels I bring with me from the Plaza, and I clean up the whole house. Then they come home at one or two in the morning, and I take the dirty towels and some of the baby's things that need washing, and, with my bundle over my shoulder, I go out and get a taxi, and the driver, he thinks I am this old washerwoman from Third Avenue, and he takes me in the taxi and talks to me with sympathy, so I am afraid to let him take me to the Plaza. I get out a block away from the Plaza and I walk home with my bundle and I wash the baby's things, and then I go to sleep."

"Daughter, you're hitting them with the bases loaded," Hemingway said earnestly.

There was a ring at the door, and a bellboy brought in a florist's box. Mrs. Hemingway opened it and took out some green orchids, which were from her mother. Mrs. Hemingway put the flowers in a vase and said it was time to order supper.

As we ate, the Hemingways and Miss Dietrich talked about the war. All three had seen it at first hand. Mrs. Hemingway, who, as

Mary Welsh, was a *Time* correspondent in London, met Hemingway there during the war, and both saw a good deal of Miss Dietrich there and, later on, in Paris. Miss Dietrich was a U.S.O. entertainer, and performed on almost every front in the European theatre. She grew a little sad as she talked about the war. She had loved entertaining the troops, and the spirit overseas, she said, was the best she had ever found in people anywhere. "Everybody was the way people should be all the time," she continued. "Not mean and afraid but good to each other."

Hemingway raised his glass in a toast to her.

"I've finally figured out why Papa sometimes gets mean now that the war is over," Mrs. Hemingway said. "It's because there is no occasion for him to be valorous in peacetime."

"It was different in the war," Miss Dietrich said. "People were not so selfish and they helped each other."

Hemingway asked her about some recordings she had made, during the war, of popular American songs with lyrics translated into German, and said he'd like to have them. "I'll give you manuscript of new book for recordings if you want to trade even, daughter," he told her.

"Papa, I don't trade with you. I love you," said Miss Dietrich.

"You're the best that ever came into the ring," Hemingway said.

Late the next morning, I was awakened by a telephone call from Hemingway, who asked me to come right over to the hotel. He sounded urgent. I had a fast cup of coffee, and when I arrived at the suite, I found the door open and walked in. Hemingway was talking on the telephone. He was wearing an orange plaid bathrobe that looked too small for him, and he had a glass of champagne in one hand. His beard looked more scraggly than it had the day before. "My boy Patrick is coming down from Harvard and I'd like to reserve a room for him," he was saying into the telephone. " 'P,' as in 'Patrick.' " He paused and took a sip of champagne. "Much obliged. He'll be down from Harvard."

Hemingway hung up and, from his bathrobe pocket, took a box of pills. He shook two of them into the palm of his hand and downed them with a mouthful of champagne. He told me that he had been up since six, that his wife was still asleep, and that he had done enough work for that morning and wanted to talk, an activity he found relaxing. He always woke at daybreak, he explained, because his eyelids were especially thin and his eyes especially sensitive to light. "I have seen all the sunrises there have been in my life, and that's half a hundred years," he said. He had done considerable revision that morning on the manuscript. "I wake up in the morning and my mind starts making sentences, and I have to get rid of them fast—talk them or write them down," he said. "How did you like the Kraut?"

"Very much," I said.

"I love the Kraut and I love Ingrid," he said. "If I weren't married to Miss Mary and didn't love Miss Mary, I would try to hook up with either of them. Each one has what the other hasn't. And what each has, I love very much." For a moment, he looked bewildered, and then he said quickly, "Would never marry an actress, on account they have their careers and they work bad hours."

I asked him whether he still wanted to buy a coat, and he said sure but he didn't want to be rushed or crowded and it was cold outside. On a serving table near the couch were two champagne coolers, each containing ice and a bottle. He carried his glass over there and held up one of the bottles and squinted at it. It was empty. He put it back in the cooler, head down. Then he opened the other bottle, and as he poured some champagne into his glass, he sang, " 'So feed me am-mu-nition, keep me in the Third Division, your dog-face soldier boy's O.K.' " Breaking off, he said, "Song of the Third Infantry Division. I like this song when I need music inside myself to go on. I love all music, even opera. But I have no talent for it and cannot sing. I have a perfect goddam ear for music, but I can't play any instrument by ear—not even the piano. My mother used to make me play the cello. She took me out of school one year to learn the cello, when I wanted to be out in the fresh air playing football. She wanted to have chamber music in the house."

His briefcase was lying open on a chair near the desk, and the manuscript pages were protruding from it; someone seemed to have stuffed them into the briefcase without much care. Hemingway told me that he had been cutting the manuscript. "The test of a book is how much good stuff you can throw away," he said. "When I'm writing it, I'm just as proud as a goddam lion. I use the oldest words in the English language. People think I'm an ignorant bastard who doesn't know the ten-dollar words. I know the ten-dollar words. There are older and better words which if you arrange them in the proper combination you make it stick. Remember, anybody who pulls his erudition or education on you hasn't any. Also, daughter, remember that I never carried Teddy bears to bed with me since I was four. Now, with seventy-eight-year-old grand-mothers taking advantage of loopholes in the G.I. Bill of Rights whereby a gold-star mother can receive her son's education, I thought of establishing a scholarship and sending myself to Har-vard, because my Aunt Arabelle has always felt very bad that I am the only Hemingway boy that never went to college. But I have been so busy I have not got around to it. I only went to high school and a couple of military cram courses, and never took French. I began to learn to read French by reading the A.P. story in the French paper after reading the American A.P. story, and finally learned to read it by reading accounts of things I had seen—*les événements sportifs*—and from that and *les crimes* it was only a jump to Dr. de Maupassant, who wrote about things I had seen or could understand. Dumas, Daudet, Stendhal, who when I read him I knew that was the way I wanted to be able to write. Mr. Flaubert, who always threw them perfectly straight, hard, high, and inside. Then Mr. Baudelaire, that I learned my knuckle ball from, and Mr. Rimbaud, who never threw a fast ball in his life. Mr. Gide and Mr. Valéry I couldn't learn from. I think Mr. Valéry was too smart for me. Like Jack Britton and Benny Leonard."

Jack Britton, he continued, was a fighter he admired very much. "Jack Britton kept on his toes and moved around and never let them hit him solid," he said. "I like to keep on my toes and never let them hit me solid. Never lead against a hitter unless you can outhit him. Crowd a boxer," he said, assuming a boxing stance and holding his right hand, which was grasping the champagne glass, close to his chest. With his left hand, he punched at the air, saying, "Remember. Duck a swing. Block a hook. And counter a jab with everything you own." He straightened up and looked thoughtfully at his glass. Then he said, "One time, I asked Jack, speaking of a fight with Benny Leonard, 'How did you handle Benny so easy, Jack?' 'Ernie,' he said, 'Benny is an awfully smart boxer. All the time he's boxing, he's thinking. All the time he was thinking, I was hitting him.'" Hemingway gave a hoarse laugh, as though he had heard the story for the first time. "Jack moved very geometrically pure, never one hundredth of an inch too much. No one ever got a solid shot at him. Wasn't anybody he couldn't hit any time he wanted to." He laughed again. "'All the time he was thinking, I was hitting him.'" The anecdote, he told me, had been in the original version of his short story "Fifty Grand," but Scott Fitzgerald had persuaded him to take it out. "Scott thought everybody knew about it, when only Jack Britton and I knew about it, because Jack told it to me," he said. "So Scott told me to take it out. I didn't want to, but Scott was a successful writer and a writer I respected, so I listened to him and took it out."

Hemingway sat down on the couch and nodded his head sharply a couple of times to be sure he had my attention. "As you get older, it is harder to have heroes, but it is sort of necessary," he said. "I have a cat named Boise, who wants to be a human being," he went on slowly, lowering his voice to a kind of grumble. "So Boise eats everything that human beings eat. He chews Vitamin B Complex capsules, which are as bitter as aloes. He thinks I am holding out on him because I won't give him blood-pressure tablets, and because I let him go to sleep without Seconal." He gave a short, rumbling laugh. "I am a strange old man," he said. "How do you like it now, gentlemen?"

Fifty, Hemingway said, on reconsideration, is not supposed to be old. "It is sort of fun to be fifty and feel you are going to defend the title again," he said. "I won it in the twenties and defended it in the thirties and the forties, and I don't mind at all defending it in the fifties."

After a while, Mrs. Hemingway came into the room. She was wearing gray flannel slacks and a white blouse, and she said she felt wonderful, because she had had her first hot bath in six months. Then she said she was going out to do her errands, and suggested that Hemingway get dressed and go out and do his. He said that it was lunchtime, and that if they went out then, they would have to stop someplace for lunch, whereas if they had lunch sent up to the room, they might save time. Mrs. Hemingway said she would order lunch while he got dressed. Still holding his glass, he reluctantly got up from the couch. Then he finished his drink and went into the bedroom. By the time he came out—wearing the same outfit as the day before, except for a blue shirt with a button-down collar—a waiter had set the table for our lunch. We couldn't have lunch without a bottle of Tavel, Hemingway said, and we waited until the waiter had brought it before starting to eat.

Hemingway began with oysters, and he chewed each one very thoroughly. "Eat good and digest good," he told us.

"Papa, please get glasses fixed," Mrs. Hemingway said.

He nodded. Then he nodded a few times at me—a repetition of the sign for attention. "What I want to be when I am old is a wise old man who won't bore," he said, then paused while the waiter set a plate of asparagus and an artichoke before him and poured the Tavel. Hemingway tasted the wine and gave the waiter a nod. "I'd like to see all the new fighters, horses, ballets, bike riders, dames, bullfighters, painters, airplanes, sons of bitches, café characters, big international whores, restaurants, years of wine, newsreels, and never have to write a line about any of it," he said. "I'd like to write lots of letters to my friends and get back letters. Would like to be able to make love good until I was eighty-five, the way Clemenceau could. And what I would like to be is not Bernie Baruch. I wouldn't sit on park benches, although I might go around the park once in a while to feed the pigeons, and also I wouldn't have any long beard, so there could be an old man didn't look like Shaw." He stopped and ran the back of his hand along his beard, and looked around the room reflectively. "Have never met Mr. Shaw," he said. "Never been to Niagara Falls, either. Anyway, I would take up harness racing. You aren't up near the top at that until you're over seventy-five. Then I could get me a good young ball club, maybe, like Mr. Mack. Only, I wouldn't signal with a program, so as to break the pattern. Haven't figured out yet what I would signal with. And when that's over, I'll make the prettiest corpse since Pretty Boy Floyd. Only suckers worry about saving their souls. Who the hell should care about saving his soul when it is a man's duty to lose it intelligently, the way you would sell a position you were defending, if you could not hold it, as expensively as possible, trying to make it the most expensive position that was ever sold. It isn't hard to die." He opened his mouth and laughed, at first soundlessly and then loudly. "No more worries," he said. He picked up a long spear of asparagus with his fingers and looked at it without enthusiasm. "It takes a pretty good man to make any sense when he's dying," he said.

Mrs. Hemingway had finished eating, and she quickly finished her wine. Hemingway slowly finished his. I looked at my wristwatch, and found that it was almost three. The waiter started clearing the table, and we all got up. Hemingway stood looking sadly at the bottle of champagne, which was not yet empty. Mrs. Hemingway put on her coat, and I put on mine.

"The half bottle of champagne is the enemy of man," Hemingway said. We all sat down again.

"If I have any money, I can't think of any better way of spending money than on champagne," Hemingway said, pouring some.

When the champagne was gone, we left the suite. Downstairs, Mrs. Hemingway told us to remember to get glasses fixed, and scooted away.

Hemingway balked for a moment in front of the hotel. It was a cool, cloudy day. This was not good weather for him to be out in, he said sulkily, adding that his throat felt kind of sore. I asked him if he wanted to see a doctor. He said no. "I never trust a doctor I have to pay," he said, and started across Fifth Avenue. A flock of pigeons flew by. He stopped, looked up, and aimed an imaginary rifle at them. He pulled the trigger, and then looked disappointed. "Very difficult shot," he said. He turned quickly and pretended to shoot again. "Easy shot," he said. "Look!" He pointed to a spot on the pavement. He seemed to be feeling better, but not much better.

I asked him if he wanted to stop first at his optician's. He said no. I mentioned the coat. He shrugged. Mrs. Hemingway had suggested that he look for a coat at Abercrombie & Fitch, so I mentioned Abercrombie & Fitch. He shrugged again and lumbered slowly over to a taxi, and we started down Fifth Avenue in the afternoon traffic. At the corner of Fifty-fourth, we stopped on a signal from the traffic cop. Hemingway growled. "I love to see an Irish cop being cold," he said. "Give you eight to one he was an M.P. in the war. Very skillful cop. Feints and fakes good. Cops are not like they are in the Hellinger movies. Only once in a while." We started up again, and he showed me where he once walked across Fifth Avenue with Scott Fitzgerald. "Scott wasn't at Princeton any more, but he was still talking football," he said, without animation. "The ambition of Scott's life was to be on the football team. I said, 'Scott, why don't you cut out this football?' I said, 'Come on, boy.' He said, 'You're crazy.' That's the end of that story. If you can't get through traffic, how the hell are you gonna get through the line? But I am not Thomas Mann," he added. "Get another opinion."

By the time we reached Abercrombie's, Hemingway was moody again. He got out of the taxi reluctantly, and reluctantly entered the store. I asked him whether he wanted to look at a coat first or something else.

"Coat," he said unhappily.

In the elevator, Hemingway looked even bigger and bulkier than he had before, and his face had the expression of a man who is being forcibly subjected to the worst kind of misery. A middle-aged woman standing next to him stared at his scraggly white beard with obvious alarm and disapproval. "Good Christ!" Hemingway said suddenly, in the silence of the elevator, and the middle-aged woman looked down at her feet.

The doors opened at our floor, and we got out and headed for a rack of topcoats. A tall, dapper clerk approached us, and Hemingway shoved his hands into his pants pockets and crouched forward. "I think I still have credit in this joint," he said to the clerk.

The clerk cleared his throat. "Yes, sir," he said.

"Want to see coat," Hemingway said menacingly.

"Yes, sir," said the clerk. "What kind of coat did you wish to see, sir?"

"That one." He pointed to a straight-hanging, beltless tan

gabardine coat on the rack. The clerk helped him into it and gently drew him over to a full-length mirror. "Hangs like a shroud," Hemingway said, tearing the coat off. "I'm tall on top. Got any other coat?" he asked, as though he expected the answer to be no. He edged impatiently toward the elevators.

"How about this one, sir, with a removable lining, sir?" the clerk said. This one had a belt. Hemingway tried it on, studied himself in the mirror, and then raised his arms as though he were aiming a rifle. "You going to use it for *shooting*, sir?" the clerk asked. Hemingway grunted, and said he would take the coat. He gave the clerk his name, and the clerk snapped his fingers. "Of course!" he said. "There was *something* . . ." Hemingway looked embarrassed and said to send the coat to him at the Sherry-Netherland, and then said he'd like to look at a belt.

"What kind of belt, Mr. Hemingway?" the clerk asked.

"Guess a brown one," Hemingway said.

We moved over to the belt counter, and another clerk appeared.

"Will you show Mr. Hemingway a belt?" the first clerk said, and stepped back and thoughtfully watched Hemingway.

The second clerk took a tape measure from his pocket, saying he thought Hemingway was a size 44 or 46.

"Wanta bet?" Hemingway asked. He took the clerk's hand and punched himself in the stomach with it.

"Gee, he's got a hard tummy," the belt clerk said. He measured Hemingway's waistline. "Thirty-eight!" he reported. "Small waist for your size. What do you do—a lot of exercise?"

Hemingway hunched his shoulders, feinted, laughed, and looked happy for the first time since we'd left the hotel. He punched himself in the stomach with his own fist.

"Where you going—to Spain again?" the belt clerk asked.

"To Italy," Hemingway said, and punched himself in the stomach again. After Hemingway had decided on a brown calf belt, the clerk asked him whether he wanted a money belt. He said no—he kept his money in a checkbook.

Our next stop was the shoe department, and there Hemingway asked a clerk for some folding bedroom slippers.

"Pullman slippers," the clerk said. "What size?"

" 'Levens," Hemingway said bashfully. The slippers were produced, and he told the clerk he would take them. "I'll put them in my pocket," he said. "Just mark them, so they won't think I'm a shoplifter."

"You'd be surprised what's taken from the store," said the clerk, who was very small and very old. "Why, the other morning, someone on the first floor went off with a big roulette wheel. Just picked it up and—"

Hemingway was not listening. "Wolfie!" he shouted at a man who seemed almost seven feet tall and whose back was to us.

The man turned around. He had a big, square red face, and at the sight of Hemingway it registered extreme joy. "Papa!" he shouted.

The big man and Hemingway embraced and pounded each other on the back for quite some time. It was Winston Guest. Mr. Guest told us he was going upstairs to pick up a gun, and proposed that we come along. Hemingway asked what kind of gun, and Guest said a ten-gauge magnum.

"Beautiful gun," Hemingway said, taking his bedroom slippers from the clerk and stuffing them into his pocket.

In the elevator, Hemingway and Guest checked with each other on how much weight they had lost. Guest said he was now down to two hundred and thirty-five, after a good deal of galloping around on polo ponies. Hemingway said he was down to two hundred and eight, after shooting ducks in Cuba and working on his book.

"How's the book now, Papa?" Guest asked as we got out of the elevator.

Hemingway gave his fist-to-the-face laugh and said he was going to defend his title once more. "Wolfie, all of a sudden I found I could write wonderful again, instead of just biting on the nail," he said slowly. "I think it took a while for my head to get rebuilt inside. You should not, ideally, break a writer's head open or give him seven concussions in two years or break six ribs on him when he is forty-seven or push a rear-view-mirror support through the front of his skull opposite the pituitary gland, or, really, shoot at him too much. On the other hand, Wolfie, leave the sons of bitches alone and they are liable to start crawling back into the womb or somewhere if you drop a porkpie hat." He exploded into laughter.

Guest's huge frame shook with almost uncontrollable laughter. "God, Papa!" he said. "I still have your shooting clothes out at the island. When are you coming out to shoot, Papa?"

Hemingway laughed again and pounded him on the back. "Wolfie, you're so damn big!" he said.

Guest arranged to have his gun delivered, and then we all got into the elevator, the two of them talking about a man who caught a black marlin last year that weighed a thousand and six pounds.

"How do you like it now, gentlemen?" Hemingway asked.

"God, Papa!" said Guest.

On the ground floor, Guest pointed to a mounted elephant head on the wall. "Pygmy elephant, Papa," he said.

"Miserable elephant," said Hemingway.

Their arms around each other, they went out to the street. I said that I had to leave, and Hemingway told me to be sure to come over to the hotel early the next morning, so that I could go with him and Patrick to the Metropolitan Museum. As I walked off, I heard Guest say, "God, Papa, I'm not ashamed of anything I've ever done."

"Nor, oddly enough, am I," said Hemingway.

I looked around. They were punching each other in the stomach and laughing raucously.

The following morning, the door of the Hemingway suite was opened for me by Patrick, a shy young man of medium height, with large eyes and a sensitive face. He was wearing gray flannel slacks, a white shirt open at the collar, Argyle socks, and loafers. Mrs. Hemingway was writing a letter at the desk. As I came in, she looked up and said, "As soon as Papa has finished dressing, we're going to look at pictures." She went back to her letter.

Patrick told me that he'd just as soon spend the whole day looking at pictures, and that he had done a bit of painting himself. "Papa has to be back here for lunch with Mr. Scribner," he said, and added that he himself was going to stay in town until the next morning, when the Hemingways sailed. The telephone rang and he answered it. "Papa, I think it's Gigi calling you!" he shouted into the bedroom.

Hemingway emerged, in shirtsleeves, and went to the phone. "How are you, kid?" he said into it, then asked Gigi to come down to the Finca for his next vacation. "You're welcome down there, Gigi," he said. "You know that cat you liked? The one you named Smelly? We renamed him Ecstasy. Every one of our cats knows his own name." After hanging up, he told me that Gigi was a wonderful shot—that when he was eleven he had won second place in the shoot championship of Cuba. "Isn't that the true gen, Mouse?" he asked.

"That's right, Papa," said Patrick.

I wanted to know what "true gen" meant, and Hemingway explained that it was British slang for "information," from "intelligence." "It's divided into three classes: gen; the true gen, which is as true as you can state it; and the really true gen, which you can operate on," he said.

He looked at the green orchids. "My mother never sent me any flowers," he said. His mother was about eighty, he said, and lived in River Forest, Illinois. His father, who was a physician, had been dead for many years; he shot himself when Ernest was a boy. "Let's get going if we're going to see the pictures," he said. "I told Charlie Scribner to meet me here at one. Excuse me while I wash. In big city, I guess you wash your neck." He went back into the bedroom. While he was gone, Mrs. Hemingway told me that Ernest was the second of six children—Marcelline, then Ernest, Ursula, Madelaine, Carol, and the youngest, his only brother, Leicester. All the sisters were named after saints. Every one of the children was married; Leicester was living in Bogotá, Colombia, where he was attached to the United States Embassy.

Hemingway came out in a little while, wearing his new coat. Mrs. Hemingway and Patrick put on their coats, and we went downstairs. It was raining, and we hurried into a taxi. On the way to the Metropolitan, Hemingway said very little; he just hummed to himself and watched the street. Mrs. Hemingway told me that he was usually unhappy in taxis, because he could not sit in the front seat to watch the road ahead. He looked out the window and pointed to a flock of birds flying across the sky. "In this town, birds fly, but they're not serious about it," he said. "New York birds don't climb."

When we drew up at the Museum entrance, a line of school-children was moving in slowly. Hemingway impatiently led us past them. In the lobby, he paused, pulled a silver flask from one of his coat pockets, unscrewed its top, and took a long drink. Putting the flask back in his pocket, he asked Mrs. Hemingway whether she wanted to see the Goyas first or the Breughels. She said the Breughels.

"I learned to write by looking at paintings in the Luxembourg Museum in Paris," he said. "I never went past high school. When you've got a hungry gut and the museum is free, you go to the museum. Look," he said, stopping before "Portrait of a Man," which has been attributed to both Titian and Giorgione. "They were old Venice boys, too."

"Here's what I like, Papa," Patrick said, and Hemingway joined his son in front of "Portrait of Federigo Gonzaga (1500-1540)," by Francesco Francia. It shows, against a landscape, a small boy with long hair and a cloak.

"This is what we try to do when we write, Mousie," Hemingway said, pointing to the trees in the background. "We always have this in when we write."

Mrs. Hemingway called to us. She was looking at "Portrait of the Artist," by Van Dyck. Hemingway looked at it, nodded approval, and said, "In Spain, we had a fighter pilot named Whitey Dahl, so Whitey came to me one time and said, 'Mr. Hemingway, is Van Dyck a good painter?' I said, 'Yes, he is.' He said, 'Well, I'm glad, because I have one in my room and I like it very much, and I'm glad he's a good painter because I like him.' The next day, Whitey was shot down."

We all walked over to Rubens' "The Triumph of Christ Over Sin and Death." Christ is shown surrounded by snakes and angels and is being watched by a figure in a cloud. Mrs. Hemingway and Patrick said they thought it didn't look like the usual Rubens.

"Yeah, he did that all right," Hemingway said authoritatively.

"You can tell the real just as a bird dog can tell. Smell them. Or from having lived with very poor but very good painters."

That settled that, and we went on to the Breughel room. It was closed, we discovered. The door bore a sign that read "NOW UNDERTAKING REPAIRS."

"They have our indulgence," Hemingway said, and took another drink from his flask. "I sure miss the good Breughel," he said as we moved along. "It's the great one, of the harvesters. It is a lot of people cutting grain, but he uses the grain geometrically, to make an emotion that is so strong for me that I can hardly take it." We came to El Greco's green "View of Toledo" and stood looking at it a long time. "This is the best picture in the Museum for me, and Christ knows there are some lovely ones," Hemingway said.

Patrick admired several paintings Hemingway didn't approve of. Every time this happened, Hemingway got into an involved technical discussion with his son. Patrick would shake his head and laugh and say he respected Hemingway's opinions. He didn't argue much. "What the hell!" Hemingway said suddenly. "I don't want to be an art critic. I just want to look at pictures and be happy with them and learn from them. Now, this for me is a damn good picture." He stood back and peered at a Reynolds entitled "Colonel George Coussmaker," which shows the Colonel leaning against a tree and holding his horse's bridle. "Now, this Colonel is a son of a bitch who was willing to pay money to the best portrait painter of his day just to have himself painted," Hemingway said, and gave a short laugh. "Look at the man's arrogance and the strength in the neck of the horse and the way the man's legs hang. He's so arrogant he can afford to lean against a tree."

We separated for a while and looked at paintings individually, and then Hemingway called us over and pointed to a picture labelled, in large letters, "Catharine Lorillard Wolfe" and, in small ones, "By Cabanel." "This is where I got confused as a kid, in Chicago," he said. "My favorite painters for a long time were Bunte and Ryerson, two of the biggest and wealthiest families in Chicago. I always thought the names in big letters were the painters."

After we reached the Cézannes and Degas and the other Impressionists, Hemingway became more and more excited, and discoursed on what each artist could do and how and what he had learned from each. Patrick listened respectfully and didn't seem want to talk about painting techniques any more. Hemingway spent several minutes looking at Cézanne's "Rocks—Forest of Fontainebleau." "This is what we try to do in writing, this and this, and the woods, and the rocks we have to climb over," he said. "Cézanne is my painter, after the early painters. Wonder, wonder painter. Degas was another wonder painter. I've never seen a bad Degas. You know what he did with the bad Degas? He burned them."

Hemingway took another long drink from his flask. We came to Manet's pastel portrait of Mlle. Valtesse de la Bigne, a young woman with blond hair coiled on the top of her head. Hemingway was silent for a while, looking at it; finally he turned away. "Manet could show the bloom people have when they're still innocent and before they've been disillusioned," he said.

As we walked along, Hemingway said to me, "I can make a landscape like Mr. Paul Cézanne. I learned how to make a landscape from Mr. Paul Cézanne by walking through the Luxembourg Museum a thousand times with an empty gut, and I am pretty sure that if Mr. Paul was around, he would like the way I make them and be happy that I learned it from him." He had learned a lot from Mr. Johann Sebastian Bach, too. "In the first paragraphs of 'Farewell,' I used the word 'and' consciously over and over the way Mr. Johann Sebastian Bach used a note in music when he was emitting counterpoint. I can almost write like Mr. Johann sometimes—or, anyway, so he would like it. All such people are easy to deal with, because we all know you have to learn."

"Papa, look at this," Patrick said. He was looking at "Meditation on the Passion," by Carpaccio. Patrick said it had a lot of strange animals in it for a religious painting.

"Huh!" Hemingway said. "Those painters always put the sacred scenes in the part of Italy they liked best or where they came from or where their girls came from. They made their girls the Madonnas. This is supposed to be Palestine, and Palestine is a long way off, he figures. So he puts in a red parrot, and he puts in deer and a leopard. And then he thinks, This is the Far East and it's far away. So he puts in the Moors, the traditional enemy of the Venetians." He paused and looked to see what else the painter had put in his picture. "Then he gets hungry, so he puts in rabbits," he said. "Goddam, Mouse, we saw a lot of good pictures. Mouse, don't you think two hours is a long time looking at pictures?"

Everybody agreed that two hours was a long time looking at pictures, so Hemingway said that we would skip the Goyas, and that we would all go to the Museum again when they returned from Europe.

It was still raining when we came out of the Museum. "Goddam, I hate to go out in the rain," Hemingway said. "Goddam, I hate to get wet."

Charles Scribner was waiting in the lobby of the hotel. "Ernest," he said, shaking Hemingway's hand. He was a dignified, solemn, slow-speaking gentleman with silvery hair.

"We've been looking at pictures, Charlie," Hemingway said as we went up in the elevator. "They have some pretty good pictures now, Charlie."

Scribner nodded and said, "Yuh, yuh."

"Was fun for country boy like me," Hemingway said.

"Yuh, yuh," said Scribner.

We went into the suite and took off our coats, and Hemingway said we would have lunch right there. He called room service, and Mrs. Hemingway sat down at the desk to finish her letter. Hemingway sat down on the couch with Mr. Scribner and began telling him that he had been jamming, like a rider in a six-day bike race, and Patrick sat quietly in a corner and watched his father. The waiter came in and passed out menus. Scribner said he was going to order the most expensive item on the menu, because Hemingway was paying for it. He laughed tentatively, and Patrick laughed to keep him company. The waiter retired with our orders, and Scribner and Hemingway talked business for a while. Scribner wanted to know whether Hemingway had the letters he had written to him.

Hemingway said, "I carry them everyplace I go, Charlie, together with a copy of the poems of Robert Browning."

Scribner nodded and, from the inner pocket of his jacket, took some papers—copies of the contract for the new book, he said. The contract provided for an advance of twenty-five thousand dollars against royalties, beginning at fifteen per cent.

Hemingway signed the contract, and got up from the couch. Then he said, "Never ran as no genius, but I'll defend the title again against all the good young new ones." He lowered his head, put his left foot forward, and jabbed at the air with a left and a right. "Never let them hit you solid," he said.

Scribner wanted to know where Hemingway could be reached in Europe. Care of the Guaranty Trust Company in Paris, Hemingway told him. "When we took Paris, I tried to take that bank and got smacked back," he said, and laughed a shy laugh. "I thought it would be awfully nice if I could take my own bank."

"Yuh, yuh," Scribner said. "What are you planning to do in Italy, Ernest?"

Hemingway said he would work part of each day and see his Italian friends and go duckhunting in the mornings. "We shot three hundred and thirty-one ducks to six guns there one morning," he said. "Mary shot good, too."

Mrs. Hemingway looked up. "Any girl who marries Papa has to learn how to carry a gun," she said, and returned to her letter-writing.

"I went hunting once in Suffolk, England," Scribner said. Everyone waited politely for him to continue. "I remember they gave me goose eggs to eat for breakfast in Suffolk. Then we went out to shoot. I didn't know how to get my gun off safe."

"Hunting is sort of a good life," Hemingway said. "Better than Westport or Bronxville, I think."

"After I learned how to get my gun off safe, I couldn't hit anything," Scribner said.

"I'd like to make the big Monte Carlo shoot and the Championship of the World at San Remo," Hemingway said. "I'm in pretty good shape to shoot either one. It's not a spectator sport at all. But exciting to do and wonderful to manage. I used to handle Wolfie in big shoots. He is a great shot. It was like handling a great horse."

"I finally got one," Scribner said timidly.

"Got what?" asked Hemingway.

"A rabbit," Scribner said. "I shot this rabbit."

"They haven't held the big Monte Carlo shoot since 1939," Hemingway said. "Only two Americans ever won it in seventy-four years. Shooting gives me a good feeling. A lot of it is being together and friendly instead of feeling you are in some place where everybody hates you and wishes you ill. It is faster than baseball, and you are out on one strike."

The telephone rang, and Hemingway picked it up, listened, said a few words, and then turned to us and said that an outfit called Endorsements, Inc., had offered him four thousand dollars to pose as a Man of Distinction. "I told them I wouldn't drink the stuff for four thousand dollars," he said. "I told them I was a champagne man. Am trying to be a good guy, but it's a difficult trade. What you win in Boston, you lose in Chicago."

—1950

7

PICTURE

1   *Throw the Little Old Lady Down the Stairs!*

THE MAKING OF THE Metro-Goldwyn-Mayer movie "The Red Badge of Courage," based on the Stephen Crane novel about the Civil War, was preceded by routine disclosures about its production plans from the columnist Louella Parsons ("John Huston is writing a screen treatment of Stephen Crane's classic, 'The Red Badge of Courage,' as a possibility for an M-G-M picture"), from the columnist Hedda Hopper ("Metro has an option on 'The Red Badge of Courage' and John Huston's working up a budget for it. But there's no green light yet"), and from Variety ("Pre-production work on 'Red Badge of Courage' commenced at Metro with thesp-tests for top roles in drama"), and it was preceded, in the spring of 1950, by a routine visit by John Huston, who is both a screen writer and a director, to New York, the headquarters of Loew's, Inc., the company that produces and distributes M-G-M pictures. On the occasion of his visit, I decided to follow the history of that particular movie from beginning to end, in order to learn whatever I might learn about the American motion-picture industry.

Huston, at forty-three, was one of the most admired, rebellious, and shadowy figures in the world of motion pictures. I had seen him a year before, when he came here to accept an award of a trip around the world for his film contributions to world unity. He had talked of an idea he had for making a motion picture about the nature of the world while he was going around it. Then he had flown back to Hollywood, and to the demands of his employers, Metro-Goldwyn-Mayer, and had made "The Asphalt Jungle," a picture about a band of criminals engaged in pursuits that Huston described somewhere in the dialogue of the movie as "a left-handed form of human endeavor." Now, on this visit, shortly after the sudden death, in Hollywood, of his father, Walter Huston, he telephoned me from his Waldorf Tower suite and said he was having a terrible time trying to make "The Red Badge of Courage." Louis B. Mayer and most of the other top executives at M-G-M, he said, were opposed to the entire project. "You know something?" he said, over the telephone. He has a theatrical way of inflecting his voice that can give a commonplace query a rich and melodramatic intensity. "They don't want me to make this picture. And I want to make this picture." He made the most of every syllable, so that it seemed at that moment to lie under his patent and have some special urgency. "Come on over, kid, and I'll tell you all about the hassle," he said.

The door of Huston's suite was opened by a conservatively at-tired young man with a round face and pink cheeks. He introduced himself as Arthur Fellows. "John is in the next room getting dressed," he said. "Imagine getting a layout like this all to your-self! That's the way the big studios do things." He nodded with approval at the Waldorf's trappings. "Not that I care for the big studios," he said. "I believe in being independent. I work for David Selznick. I've worked for David for fifteen years. David is independent. I look at the picture business as a career. Same as banking, or medicine, or law. You've got to learn it from the ground up. I learned it from the ground up with David. I was an assistant director on 'Duel in the Sun.' I directed the scene of the fight between two horses. Right now, I'm here temporarily on publicity and promotion. David—" He broke off as Huston strode into the room. Huston made his entrance in the manner of an actor who is determined to win the immediate attention of his audience.

"Hel-lo, kid," Huston said as we shook hands. He took a step back, then put his hands in his trouser pockets and leaned forward intently. "Well!" he said. He made the word expand into a major pronouncement.

Huston is a lean, rangy man, two inches over six feet tall, with long arms and long hands, long legs and long feet. He has thick black hair, and it had been slicked down with water, but some of the front strands fell raffishly over his forehead. He has a deeply creased, leathery face, high cheekbones, and slanting reddish-brown eyes. His ears are flattened against the sides of his head, and the bridge of his nose is bashed in. His eyes looked watchful, and yet strangely empty of all feeling, in weird contrast to the heartiness of his manner. He took his hands out of his pockets and yanked at his hair. "Well!" he said, again as though he were making a major pronouncement. He turned to Fellows. "Art, order some Martinis, will you, kid?"

Huston sat down on the arm of a chair, fixed a long brown cigarette in one corner of his mouth, took a kitchen match from his trouser pocket, and scraped the head of the match into flame with his thumbnail. He lit the cigarette and drew deeply on it, half closing his eyes against the smoke, which seemed to make them slant still more. Then he rested his elbows on his knees, holding the cigarette to his mouth with two fingers of one hand, and looked out the window. The sun had gone down, and the light coming into the suite, high in the Tower, was beginning to dull. Huston looked as though he might be waiting—having set up a Huston scene—for the cameras to roll. But, as I gradually grew to realize, life was not imitating art, Huston was not imitating himself, when he set up such a scene; on the contrary, the style of the Huston pictures, Huston being one of the few Hollywood directors who manage to leave their personal mark on the films they make, was the style of the man. In appearance, in gestures, in manner of speech, in the selection of the people and objects he surrounded himself with, and in the way he composed them into individual "shots" (the abrupt closeup of the thumbnail scraping the head of a kitchen match) and then arranged his shots in a dramatic sequence, he was simply the raw material of his own art; that is, the man whose personality left its imprint, unmistakably, on what had come to be known as a Huston picture.

"I just love the light at this time of the day," Huston said as Fellows returned from the phone. "Art, don't you just love the light at this time of the day?"

Fellows said it was all right.

Huston gave a chuckle. "Well, now," he said, "here I am, spending the studio's money on this trip, and I don't even know whether I'm going to make the picture I'm here for. I'm auditioning actors at the Loew's office and talking production up there and doing all the publicity things they tell me to do. I've got the 'Red Badge' script O.K.'d, and I'm going down South to pick locations for the picture, but nothing is moving. We can't make this picture unless we have six hundred Confederate uniforms and six hundred Union uniforms. And the studio is just not making those uniforms for us. I'm beginning to think they don't *want* the picture!"

"It's an offbeat picture," Fellows said politely. "The public wants pictures like 'Ma and Pa Kettle.' I say make pictures the public wants. Over here," he said to a waiter who had entered with a tray holding six Martinis in champagne glasses. "No getting away from it, John," Fellows went on, handing Huston a drink. "Biggest box-office draws are pictures catering to the intelligence of the twelve-year-old."

People underestimated the intelligence of the twelve-year-old, Huston said. He said he had an adopted son in his early teens, a Mexican-Indian orphan, Pablo, whom he had found while making "Treasure of Sierra Madre" in Mexico a few years ago, and his boy had excellent taste in pictures. "Why, my boy Pablo reads Shakespeare," he said. "Do you read Shakespeare, Art?"

"Television, John," said Fellows. "The junk they go for on television."

Huston asked him vaguely what the talk was in New York about television.

Television was booming, Fellows said, and all the actors, singers, dancers, directors, producers, and writers who hadn't been able to get work in Hollywood were going into television in New York. On the other hand, all the actors, singers, dancers, directors, producers, and writers who had gone into television in New York were starving and wanted to go back to Hollywood. "Nobody really knows what's happening," said Fellows. "All I know is television can never do what pictures can do."

"We'll just make pictures and release them on television, that's all. The hell with television," Huston said. "Do you kids want the lights on?" The room was murky. It made a fine tableau, Huston said. Fellows and I agreed that it was pleasant with the lights off. There was a brief silence. Huston moved like a shadow to a chair opposite mine and lit another brown cigarette, the quick glow from the match lighting up his face. "Been to the races out here, Art?" he asked.

A few times, Fellows said, but David Selznick had been keeping him so busy he hadn't had much time for horses.

"The ponies have me broke all the time," Huston said. "You know, I can't write a check for five hundred dollars. I am always broke. I can't even take an ordinary vacation. But there's nothing I'd rather spend my money on than a horse, especially when the horse is one of my own. There's nothing like breeding and raising a horse of your own. I've got four horses racing under my colors right now, and in a couple of years I'll have more, even if I have to go into hock to support them. All I want is one good winner of my own. Everybody I know is conspiring to take my horses away from me. Someday I'll have one good winner, and I'll be able to say, 'Well, you bastards, this is what it was all about!' "

Financial problems, Huston said, had prevented him from taking the trip around the world. Although his M-G-M salary was four thousand dollars a week while he was making a picture, he had had to get the company to advance him a hundred and fifty thousand dollars, which he was paying off in installments. He was bound by his contract to make at least one picture a year for the next three years for M-G-M. He was a partner in an independent company, Horizon Pictures, which he had started a couple of years before with a man named Sam Spiegel, whom he had met in the early thirties in London. Huston had directed one picture, "We Were Strangers," for Horizon, and he was scheduled to direct another— "The African Queen," based on the novel by C. S. Forester—as soon as he had completed "The Red Badge of Courage" for M-G-M. Huston said he thought "The African Queen" would make money, and if it did, he would then make some pictures on his own that he wanted to make as much as he did "The Red Badge of Courage." The reason L. B. Mayer and the other M-G-M executives did not think that "The Red Badge of Courage" could be a commercial success, Huston said, was that it had no standard plot, no romance, and no leading female characters, and, if Huston had his way in casting it, would have no stars. It was simply the story of a youth who ran away from his first battle in the Civil War, and then returned to the front and distinguished himself by performing several heroic acts. Huston, like Stephen Crane, wanted to show something of the emotions of men in war, and the ironically thin line between cowardice and heroism. A few months earlier, Huston and an M-G-M producer named Gottfried Reinhardt, the son of the late Max Reinhardt, had suggested to Dore Schary, the studio's vice-president in charge of production, that they make the picture.

"Dore loved the idea," Huston said. "And Dore said he would read the novel." A couple of weeks later, Schary had asked Huston to write a screen treatment—a rough outline for the detailed script. "I did my treatment in four days," Huston said. "I was going down to Mexico to get married, so I took my secretary along and dictated part of it on the plane going down, got married, dictated some more after the ceremony, and dictated the rest on the plane trip back." Schary approved the treatment, and the cost of making the picture was estimated at a million and a half dollars. Huston wrote the screenplay in five weeks, and Schary approved it. "Then the strangest things began to happen," Huston said. "Dore is called vice-president in charge of production. L. B. is called vice-president in charge of the studio. Nobody knows which is boss." His voice rose dramatically. "We were told Dore had to O.K. everything. We got his O.K., but nothing moved. And we know that L.B. hates the idea of making this picture." His voice sank to a confidential whisper. "He just hates it!"

For the role of the Youth, Huston said, he wanted twenty-six-year-old Audie Murphy, the most-decorated hero of the Second World War, whose film career had been limited to minor roles. Huston said he was having some difficulty persuading both Schary and Reinhardt to let Murphy have the part. "They'd rather have a star," he said indignantly. "They just don't see Audie the way I do. This little, gentle-eyed creature. Why, in the war he'd literally go out of his way to find Germans to kill. He's a gentle little killer."

"Another Martini?" Fellows asked.

"I hate stars," Huston said, exchanging his empty glass for a full one. "They're not actors. I've been around actors all my life, and I like them, and yet I never had an actor as a friend. Except Dad. And Dad never thought of himself as an actor. But the best actor I ever worked with was Dad. All I had to tell Dad about his part of the old man in 'Treasure' was to talk fast. Just talk fast." Huston talked rapidly, in a startling and accurate imitation of his father. "A man who talks fast never listens to himself. Dad talked like this. Man talking fast is an honest man. Dad was a man who never tried to sell anybody anything."

It was now quite dark in the room. We sat in the darkness for a while without talking, and then Huston got up and went over to the light switch. He asked if we were ready for light, and then snapped the switch. He was revealed in the sudden yellow brightness, standing motionless, a look of bewilderment on his face. "I hate this scene," he said. "Let's go out and get something to eat."

Huston finished his drink in a gulp, set the glass down, and put a gray homburg on his head, and the three of us rode down in the elevator. It was a warm, drizzly evening. The Waldorf doorman got us a cab, and Huston told the driver to take us to "21." He raised one of the jump seats and rested his knees against it. "You know, I just love New York when summer is coming in," he said, emphasizing each word possessively. "Everything begins to slow down a little. And later on, the clatter and hassling sort of comes to a stop. And the city is quiet. And you can take walks!" he said in a tone of amazement. "And you pass bars!" he said, as though this were even more astonishing. "And the doors of the bars are open," he said, holding up his hands, palms toward each other, framing a picture of an open door. "You can go anywhere alone, and yet you're never alone in the summer in New York," he said, and dropped his hands to his lap.

Huston first came to New York in 1919, when he was thirteen, to spend the summer with his father, who had been divorced from his mother several years before. John was born in the town of Nevada, Missouri, and had spent the better part of his childhood with his mother, first in Weatherford, Texas, and then in Los Angeles. His mother, who died in 1938, had been a newspaper-woman. For three years before coming to New York, Huston had been bedridden with what was called an enlarged heart, and he also suffered from an obscure kidney ailment. When he recovered, he went to visit his father. He had a marvellous birthday in New York the summer he turned eighteen, he said. He had come East again from Los Angeles, where he had won the amateur light-weight boxing championship of California, and he had moved into a small fourth-floor apartment on Macdougal Street; the apartment above was occupied by Sam Jaffe (the actor who, years later, played the part of the German safe-cracker in "The Asphalt Jungle"). Huston's father, who was appearing on Broadway in "Desire Under the Elms," came to the birthday celebration. Jaffe had asked John what he wanted as a present, and he had said a horse. "Well," he said, "Sam"—and there was great affection in his pronouncing of the name—"the kindest, most retiring guy in the world, had gone out and bought the oldest, saddest, most worn-out gray mare. It was all wonderful. The best birthday I ever had. Art, don't you just love New York in the summer?"

Not to live in, Fellows said, and Huston said, with a sigh, that it would be difficult to keep horses in New York, and besides, when you came right down to it, he really liked the way of life in the motion-picture world.

"It's the jungle," he said. "It appeals to my nature. Louella Parsons and her atavistic nonsense. I really like Louella. She's part of the jungle. It's more than a place where streets are named after Sam Goldwyn and buildings after Bing Crosby. There's more to it than pink Cadillacs with leopard-skin seat covers. It's the jungle, and it harbors an industry that's one of the biggest in the country. A closed-in, tight, frantically inbred, and frantically competitive jungle. And the rulers of the jungle are predatory and fascinating and tough. L. B. Mayer is one of the rulers of the jungle." He lowered his voice impressively. "I like L.B. He's a ruler now, but he has to watch his step or he'll be done in. He's shrewd. He's big business. He didn't know a thing about horses, but when he took up horses, he built up one of the finest stables in the country. L.B. is tough. He's never trying to win the point you're talking about. His aim is always long-range—to keep control of the studio. He loves Dore. But someday he'll destroy Dore. L.B. is sixty-five. And he's pink. And healthy. And smiling. Dore is about twenty years younger. And he looks old. And sick. And worried. Because L.B. guards the jungle like a lion. But the very top rulers of the jungle are here in New York. Nick Schenck, the president of Loew's, Inc., the ruler of the rulers, stays here in New York and smiles, watching from afar, from behind the scenes, but he's the real power, watching the pack close in on one or another of the lesser rulers—close in, ready to pounce! Nick Schenck never gets his picture in the papers, and he doesn't go to parties, and he avoids going out in public, but he's the real king of the pack. And he does it all from New York!" He uttered an eerie, choked laugh through clenched teeth. "God, are they tough!"

The taxi drew up before "21." "Mr. Huston!" the doorman said, and Huston shook hands with him. "Welcome back, Mr. Huston."

It was close to midnight when Huston and Fellows and I emerged. Huston suggested that we walk, because he loved to walk at that time of the night. The drizzling rain had stopped and the air was clear, but the street was wet and shining. Huston said he wanted to go over to Third Avenue, because he liked to see into the bars there and because nobody over there looked like a studio vice-president. We headed for Third Avenue.

As we walked down Third Avenue, Huston started to take

fast, important strides. "You know what I like about making this picture, Art?" he said. "I'm going to be out in the country. On location." Walking along, he glanced into shop windows displaying silver plate and paintings. He stopped for a moment in front of the dusty window of an art shop and looked at a reproduction of a painting. "Modigliani," he said. "I used to spend hours in this town looking at Modiglianis." He had once done considerable painting himself, he said, but in recent years he had done little. We moved on, and suddenly, in the middle of the wet, glistening walk, we saw a man lying motionless, face down. He had one arm in the sleeve of a torn brown overcoat, and the other arm was underneath him, the empty sleeve of the coat folded back over his head. His shoes were scuffed and ragged and they were pointed in toward each other. Half a dozen spectators stood gazing silently at the figure on the sidewalk. Huston immediately took charge. Putting his hands in his trouser pockets, he gave a peculiar quarter twist to his body. He took just a moment to push his hat back on his head, then squatted beside the motionless figure. He let another moment go by without doing anything, while the group of spectators grew. Everyone was very quiet. Huston lifted the hand in the overcoat sleeve and felt for the pulse. The Third Avenue "L" rattled noisily by overhead, and then there was silence again. Huston held the man's wrist for quite a long time, never looking up at the crowd. Then he took quite a long time putting the man's arm back in its original position. Huston rose slowly to his feet. He fixed his hat forward. He put his hands back in his pockets. Then he turned to the audience, and, projecting his words with distinct care, he said, "He's—just—fine!" He gave a thick, congested laugh through his closed teeth. He tapped his hat forward with satisfaction, and jauntily led us away. It was a scene from a Huston movie.

Five weeks later, Huston was back at the Waldorf, in the same suite. When he telephoned me this time, he sounded cheerful. During his absence, "The Asphalt Jungle" had opened in New York and had been reviewed enthusiastically, but he didn't mention that; what he felt good about was that he had just bought a new filly from Calumet Farms. When I went over to see him that evening, he was alone in his suite. Two days before, he had found a superb location for "The Red Badge of Courage" outside Nashville.

When Huston had returned to the studio after his Eastern trip, he told me, he had found that no preparations at all were under way for "The Red Badge of Courage." "Those uniforms just weren't being made!" he said with amazement. "I went to see L.B., and L.B. told me he had no faith in the picture. He didn't believe it would make money. Gottfried and I went to see Dore. We found Dore at home, sick in bed. The moment we entered, he said, 'Boys, we'll make this picture!' Maybe it was Nick Schenck who gave Dore the go-ahead sign. Anyway, that night Dore wrote a letter to L.B. and said in the letter he thought M-G-M ought to make the picture. And the next morning L.B. called us in and talked for six hours about why this picture would not make any money. You know, I like L.B. He said that Dore was a wonderful boy, that he loved Dore like his own son. And he said that he could not deny a boy who wrote that kind of letter to him. And when we came out of L.B.'s office, the studio was bubbling, and the uniforms were being made!" Huston chortled. He picked up a pad of paper and started sketching horses as he talked. He and Reinhardt, he said, had found a marvellous actor named Royal Dano to play the part of the Tattered Man, and Dano had that singular quality that makes for greatness on the screen. Charlie Chaplin and Greta Garbo have that quality, he said. "The screen exaggerates and magnifies whatever it is that a great actor has," he said. "It's almost as though greatness were a matter of quality rather than ability. Dad had it. He had that something people felt in him. You sense it every time you're near it. You see it in Audie Murphy's eyes. It's like a great horse. You go past his stall and you can feel the vibration in there. You can feel it. So I'm going to make the picture, kid. I'm going to direct it on horseback. I've always wanted to direct a picture on horseback."

The expenses at the Nashville site, he said, would be less than at the one he had originally hoped to get, in Leesburg, Virginia, and its terrain lent itself perfectly to the kind of photography he wanted

—a sharply contrasting black-and-white approximating the texture and atmosphere of the Brady photographs of the Civil War.

"Tell you what," Huston said, in his amazed tone. "I'm going to show you how we make a picture! And then you can come out to Hollywood and you can see everything that happens to the picture out there! And you can meet Gottfried! And Dore! And L.B.! And everybody! And you can meet my horses! Will you do it?"

I said I would.

Several weeks later, Huston telephoned again, this time from California. He was going to start making "The Red Badge of Courage" in a month, and the location was not going to be in Tennessee, after all, but on his own ranch, in the San Fernando Valley. He didn't sound too happy about it. "You'd better get out here for the fireworks," he said. "We're going to have the Civil War right here on the Coast."

When I arrived on the West Coast, Huston set about arranging for me to meet everybody who had anything to do with "The Red Badge of Courage." The day I met Gottfried Reinhardt, the thirty-nine-year-old producer of "The Red Badge of Courage," he was sitting in his office at the Metro-Goldwyn-Mayer studio in Culver City, studying the estimated budget for the picture. It would be the fifteen-hundred-and-twelfth picture to be put into production since Metro-Goldwyn-Mayer was founded, on May 24, 1924. The mimeographed booklet containing the estimate was stamped "Production No. 1512." (The estimate, I learned later on, informed Reinhardt that the picture would be allotted nine rehearsal days and thirty-four production days; the footage of the finished film was expected to come to 7,865 feet; the total cost was expected to be $1,434,789.) Reinhardt's office was a comfortable one. It was a suite, which included a small bath and a conference room furnished with leather armchairs. A brass plate engraved with his name was on the door. In his private office, in addition to a desk and several green leather armchairs and a green leather couch, he had a thick brown carpet, a bookcase with a set of the Encyclopædia Britannica, and a potted plant six feet high. The walls were hung with old prints. On his desk, near several large cigarette lighters, a couple of ball-point pens, and a leather cigar box, stood a framed photograph of Max Reinhardt. The elder Reinhardt had a look of gentle but troubled thoughtfulness. There was a considerable resemblance between father and son.

"Where you have your office is a sign of your importance," Reinhardt told me as we sat around talking. "I'm on the first floor. Dore Schary is two floors up, right over me. L.B. is also two floors up. I have a washbasin but no shower in my office. Dore has a shower but no bathtub. L.B. has a shower and a bathtub. The kind of bath facilities you have in your office is another measure of the worth of your position." He smiled sardonically. "An important director is almost as important as a producer," he continued, getting up and straightening one of the prints. "John's office is a corner one, like mine."

Reinhardt is a paunchy man with a thick mane of wavy brown hair; in his cocoa-brown silk shantung suit, he looked like a Teddy bear. There was a cigar in his mouth and an expression of profound cynicism on his face. A heavy gold key chain hung in a deep loop from under his coat to a trouser pocket. He speaks with a German accent but without harshness, and his words come out pleasantly, in an even, regretful-sounding way. "We promised Dore that we would make our picture for one million five or under, and that we would make it in about thirty days," he said, sitting down at his desk again. He put a hand on the estimate and sighed heavily. "The producer's job is to save time and money." He bobbed his head as he talked. A strand of hair fell over his face. He replaced it and puffed at his cigar in a kind of restrained frenzy. Then he removed the cigar and, bobbing his head again, said, "When you tell people you have made a picture, they do not ask, 'Is it a good picture?' They ask, 'How many days?' " He tapped the ash from his cigar tenderly into a tray and gave another heavy sigh.

Reinhardt, who was born in Berlin, arrived in the United States in 1932, at the age of nineteen, for a visit. He had been over here a few months when Hitler came to power in Germany, and he decided to stay. Ernst Lubitsch, who had worked with the elder Reinhardt in Europe, offered Gottfried a job, without pay, at Paramount, as his assistant on a film version of Noel Coward's "Design for Living," starring Fredric March, Miriam Hopkins, and Gary Cooper. In the fall of 1933, Reinhardt moved to Metro, as a hundred-and-fifty-dollar-a-week assistant to Walter Wanger, then a producer at that studio. Not long afterward, Wanger left and Reinhardt was made assistant to Bernard Hyman, who was considered a right-hand man of Irving Thalberg. Reinhardt became first a film writer ("The Great Waltz") and then, in 1940, a producer ("Comrade X," with Clark Gable and Hedy Lamarr; "Rage in Heaven," with Ingrid Bergman and Robert Montgomery; "Two-Faced Woman," with Greta Garbo, the last picture she appeared in). In 1942, he went into the Army. He worked on Signal Corps films for four years, and then returned to Metro and produced pictures featuring some of the studio's most popular stars, including Clark Gable and Lana Turner. His recent pictures, however, had not been regarded as box-office hits by the studio. At the age of seventy-two, Reinhardt's mother, a celebrated German actress named Else Heims, is still appearing in plays in Berlin. His father, who died eight years ago, came to Hollywood in 1934 to direct a stage production of "A Midsummer Night's Dream" at the Hollywood Bowl. (The production became famous because it presented an unknown young woman named Olivia de Havilland, who had never acted in public before, as a last-minute replacement for the star, who, for some reason or other, was unable to go on.) Max Reinhardt was then invited by Warner Brothers to direct a movie production of "A Midsummer Night's Dream." This picture was not a hit. For the next five years, he ran a Hollywood school known as Max Reinhardt's Workshop; for a short while in 1939, John Huston conducted a course in screen writing there. Max Reinhardt never got another directorial job in the movies. For many months he tried to obtain an appointment with L. B. Mayer, but Mayer was always too busy to see him.

At Metro-Goldwyn-Mayer, Gottfried Reinhardt had witnessed a succession of struggles for power among the executives at the studio. He had learned many lessons simply by watching these battles, he told me. "M-G-M is like a medieval monarchy," he said. "Palace revolutions all the time." He leaned back in his swivel chair. "L.B. is the King. Dore is the Prime Minister. Benny Thau, an old Mayer man, is the Foreign Minister, and makes all the important deals for the studio, like the loan-outs of big stars. L. K. Sidney, one vice-president, is the Minister of the Interior, and Edgar J. Mannix, another vice-president, is Lord Privy Seal, or, sometimes, Minister Without Portfolio. And John and I are loyal subjects." He bobbed his head and gave a cynical laugh. "Our King is not without power. I found, with 'The Red Badge of Courage,' that you need the King's blessing if you want to make a picture. I have the King's blessing, but it has been given with large reservations." He looked at me over his cigar. "Our picture must be a commercial success," he said flatly. "And it must be a *great* picture."

There was a stir in Dave Chasen's Restaurant in Beverly Hills when Dore Schary walked in. Chasen's is run by the former stage comedian whose name it bears, and it is popular with people in the motion-picture industry. The restaurant is divided into several sections. The first one, facing directly upon the entrance, contains semicircular booths. This section leads to a long bar opposite another section of booths. There are additional sections behind and to the sides of the first two. The headwaiter immediately led Schary to a front booth. Two waiters took up sentrylike positions there, facing each other across the table. All the other patrons focussed their attention on Schary. They seemed to be looking around at everybody except the people they were with and with whom they were managing to carry on conversations.

"I'll read you Ben's letter," a man near us was saying. "He writes, 'Whenever I think of Byzantium, I remember you. I hope you survive the court intrigues of Hollywood's twilight, and when the place crumbles, may you fall from a throne.'"

"I have news for you," said his companion. "It's not twilight yet. It's only smog."

"I have news for you," the first man said, staring without restraint at Schary. "Ben will be back here. He *likes* the court intrigues."

Schary was not a bit self-conscious. He had an aura of immense self-assurance, as though he had reached a point where he could no longer be affected by anything that might happen in Chasen's. He is an optimistic man, and he was talking to me optimistically about the movies. He respected foreign movies, he said, but he believed that the American picture industry provided more entertainment and enlightenment than any other movie-makers in the world. "Our scope is international," he said. "Our thinking is international, and our creative urges and drives are constantly being renewed with the same vigor that renews so many things in the American way of life." The motion-picture community generically referred to as Hollywood, he told me, is no different from any other American community that is dominated by a single industry. "We're the same as Detroit," he said. "We just get talked about more, that's all." He was almost the only man in Chasen's who was not at that moment looking around at someone other than the person he was talking to.

Dave Chasen, a small, solemn man with soft, wistful eyes, came over and told Schary how happy he was to see him there.

"How are you, doll?" Schary said.

"You're looking good," Chasen said sadly.

Schary gave him a genial grin and went on talking to me about the picture industry. A man who seems to be favorably disposed toward the entire world, Schary has a chatty, friendly, homespun manner reminiscent of the late Will Rogers', but there is in it a definite hint of a firm-minded and paternalistic Sunday-school teacher. He is six feet tall, and he has a big head, a high, freckled forehead, and a large nose, shaped like a Saint Bernard's. He spoke earnestly, as though trying to convey a tremendous seriousness of purpose about his work in motion pictures. "A motion picture is a success or a failure at its very inception," he told me. "There was resistance, great resistance, to making 'The Red Badge of Courage.' In terms of cost and in other terms. This picture has no women. This picture has no love story. This picture has no single incident. This is a period picture. The story— Well, there's no story in this picture. It's just the story of a boy. It's the story of a coward. Well, it's the story of a hero." Schary apparently enjoyed hearing himself talk. He was obviously in no hurry to make his point. "These are the elements that are considered important in determining success or failure at the box office," he said, and paused, as if he felt slightly bewildered by the point he was trying to make. He finally said that there had been successful pictures that did not have these so-called important elements. "Crossfire," which he had made, was one, and "All Quiet on the Western Front" was another. "Lew Ayres was the German equivalent of our boy," he said. "I'll almost bet you that Remarque knew 'The Red Badge of Courage.' In the main, when you set out to make a picture, you say, 'I just have a hunch about this picture.' And that's what I felt about this one. Call it instinct if you will. I felt that this picture is liable to be a wonderful picture and a commercial success."

A man who had been standing at the bar picked up his Martini and strolled over to a front booth near us. "I have a great story for you," he said to the group seated there. "This actor comes back from a funeral and he's bawling and carrying on, the tears streaming down his face. So his friend tells him he never saw anybody take a funeral so hard. The actor says, 'You should have seen me at the grave!' " The storyteller gave an explosive burst of self-appreciation. He took a sip of his Martini and caressed the stem of the glass. "This old actor dies," he said, his eyes moving away from his audience as Walter Pidgeon entered with a large party and was seated in the front section. "Two other old actors come to see him laid out in the coffin. 'Joe looks terrific,' says one. 'Why not?' says the other one. 'He just got back from Palm Springs!' "

Schary began talking about L. B. Mayer. "I know Mayer," he said. "I know this man. I know Mayer because my father was like him. Powerful. Physically very strong. Strong-tempered and willful. Mayer literally *hits* people. But my father made this guy look like a May party." He gave me an easy grin.

Just then, a young man rushed over to the table, grabbed Schary's hand, and cried, "Dore! Wonderful to see you, Dore!" He held on to Schary's hand, giving him an incredulous, admiring stare. "You look wonderful, Dore! You look wonderful!"

"Sweetie, how are ya?" Schary said amiably.

The young man continued to stare at Schary; he seemed to be

waiting for confirmation of something. Then he said, "You remember me, Dore! Dave Miller!"

"Of course, doll," Schary said.

"R.K.O.!" Miller announced, as though he were calling out a railroad stop, and in the same tone he announced that he was directing a picture at Columbia. Schary gave him a broad, understanding grin.

Miller shook his head unbelievingly several times and then, reluctantly, started to back away. "You're doing wonderful things now, Dore. Wonderful! The best of everything to you, Dore," he said. "The best."

The maze of paths followed by all the individuals at M-G-M working together to make a motion picture led inexorably to the office of Louis B. Mayer, and I found him there one day, behind a series of doors, talking to Arthur Freed, a producer of musicals for the studio. Mayer's office was about half as large as the lounge of the Music Hall, and he sat behind a huge cream-colored desk overlooking a vast expanse of peach-colored carpet. The walls of the office were panelled in cream-colored leather, and there was a cream-colored bar, a cream-colored fireplace with cream-colored fire irons, cream-colored leather chairs and couches, and a cream-colored grand piano. Behind Mayer's desk stood an American flag and a marble statue of the M-G-M lion. The desk was covered with four cream-colored telephones, a prayer book, several photographs of lions, a tintype of Mayer's mother, and a statuette of the Republican Party's elephant. The big desk hid most of Mayer, but I could see his powerful shoulders, decked in navy blue, and a gay, polka-dot bow tie that almost touched his chin. His large head seems set upon the shoulders, without an intervening neck. His hair is thick and snow-white, his face is ruddy, and his eyes, behind glasses with amber-colored frames, stared with a sort of fierce blankness at Freed, who was showing him a report on the box-office receipts of his latest musical, then playing at the Radio City Music Hall.

"Great! I saw it!" Mayer said, sweeping Freed back with his arm. "I said to you the picture would be a wonderful hit. In here!" he cried, poking his index finger at his chest. "It wins the audience in here!" He lifted his snowy head and looked at the cream-colored wall before him as though he were watching the Music Hall screen. "Entertainment!" he cried, transfixed by what he seemed to see on that screen, and he made the face of a man who was emotionally stirred by what he was watching. "It's good enough for you and I and the box office," he said, turning back to Freed. "Not for the smart alecks. It's not good enough any more," he went on, whining coyly, in imitation of someone saying that winning the heart of the audience was not good enough. He pounded a commanding fist on his desk and looked at me. "Let me tell you something!" he said. "Prizes! Awards! Ribbons! We had two pictures here. An Andy Hardy picture, with little Mickey Rooney, and 'Ninotchka,' with Greta Garbo. 'Ninotchka' got the prizes. *Blue* ribbons! *Purple* ribbons! Nine bells and seven stars! Which picture made the money? 'Andy Hardy' made the money. Why? Because it won praise from the heart. No ribbons!"

"Hah!" Mr. Freed said.

"Twenty-six years with the studio!" Mayer went on. "They used to listen to me. Never would Irving Thalberg make a picture I was opposed to. I had a worship for that boy. He worked. Now they want cocktail parties and their names in the papers. Irving listened to me. Never satisfied with his own work. That was Irving. Years later, after Irving passed away, they still listened. They make an Andy Hardy picture." He turned his powerful shoulders toward me. "Andy's mother is dying, and they make the picture showing Andy standing outside the door. *Standing.* I told them, 'Don't you know that an American boy like that will get down on his hands and knees and *pray?*' They listened. They brought Mickey Rooney down on his hands and knees." Mayer leaped from his chair and crouched on the peach-colored carpet and showed how Andy Hardy had prayed. "The biggest thing in the picture!" He got up and returned to his chair. "Not good enough," he said, whining coyly again. "Don't show the good, wholesome American mother in the home. Kind. Sweet. Sacrifices. Love." Mayer paused and by his expression demonstrated, in turn, maternal kindness, sweetness, sacrifice, and love, and then glared at Freed and me. "No!" he cried. "Knock the mother on the jaw!" He gave himself an uppercut to the chin. "Throw the little old lady down the stairs!" He threw himself in the direction of the American flag. "Throw the mother's good, homemade chicken soup in the mother's face!" He threw an imaginary plate of soup in Freed's face. "*Step* on the mother! *Kick* her! That is *art*, they say. Art!" He raised and lowered his white eyebrows, wiggled his shoulders like a hula dancer, and moved his hands in a mysterious pattern in the air. "Art!" he repeated, and gave an angry growl.

"You said it," said Freed.

" 'Andy Hardy'! I saw the picture and the tears were in my eyes," Mayer said. "I'm not ashamed. I'll see it again. Every time, I'll cry."

"In musicals, we don't have any of those phony artistic pretensions," Freed said.

Mayer gave no sign that he had heard Freed. "Between you and I and the lamppost," he said, straightening his bow tie, "the smart alecks around here don't know the difference between the heart and the gutter. They don't want to listen to you. Marie Dressler! Who thought you could take a fat old lady and make her a star? I did it. And Wally Beery. And Lionel Barrymore." He leaned back in his chair, one hand tucked into his shirt, his eyes squinting, his voice turning into the querulous rasp of Dr. Gillespie informing Dr. Kildare of his diagnosis of the disease. Then, resuming his natural manner, he said, "The audience knows. Look at the receipts. Give the audience what they want? No. Not good enough." He paused.

"Thoreau said most of us lead lives of quiet desperation," Freed said quickly. "Pictures should make you feel better, not worse."

Again Mayer did not seem to hear. " 'The Red Badge of Courage,' " he said. "A million and a half. Maybe more. What for? There's no story. I was against it. They wanted to make it. I don't say no. John Huston. He was going to do 'Quo Vadis.' What he wanted to do to the picture! No heart. His idea was he'd throw the Christians to the lions. That's all. I begged him to change his ideas. I got down on my hands and knees to him. I sang 'Mammy' to him. I showed him the meaning of heart. I crawled to him on hands and knees. 'Ma-a-ammy!' With tears. No! No heart! He thanked me for taking him off the picture. Now he wants 'The Red Badge of Courage.' Dore Schary wants it. All right. I'll watch. I don't say no, but I wouldn't make that picture with Sam *Goldwyn's* money."

In the few days remaining before rehearsals started, Huston had to attend budget and production conferences, he had to examine, with his cameraman and technical crew, the exact spots on his San Fernando Valley ranch where the battle scenes for the picture would be shot, and he had to make a number of revisions in the screenplay, including some suggested by the Production Code Administrator of the Motion Picture Association of America, which had come to him in a copy of a letter addressed to Mayer:

Dear Mr. Mayer:

We have read the script for your proposed production THE RED BADGE OF COURAGE, and beg to report that the basic story seems to meet the requirements of the Production Code. Going through the script in detail, we call your attention to the following minor items.

Page 1A: Here, and throughout the script, please make certain that the expression "dum" is pronounced clearly, and does not sound like the unacceptable expletive "damn."

Page 21: The expression "damn" is unacceptable.

Page 41: The same applies to the exclamation "Lord," the expression "I swear t' Gawd."

Page 42: The same applies to "Lord knows" and the exclamation "Gawd."

Page 44: The exclamation "Good Lord" is unacceptable.

Page 65: The expression "hell to pay" is unacceptable.

Joseph I. Breen, the writer of the letter, stated that three other uses of the word "Lord" in the script were unacceptable, along with one "in God's name," two "damn"s, and three "hell"s, and, before signing off—cordially—reminded Mr. Mayer that the final judgment of the Code Administrator would be based upon the finished picture.

Hedda Hopper, in the Los Angeles *Times,* headlined one of her daily columns with the news that Audie Murphy would star in "The Red Badge of Courage." "The happiest and most appropriate casting of the year took place at M-G-M yesterday when Dore Schary gave Audie Murphy, the most decorated hero of World War II, the leading role in 'The Red Badge of Courage,' with John Huston directing," she wrote. "For a change, we'll have a real soldier playing a real soldier on the screen. It couldn't happen at a better time."

The administrative headquarters for the M-G-M studio is a U-shaped white concrete building identified, in metal letters, as the Irving Thalberg Building. The steps leading to the Thalberg Building, between broad, shrub-bordered lawns, are wide and smooth, and they shone whitely under the midsummer sun, as cool and as stately as the steps to the Capitol in Washington, as I headed for them one morning. A taxi drew over to the curb and jerked to a halt. The door opened and Huston leaped out. He plunged a hand into a trouser pocket, handed the driver a wadded bill, and rushed toward the steps. He had stayed in town the night before, he said, at one of his three places—a small house in Beverly Hills he rented from Paulette Goddard—and he had expected his secretary to telephone him and wake him up. She had not telephoned, and he had overslept. He seemed angry and tense. "Audie's waiting for me," he said irritably.

We went into a large reception room with gray-checkered linoleum on the floor, and Huston strode across it, nodding to a young man seated at a semicircular desk between two doors. "Good morning, Mr. Huston," the young man said brightly. At once, the catches on both doors started clicking, and Huston opened the one on the right. I hurried after him, down a linoleum-floored corridor, whose cream-colored walls were lined with cream-colored doors. On each door was a slot holding a white card with a name printed on it. At the end of the corridor, we turned to the right, down another corridor, and at the end of *that* we came to a door with his name on it, engraved in black letters on a brass plate. Huston opened it, and a young lady with curly black hair, seated at a desk facing the door, looked up as we came in. Huston turned immediately to a bench adjoining the entrance. Audie Murphy was sitting on it. He stood up.

"Hello, Audie. How are you, Audie?" Huston said gently, as though speaking to a frightened child. The two men shook hands. "Well, we made it, kid," Huston said, and forced an outburst of ho-ho-hos.

Murphy gave him a wan smile and said nothing. A slight young man with a small, freckled face, long, wavy reddish-brown hair, and large, cool gray eyes, he was wearing tan twill frontier riding pants, a matching shirt, open at the collar, and Western boots with pointed toes and high heels.

"Come in, Audie," Huston said, opening the door to an inner office.

"Good morning," the secretary behind him said. "Publicity wants to know what do you do when you hit a snag in writing a script?"

"Tell publicity I'm not here," Huston said in a tone of cold reproach. Then, his voice gentle again, he said, "Come in, Audie."

Huston's office had oak-panelled walls, a blue carpet, and three windows reaching from the ceiling to the floor. There was a long mahogany desk at one end of the room, and at the opposite end, facing it, was a blue leather couch. Several blue leather armchairs were scattered around the office.

"Sit down, guys," Huston said, and himself sat down behind the desk, in a swivel chair with a blue leather seat. "Well," he said, clenching his hands and resting his chin on them. He swung from side to side in his chair a few times, then leaned back and put his feet on the desk on top of a stack of papers.

Murphy sat down in an armchair facing one of the windows and ran a forefinger across his lower lip. "I've got a sore lip," he said. " 'Bout six this morning, I went riding on my colt. I went riding without my hat, and the sun burned my lip all up." He spoke with a delicate plaintiveness, in the nasal, twangy drawl of a Texan.

"I've got the same thing, kid," Huston said, pursing his lips. "Tell you what, Audie. Bring your colt out to my ranch. You can have your colt right there with you, any time you want to ride while we're making the picture."

Murphy fingered his sore lip, as if trying to determine whether Huston's pleasant offer did anything for his affliction. Apparently it didn't, so he looked sadly out the window.

"We'll do a lot of riding together, kid," Huston said. "That's good riding country there in the hills, you know."

Murphy made a small, sighing noise of assent.

"I want you to hear this, Audie," Huston said, nervously unfolding a sheet of paper he had taken from his jacket. "Some new lines I just wrote for the script." He read several lines, then laughed appreciatively.

Murphy made another small noise of assent.

Huston continued to laugh, but his eyes, fastened on Murphy, were sombre. He seemed baffled and worried by Murphy's unresponsiveness, because usually actors were quick to respond to him. He took his feet down from his desk and picked up a slip of blue paper one heel had been resting on. " 'Interoffice Communication,' " he read aloud, and glanced quickly at Murphy to get his attention. " 'To Messrs. Gottfried Reinhardt, John Huston . . . SUBJECT: Hair for RED BADGE OF COURAGE Production. As per discussion this morning, we are proceeding with the manufacture of: 50 Hook-on Beards at $3.50 each, 100 Crepe wool Mustaches at 50¢ each, 100 Crepe wool Falls at $2.50 each—for Production No. 1512—RED BADGE OF COURAGE. These will be manufactured in the Makeup Department.' "

Huston stopped reading, looked at Murphy, and saw that he had already lost his attention. "Well, now," Huston said. "Let's go get some breakfast. I haven't had any breakfast yet."

The door opened, and a stoop-shouldered young man with enormous, eager-looking eyes came in. He was introduced as Albert Band, Huston's assistant. Huston moved toward the door.

"Where you going?" Band asked, blinking his eyes. His eye-lashes descended over his eyes like two dust mops.

"Breakfast," said Huston.

Band said that he had had his breakfast, but he would come along and watch Huston have his.

We went out a side door to the studio gates, where a policeman in a stone hut looked carefully at each of us as we filed through. "Mr. Huston," he said.

"Good morning," Huston said, giving full weight to each sylla-ble.

We went down a narrow street between low, gray-painted build-ings of wood or stucco, which had shingles identifying them as "Men's Wardrobe," "International Department," "Casting Of-fice," "Accounting Department," and "Danger 2300 Volts." Far-ther along the street were the sound stages, gray, hangarlike buildings. We passed a number of costumed actors and actresses, and people in casual summer dress who exchanged nods with Huston and looked piercingly at Murphy, Band, and me.

A portly gentleman in a gray pin-striped suit stopped Huston and shook hands with him. "Congratulate me," he said. "My pic-ture opens next week in New York."

"Music Hall?" Huston asked.

"I have news for you," the man said in a dry tone. "Dore Schary personally produces a picture, *it* gets into the Music Hall. I got Loew's State."

The M-G-M commissary is a comfortable restaurant with soft lighting, cream-colored walls, an aquamarine ceiling, and modern furnishings. When Huston, Murphy, Band, and I entered, about a third of the tables were occupied, and most of the people sitting at them stared at our party without restraint. We took a table, and Huston ordered orange juice, a hard-boiled egg, bacon, and coffee. Murphy fingered his sore lip.

"How about some coffee, *amigo?*" Huston asked him.

Murphy nodded wistfully.

"Gottfried told me a great story yesterday," Band said, batting his enormous eyes at Huston. "Two producers come out of the projection room where one has just shown the other his picture, and he asks, 'Well, how did you like the picture?' 'Great,' the other producer says. 'What's the matter—you didn't like it?' the first producer asks. Isn't that a great story?" Band said with a short laugh.

"A great story, Albert," Huston said, putting a brown cigarette in one corner of his mouth.

"I've got another one," Band said. He took a kitchen match from his pocket, scraped the head of it with his thumbnail, and held the flame to Huston's cigarette. "This producer doesn't like the score that has been composed for his picture. 'The music isn't right,' he says. 'It's a picture about France,' he says, 'so I want a lot of French horns.'" Band laughed again.

"Got a newspaper, Albert?" Huston said. Band said no. "Get me a paper, Albert," said Huston. "I want to see the selections." He did not look up as Band went out. Drawing deeply on his cigarette, he looked down through the smoke at the table and brushed away some shreds of tobacco.

Murphy fixed his gaze on the windows along the far wall.

Huston looked at him. "Excited, kid?" he asked.

"Seems as though nothing can get me excited any more—you know, enthused?" he said. "Before the war, I'd get excited and enthused about a lot of things, but not any more."

"I feel the same way, kid," said Huston.

The waitress brought Huston's breakfast and Murphy's cup of coffee. Huston squinted at Murphy over his drooping cigarette and told him that his hair looked fine. "You might taper the sideburns a bit, kid," he said, taking the cigarette from his mouth and resting it on an ashtray. "That's all we need to do, kid." He took a few sips of orange juice and then pushed the glass aside, picked up the hard-boiled egg, and bit into it. "Audie, ever been in Chico, up north of San Francisco, near the Sacramento River?" he asked expansively. "Well, now, we'll be going up there on location to do the river-crossing scene and other stuff for the picture. And while we're there, we'll go fishing, kid."

Band returned and handed Huston a newspaper. Huston took a

couple of quick swallows of coffee and pushed his breakfast aside. Opening the paper on the table, he said that his filly Tryst was running that day and that he wanted to know what the handicappers had to say about her. He picked up the paper and held it in front of his face. The headline facing us read, "CHINESE REPORTED AIDING FOE."

Murphy stared vaguely at the paper. "I'd like to go fishing," he said.

From behind the newspaper, Huston grunted.

"You going fishing?" Band asked.

"When we get to Chico," said Murphy.

At an adjoining table, a young man was saying loudly, "He comes out here from Broadway and he thinks he's acting in movies. Today on the set, I'm doing a scene with him, and he says to me, 'I don't feel your presence.' 'So reach out and touch me,' I said."

"Look, I know you're busy, I don't wanna butt in, but this I gotta tell you," a roly-poly little man said, going up to the young man's table. "I'm at Sam Goldwyn's last night and he says he's got a new painting to show me. So he takes me over to the painting and points to it and says, 'My Toujours Lautrec!' "

Huston closed the newspaper and folded it under his arm. "Let's get back, guys," he said. He instructed Band to place a token bet on Tryst for him, and Band walked off.

Back in the Thalberg Building, Huston invited Murphy and me to see a number of test shots he had made on his ranch for "The Red Badge of Courage." He had seen the tests and, with Reinhardt and Schary, had made the final decisions on the leading players in the cast. In addition to Audie Murphy as the Youth, there would be Bill Mauldin as the Loud Soldier, John Dierkes as the Tall Soldier, and Royal Dano as the Tattered Man. We trooped downstairs to a carpeted lounge in the basement and went into a projection room that contained two rows of heavy, deep leather armchairs. Beside the arm of one of the center chairs was a board holding a telephone and a mechanism called a "fader," which controls the volume of sound. The first shot showed the Youth, who had returned to his regiment after running away from battle, having his head bandaged by his friend the Loud Soldier. Mauldin, dressed in Union blue, his ears protruding horizontally from under a kepi, said as he bound a kerchief around Murphy's head, "Yeh look like th' devil, but I bet yeh feel better."

In the audience, Murphy said in a loud whisper, "I was biting my cheek so hard trying to keep from laughing."

"Yes, Audie," said Huston.

The next scene showed Murphy carrying a gun and urging some soldiers behind him to come on. "Let's show them Rebs what we're made of!" Murphy called fiercely, on the screen. "Come on! All we got to do is cross this here field! Who's with me? Come on! Come on!" Murphy advanced, and Huston's voice came on the sound track, laughing and saying, "Very good."

"I was biting my cheek so hard my whole cheek was sore," Murphy said.

"Yes, Audie," Huston said.

Next there was a scene between Murphy and the Tall Soldier, played by John Dierkes. The Tall Soldier died, his breath rasping and then ceasing, and his hair blowing long and wild. The Youth wept.

The lights came on. "We're going to be just fine," Huston said.

Back in his office, where we found Band waiting for us, Huston, taking another cigarette, said that Dierkes would be just wonderful in the picture.

"Just great," said Band.

Murphy was back in his armchair, staring out the window as though lost in a distant dream. Huston gave him a sharp glance, then sighed and put his long legs up on the desk. "Well, now, Audie, we're going to have such fun making this picture on my ranch!" he said. "Let me tell you kids all about the ranch." There was a compelling promise in his tone. He waited while Murphy shifted his gaze from the window to him. Huston deliberately took his time. He drew on his cigarette, and blew the smoke away. He began by telling us that he had four hundred and eighty acres— rolling fields, pasture, a brook, and hills harboring mountain lions and jaguars. He had paddocks and stables for his horses, a pen for eight Weimaraner puppies, doghouses for the Weimaraner parents and three other dogs (including a white German shepherd named Paulette, after Paulette Goddard), and a three-room shack for himself, his adopted son, Pablo, and a young man named Eduardo, who managed the ranch. Huston's wife, the former Ricki Soma, and their infant son lived at Malibu Beach, and Huston commuted between the two establishments. At the ranch, Huston had a cowboy named Dusty, and, with a good deal of laughter, he described Dusty's gaunt and leathery face and his big black ten-gallon hat. "Oh, God!" he said, with a shake of his head. "Dusty wants to be in the picture." He coughed out a series of jovial ho-ho-hos. Murphy, who had given him a quiet smile, developed the smile into hollow-sounding laughter. Huston seemed satisfied that he had finally got a response out of Murphy.

The door opened, and Reinhardt stood there, an expression of cynical bewilderment on his face, a large cigar between his lips.

"Come in, Gottfried," said Huston.

"Hello, Mr. Reinhardt," Murphy said, standing up.

Reinhardt took a few steps forward, bobbing his head paternally at everyone. "There's going to be trouble, John," he said, in a tone of dry, flat amiability. He chewed his cigar around to a corner of his mouth to let the words out. "The production office thought the river for the picture was a stream. In the script, it says, 'The regiment crosses a stream.' Now they want to know what you mean you need hundreds of men to cross the Sacramento River?" He bobbed his head again.

"Ho! Ho!" Huston said, crossing his legs on top of his desk. Murphy sat down again. Band paced the carpet in front of Huston's desk.

"Trouble!" Reinhardt said.

"Well, now, Gottfried, you and I are used to trouble on this picture," Huston said. He put a brown cigarette in his mouth. Band held a kitchen match to it. Huston cocked his head over the flame and gave Murphy a wry smile. "They're afraid the soldiers will get their little tootsies wet," he said, with a titter.

Murphy smiled sadly. Band laughed and batted his eyes first at Huston, then at Reinhardt.

"Now, *Albert* wouldn't be afraid to cross the river, would you, Albert?" Huston asked.

Murphy smiled.

"I have news for you," Band said. "I'm *going* to cross it. You promised me I could have a part in this picture."

Reinhardt laughed, the upper part of his body bouncing energetically. As Band continued pacing in front of Huston's desk, Reinhardt fell in ahead of him, and the two men paced together. Reinhardt's gold key chain looped into his trouser pocket flopped noisily as he paced. "Everybody in Hollywood wants to be something he is not," he said as Huston watched him over the tips of his shoes. "Albert is not satisfied to be your assistant. He wants to be an actor. The writers want to be directors. The producers want to be writers. The actors want to be producers. The wives want to be painters. Nobody is satisfied. Everybody is frustrated. Nobody is happy." He sighed, and sat down heavily in a chair facing Murphy. "I am a man who likes to see people happy," he muttered through his cigar.

The door opened, and John Dierkes entered. "Hi, John! Hi, everybody!" he said cheerfully, in a rasping drawl. He had a thick shock of stringy orange hair. "Hi, sport!" he said to Murphy. "Hedda sure likes you, sport. Didja see what she said about you today?"

"Did you let your hair grow?" Reinhardt asked him.

"Sure did, Gottfried," said Dierkes. "It's been growin' and growin' for weeks." He sat down, clasped his hands between his knees, and beamed at Murphy. "You learnin' your lines, sport?" he asked.

Huston recrossed his legs impatiently and said that he had just seen Dierkes' screen test. "You look like an ugly bastard," Huston said. "You're the only man I know who is uglier than I am."

Dierkes dropped his long chin in an amiable smile. "That's what you said the first time we met, John," he said. "In London. I was in the Red Cross and you were sure spiffy in your major's uniform. 1943."

"I was on my way to Italy," Huston said. "That's when we made 'The Battle of San Pietro.'"

Reinhardt turned to Murphy. "Did you ever see the picture 'K-Rations and How to Chew Them'?" he asked in a loud voice. He tilted his cigar to a sharp angle and pointed a finger at himself. "Mine," he said.

"England was just wonderful in the war," Huston said. "You always wanted to stay up all night. You never wanted to go to sleep."

Reinhardt said, "I'll bet I'm the only producer who ever had Albert Einstein as an actor." Attention now focussed on him. He said that he had been making an Army film called "Know Your Enemy—Germany," the beginning of which showed some notable German refugees. "Anthony Veiller, a screen writer who was my major, told me to tell Einstein to comb his hair before we photographed him. I said, 'Would you tell Einstein to comb his hair?' He said no. So we photographed Einstein with his hair not combed." Reinhardt bounced merrily in his chair and laughed.

"God, those English bootmakers!" Huston said. "The love and affection they lavish on their boots! Whenever I go to London, I head straight for Maxwell and order boots made."

Reinhardt got up and went to the door, saying that in the afternoon there was going to be a conference of the key members of the crew assigned to the picture. The cost of making a picture depended largely on the time it took, he observed. The director and his actors might work together only three hours of an eight-hour day; the balance of the time would be spent waiting for scenes to be prepared. Reinhardt wanted to discuss what he called the leap-frog method, which meant having an assistant director line up shots in advance, so that Huston could move from one scene to another without delay. "We bring this picture in early, we will be real heroes," Reinhardt said.

"Don't worry, Gottfried," Huston said.

"I will see you later?" Reinhardt asked.

"I'll be there, Gottfried. Don't worry," Huston said.

Huston gave me a copy of the script for "The Red Badge of Courage" and left me alone in his office to read it. The script was a mimeographed booklet in a yellow paper cover, which was stamped with the seal of M-G-M. Also on the cover were the words

"Production No. 1512" and the names of the film's producer, Gottfried Reinhardt, and its director, John Huston. A notation on the
flyleaf stated that the number of pages was ninety-two. Each shot
described in the script was numbered. I turned to page 92. The last
shot was numbered 344, and its description read:

CLOSE TRUCKING SHOT—THE YOUTH

As he trudges from the place of blood and wrath, his spirit
changes. He is rid of the sickness of battle. He lifts his head
to the rain, breathes in the cool air, hears a sound above him.
CAMERA PANS UP to a tree and a bird is singing.

FADE OUT

I turned to page 73, one the Breen Office had found unacceptable expressions on:

CLOSE SHOT—LIEUTENANT

Lieutenant

Come on, men! This is no time to stop! In God's name,
don't just stand there! We'll all get killed. Come on! I never
seed sech lunkheads! Get movin', damn yeh— Oh, yeh cowards.—Yeh rotten little cowards!

I turned back to the beginning and settled down to read:

FADE IN:

MED. LONG SHOT—EMBANKMENT ACROSS A RIVER—NIGHT

Low fires are seen in the distance, forming the enemy camp.
Trees and bushes. A LOW WHISTLE IS HEARD from across the
river.

MED. SHOT—THE OTHER SIDE OF THE RIVER

Moonlight reveals some bushes and trees, and a sentry walking into view. Crickets sing in the still night. The low whistle
is repeated. The sentry puts his rifle to his shoulder, stands
staring into the gloom.

CLOSE SHOT—SENTRY—IT IS THE YOUTH

The Youth

Who goes there?
MED. LONG SHOT—ACROSS THE RIVER
Southern Voice
Me, Yank—jest me. . . . Move back into the shadders,
Yank, unless you want one of them little red badges. I
couldn't miss yeh standin' there in the moonlight.

The script took me a couple of hours to read. It included several
scenes written by Huston that did not appear in the novel, but
for the most part the screenplay indicated that Huston intended
to embody in his picture the Youth's impressions of war exactly as
Crane had described them.

After finishing the script, I went into a sort of back room of
Huston's office, used as a conference and poker room, where I
found Mrs. Huston. Mrs. Huston had not seen her husband for
several days. She is a striking girl with an oval face and long
dark hair drawn back tight from her face, parted in the middle,
and done up in a bun in back. She was formerly a ballet dancer in
New York, and is now an actress. She showed me around the
room. There were a sofa and several chairs covered in brown
leather. There were photographs of horses on the walls. There
was a framed picture, clipped from a magazine, showing Huston
with his father and captioned, "John Huston—for the last three
years a major in the Army's Signal Corps—has produced an important and engrossing documentary film, 'Let There Be Light.'
His father, Walter Huston, does an equally fine narration for this
picture on the crackup and treatment of neuropsychopathic soldiers." There were certificates of awards: the One World Flight
Award for Motion Pictures, and the Screen Writers Guild Award
to Huston for his "Treasure of Sierra Madre," which was described
in the citation as "the best-written Western of 1948," and two
Motion Picture Academy statuettes—one for the best screenplay
of 1948, the other for the best-directed film that year. A silver tray
on a corner table was inscribed "To John Huston, One Hell of a
Guy. The Macadamized Award from all the Members of the
Asphalt Jungle."

Albert Band came into the room. He said there ought to be a lot of fun with the new picture, especially when the company went on location at Chico.

Mrs. Huston said that she was going along to Chico, where she would do some fishing. "I just *love* fishing," she went on, as if trying to convince herself.

Huston entered, greeted his wife, and announced that everybody ought to have a drink. He called his secretary in and told her that the key to the liquor was under one of the Oscars.

"How's the young man?" Huston asked his wife.

The baby was fine, she said.

"Did you bring my car, honey?" he asked.

The car was outside.

"Tryst is running today, honey," Huston said tenderly.

"I have news for you," Band said. "Tryst ran out of the money."

Huston looked astonished and, after a moment, laughed in a strained way. "Albert," he said, "get over to Gottfried's office and find out when that goddam meeting is supposed to start."

Since most of the film was to be shot about thirty miles from Hollywood, on Huston's ranch, in the San Fernando Valley, Huston arranged to look over the terrain one day with Reinhardt and the production crew. I arrived at the ranch about eleven o'clock in the morning, and a few minutes later the crew drove up in a large black limousine. Huston came out of his ranchhouse to greet us, dressed in a red-and-green checked cap, a pink T shirt, tan riding pants flapping out at the sides, tan leggings, tan suspenders, and heavy maroon shoes that reached to his ankles. Included in the crew were the cameraman, Harold Rosson, a short, stocky, gum-chewing middle-aged man with a sharp face; the unit manager, Lee Katz, a heavyset man in his late thirties, with thin blond fuzz on his head, a brisk, officious manner, and a perpetual ingratiating smile; the "leapfrog" director, Andrew Marton, a serious, pedantic Hungarian-American with a heavy accent and a nervous, solicitous manner, whose job it would be to arrange things so that Huston would not have to wait between scenes; the art director, Hans Peters, a stiff, formal German with cropped hair, who also had a heavy accent; another assistant director, Reggie Callow, a harassed-looking man with a large red face, a bowl-shaped midriff, and the gravelly voice of a buck sergeant; and the technical adviser, Colonel Paul Davison, a retired Army officer with a mustache, dark glasses, and a soldierly bearing. All were carrying copies of the script.

Rosson clapped Huston on the shoulder. "Happy birthday, pal," he said.

"I almost forgot," Huston said. "Thanks, Hal. Thanks very much, kid."

Reinhardt and Band drove up in a gray Cadillac convertible with the top down. Reinhardt had a navy-blue beret on his head and a cigar in his mouth. He came over and pumped Huston's hand. "Happy birthday, John," he said.

"Oh, yes. I almost forgot," Huston said. "Well, gentlemen, let's get started."

Everybody was wearing rough clothes except Reinhardt, who wore neat gabardine slacks of bright blue and a soft shirt of lighter blue. Band had on Russian Cossack boots, into which were tucked ragged cotton pants. Marton wore dungarees and a khaki bush jacket, which, he said, he had brought from Africa, where he had recently worked as co-director of "King Solomon's Mines." Colonel Davison wore Army fatigues.

Dusty, the Huston-ranch cowboy who wanted to play in the picture, stood around while the crew got organized. He went into the stables and returned leading a large black horse, saddled and bridled. Huston mounted it, and then Dusty brought out a white-and-brown cow pony.

"I'll ride Papoose, pal," Rosson said to Huston, and heaved himself aboard the cow pony.

"He was once married to Jean Harlow," Band said to Colonel Davison, pointing to Rosson.

"Let's go, gentlemen!" Huston called, waving everybody on. He walked his horse slowly down the road.

"John can really set a saddle," Dusty said, watching him go.

Rosson started after Huston. Reinhardt and Band followed in the Cadillac. The rest of us, in the limousine, brought up the rear of the cavalcade.

Marton peered out the window at Rosson, rocking along on the cow pony. "He used to be married to Jean Harlow," he said thoughtfully. "Reggie, what do we do first?"

Callow said that they were going to stop at the location for the scene showing the Youth's regiment on the march, to determine how many men would be needed to give the effect of an army on the march. It was Scene 37. All the script had to say about it was "MEDIUM LONG SHOT—A ROAD—THE ARMY ON THE MARCH—DUSK."

"The mathematics of this discussion is important," Callow said.

Katz, whose primary job was to serve as a liaison man between the crew and the studio production office, was sitting up front. He turned around and said, smiling, "Mathematics means money."

"Everything is such a production," said Marton. "Why can't they just turn Johnny loose with the camera?"

Colonel Davison, who was sitting in a jump seat next to Peters, cleared his throat.

"What, what?" Katz said to him.

"Warm today," the Colonel said, clearing his throat again.

"Nothing," Marton said. "In Africa, we had a hundred and fifty degrees in the shade."

"That so?" said the Colonel.

Katz turned around again. There were beads of perspiration on his forehead and in the fuzz on his head. "You boys are going to have a time climbing these hills today," he said cheerily. "Hot, hot."

Peters said, without moving his head, "Very warm."

"It's going to be a tough war," Callow said.

The road for the MEDIUM LONG SHOT was a dirt one curving around a hill and running through sunburned fields. A large oak tree at the foot of the hill cast a shadow over the road. Huston and Rosson sat on their horses near the top of the hill, waiting for the rest of the party to struggle up to them through dry, prickly grass. Reinhardt was carrying a sixteen-millimetre movie camera. A hawk flew overhead, and Reinhardt stopped, halfway up the hill, and trained his camera on it. "I like to take pictures of birds," he said. When everyone had reached Huston and was standing around him, Huston pointed to the bend in the road.

"The Army comes around there," he said commandingly. He paused and patted the neck of his horse. "Colonel," he said.

"Yes, sir!" Colonel Davison said, coming to attention.

"Colonel, how far apart will we put the fours?" Huston asked.

"About an arm's length, sir," said the Colonel.

"Get away from my script!" Callow said to Huston's horse, who was attempting to eat it.

Huston gave Callow a reproachful look and patted the horse's neck. "Never mind, baby," he said.

"Gentlemen," Rosson said, "keep in mind we must not have these Western mountains in what was primarily an Eastern war." He dismounted and gave the reins of his pony to Band, who clambered clumsily into the saddle. The pony started turning in circles.

"It's only me, little baby," Band said to it.

"Albert!" Huston said. Band got off the pony, and it calmed down.

"Gentlemen," Huston said. "The finder, please."

Marton handed him a cone-shaped tube with a rectangular window at the wide end. It would determine the kind of lens that would be needed for the shot. Huston looked at the road through the finder for a long time. "A slow, uneven march," he said dramatically. "The Union colonel and his aide are leading the march on horseback. Looks wonderful, just wonderful. Take a look, Hal." He handed the finder to Rosson, who looked at the road through it.

"Great, pal!" Rosson said, chewing his gum with quick, rabbit-like chomps.

"Doesn't it look like a Brady, kid?" Huston said to Rosson.

"Great, pal," said Rosson.

The two men discussed where the camera would be set up, how the shot of the column of soldiers would be composed, when the shot would be taken (in the early morning, when the light on the troops would be coming from the back). They also discussed the fact that the scene, like most of the others in the picture, would be photographed as if from the point of view of the Youth. Then they got to talking about how many men would be needed for the scene.

"How about four hundred and fifty?" said Katz.

"Eight hundred," Huston said immediately.

"Maybe we could do with six hundred and fifty," Reinhardt said, giving Huston a knowing glance.

Katz said that the column would be spaced out with horses and caissons, and that they could get away with less than six hundred and fifty infantrymen.

Huston gave Colonel Davison a sly glance and winked.

The Colonel quickly cleared his throat and said, "Sir, to be militarily correct we ought to have a thousand infantry."

"God!" Reinhardt said.

"Never, never," Katz said.

"Make the picture in Africa," Marton said. "Extras cost eighteen cents a day in Africa."

"That's exactly fifteen dollars and thirty-eight cents less than an extra costs here," Callow said. "We could change it to the Boer War."

"Is it to be six hundred and fifty, gentlemen?" Huston said impatiently.

"If that's the way you want it," Katz said. "Anything I can do for you."

We went from one site to another, trudging up and down hills and breaking paths through heavy underbrush. The afternoon sun was hot, and the faces of the crew were grimy and wet, and their clothes were dusty and sprinkled with burs and prickly foxtails. Only Reinhardt seemed unaffected by his exertions. His blue slacks were still creased, and a fresh cigar was in his mouth as he stood beside Huston examining the site for a scene—to be shot some afternoon—that would show the Youth coming upon a line of wounded men, who would be moving down a path on a slope. Huston and Reinhardt looked at a grassy slope that led down to a road and a patch of trees. The distance from the top of the slope to the road was two hundred and seventy yards, Callow told Huston and Reinhardt. The three men estimated that they would need a hundred extras to make an impressive line of wounded men.

Huston looked through the finder at the slope. "The Youth sees a long line of wounded staggering down," he said, in a low voice.

"We've got to have something for these men to do in the morning," Katz said. "We can't have a hundred extras on the payroll and have them stand around with nothing to do for half a day."

Huston lowered the finder. "Let's just put the figures down as required for each shot, without reference to any other shot," he said coldly.

Katz smiled and threw up his hands.

"And if we find we need twenty-five more men—" Huston began.

"I will appeal to Mr. Reinhardt," Katz said.

"You have great powers of persuasion," said Huston.

Reinhardt bobbed his head and laughed, looking at his director with admiration.

Callow sat by the side of the path, laboriously pulling foxtails out of his socks. "I'm stabbed all over," he said. "I fought the Civil War once before, when I was assistant director on 'Gone with the Wind.' It was never this rough, and 'Wind' was the best Western ever made."

Reinhardt was aiming his camera at a small silver-and-red airplane flying low overhead.

"That's no bird; that's Clarence Brown," said Band.

"Clarence is up there looking for gold," Marton said.

"There is a great story about Clarence Brown," Reinhardt said. "A friend says to him, 'What do you want with all that money, Clarence? You can't take it with you.' 'You can't?' Clarence says. 'Then I'm not going.'" Band and Marton agreed that it was a great story, and Reinhardt looked pleased with himself.

Katz was saying that the first battle scene would have four

hundred infantrymen, fifty cavalrymen, and four complete teams of artillerymen and horses, making a total of four hundred and seventy-four men and a hundred and six horses.

"More people than we ever had in 'Wind,' " Callow said.

Huston, now on his horse, leaned forward in the saddle and rested the side of his face against the neck of the horse.

"We accomplished a lot today," Reinhardt said.

Huston said, with great conviction, "It looks just swell, Gottfried, just wonderful."

"It must be a great picture," Reinhardt said.

"Great," Band said.

Huston wheeled his horse and started across the slope at a canter. He approached a log on top of a mound of earth, spurred his horse, and made a smooth jump. Reinhardt trained his camera on Huston until he disappeared around a wooded knoll.

That night, John Huston celebrated his forty-fourth birthday at a formal dinner party in Hollywood attended by a couple of dozen of his closest friends and associates. The party was given by Reinhardt, in the private dining room of Chasen's Restaurant. The host stood near the door. He looked cynical, and scornful of everything about him, as he pumped the hand of each arriving guest, but he managed, with a half-smoked cigar fixed firmly in a corner of his mouth, to beam with delight. The guests all exuded an atmosphere of exclusiveness and intimacy. It seemed to have nothing to do with Huston's birthday. The birthday, apparently, was merely the occasion, not the cause, of the guests' effusions. Good will was stamped on the faces of all, but there was no indication as to whom or what it was directed toward. As they entered, the guests exchanged quick glances, as though they were assuring each other and themselves that they were there.

At one end of the room, a couple of bartenders had set up a double file of champagne glasses on the bar. Waiters circulated with platters of canapés. Reinhardt's wife, a slender, attractive, sardonic-looking lady with large, skeptical brown eyes and a vaguely Continental manner, moved with a sort of weary impishness among the guests. She was wearing a gossamer blue dinner gown embroidered with silver. The other ladies at the party—all wives of the friends and associates—were almost as festively adorned, but there was about many of them an air of defeat, as though they had given up a battle for some undefined goal. They stood around in groups, watching the groups of men. Mrs. Reinhardt, with the air of one who refuses to admit defeat, bore down on Edward G. Robinson, John Garfield, and Paul Kohner, who was Huston's agent. Robinson, who had recently returned from abroad, was talking about his collection of paintings. Garfield was acting exuberant. Kohner was a genial, tolerant onlooker. At Mrs. Reinhardt's approach, Robinson abandoned his paintings and, starting to hum, fixed on her a broad smile of welcome. "Silvia," he said, and continued to hum.

"There is a rumor making the rounds," she said, pronouncing each syllable slowly and emphatically. "The men are going to play poker after dinner, and the ladies will be given the brush. You know what I am talking about?"

Robinson smiled even more broadly.

Garfield said, "The girls can go to a movie or something. Eddie, you buy any paintings in Europe?"

"Julie, you are not playing poker," said Mrs. Reinhardt to Garfield.

"I have news for you," said Garfield. "I am. Eddie?"

"Not this trip," Robinson said, without ceasing to grin at Mrs. Reinhardt. "In New York, a Rouault. The time before in Europe, a Soutine."

"Last night, I met somebody owned a Degas," said a tall and glamorous-looking but nervous girl with red hair, who had detached herself from a group of ladies and was now at Robinson's elbow. Mrs. Reinhardt and the three men did not bother to acknowledge her remark. "This Degas," the red-haired girl said miserably, "it's getting out of the bathtub, for a change, not in."

"You are playing, too, Paul?" Mrs. Reinhardt asked Kohner as the red-haired girl, still ignored, moved back to her group.

"Maybe I'll go to Europe, Eddie," Garfield said. "I think I need Europe."

Mrs. Reinhardt joined her husband. "Gottfried! Did they make the crêpes Hélène, Gottfried?"

"Yes, darling. I personally showed them how," he said, giving his wife a pat on the head. "Mingle with the wives. You must mingle."

"I won't mingle," said Mrs. Reinhardt. "I have an odd interior climate." She wandered off.

Huston, very sunburned, arrived with his wife. In the lapel of his dinner jacket he wore the ribbon of the Legion of Merit, awarded to him for his work on Army Signal Corps films in the war. "Well!" he said, looking oppressed, and slightly alien to the overflowing intimacy that was advancing toward him.

"John!" Reinhardt said, as though it had been a couple of years instead of a couple of hours since they had last met. "Ricki!" he said, greeting Mrs. Huston with the same enthusiasm.

As Huston confronted the party about to envelop him, his face was contorted, like that of a baby about to explode into tears; then he relaxed into a slouch and went forward to meet his celebrators.

"Johnny!" someone said, and he quickly became the hub of a wheel of admirers. Mrs. Huston, looking tremulous and beautiful, started uncertainly after him but stopped behind the circle, which included a director, William Wyler; a writer, Robert Wyler; Huston's lawyer, Mark Cohen; and Paul Kohner. As Mrs. Huston joined a group of wives, there was a good deal of laughter in the circle around her husband. Cohen, a scholarly-looking gentleman with pince-nez, laughed good-naturedly at everything everybody said. Robert Wyler, William's elder brother and husband of an actress named Cathy O'Donnell, laughed at everything William said. Huston laughed without waiting for anything to be said.

"God love ya, Willie!" Huston said to William Wyler, putting a long arm all the way around his friend's shoulders and shaking him.

Wyler, a short, stocky, slow-speaking man with a self-absorbed expression, drew back and looked up at him. "Johnny, you're getting older," he said.

Laughter, led by Robert Wyler, thundered around the circle.

"Ho! Ho! Ho!" Huston said, forcing each laugh out with tremendous care. "I've had nine lives so far, and I regret every one of them."

At the door, Reinhardt greeted Sam Spiegel, Huston's partner in Horizon Pictures, and Spiegel's wife, Lynne Baggett, a tall, statuesque actress with fluffy blond curls piled up on top of her head.

"So, Gottfried, you start rehearsals next week," Spiegel said, his eyes flickering busily around at everybody except the man he was talking to. Spiegel, whose professional name is S. P. Eagle, is a stout, hawk-nosed man in his late forties with sad, moist eyes, an expression of harried innocence, and a habit of running his tongue swiftly along his upper lip. He was born in Austria, came to America in 1927, was working in Berlin for Universal Pictures when Hitler came to power, in 1933. He met Huston later that year, when both were looking for work in the British motion-picture industry. In 1947, learning that Huston was looking for fifty thousand dollars, Spiegel got the money and gave it to him in exchange for a promise to found an independent motion-picture company—Horizon Pictures—and to put half the money into it. Spiegel then promoted, from the Bankers Trust Company in New York, a loan of nine hundred thousand dollars for Horizon's first film. He went on to promote for himself an extensive knowledge of what all the other producers in Hollywood were up to, and a proprietorship over Huston that most of them were jealous of. Reinhardt beamed at him as warmly as he had at the other guests. Mrs. Reinhardt welcomed the Spiegels with an intensely playful air of surprise at their presence. Spiegel lingered at the door, stared at the admirers surrounding Huston, and told Reinhardt, without being asked, that he had just finished producing a Horizon film starring Evelyn Keyes, Huston's third wife (the present Mrs. Huston is his fourth), and that he planned to make two more pictures while he was waiting for Huston to complete his Metro assignment with Reinhardt. "Then John will make 'The African Queen' with me," Spiegel said. "I get him next, Gottfried."

"Fine," Reinhardt said, bouncing up and down like an amiable bear.

" 'The African Queen' can be a commercial success. It will give John the kind of commercial hit he had when he made 'The Maltese Falcon' in 1941," Spiegel said blandly.

"Fine," Reinhardt said, ignoring the implication that "The Red Badge of Courage" would be a commercial failure.

"When do we start the poker game?" Spiegel asked.

"Fine," said Reinhardt, still bouncing.

"Gottfried," Spiegel said, "when is the poker?"

"Gottfried!" Mrs. Reinhardt said.

"Poker?" Reinhardt said. "After dinner."

Mrs. Spiegel spoke for the first time. "What do we do?" she asked.

"You go to a movie or something, baby," said Spiegel. "A nice double feature." He tapped her arm, and they moved on into the room.

Mrs. Reinhardt, watching them go, gave a cry of mock hysteria. "Gottfried, nobody ever listens to anybody else!" she said. "It's a condition of the world."

"Fine," Reinhardt said to her, and turned to greet a couple of latecomers. They were Band and his wife, a pert, slim girl, formerly a photographer's model, whose picture had appeared twice on the cover of a magazine called *Real Story*. The Bands were late because they had stopped to pick up a present for Huston. The present was a book of reproductions of French Impressionists.

"I believe in friendship," Band said to Reinhardt, then made his way to Huston and delivered the present.

Huston unwrapped his present. "This is just swell, amigo—just wonderful," he said to Band. He closed the book and took a cigarette box out of his pocket. It was empty. "Get me some cigarettes, will ya, kid?" he said.

Band rushed off for cigarettes.

Dave Chasen came into the room, sucking at a pipe, and asked Reinhardt if everything was all right.

"Fine," said Reinhardt.

"I'll stay a minute," Chasen said, and sighed. "What I have to listen to out there! And everybody wants to sit in the front. If I put everybody in the front, who will sit in the back?" He went over to Huston, saying "John!"

"Dave! God love ya, Dave!" Huston said, giving the restaurateur his long-armed embrace.

"Dave!" half a dozen voices called. "Dave! Dave!" Everybody seemed to make it a point to sound his name, but only Mrs. Reinhardt appeared to have anything to say to him. She told him that she was worried about her black French poodle. "Mocha is so neurotic, Dave, he refuses to eat. Dave, he wants lobster. Can I take home some lobster for Mocha, Dave?"

Chasen said all right, sighed again, and returned to his duties.

At dinner—before the men started their poker game and the women went to a movie—the guests sat at circular tables seating six, and between courses they moved from table to table, discussing the party as compared to other parties. Everybody was talking about the decline of big parties. People were cutting down on the big parties, they said. When did Nunnally Johnson give that big tent party? Four years ago. The tent alone, put up over his tennis court, had cost seven hundred dollars. The tent was of Pliofilm, and you could look up and see stars in the sky through it. You hardly ever found a party any more where the host rented a dance floor from that company that rented terrific dance floors. It was easier, and less expensive, to give a party at Chasen's.

"We entertain each other because we never know how to enjoy ourselves with other people," Reinhardt said to the guests at his table. "Hollywood people are afraid to leave Hollywood. Out in the world, they are frightened. They are unsure of themselves. They never enjoy themselves out of Hollywood. Sam Hoffenstein used to say we are the croupiers in a crooked gambling house. And it's true. Every one of us thinks, You know, I really don't deserve a swimming pool."

The guests did not seem to mind what he had said, but, on the other hand, there was no indication that anyone had listened to him.

2   Everything Has Just Gone Zoom

THE WEEK BEFORE REHEARSALS STARTED on "The Red Badge of Courage," Reinhardt and Huston found it a little hard to believe that they actually had a starting date (August 25, 1950) and a work schedule (nine rehearsal days and thirty-four shooting days). As the rehearsals approached, Reinhardt kept repeating to Huston that they would make "a great picture;" the picture would be profitable to Loew's, Inc., and at the same time it would duplicate the quality of the Stephen Crane novel and be great artistically. Huston, in turn, kept repeating that the picture had "a wonderful cast, with wonderful faces." Whenever Huston or Reinhardt received an interoffice communication from one of the thirty-two departments involved in the production of the picture, he was able to reassure himself of the reality of the project by noting that on the memo the "Subject" was described, convincingly, as "Production No. 1512" and that copies were going to all the key executives, including Schenck himself, in New York. If a memo went to Schenck, it was real. A couple of times, when Huston was looking over a memo, he said to Reinhardt, "You know, we're really going to make the picture."

On the eve of the first rehearsals, I dropped in on Reinhardt and Huston at Reinhardt's house, where they were working on the script. Reinhardt lived in Bel Air, on a winding, narrow road high in the hills overlooking Beverly Hills. The house was in a hollow, and it resembled the English mansion in the movie version of "Wuthering Heights"—gabled, dark, and forbidding. I found the two men in a study that had deep leather armchairs, two love seats, and a green-tiled fireplace, in which stood a couple of tropical plants. Beyond a wide archway was a gloomy, cavernous room where the outline of a grand piano was visible. Reinhardt, holding a copy of the script, was pacing back and forth in front of an armchair in which Huston, comfortably dressed in a pink-checked cotton shirt, gray flannel slacks, and loafers, lay sprawled, his long legs stretched out and a copy of the script on his lap. Reinhardt's collar was unbuttoned and his necktie hung loosely around his shoulders. A long strand of hair had fallen over his right eye, and the stub of a cigar was in his mouth. He explained to me that they were devising dialogue for a scene in which the Youth and his comrades, marching to their first battle, are taunted by battle-scarred veterans.

"You got anything?" Reinhardt asked Huston, stepping over his legs. Albert Band entered the room and started pacing behind Reinhardt. Huston was rhythmically banging his chin against his chest. Then, after drawing little sketches of Reinhardt in the margin of his script, he scribbled some words. "Write this down, Albert," he said. " 'Hang your clothes on a hickory limb, and don't go near the battle!' "

"Good," Band said, writing it down. "Very good."

"Now!" Reinhardt said, standing still for a moment. "We need words for Scene 110. Or you can ad-lib it on the set."

Huston turned the pages of the script, a mimeographed booklet stamped on the cover with the words "Production No. 1512," to the scene:

MEDIUM SHOT—BACK OF THE LINE OF FIRING MEN

A private is fleeing, screaming, from his place in the line. He is met and stopped by the captain of the reserves who grabs him by the collar. The private is blubbering and staring with sheeplike eyes at the captain, who is pounding him.

Huston said, "I think this would be good if it's not said. Just have this little bit of action."

"You have to say *something*," Reinhardt said.

"We'll do it on the set," said Huston. "I want to see how it looks first."

Reinhardt rotated the cigar stub in his mouth. "Albert, go tell the cook we'll eat in half an hour," he said, and Band left the room.

Huston shifted to a love seat and lay back, his hands clasped behind his head. He seemed lost in some remote thought. Suddenly he jerked his head in a conspiratorial way at Reinhardt and, taking a piece of paper from his pocket, said he wanted to read something aloud. On April 23, 1863, he said, his great-grandfather Colonel William P. Richardson received a silver-sheathed sword from the noncommissioned officers and privates of the 25th Regiment, Ohio Volunteer Infantry, and he was going to put the sword in the movie; it would be worn by the actor playing the part of the Youth's general. "We ought to put this kind of talk in the picture, too," he said. "Listen. This is from the speech my great-grandfather's superior officer made when he presented it to him: 'Wealth, influence, or favoritism might procure such a gift as this, but the esteem and confidence of brave men cannot be bought.' Jesus, Gottfried, people don't talk like that any more!"

Reinhardt nodded, then glanced impatiently at his script.

"My mother had that speech copied," Huston said. "He was her grandfather. I've got a Brady of him."

"Your mother would have been pleased to know that you're making 'The Red Badge of Courage,' " Reinhardt said. He looked rather taken with his own adroitness in bringing his director back to the task of the hour.

"Nothing I ever did pleased my mother," Huston said.

Band came back, and Reinhardt said that they would have to work on the script every night after rehearsals. Huston told him they were farther ahead than he seemed to think.

"We accomplished a lot today," Band said.

"We really must finish," Reinhardt said, with restrained desperation.

"Don't worry about it, amigo," said Huston.

"Remember that night in this room when we both said we wanted to make the picture?" Reinhardt said. "I said to you, 'What about making "The Red Badge of Courage"?' And you said, 'That's my dream.' And we shook hands." Reinhardt looked very serious. "L.B. begged me not to do this picture," he said. "He was like a father to me."

Mrs. Reinhardt came in, wearing black jersey ballet tights and shirt, and ballet slippers. She had a black apron tied over the tights, and the apron strings floated behind her like a tail. She was accompanied by Mocha, her black French poodle. Band started to sit down in an armchair, but Mocha beat him to it.

"Today, Mocha ate four bananas," Mrs. Reinhardt said.

Reinhardt did not look at her. He said to Huston, "L.B. called me into his office and talked for hours about the kind of pictures that make money. He said he was telling me for my own good. I thought he would weep."

"L.B. is weeping?" Mrs. Reinhardt said.

"He didn't want us to make the picture, honey," Huston said.

Mrs. Reinhardt said, "Gottfried, should I let Mocha eat strawberries?"

Reinhardt said, "L.B. told Dore if he thought we should make the picture, to go ahead and make it."

"Hang yourselves, boys, in other words," Huston said cheerfully.

Reinhardt looked at him shyly and laughed. "Now L.B. puts Dore on the spot with this picture," he said. "He has his arm around Dore. And he says he loves Dore." He laughed, and then he looked serious. "Frankly, I'm worried," he said. "The book is about the *thoughts* of the Youth. Will we show what really goes on inside the boy?"

"Audie Murphy will show it, Gottfried," Huston said.

"You wanted Audie," said Reinhardt.

"Yes," Huston said in a patient tone.

"Montgomery Clift—" Reinhardt began.

"Don't worry, Gottfried," Huston said.

"This must be a *great* picture," Reinhardt said.

"Don't worry, Gottfried," Huston said.

Around the same time, Huston's agent, Paul Kohner, submitted the script to a local psychologist for reassurance that the theme of "The Red Badge of Courage"—that of a boy who runs away from his first battle and then, when he returns to his comrades, performs heroic acts in his next battle—was valid. The psychologist turned in a typewritten report stating that the script told the story of a soldier who surmounts his fear complex and becomes a hero, in accordance with the established theory that a courageous action can be a direct reaction to cowardice.

"Of course, it is presupposed dramaturgically that the psychosis of fear is taken as a fact," he wrote. "And so automatically the question arises as to whether such a conception can be generalized. . . . Since the motives of his heroism are of purely psychopathic origin it should be stated that the filmic description of the psychological evolution fails to convince at the important moments. This is a cardinal fault in regard to the conception of the matter." He then suggested several additional scenes that would explain the Youth's change from cowardice to heroism in battle. "These differentiated psychological Zwischentöne have to be plastically formed," he wrote, and added that if his suggestions were followed, "the picture could be the outstanding one of the year."

Huston and Reinhardt read the analysis, exchanged bleak looks, and had it filed.

The morning of the day rehearsals were to start, on Huston's ranch, Huston, a red-and-green checked cap on his head, a brown cigarette in his mouth, and his arms folded on the top bar of a white rail fence separating his ranchhouse from his stables, watched his adopted son, Pablo, saddle a big black horse. It was the horse from whose back Huston intended to direct the picture. The horse moved impatiently under the saddle.

"All right, baby," Huston said soothingly.

"Take it easy, baby," said Pablo. "Dad, you want me to walk him a little bit?"

"Just hold him there, Pablo," said Huston, and exhaled a stream of cigarette smoke with an expression of happy fulfillment. He mounted the horse, and with a quick, dramatic gesture he pulled his cap down farther over his forehead, and then, taking the reins in both hands, he sat facing the dry, rutty dirt road leading away from the stables. The big horse stood motionless. Huston sat in silence, staring grimly ahead for a moment. "Well, now, Pablo," he said, with intense emphasis on each syllable. "Keep an eye on everything back here, amigo." Then he started the horse down the road (MEDIUM SHOT) at an easy, rocking walk, stirring up a cloud of dust in his wake.

Huston stopped his horse beside a large oak tree next to a dry, barren yellow field. Studio limousines and a large studio bus were parked in the field. A pyramid of rifles was stacked near the bus. Under the oak tree sat Harold Rosson, the cameraman, with Reggie Callow, assistant director; Lee Katz, unit manager; Andrew Marton, the "leapfrog" director; Colonel Paul Davison, the technical adviser; and Albert Band.

Callow stepped forward and gave a brisk salute. "The troops are in good shape, Mr. Huston, sir," he said. "Been drilling them for an hour."

"Very good, amigo," Huston said.

"Rough day," Katz said. "Hot, hot."

A dozen of the studio's stock actors, in blue uniforms and kepis, lounged about on the grass. Not far from them was another group, consisting of a script clerk, a still photographer, a few assistant and second assistant directors, a few assistant and second assistant cameramen, grips (the movie equivalent of stagehands), and property men. The leading members of the cast, all in blue uniforms, sat in a circle on the ground playing poker: Audie Murphy, the Youth; Bill Mauldin, the Loud Soldier; John Dierkes, the Tall Soldier; Royal Dano, the Tattered Man; and Douglas Dick, the Lieutenant.

"All right, lads," Huston said. He dismounted, tied his horse's reins to a branch of the tree, and spent the next hour conferring with Rosson on camera problems. The stock players lolled about, blank-faced and resigned. They were being paid a hundred and seventy-five dollars a week, and audiences wouldn't notice them enough to remember their faces. Some were on the way up; that is, they were being given work more and more regularly. Others were on the way down. All of them had the manner of men who expected no major surprises. The leading actors made a great show of casualness and boredom, and then became genuinely bored, genuinely casual, and gave up the poker game. Bill Mauldin, his kepi pushed back and a cigarette holder stuck jauntily in his mouth, held the others' attention for a while with a series of jokes.

"Hell, this is ditch-diggin' work," Mauldin remarked at one point. "I'm just here raisin' scratch, so's I can go back home and work on my play." He started to roll a cigarette.

Dano took a pack from his pocket and held it out.

"Hell," Mauldin said, "I was rollin' my own when you was in three-cornered pants."

"Gosh, Bill," Dierkes drawled. "You talk just like the Loud Soldier."

"Hell," Mauldin said, looking proud and pleased, and ducked his head.

Dano remarked amiably that working in pictures was fine with him. He seemed at ease and as well suited to the role of the Tattered Man as Mauldin was to the Loud Soldier. He was unshaven and gaunt—so skinny that his bones protruded. He had large dark eyes, long lashes, and black hair, which was hanging raggedly over his ears. His uniform was torn and his shirttail was outside his trousers. He looked as though he had always worn tatters. He yawned, stretched out on the ground with his head on a rock, and went to sleep.

Dierkes turned to Murphy, who, with a troubled expression, was staring at the top of a tree, and asked him how he felt.

Murphy said that his malaria was acting up again, that he had had an attack of nausea while driving out to the ranch, and that he was going to lie down in Huston's ranchhouse.

As Murphy walked slowly away, Dierkes shook his head and said to Mauldin that he was amazed whenever he realized that Murphy was the most-decorated soldier of the last war. "When the war ended, he wasn't even old enough to vote," he added. In a tone of deep respect, Dierkes, who has an enormous interest in other people, said that Murphy was one of nine children of a Texas sharecropper, who abandoned his family when Murphy was fourteen. The mother died two years later. Murphy was working in a radio-repair shop when the war came. He tried to enlist in the Marines and then in the paratroops but was turned down because he was underweight. He finally got into the infantry. Among his decorations were the Medal of Honor, the Distinguished Service Cross, the Silver Star, the Legion of Merit, the Bronze Star, the Croix de Guerre, and the Purple Heart. "Now look at the little sport," Dierkes said.

"Hell, *amigo*, he's in a war picture, ain't he?" Mauldin said.

"All right, lads!" Huston called. They woke Dano up, and the first rehearsal began.

The rehearsals concentrated less on the acting than on preparations for getting the actors photographed. Huston studied his actors from various points through a finder, and conferred with Rosson about the placing of the camera, composing the basic plan of each scene with the meticulous care of a painter at work on a picture. A scene in which the Loud Soldier was to run up to a group of comrades and shout that the army was moving into battle would have to look as if it were near a river where, in the previous scene, the Loud Soldier had heard the news. The latter scene would be filmed at the Sacramento River location, near Chico, several hundred miles north of the ranch. At the end of the nine-day rehearsal period, the company would go up to Chico for several days of additional rehearsal and shooting.

After a couple of hours, the cast and crew had lunch, provided by an M-G-M catering truck, in the field. Lee Katz told Huston that in the course of making the picture ten thousand five hundred box lunches would be served, at a cost to Metro of $15,750— one of the smaller items in the picture's budget. During lunch, a prop man brought Huston a box containing old-fashioned watches of several styles and asked him to choose one for a scene in which the Loud Soldier, fearing that he will be killed in battle, gives his watch to the Youth. Another prop man carried over three small, squealing pigs and asked Huston to choose the one that would be stolen from a farm girl in a scene featuring a soldier pillaging a farmyard. Huston chose a watch and cast a pig, and then called for a rehearsal of a scene between Murphy and Mauldin just before their first battle.

Murphy sat under an oak tree, and Mauldin sat several yards behind the tree. Huston and Rosson squatted in front of them. Callow, his script open to the scene, stood behind Huston. The script clerk, whose name was Jack Aldworth, conferred with Callow about time schedules. Colonel Davison sat at the roadside with Marton, who began to tell how he had narrowly escaped death at the hands of African natives while making "King Solomon's Mines." The stock players lolled nearby.

"All right, Billy, come on down," Huston said to Mauldin, putting the finder to his eyes. Through it he watched Mauldin come down and lean over Murphy's shoulder, saying, "Why, hello, Henry. Is it you? What yeh doin' here?"

"Oh, thinkin'," said Murphy.

Huston did not seem to be paying any attention to the performances of the actors. Occasionally, he interrupted to ask them to look in this direction or that, and he discussed with Rosson where the camera should be placed and how much of the tree should be in the picture.

After the rehearsal of the scene was over, Huston made his first comment on the acting. He drew Murphy aside and told him that there was a humorous aspect to the Youth's fear. "Fear in a man is something tragic or reprehensible, you know, Audie?" he said. "But fear in a youth—it's *ludicrous*."

Murphy nodded solemnly.

"All right, *amigo*," Huston said, clapping him on the shoulder. "You just work it out for yourself."

"Here comes the producer, boys!" someone shouted. "Act busy!"

Reinhardt plodded slowly across the sun-baked yellow field. A fresh cigar was in his mouth, and a blue beret was on his head. He shook Huston's hand and asked him how things were going.

"Wonderful, Gottfried," said Huston. "Just wonderful."

As the rehearsals progressed, Huston seemed to show a greater interest in the acting of some scenes, and he was particularly interested in one in which Murphy discovered his comrade the Tall Soldier, Dierkes, in the line of wounded men straggling away from the battle the Youth had run away from. Dano, the Tattered Man, trudged along a dirt road, one arm dangling at his side. Murphy came from behind a clump of bushes and fell in with him. The Tattered Man looked fervently at him. "Th' boys ain't had no fair chancet up t' now, but this time they showed what they was," Dano said. "I knowed it'd turn out this way. Yeh can't lick them boys. No, sir! They're fighters, they be. Where yeh hit, ol' boy?" Dierkes came shuffling past them. Murphy started after him, calling his name, and put a hand on his arm.

At this point, Huston fell into step with Murphy and Dierkes, his face signalling grotesque and terrible emotions, which were not apparent in the faces of the actors. Band brought up the rear, following the lines in the script.

"I was allus a good friend t' yeh, wa'n't I, Henry?" Dierkes said, in a kind of delirium. "I've allus been a pretty good feller, ain't I? An' it ain't much t' ask, is it? Jest t' pull me along outer th' road? I'd do it fer you, wouldn't I, Henry?"

Murphy tried to get Dierkes to lean on him for support.

"No, no, no, leave me be," Dierkes said, pulling away.

Huston elbowed Dierkes aside and put Murphy's hand on his own arm. "When you say 'No, no, no, leave me be,' start to go down and make him let go of you," he told Dierkes. He stumbled and fell forward, loosening Murphy's grip. "All right, try it again—by yourselves this time."

Huston lit a brown cigarette as the actors moved back up the path to do the scene again. Inhaling deeply, as though in anger, he said that Dano was wonderful. "That boy is an actor," he said. "He's a great actor. I don't have to tell him a goddam thing. The only other actor I've known who had that was Dad. But Dierkes will be wonderful in the picture. That face! Even when an actor is limited in his acting experience, you can cover for him. You can get him to do things that don't require acting." He threw his cigarette down and ground it out. "You make him let go of you as you start to go down," he said to Dierkes in a soft voice.

Dierkes looked puzzled. "Don't I pull my arm away from him?"

"Do whatever you want to do with your goddam arm," said the director. "The point is you make him let go of you by falling."

Dierkes looked more puzzled. "I see, John," he said.

"Once more," Huston said crisply.

. . .

There were only a few days left of the allotted rehearsal time. The company had become tense. With a certain air of impatience with the problem, Huston had tried to communicate to the others his ideas and feelings for composing the various shots, and he had talked about the way things might eventually look on the screen. The others had tried to demonstrate that they understood just what he was driving at. But the strain was beginning to tell. One joke that made the rounds of the cast and crew was "This is getting to be a long war." The most popular one was "Did you hear about the coward who quit M-G-M to join the Army?"

Reinhardt was becoming dissatisfied with the script. He acted like a man under pressure. He lost weight, and smoked more cigars every day. Huston showed no sign of being under any pressure. He was able to turn from one thing to another with ease, good humor, and concentration. In a single hour one day, he did the following: When Dusty, the official cowboy on Huston's ranch, wanted to know when he would be given a part in the picture, Huston entered into a long, involved discussion with him about why it was necessary for a man to choose between a career in pictures and life on the range, and how much better the latter was in the long run. From Dusty, he turned to Audie Murphy, and asked him to look through the finder at the hilltop where the Tall Soldier would die. "He goes to die in the open, Audie," Huston said. "Do you feel the sense of expanse up there?" He went into a long, involved explanation of why a man chooses to die in the open. From Murphy, Huston turned to Rosson, to work out the details of placing the camera on a dolly, or wheeled platform, and of building dolly tracks for scenes in which the camera would have to roll along with moving actors. From Rosson, Huston turned to a telephone to take a call from Sam Spiegel, his partner in Horizon Pictures; he told Spiegel he might be free to work on Horizon's next picture, "The African Queen," in four months. From the telephone, he turned to Hans Peters, the art director, to inquire whether a night scene filmed on a set at the studio would look as real as one filmed outdoors. From Peters, Huston turned to a newspaper photographer who wanted him to pose with Mrs. Huston, who was watching rehearsals, for what he called a happy-go-lucky family shot, and he agreed to pose later that day. From the photographer, Huston turned to a tree branch lying in the road and demonstrated with it how a jockey twirls a whip. From the tree branch, Huston turned to his wife, who told him that he was expected to appear in an hour, in black tie, at a dinner party at the home of L. B. Mayer.

The operating budget for Production No. 1512 was by now complete. It showed that the total cost was supposed to come to $1,-434,789, including:

Direction	$156,010
Story and Continuity	41,992
Cast	82,250
Departmental Overhead	238,000
Rent and Purchase Props	80,800
Extras	145,058
Cameramen	25,500
Sound	35,177
Cutters and Projectionists	15,650
Producer's Unit Charge	102,120
Production Staff	30,915
Stills and Stillmen	6,995
Picture Film and Dev.	17,524
Sound Film and Dev.	8,855
Music	12,620
Wardrobe	43,000
Makeup and Hairdressers	13,915
Auto and Truck Hire	49,125
Meals and Lodging	35,385
Travel and Transportation	6,360
Location Fees and Expenses	18,255
Misc.	23,850

In a breakdown of these figures, the estimate showed that Audie Murphy was scheduled for forty-seven working days at a salary of

$2,500 a week; his cost to the production would be $25,000. Bill Mauldin, working the same number of days at $2,000 a week, would cost $15,667. John Dierkes, working thirty days at $600 a week, would cost $3,000; Douglas Dick, forty-six days at $800 a week, would cost $6,133; Royal Dano, twenty-four days at $750 a week, would cost $3,000. The Story and Continuity cost included $10,000 paid to the estate and the publisher of Stephen Crane for the rights to film the novel, and $28,000 paid to the writer of the screenplay—Huston. The Directorial charges included Huston's $4,000-a-week salary, totalling $137,334.

The Rent and Purchase Props included $33,370 for the use of horses and the services of their trainers. The figures for the battle scenes indicated that they would be violent as well as expensive: eighty thousand rounds of ammunition, at $110 per thousand, would come to $8,800; three caissons had to be reconditioned at $25 each; two hundred and fifty 45-70 rifles with bayonets and slings would come to $200. There would be ten Confederate flags ($65) and two Union flags ($13). Six dummy horse carcasses were to be bought at $275 each. Among the battle regalia that were being rented were two Union battle drums, at $5 each per week; two short bugles, at $3.50 each per week; twenty pairs of carbine boots, at $1.50 a pair per week; thirty nose bags, at one dollar each per week; a hundred infantry packs and blanket rolls suitable for foreground use, at $1.50 each per week; and twenty-five cavalry sabres, at $5 each per week. The Production Staff charge of $30,-915 included the cost of Lee Katz ($8,718), of two assistant directors ($5,366, half of which represented Reggie Callow's cost to the picture), of two second assistant directors ($2,609), and of Jack Aldworth, the script clerk ($1,430). The estimate explained that Aldworth would be paid $160 a week while on location, and $140 a week at the studio. Of the money to be paid to the cameramen, Rosson, at a weekly salary of $750, would receive $11,250.

The Sound charges were broken down in this fashion: twenty-nine days of recording at the studio would cost $7,337; two days of playback, $506; the use of the public-address system for fifty-eight days, $4,002; and 30,000 feet of re-recording, or dubbing, at sixteen cents a foot, $4,800. The estimate for Picture Film and Dev.

showed the expenses involved in buying and processing both nega-
tives and positives, and showed that the job would take more than
forty times as much film as was expected to appear in the final
product. The 180,000 feet of black-and-white negative, at 4.1 cents
a foot, would cost $7,380; the processing of 165,000 feet of black-
and-white negative, at 2.5 cents a foot, would cost $4,125; 155,000
feet of black-and-white positive, at 1.283 cents a foot, would cost
$1,989; and the processing of it, at 2.6 cents a foot, would cost
$4,030.

The breakdown of the Wardrobe charges of $43,000 revealed
that uniforms for officers would cost more than those for soldiers
in both the Union and the Confederate Armies. In addition to old
uniforms on hand in the wardrobe department, there would be a
hundred and twenty-five new ones for Union soldiers, at $50 each
($6,250); twenty-five new Union officers' outfits, at $75 each ($1,-
875); and ten Confederate officers' uniforms, at the same price
($750). The cost of Music, including a thirty-five-piece orchestra,
was figured on a basis of $600 an hour. Box lunches, as Lee Katz
had pointed out, would cost $15,750.

The cost of extras and bit players was broken down scene by
scene:

> EXT. Fording River (Chico)
> Sc. 65-66—soldiers slide down bank, cross stream, and
> climb hill—$2,850
> EXT. Farm (Ranch)
> Sc. 43-47—soldiers side with farm girl as she berates fat
> soldier for attempting to snatch pig
> fat soldier $150
> girl $150
> ad-libs (4) @ $55 $220
> extras—total $2,431

One of the least expensive shots would show the body of a dead
soldier in the woods. (The Youth would come upon the body after
he had run away from the battle.) The only cost for this, other
than the overhead and Murphy's salary, would be the wages of the

extra who would play dead—$25. Extras who spoke lines would be paid an additional $23 for each day they spoke. The battle scenes would be the most expensive. The Confederate charge that causes many Union soldiers, including the Youth, to flee would cost $16,469.

Reinhardt, Huston, and the cast and crew of "The Red Badge of Courage" were accompanied to Chico, for the first shooting on the film, by Mrs. Huston, Pablo, and Mrs. Reinhardt. The Hustons, the Reinhardts, and the leading members of the cast were quartered in the Oaks Hotel there. (The other members of the company were scattered about the town.) The Oaks is a small, neat, rectangular building in the center of a small, neat, rectangular town.

Late in the morning of the first day, Mrs. Reinhardt sat gloomily in a high-backed chair in the lobby. She was wearing a high-necked dress of mossy-green sheer silk with a golden butterfly at the throat, and high-heeled black pumps. She looked chic and elegant. The other lobby-sitters were for the most part gentlemen dozing under ten-gallon hats. A newspaper lay in Mrs. Reinhardt's lap; a black banner head stretched from one side to the other: "AMERICANS SMASH RED ROADBLOCK." Huston and Reinhardt were on the Sacramento River, eight miles away, with some stunt men who were trying to find a safe and cinematically attractive site for the scene in which the Youth's regiment would cross a river. The actors were rehearsing in a park four miles away. It was a twenty-four-hundred-acre park, and Mrs. Reinhardt told me she did not have the faintest notion where to find anybody in it, even if she were dressed for the excursion.

"It's wilderness and you need trousers," she said to me. "Gottfried loathes me in trousers. The temperature outside is one hundred and five degrees. Have you read the news?" She opened the newspaper and pointed to a headline reading, "MOVING PICTURE CREWS ARRIVE IN CHICO FOR FILMING OF CIVIL WAR DRAMA SHOTS."

"We are famous," Mrs. Reinhardt said dryly. She closed the newspaper and sighed in utter despair. "Why am I here?" she asked.

.   .   .

Huston was in an expansive mood. He was sitting behind the desk in a room in the Oaks Hotel, his chair tipped back and his heels resting on the desk, and looking over some local citizens who, in response to advertisements, were applying for bit parts in the picture. He loved to use the faces of nonprofessional actors in his pictures, he told me, and besides it cost less to hire bit-part players and extras—a couple of hundred men would be engaged, at $10 a day each, to appear as members of the Youth's regiment in the Union Army—locally than it would to transport them from Hollywood. The first applicant to come in was an eager, hard-breathing young man named Dixon Porter. He had a round, innocent face and an incongruously heavy black beard. Huston gave him a gracious nod. "Nice beard you've got there, Dixon," he said. He picked up a long pad of yellow paper and started making sketches of Dixon and various types of beards.

Reggie Callow, who was attending the audition, along with Colonel Davison and the other assistant director, Joel Freeman, said that beards were almost as important as talent for these bit parts.

"M-G-M offers a five-dollar bonus to every man with a good beard!" Callow said, in a raucous voice. "Go ahead, Dixon. Read."

Dixon Porter read, " 'Ain't they a sight to behold, in their brand-new uniforms! Hang yer clothes on a hickory limb and don't go near the battle!' "

"Thank you, Dixon," Huston said. "Very good, Dixon. Thank you very much."

"We'll let you know, Dixon," Callow said mechanically, ushering the applicant out.

"That boy is good," Huston said. "Not tough but good. We'll find some use for him. Now let's get some real grizzled sons of bitches." He went back to his sketching.

The next applicant was a thin young man with a long, dolorous face, horn-rimmed glasses, and a soft beard. He said he belonged to a local little-theatre group. After he had read and departed, Huston told Callow they needed tougher-looking men, tough as hell.

"Every time you get little-theatre, you get these delicate fellas," Callow said.

The third applicant, who was accompanied by his three-year-old daughter, explained earnestly that he hadn't been able to get a baby-sitter. Huston tore off the page he had been sketching on, crumpled it up, and threw it on the floor. The earnest father and the three-year-old went out again.

"Joel!" Huston said sternly to the other assistant director, a serious young man with a crew haircut. "Joel, you go out tonight to the poolrooms! To the gas stations! Find the tough guys and bring them back. We need guys who look tough."

"You mean guys who look—" Freeman began.

"Tough!" said Huston.

Reinhardt had finally pinned Huston down to the job of revising the script with him. They worked in Huston's hotel room, with Albert Band, making some changes requested by Joseph I. Breen, the Motion Picture Production Code Administrator. Huston lay on the bed, his back resting against the headboard, and sketched thoughtfully on a yellow pad as Band read off the lines that were considered objectionable.

" 'Gawd, he's runnin',' " Band read.

" 'Look, he's runnin',' " Huston said, in a bored voice.

" 'It'll be hell to pay,' " Band read.

" 'It'll be the devil to pay,' " said Huston.

"You can't say that," Reinhardt said.

Huston said, "The hell you can't."

"Joe Breen—" Reinhardt began.

"All right," Huston interrupted. " 'It'll be the *dickens* to pay.' "

" 'Damn tobacco,' " Band continued.

"Take 'damn' out," said Huston.

"That takes care of your censor problem for now," said Band.

Reinhardt directed him to make copies of the changes and send them to Metro's Script Department. Then he looked uncertainly at Huston. "You don't like to write?" he asked.

"When I put pencil to paper, I find myself sketching," Huston said. "I can't write alone—I get too lonely. I have to dictate."

Reinhardt asked him to try to write some dialogue for the Youth's officers just before the regiment goes into action, to give the audience an idea of the position of the Youth's regiment in relation to the battle. Reluctantly, Huston set to work. Reinhardt went to his own room for a cigar. When he returned, Huston said, "Here's a speech. The Colonel rides up behind the lines and says to the Captain, 'Captain, the Rebs are on that hill over there. We're goin' to try an' push them off. Maybe we will, maybe we won't. Anyway, take positions on that road down there and hold it whatever happens!' Captain says, 'We'll stand, Colonel, sir!' "

"Good!" Reinhardt said explosively.

"It's got to be kept simple," Huston said, looking pleased.

"Good!" Band said explosively.

The telephone rang. Band answered it and told Huston it was Sam Spiegel, calling from Hollywood. Huston said to say he wasn't in. Reinhardt bit off the end of his cigar and smiled happily.

Late in the afternoon of the day before the shooting of the picture was to start, Huston asked Harold Rosson if he wanted to go fishing. Rosson said no, adding that he had been bitten by a wasp, burned by the sun, and exhausted by tramping through underbrush in search of locations, and besides he had a bad dust cold; he was going to bed. Undaunted, Huston said that he was going fishing. Pablo escorted Mrs. Reinhardt on a shopping trip, from which she returned with an outfit, recommended by Pablo, to wear on location—a pair of Army suntans, a green T shirt, and a green porkpie hat. At the Oaks, Andrew Marton passed around a copy of the *Hollywood Reporter* in which the column "Trade Views," written by W. R. Wilkerson, the paper's owner, was devoted entirely to the leapfrog method being used in making "The Red Badge of Courage." (This was a reference to Marton's job of getting scenes lined up for Huston so that they could be shot without delay.) The column said, "Reinhardt and Huston are trying to make the picture with as little cost as possible. Such activity is to be congratulated and given every encouragement."

At two o'clock in the morning of the day the shooting was to start, Reinhardt sat down and wrote a letter to Huston:

Dear John:

Well—today is the day! After all the cliffs and shallows we have had to circumnavigate, it seems almost miraculous that this day should have come at all and so soon. How well I remember that night in my house, when at two o'clock we suddenly, enthusiastically, almost recklessly decided on "The Red Badge of Courage"! Well, the first phase is completed. We didn't "run." However, taking a leaf from our book, that isn't enough. We now must prove that we are real heroes. Or better, you must prove it. For I, the more or less unarmed lieutenant, can merely egg you on. It is you who will have to engage the enemy from today on, and I know that you will give a wonderful account of yourself. To that end you have my very best wishes, my unshakable confidence, and, if you want, my help.

I needn't tell you that the course ahead will be far from an easy one. The deep waters we have reached offer far greater dangers than the petty little political cliffs and financial shallows we were able to avoid. And they require much more than your amazing talents (which are a pleasure to watch) or whatever circumspection I was able to lend our venture. They require your constant, untiring watchfulness.

Let me—on this day—point out the main problems as they come to mind one by one:

(1) Audie Murphy. He needs your constant attention, all your ingenuity (photographically and directorially), all the inspiration you can give him. He shouldn't be left alone for a single second. Nothing should be taken for granted. At the risk of making myself a tremendous bore, CONCENTRATE ON AUDIE MURPHY! I watched him. I believe he will be good. How good (and the whole picture depends on the degree) depends entirely on the support you give him.

(2) Variety. Change of pace. At the speed you are going to do this in all respects terribly difficult picture and the

crazy continuity you will shoot it in, there is the danger of losing the rhythm of the continuity; the tempo might become too even, the moods too similar. In view of the general sameness of the background and the subtlety and introspectiveness of the development, I beg you to examine and re-examine every scene in the light of what precedes and follows the action. This may sound like childish advice. But I know how easy it is to get bogged down in the physical difficulties alone.

(3) Humor. Wherever you see the opportunity, bring it out; wherever you can, inject it!

(4) Geography. I know you are aware of that. But I repeat: it is imperative that we always know where we are. Especially the transitions from one locale to another must be smooth and clear.

(5) Script. Every hour you can spare (and I know this is going to be tough from now on) you ought to spend on the script until, from beginning to end, it is in a shape to your own satisfaction. Needless to say, I am at your disposal all the time. You have no idea—or maybe you have—how the days and hours you spent on the script (away from the set) in the last few weeks improved it.

That is all. Regarding the last point, I must add that you made me very unhappy last night. You know I was waiting for you. But it wasn't so much your failure to tell me that you went fishing which disturbed me (although it wouldn't have hurt if you had done it), but I know we would have accomplished a lot, maybe finished the script, if you had kept our appointment. Now that the shooting starts it will be twice as difficult. After all, that is the main reason why I came. If we can't get together, I might as well pack up and go home. I hope you won't mind my frankness in telling you this. You asked me once to be your "boss." I can't do that. I can only be your accomplice and friend. And in those capacities, I am anxious and ready to lend you whatever assistance I can.

And now, good luck! I have a feeling something quite

extraordinary is likely to come out of all this. But whatever will be the outcome, I can tell you one thing already: it has been a great experience to be associated with you. And somehow I am quite calm: we will steer our ship safely and proudly into port.

Always,
Gottfried

Reinhardt's letter was not the only one Huston received in the morning. At breakfast with Murphy and Mauldin, he read a letter from Dore Schary that said, "Today's your day, and with it goes all my best to you. I'm sure, John, we'll get a damned good movie out of 'Red Badge'—one that we'll all be proud of. Good luck and good shooting. Sincerely, Dore." Joe Cohn, the head of Metro's Production Office (logistics, budgets, etc.), wired Huston, "YOU ARE DOING A WAR PICTURE. SHOOT—SHOOT—SHOOT."

The atmosphere at the breakfast table was one of readiness. Murphy and Mauldin, the two leading men, had on their blue uniforms and kepis. They listened abstractedly as Huston, putting his correspondence aside and playing nervously with a couple of quarters, told them about Nate Leipsig, who he said was the greatest coin manipulator in history. Then Huston, who was wearing regulation Army suntans, stood up, put a Mexican straw hat on, took a gulp of coffee, and said he would see the boys outside. A few minutes later, Huston and Reinhardt, who wore blue cotton slacks and a matching knit shirt and carried a pith helmet, came out. Both men were looking grim. "I want to ride out with you, Gottfried," Huston was saying. Reinhardt nodded benignly and clapped the helmet on his head.

The first scene to be shot, No. 72, read:

MEDIUM SHOT—NEW ANGLE

The regiment encounters the body of a dead soldier and the ranks open covertly to avoid the corpse.

It was being set up on a dirt road running through the thickly wooded park. A couple of hundred Chicoans, many of them sporting five-dollar-bonus beards and all of them dressed in Union blues and carrying rifles or swords, were lined up on the road in a column of fours. Near the head of the column stood Dixon Porter, wearing the sword and red sash of a lieutenant; he was one of the extras. A long dolly track, with wooden rails, had been laid beside the road. The camera, fixed on a tripod, stood on a rubber-wheeled dolly at one end of the track. The trees lining the road arched high over the heads of the warlike array. Everybody in Huston's crew seemed, with a harassed awareness of the dollar value of every minute, to be rushing everyone else. Rosson, standing on the dolly and peering through the camera at the line of soldiers, gave hurried signals to assistants helping him get the camera in position. Huston and Reinhardt made a hasty inspection of the Chicoan army. Marton dashed at Mauldin, collared him, and thrust him into the Union ranks behind Murphy and Dierkes. The time was 8:38 A.M.

In the road, ahead of the troops, lay a soldier, face down, his uniform dishevelled, a rifle under his limp arm, his legs sprawled. Callow was arranging and rearranging the legs. A still photographer aimed a Speed Graphic at the dead man; his flash bulb popped, and he quickly turned his camera on the waiting troops. Band arrived and began to tag after Huston, who walked over to the camera.

"Good morning, boys," Huston said to Rosson and his assistants. "Good luck, gentlemen!"

Jack Aldworth was writing in a hard-covered notebook. The first page was headed "LOG—PROD. NO. 1512—HUSTON." Under the heading, he had already written:

    7:45-8:00—Travel to Location
    8:00-8:20—Spot Equip. and Unload Trucks
    8:20-8:32—Line up Dolly Shot with Soldiers

He now wrote:

    8:32-8:40—Set up camera with it on dolly—meanwhile reh [rehearse] and drill soldiers.

Aldworth would submit his daily log to Reinhardt and to Callow, who would submit it to Lee Katz, who would submit copies of it to Joe Cohn, Dore Schary, and L. B. Mayer, in Culver City, and to Nicholas Schenck, in New York. (Along with the daily log would go a daily report on the time the crew left for location, the time shooting started and finished, the number of scenes filmed, and the number of extras used.) Reinhardt was standing beside the camera, reading a letter that had just been handed to him by a messenger:

> Dear Gottfried:
>   Well, we're off! And we're off to a good start. I'm certain it will be good, Gottfried, damned good. We'll make it so. Good luck and my best.
>
> Sincerely,
Dore

The rehearsal began. Callow yelled, "Here we go, boys! Get in line!" The troops started marching toward the man lying in the road. Callow told them to pause and look down at the body as they passed it. Huston peered into the camera and watched the procession, then called to the troops that this was the first dead man they had ever seen, and told them to keep this in mind when they looked down at the body. The time was 8:56.

For all the tension, hurry, and confusion, it was very quiet. At Callow's command, the Union soldiers, having passed the body, moved back to their starting point. They were silent, and their silence was respectful. A smoke machine mounted on a truck, which had been hidden in the woods off the road, started up with a clatter, and smoke drifted slowly among the trees in the almost windless heat of the morning.

Huston moved about quickly and smoothly. He strode over to the dead man in the road and called for a bucket of water. A prop man scurried off, and was back with it in a few seconds. Huston quickly mussed the man's hair and sprinkled dirt over his hair, face, and knapsack. Reinhardt looked down with a cynical smile as Huston mixed a handful of earth with water and daubed mud over the man's face and hands. Huston stood up. Aldworth was holding out a clean white handkerchief. Huston wiped his hands on it and called for blood. A makeup man sprinted over with a tube of "panchromatic blood"—mineral oil with vegetable coloring. Huston, thumbs hooked in the back of his belt, directed the bloodying process. Callow rushed up and said, "Mr. Huston, have the troops lost their knapsacks by this time or haven't they?" Huston, thoughtfully staring at the dead man, said they still had knapsacks. He sprinkled another handful of dirt over the man. Marton hurried up and asked whether the troops still had their knapsacks on, and Huston gave him the same answer he had given Callow. It was 9:10.

Colonel Davison came up to tell Huston that the drummer boys in the column looked too naked with only their drums. Huston directed a prop man to put packs on the boys. Aldworth was writing:

8:40-9:12—Cont. line up Dolly Shot

A makeup man fussed with Mauldin's wig under his kepi until it covered the better part of his neck. Huston saw the wig and said it was all wrong. The wig was removed, and a smaller one was substituted. Smoke now lay over everybody and everything. The smoke machine sounded like a couple of steam shovels. "Kill that motor!" Callow bawled.

A man carrying a loudspeaker box on his shoulder and a microphone in his hand walked over to Huston. "All right," Huston said in a dramatically calm voice into the mike. "All right, boys." Everybody looked at him. "The idea is these troops are coming into a battle area," he said. "This is the first time you have heard gunfire. I'm going to fire a revolver. This will be the first shot you have ever heard. Each soldier as he passes the dead man will slow down. This is the first dead man you have ever seen. All right." The time was 9:26.

There was a brief silence—a lull before a battle. Huston told a smoke man not to make smoke, because this would be a rehearsal. Callow reminded the troops that they were not to step over the dead man but to pass around him. Huston went over to the camera and called for action. Callow told the men to get going. They began to shuffle toward the dead man. The camera trained on them rolled on ahead, pulled along the dolly track by grips. Huston walked backward behind the dolly, looking intently at the faces of the troops. He gave the Chicoans a menacing look, and slowly raised the revolver over his head. He fired the revolver, still watching grimly, then fired again. The troops shuffled uneasily around the body of the dead man. Callow called "About face!" and the men returned to their starting position. Huston went over to the dead man and sprinkled more dirt on him. Reinhardt laughed. "How he loves to do that!" he said.

The time was 9:35. Jack Aldworth was writing:

9:12-9:35—Reh

Katz said to Reinhardt, "Joe Cohn asked me last night when you were coming back."

"I wish I knew," Reinhardt said.

"Consider the whole thing unasked," said Katz. At the end of each day, he told Reinhardt, the film that had been shot would be flown back to Culver City for developing.

Reinhardt said he wanted to see each day's film—called rushes, or dailies—the following day. He didn't want to wait two or three days. "I don't care how they feel about spending the money," he added.

"May I quote you?" Katz asked, smiling.

"It's important," said Reinhardt.

"Let me just find my studio notes," Katz said, digging in his pockets.

"If we can get them two *hours* sooner, I want them," said Reinhardt.

Katz took out his notes and studied them. "It would mean a difference of ten or twelve dollars a night," he said. "I'll talk to Joe Cohn about it."

"All this for two lines in the script," Albert Band said. "Would television go to all this trouble for two lines in a script?"

Callow announced that everyone was to be very quiet, because they were going to start shooting. A prop man was chalking on a small slate:

Huston   Scene 72
Prod 1512   Set 01
EXT ROAD AND DEAD SOLDIER

The smoke machine started again. Aldworth wrote:

9:35-9:40—Put in smoke effect in BG [background]

Pistol in hand, Huston knelt directly in front of the camera.
"Quiet and roll it!" Callow shouted.
The camera buzzed. The prop man held his slate in front of the camera for a moment.
"*Action!*" Huston said. The soldiers moved forward. The camera moved ahead of them.
Reinhardt looked at Huston with a long sigh. "Now there is no turning back," he said. "We are committed."
On their fourth encounter with the body since the shooting had begun, the troops apparently gave the performance Huston wanted. "Cut! That's it," he said. "Print it!"
Aldworth wrote down:

9:40-10:00—Shoot four takes (Takes 1-2-3—NG [no good] action)

The dead man got up and wiped a muddy palm over his muddy face. He asked Band whether he would be paid extra for lying in the road a couple of hours.
"Over Joe Cohn's dead body," Band said.

At 2:30 P.M., the temperature in the woods was a hundred and eight. Eight Chicoans had collapsed while Huston was rehearsing a scene that required some troops to run off the road and into the forest and start digging ditches, as the Lieutenant of the Youth's platoon, played by Douglas Dick, walked toward the camera, smoothing his mustache, youthfully arrogant as he looked forward to his first taste of battle. At 2:32, Huston ordered his crew to print the shot of the troops.

At 4:02, Huston began working on a closeup of Dick smoothing his mustache. Huston lifted his own shoulder slightly to signify youthful arrogance, and encouraged Dick to imitate him. At 4:28, after seven takes, Huston said, "That's it."

At 4:45, Huston started working on closeups of the soldiers digging in.

"Do we expect an attack?" Dixon Porter asked him.

"You don't know what the hell to expect. That's why you're digging," said Huston.

Katz came over and said he didn't want to rush anybody, but the film had to be flown out of Chico at 6:30. Huston nodded curtly.

Huston directed the camera to be set up behind an elderly Chicoan who was digging in. The man had a long, deeply lined face. Kneeling alongside the camera, behind the man, Huston ordered him to relax and said he would tell him exactly what to do. "Action!" he called. "All right, sir. Move a little forward, sir. Now turn around and look behind you, slowly. That's right. Now dig. With your scabbard. Hard at it. Now with your plate! Hard. Harder. Very good. Cut!" He thanked the man and looked very happy. It was a face he liked.

Huston was rehearsing a group of soldiers in a digging scene when Rosson told him that they were fighting a losing battle with the sun. In the scene, Arthur Hunnicutt, an actor with a care-worn face, was leaning on his rifle, watching half a dozen comrades dig a hole. "I don't hold with layin' down and shootin' from behint a little hill," he was saying. "I wouldn't feel a bit proud doin' it. I aim t' do my fightin' standin' up." One of the soldiers digging said, "If yeh want t' get shot that's yer own business." Hunnicutt said, "Well, I ain't goin' t' lay down *before* I'm shot—and that's all there is to it!"

"Light's going!" Rosson cried. "Let's take it."

Jack Aldworth wrote:

6:10-6:17—Moving camera and actor to get sunlight

At 6:20, Huston took his last shot of the day. Then he walked over to a rotting log and sat down. He put his elbows on his knees and cupped his face in his hands.

Jack Aldworth noted in his report—a copy of which would be in Nicholas Schenck's New York office the next day—that eleven scenes had been shot for "The Red Badge of Courage," out of a total of three hundred and forty-seven.

On the second day of shooting, John Dierkes, the Tall Soldier, arrived at the day's location ahead of the other actors. A dusty dirt road wound through patches of wood and brush to the location, which was a broad, level, barren field beside the Sacramento River. Near the riverbank, grips were working on a twenty-five-foot-high tower of steel scaffolding, from which the camera would shoot scenes of the Union soldiers drilling on the field. A dolly track ninety feet long ran across the field at right angles to the river. On the track was the camera, which was to photograph a scene of soldiers drilling before a row of Army tents. Dierkes walked to the far end of the dolly track and sat down on one of the rails. He rubbed the back of one hand over an orange stubble of beard, and with the other he unbuttoned the stiff, high collar of his tunic. He took his kepi off and put it on the ground. With a crumpled bandanna, he wiped the perspiration from his neck. The sun was already hot in the clear sky, and the morning air was humid and buzzing with swarms of giant flies. Two trucks were lumbering past, manned by eight grips, who all had wrestlers' muscles. Dierkes stood up and saluted them. The grips did not return the salute. They seemed detached and superior, impervious to heat, humidity, flies, and isolation, fixed as though forever in one another's company, and completely absorbed in their truckloads of tools, ladders, ropes, reflectors, two-by-fours, and tripods. The trucks stopped. The head grip shouted that some small trees were needed. The grips took saws and axes, and headed for a patch of woods. A sound truck was being maneuvered into position near the camera. As it came to a halt, a young man jumped out and set up a microphone boom by the camera. In a little while, a property truck came up. The barrel-chested man in charge of it was stripped to the waist, revealing tattoos on his arms, chest, and back. Cheerfully, he let the truck's tailboard bang down; inside were stacks of rifles, swords, kepis, and extra uniforms. A few minutes later, buses arrived with the blue-coated army of Chicoans, and they lined up to get their rifles from the prop man. Then the studio limousines brought the other leading players and Huston.

Huston made a brisk tour of inspection past the row of tents, their pyramids of rifles stacked in front of them. Behind Huston came Reinhardt, his pith helmet pulled down over his forehead, and behind him, under another pith helmet, came Band. Huston conferred briefly with Reinhardt, then walked toward Audie Murphy. Dierkes slapped his kepi back on and went over to one of the studio's limousines and put his head in at the window. The driver was dozing over a newspaper.

"They workin' ya hard, Ferd?" Dierkes asked the driver.

Ferd looked up. "Am I burned up!" he said. "I was all set to get a couple of guys tomorrow and drive to Reno and hit them ever-lovin' crap tables. Then I hear they got news for me. We work. On Sunday."

"Gosh, Ferd," said Dierkes.

"Sunday is supposed to be a day of rest," said Ferd.

"I guess they don't want the picture to get behind schedule," said Dierkes.

"Behind schedule is all I hear," Ferd said, and returned to his paper.

Over the loudspeaker, Callow was bellowing for the actors to form ranks preparatory to drilling. Dierkes, on his way to pick up a rifle, walked past the camera dolly. Huston was standing on it, talking to the cameraman. Dierkes stopped, took off his kepi, and mopped his face again. Huston kept on talking to the cameraman.

Dierkes got his rifle and took the long way around to the drill field, past the dolly again. He waited a moment, then said good morning to Huston and the cameraman. Huston returned the greeting exuberantly but mechanically. Then, as though something had just occurred to him, he stepped down from the dolly and motioned Dierkes to come closer with one of his conspiratorial gestures. The two men squatted on the ground. "I just want to tell you how glad I am to have you in the picture," Huston said, with slow, dramatic emphasis. "I just know you'll be good, John."

The orange stubble of beard appeared to redden as Dierkes said, "Thanks." Then he added, "I sure wish the picture was shot."

"It'll be over before you know it," said Huston. "It always is. Too soon."

"A picture, if it is a hit, is the director's hit," Reinhardt said over dinner that night. "If it is a flop, it is the producer's flop." He was confident that "The Red Badge of Courage" would not be a flop—that it would, in fact, be both a work of art and a commercial success. The film shot the first day had been developed, and M-G-M's head cutter, Margaret Booth, whose official title is Executive Film Editor, had telephoned to tell him she had seen the first rushes.

"Margaret says everything looks fine," Reinhardt reported to Huston. "The march into the forest she loves. She says the trees look terrific, and Audie, too. The dead-man shot is very interesting, she says."

"That's something, if this dame says it's good," said Huston. "People put more stock in what she says than anybody else. She's tough as hell."

"And she told Dore," Reinhardt said.

On the third day of shooting the picture, the nervous excite· ment that had permeated the company at the start abruptly disappeared. Even the army of Chicoans seemed suddenly to lose all their eager anticipation. "Pretty cheap outfit, M-G-M," said one during a break in marching around on the hot drill field. "Ten dollars a day, and it turns out to be work."

Dixon Porter said to a friend, "I suppose out of all this chaos comes order eventually."

His friend said, "All this hurry up and wait. It's just like the Army."

Reinhardt had brought along a 16-millimetre motion-picture camera, and he was shooting his private movie of the making of the movie. "Mine will be in Technicolor," he told me.

His wife arrived on the set wearing her newly purchased trousers and porkpie hat. Reinhardt groaned when he saw her outfit. "Gottfried!" she announced. "I will keep you supplied with bottles of soda pop."

Mrs. Reinhardt put a brown cigarette in the corner of her mouth. "Silvia!" Reinhardt cried in horror.

"We are in a constant state of osmosis," Mrs. Reinhardt said, paying no attention to Reinhardt's agitation. "Osmosis has been going on for a very long time. A liquid of a lesser density flowing toward a liquid of a greater density through a thin membrane." She uttered a shrill, hopeless laugh and gave a hitch to her Army suntans.

Reinhardt wiped his face with a large silk handkerchief. It was immediately soaked with perspiration. He looked morosely at the wet silk as Katz came over to him, smiling gaily. "This is a scorcher, in case you haven't noticed," Katz said. "Anything I can do you for?"

Reinhardt asked him whether the studio had given permission for the army to ford the Sacramento River.

"Insurance men are studying the river for safety," Katz said. "They're going into it themselves."

"I will go in with them," Reinhardt said.

"Good, good," said Katz.

Huston came along and asked about the river crossing.

"Maybe if I were made head of the studio, I would go to you and say, 'No river crossing!'" Reinhardt said.

"Watch out, or that may happen," said Huston. He gave his choked kind of laugh.

"Then let's do the river crossing quickly," said Reinhardt.

.   .   .

A few minutes before midnight that night, I accompanied Huston and Reinhardt to the Vecino Theatre, on Main Street, in Chico. The marquee was flashing the current attraction in electric lights—Jack Carson in "The Good Humor Man." Waiting under the marquee were Rosson, Marton, Callow, and Band. After the regular program was over, we were going to see the first rushes of "The Red Badge of Courage." The rushes were being returned in forty-eight, rather than twenty-four, hours.

"This is it, pals," Rosson said in a low voice as we joined them.

For a few moments, nobody said anything. The men looked at one another nervously. They seemed held together by the same tense expectancy that had marked the first day of shooting. "Let's go, guys," Huston said, finally.

We followed Huston into a roaring darkness; on the screen several men and a girl were hitting each other over the head with sticks. We found seats in the rear. On the screen, a donkey kicked a man, and the crashes on the sound track mixed with the crashing laughter of the audience. Then Jack Carson was holding a girl in his arms, there was a final blast of music, and the house lights went on. "Christ!" Huston said. He stared blankly at the audience making its way out of the theatre.

Katz came in, and Reinhardt, sitting on the aisle, started to rise to let him pass.

"Sit yourself still," Katz said, and sat down behind him.

"Cigarette, Albert," Huston said. Band quickly gave him one and lighted it.

"You gentlemen ready?" a man called from the projection booth.

"Go ahead," Huston said, in a voice that sounded very loud in the now empty theatre. He slumped in his seat, putting his long legs over the back of the seat in front of him. Reinhardt knocked the ash off his cigar and sighed deeply. The house lights went off.

On the screen, the Chicoan army shuffled along the road; the faces reflected the feeling of tense expectancy that had marked the entire first day's shooting, and somehow the effect on the screen was just right dramatically. After the raucousness of Jack Carson, the shuffling of soldiers' feet sounded weirdly subdued.

There was a cut to a closeup of the dead man in the road and then to one of Audie Murphy, starting at the sound of Huston's revolver. The scene of the column scattering into the woods was followed by two closeups of Douglas Dick smoothing his mustache. In the first one, Dick held his shoulders rigid, and the fingers he passed over his mustache seemed unsure of where they were going, of where the mustache was. In the second scene, he lifted one shoulder arrogantly, in an approximation of the way Huston had shown him how to play it. Huston exhaled some smoke and changed his position so that his knees pressed against the seat in front of him. "We use the second one, Albert," he said. "Make a note."

When the house lights came on, Huston and Reinhardt walked out of the theatre rapidly.

"Well, now, the stuff looks very good, very good, Gottfried," Huston said.

Reinhardt agreed that most of the scenes looked good, but he did not like the shot of the regiment coming upon the dead soldier. There wasn't shock in the scene, he said. It didn't serve its purpose—to show the Youth's first frightening impression of war.

Huston said that the shot would be just fine—all it needed was a darker print. "The body is too light, that's all," he said impatiently.

Reinhardt still looked troubled. "There is no *surprise*," he said.

"It'll be fine, Gottfried," Huston said.

Dixon Porter had been promoted from extra to bit player. He was now one of the ragged veteran soldiers taunting the Youth and the other recruits. Huston sprayed Porter's face with water, then threw dirt in his face, and finally told him to roll around in a puddle of mud, all of which was intended to make him look tough. Another veteran was the man who had played dead. He was a painter and steeplejack named Jack O'Farren, and while he was waiting for the shot to be taken, he handed out business cards reading "The Sky's the Limit with Jack O'Farren" to all the recruits. Two of the other veterans, a real-estate salesman named Smith and a Chico State College art student named Feingold, rolled in patches of river moss, on their own initiative, after Huston had ordered them to roll in mud. They looked wonderful, he told them. He seemed exhilarated. He led the veterans in loud, boisterous laughter for their scene, slapping his knee and guffawing, and told the veterans they were great, just great; after the shot was taken, he led the spectators in applause for the performance.

With a good deal of zest, Huston then prepared to film the scene in which the Youth comes upon the body of a dead officer propped up against a tree at the edge of the woods. The effect, according to the script, was to be that of a cathedral interior, with the rays of the sun breaking through a thick haze of battle smoke. Huston showed the extra playing the dead man how he should stare open-eyed in death at the tops of the tall trees, and then he showed Murphy how he should approach the sight and move back in slow, hypnotized fascination. Then Huston switched back to the role of the dead officer. He seemed to do more than identify himself with the characters; the identification extended to the scene as a whole, including the tree. He sat against the tree, his hand clutching his sword, and again the look of death came into his eyes. Quickly he rose and strode back to the Youth's position, and again he demonstrated his idea of how one reacted when one came upon the horror of death. Reinhardt stood by watching. Huston did not talk to him.

That afternoon, Reinhardt appeared depressed. Because he was impatient to have a look at the latest rushes, he went to see them in the afternoon, while Huston was still shooting. I accompanied him to the theatre. Katz was standing outside. He told us to go on in and sit down, and said he would bring Reinhardt a soft drink.

"He'll bring the wrong thing, you'll see," Reinhardt said to me. "He'll bring me root beer and I hate root beer."

Katz returned with a bottle of root beer, and the house lights dimmed. There were scenes of the soldiers drilling, of Dierkes marching with Murphy and Mauldin, and of Murphy running through the woods, and, at the end, another take of the dead-man shot that had disappointed Reinhardt. "Much better," Reinhardt said to me. "I had them print this other take." He seemed to be working himself toward a more cheerful evaluation of the picture. The drill field, he said, looked just like a Brady photograph. Great atmosphere, he told Katz, but they should have used more men in the scene.

"It looks like a lot of people," Katz said. "It looks almost crowded."

Reinhardt did not argue the point. Dierkes looked wonderful, he said. Huston had certainly known what he was doing when he picked him. And in the second print the dead soldier looked like a dead soldier and produced a more startling, shocking effect. Murphy would be very good. "John can charm anybody into anything," he added.

When we returned to the set, Reinhardt told Huston that the rushes were wonderful. Huston seemed pleased. They walked to a shady spot and sat down.

"Tell me all about it, Gottfried," Huston said.

"The dead soldier is all right now," Reinhardt told him. "If I had seen that take, I wouldn't have kicked at all."

"It's all right now, then, Gottfried?" Huston asked, grinning at him for the first time since they had seen the first rushes together.

Reinhardt laughed a relieved laugh and said yes. "And it is really Virginia, because there is a cloud," he said.

Mrs. Huston and Mrs. Reinhardt had gone back home. "I leave in a great rush, in confusion, in a sudden gust of ambivalence toward Chico, actors, directors, producers, and the Civil War," Mrs. Reinhardt wrote in a terse note of farewell to me. "I am returning to Mocha, who understands me."

The legal department of M-G-M had finally given permission for two hundred and fifty uniformed, armed Chicoans to walk across the Sacramento River while two cameras turned. It was to be one of the most important scenes in the picture, Reinhardt told me, and it had been saved for the last day in Chico. At four that morning, Huston went fishing with Murphy. Four hours later, I drove out to the site of the river crossing with Reinhardt and Band. A hired motor launch took us across the river, and we landed near the spot where the camera had been set up, on a platform. Huston was not around. Rosson, wearing only a pair of swimming trunks, was hovering over his camera, surrounded by his assistants, and Callow was supervising the setting up of a fairly elaborate public-address system, over which he and Huston would call out orders to the men crossing the river. Reinhardt was getting his own movie camera ready for the big scene. "I wish Dore could see this," he said.

On the other side of the river, the soldiers were lining up.

"Everybody ready for D Day?" one of the cameramen shouted.

Rosson said they had to wait for Huston. He stepped down from the camera platform and hunted around in the tall grass along the riverbank, and there he came upon Huston, sound asleep. Rosson woke Huston, who followed him back to the camera, shaking his head sleepily. The director climbed onto the platform and sat there, complaining that he and Murphy had not caught a single fish. He looked around glumly at the frenzied preparations for the crossing.

"Let's go, pals!" Rosson called.

"I'm scared to death," Reinhardt said, putting his 16-millimetre camera to his eye.

Huston, over the public-address system, ordered the crossing to begin. The Chicoan army crossed the river and emerged soaked but triumphant. Huston stepped to the public-address system and told the men that they had been just great. "When you see this picture, you're going to see one of the most impressive scenes ever filmed," he said. "Now we need some volunteers for another shot. It means going back into the river part of the way."

"I'll go," Dixon Porter said, right up front, as usual.

"Good boy, Dixon," said Huston.

Porter brightened. "Had to chop water all the way across the first time," he said.

"You looked wonderful, just wonderful," said Huston.

Albert Band turned up in a blue uniform, grabbed a rifle, and went into the river with the volunteers, as he had once warned

Huston and Reinhardt he would. "It felt wonderful," he said when he came out.

During the day, a new joke made the rounds. Everybody told everybody else that the river-crossing scene would have to be re-shot because one wig had been wrong. Reinhardt put in a call to Dore Schary as soon as he had returned to his hotel. The next time Reinhardt saw Huston, he said he had given Schary a full report on the river crossing.

"Dore said to me, 'O.K., baby,' " Reinhardt told Huston.

Jack Aldworth had made his final log note for the work in Chico ("Wrap up—return to hotel—crews start loading equipment for return to studio"), and the company was getting ready to go back to Los Angeles. Huston, Reinhardt, and Band were going to drive back in Reinhardt's convertible, and they offered me a lift.

Band seemed to have been highly stimulated by his recent military experience. "One-hup-reep-foh-lelf-righ-lelf! One-hup-reep—" he chanted, marching in soldierly circles around Reinhardt.

"Albert!" Reinhardt said.

Band stopped and saluted.

"Get my camera, Albert," said Reinhardt.

Band saluted again and went off, chanting his drill-field refrain. Huston showed up shortly afterward, and read a newspaper while Band stowed the luggage. Reinhardt put his movie camera to his eye and focussed on Huston reading the headline "u.s. TROOPS ATTACK REDS."

"Put the camera in the back seat, Albert," said Reinhardt. He sighed and said he was fed up with taking his own movies. "I've spent a fortune on this picture already," he added.

Band climbed into the rear seat, and the rest of us sat up front.

"Well!" Huston said as we started off. "How much ahead of schedule are we, Gottfried?"

"A day and a half," said Reinhardt. "Reggie says if we had done that shot of the river crossing in the tank at the studio, it would have cost twelve thousand dollars more than this did. Albert, the box of cigars. Under my coat, next to you."

"We can have the river crossing on the screen for a minute," Huston said.

"That long?" asked Reinhardt, who was driving.

"It's worth it," Huston said. He slumped down in his seat, arranging his long legs in a comfortable position. Reinhardt stepped on the gas. "Don't rush," Huston said, looking out at passing fields of haystacks. "We're in no hurry, Gottfried. I like to see this kind of country. I just love to see this."

Nobody spoke for a while, and then Huston said, "I'm so happy about what we did in Chico."

"It was not so bad, was it?" Reinhardt said.

"One-hup-reep-foh—" Band said from the rear.

Huston sat up and said slowly, "I made a mistake."

Reinhardt started.

"On the veterans' closeups," said Huston. "I forgot to dolly. The long shot was a dolly shot. I forgot that on the closeups."

Reinhardt closed his lips around the cigar. Maybe they could do some retakes when they returned to the ranch, Huston said. He closed his eyes and went to sleep. Reinhardt stepped on the gas.

One of the first things Reinhardt did when he got back to his office at Metro-Goldwyn-Mayer was to write a letter to Dore Schary:

> Dear Dore:
>
> Upon returning from the wilds of Chico, I find that in the heat of fighting the Civil War (and I mean "heat"!) I missed your birthday so please let me send you my very best wishes belatedly today. Your presents are the rushes and the time in which they were shot.
>
> With kindest personal regards,
>
> Yours,
>
> Gottfried
>
> P.S. And I mean "fighting." I even forded single-footed the Sacramento River in order to convince the insurance man that it could be done without too big a risk. After all,

what nobler gesture can a studio make than risk the lives of its producers?

The scenes that were shot at Chico had been pieced together in approximately the order they would follow in the finished picture, and Reinhardt had seen them in this form. Now Huston was looking at the film in a projection room at the studio, and Reinhardt was waiting for him in his own office. Schary had seen the film, too, he said, but Mayer would not see any part of the movie until it was previewed. "Mayer really *hates* the picture," he said. "He will keep on hating it as long as he thinks we do not have a story. He would like to see us rewrite the script and give Stephen Crane's story a new *twist*." He laughed sadly. "It reminds me of the time Sam Hoffenstein was given a Tarzan picture to rewrite. He was told to give it a new twist. He rewrote it—he put it all into Yiddish." He gave a shy smile. "I love that story. It's a great story."

Huston burst into the office, followed by Albert Band.

"The stuff looks awfully good, Gottfried," Huston said. "It'll cut like a cinch. I have very few criticisms."

"What criticisms do you have?" Reinhardt asked.

"Well, practically nothing, *amigo*," said Huston. He sat down and, tilting back, put his feet on Reinhardt's desk.

Reinhardt leaned back and put his feet up on the desk, too. "This is an American custom I have embraced wholeheartedly," he said. "What criticisms?"

"I'll say right now Audie is superb," said Huston. "He's just marvellous. Sensitive. Alive. This boy is something."

Reinhardt said, "Will you do me a favor, John?"

"What?" Huston asked.

"Get Audie to smile in the picture," Reinhardt said. "Just once."

"All right, Gottfried," Huston said graciously.

A few days later, it was Huston, rather than Reinhardt, who seemed to have become dissatisfied. He was worried about the script for his picture. Specifically, he told Reinhardt that day, he was worried about the way the picture seemed to be turning into an account of the struggle between the North and the South in the Civil War. "All we want to show is that what the Youth is doing has nothing to do with the big battle," he said. "The battle has gone on for three days and it's going to go on for another three days. The Youth gets on the roulette wheel and stays for a little while and then he's thrown off, and that's all we have to be concerned with. We have to get something for the end that will show that." All they had at the end now, Huston said, was a scene in which the Youth's regiment took a stone wall held by the Confederates, and that was the last action scene in the picture. It bothered him, he said, that there was no big scene at the finish. He felt that something was missing.

Reinhardt said it was better not to strive for climaxes. "Sometimes the quiet ending is the more impressive," he said. "I always think of the strong effect of the quietness of 'Till Eulenspiegel.' The average motion-picture guy would say that it is an anticlimax. I do not think so." Reinhardt seemed to be getting immense enjoyment out of this kind of discussion.

Huston, ignoring the reference to "Till Eulenspiegel," merely repeated that they would have to get something new for the ending. "I'd just like the situation to be clarified," he said. "The Youth and his comrades have been fighting all that day and the day before. Now we open the last battle by following the general on his white horse riding along the lines. We go to the Youth and his regiment. They're part of this big thing. They capture a fragment of the wall. We begin with a big thing and end with a little thing. If the battle depended on this wall, then we would know what the situation is. But we don't know quite what happens."

Reinhardt said, "They take the wall. You think, This is the big thing. They take prisoners. Suddenly they get a command to fall in and march away, and they watch as another regiment is committed."

"I'd like to know from the standpoint of the battle itself what's happening," Huston said. "And I don't know. *I* don't even know." He laughed, and said he would think of something. "Another thing, Gottfried," he said, at the end of the discussion, "I don't like the dead officer Audie finds in the woods. It looks too stagy."

Reinhardt protested that he liked the scene.

Huston said that he would do it over.

In his living room every night after dinner, Dore Schary ran the rushes of all the pictures in production at M-G-M, and one night he invited me to come over and see the rushes of "The Red Badge of Courage." Schary lives in Brentwood, a fashionable residential district, where he has a cream-colored English stucco house. The doormat at the front door bears the words "Schary Manor"—the name of his parents' Newark home, from which they ran a catering business. In the summer of 1950, Schary was forty-five—one year older than Huston, seven years older than Reinhardt, and twenty years younger than Mayer. He was born in Newark, the youngest of five children. He attended public grade school, quitting at the age of thirteen after an argument with a teacher about a problem in algebra. Six years later, having meanwhile worked off and on in the family business, been a necktie salesman, and tried other jobs, he returned to school and, by attending day and night, went through high school in a year. In 1928, he joined the Stuart Walker Stock Company, in Cincinnati, as an actor, and remained there for one season. He subsequently spent a summer as assistant recreation director at the Flagler Hotel, in the Catskills (the director was Moss Hart), and from that he went on to play small parts in the Broadway productions of "Four Walls" and "The Last Mile." Schary wrote a play that was not produced but was read by Walter Wanger, who signed him to a hundred-dollar-a-week contract as a writer at Columbia Studio in 1932. He took the job, but at the end of twelve weeks Wanger didn't pick up his option. Schary stayed on in Hollywood, and several months later he helped write the script of M-G-M's "Big City," starring Spencer Tracy. Then, also for M-G-M, he collaborated on the writing of "Boys Town," for which he won an Academy Award. He next collaborated on "Young Tom Edison" and "Edison, the Man," and was given a job at M-G-M supervising a studio production unit, which made "Joe Smith, American,"

"Journey for Margaret," and "Lassie, Come Home." After this, Schary joined David O. Selznick's independent producing company, where he produced "The Farmer's Daughter" and "The Bachelor and the Bobby-Soxer." The success of these films led to Schary's appointment as head of production at R.K.O., and for that company he made "Crossfire" and "Mr. Blandings Builds His Dream House." He returned to M-G-M in the summer of 1948, at the invitation of L. B. Mayer. Before long, in addition to serving as superintendent of production for the whole studio, he himself produced "Battleground," starring Van Johnson, and "The Next Voice You Hear . . ."

Schary met me at the door of his house with an easygoing, homespun grin and told me that he was just about to view the last of the day's rushes. He was wearing gray flannel slacks and a blue blazer with white buttons. He took me into a large sitting room. At one end of the room were his wife, who paints under the name Miriam Svet; his three children (Jill, fifteen; Joy, thirteen; and Jeb, eleven); and M-G-M's chief cutter, Margaret Booth, a thin woman with a thin, bony face. Schary led me to a chair near them, and snapped his fingers. A wide panel in the wall at the opposite end of the room slid up, exposing a white screen, and the room was darkened. A projectionist in a booth behind us showed us "The Red Badge of Courage" scenes. These were followed by Technicolor scenes of Clark Gable and an Indian girl making love on a mountaintop. Schary told Miss Booth how he wanted the scenes trimmed, and the lights came on. The children thanked their father for being allowed to see the movies. He kissed them and sent them off to bed, adding that if they were good they could see the rushes the next night, too. Miss Booth said she had a date to go to a movie, and left. Mrs. Schary excused herself, saying that she had to work on a painting.

Schary sat down. The rushes of "The Red Badge of Courage" had been magnificent so far, he told me. "John and Gottfried have proved their point that they could make this picture," he said. "The original estimate on this picture was close to two million, and our estimators said it would take forty-eight days. John and Gottfried said they could do it in thirty and hold the cost down to a million five. Nobody believed it. But I believed it. I believe that no picture is like any other picture. So I believed the boys could do what they wanted to do. I believe that one of the most debilitating things is to have too large a frame of reference."

Before production started, Schary said, Huston and Reinhardt had seemed almost overwhelmed with doubt, and he had had to steady them. They had come to see him at home, when he was ill. "They were so concerned I went over the whole thing with them. I said, 'I have no way of comforting you guys by telling you that this is going to be a great picture. I only know that John is a brilliant director. The script is wonderful. This can be an inspiring picture. I don't think anybody will be able to say it's a bad picture. Let's follow our first hunches and first instincts, and let's make the picture! Let's make it as efficiently and as economically and with as much enthusiasm as we can. Let's stop thinking about it as an if picture. It's to be made. That's all.' From that time on, everything has just gone zoom."

Schary gave me a candid look. "I love John," he said. "That guy will live forever. He's a hearty, tough soul. When he wants something from you, he sits down next to you and his voice gets a little husky, and pretty soon you're a dead pigeon. He wanted Audie for the Youth and he got him." He shrugged benevolently. "A creative man, when he wants to win a point, he uses effective and dramatic arguments." Schary shrugged again. "I love to do this imitation of John when he says hello to you," he said. He did the imitation—getting up and giving a quarter twist to his body and saying "hel-lo"—and then sat down and chuckled at his performance. "I had visualized the Youth as a taller, blonder, freckle-faced kind of kid, sort of a younger Van Johnson," he continued. "I said, 'John, you're a big ham. If you were twenty years younger, you'd love to play this part yourself.' He said I was right. That's the kind of guy I had in mind—a guy with an odd, interesting kisser, with hair that falls down in front. But in the final test, I was sold on Audie. John never lost his hunch, and now he's got something there. Great guy, John. He's always flying back and forth. He goes here, there, everywhere in a plane. A schlemiel like myself gets on a plane and it crashes. I love John."

Schary grinned broadly. "Show business!" he said. "I'm crazy about show business. I'm crazy about making pictures. All kinds of pictures. But my favorites are the simple, down-to-earth pictures, the ones about everyday life. 'The Next Voice You Hear . . .' was that kind of picture. I'm crazy about that picture. I *love* it." Schary went on to say that he enjoyed seeing the rushes every night. "I like to reaffirm myself," he said. "The biggest job is the transfer of an image to the screen. For 'The Red Badge of Courage' I had an image in mind of dark-blue uniforms against light, dusty roads. This was an image that John moved successfully into the realm of production." Schary gave a professorial nod. "The boys are making an impressive picture. The only controversy about 'The Red Badge of Courage' is whether it will be a success or a failure. It's as simple as that."

3   Piccolos Under Your Name, Strings Under Mine

"THE RED BADGE OF COURAGE" was a day and a half ahead in its thirty-four-day shooting schedule when, early in September, the cast and crew reported at Huston's ranch to start on the major battle scenes. In their two weeks at Chico, Huston and Reinhardt had completed eighty of the three hundred and forty-seven scenes outlined in the script—mostly shots showing the Youth drilling in camp, marching through woods, crossing a river with his regiment, and fleeing through a forest. Reinhardt had not entirely liked one scene that Huston wanted to keep (the Youth's regiment coming upon the body of a soldier in a road) and

Huston had not entirely liked one scene that Reinhardt wanted to keep (the Youth coming upon a dead officer seated upright in a forest), but for the most part the two men agreed that they had made a good beginning. The eighty scenes had been seen, and praised, by Schary, who said that the film indicated that "The Red Badge of Courage" would be an impressive and inspiring picture, and that Reinhardt and Huston were fulfilling their promise to him to produce the movie at a maximum cost of $1,500,000, to finish it on schedule, and to try to make it a commercial success. Neither Mayer nor Schenck had seen any part of the film, but, by frequent long-distance telephone talks with Schenck, Schary kept in close touch with him about reports on Production No. 1512 that came to Schary's desk (duplicates of which came to Mayer's desk) at the studio; these showed that, of the total cost of $1,434,789 estimated for the movie, $468,044 had been spent up to the time Huston prepared to shoot his first battle scene. (Other reports of around the same time revealed that the studio's musical film "An American in Paris," Production No. 1507, would have a thirteen-minute ballet sequence costing $400,000, and that "Quo Vadis," Production No. 1312, would cost $8,500,- 000 but was expected to show a net profit of $12,000,000.) The first battle scene, which would give the Youth his first sight of combat, was going to cost Loew's, Inc., $155,000.

The battle scene was filmed from the top of a long, steep hill that faced another hill, which was longer but not so steep. The hills ran down to a shallow ravine, and this ravine was where the Youth would see his first fighting. From the top of the steeper hill, he would watch the clash of the Union and Confederate cavalry, amid bursting shells. Stuffed dummies of men and horses had been strewn over the battlefield. A studio ambulance was parked out of range of the camera; any actual casualties, it was announced, would be delivered to Los Angeles Hospital in forty minutes. Lee Katz, unit manager, the liaison man between Production No. 1512 and the studio Production Office, headed by vice-president Joe Cohn, climbed to the top of the hill and, panting, asked Huston if he was all ready for the battle. "Some battle!" Katz said. "It's costing a hundred and fifty-five thousand dollars."

"Doesn't it look just wonderful?" Huston said.

A great many people were on hand for the battle. A couple of hundred extras in Union blue lounged around with rifles and waited to be assigned their places. (As the shooting of the picture progressed, most of the extras were scheduled to change into gray uniforms from time to time and fight as Confederate soldiers.) Bill Mauldin, John Dierkes, and minor character actors stood off to one side; along with Audie Murphy, they were to be placed so that one of the three cameras being used would register their reactions to the battle.

"The new Mike Romanoff's will have only one section," one of the character actors was saying. "All tables will be on a par with each other. Everybody will be equal."

Andrew Marton, the "leapfrog" director, seemed to have abandoned future battles for the one on hand. He thoughtfully examined the faces of the soldiers, and then thoughtfully examined the sight below, and nodded with approval. "Johnny likes this sort of thing to look menacing and forbidding," he said.

"This will be greater than 'Gone with the Wind,'" said Albert Band.

Audie Murphy was off by himself studiously thrusting a bayonet into the ground. "All set for the big battle?" Colonel Davison asked him. Murphy smiled politely and said yes.

Huston, who was wearing Army suntans and a red-and-green checked cap, ran up and down the long hills without losing his wind; he was arranging the Union soldiers in jagged lines and hurrying back to check with Harold Rosson on how they looked through the camera.

"Where's your horse, pal?" Rosson asked, chewing gum rapidly.

Huston said that he had found directing the picture on horseback, as he had started out to do, too hard on his horse. "Christ, Hal, doesn't it look great?" he said as he surveyed the troops.

"We're getting it to look like Brady, all right, pal," Rosson said.

Huston laughed. The irony of the Youth's flight from his initial battle and his heroic deeds in a later battle must be made clear in the picture, he told the cameraman—his war in the movie must not appear to be a North vs. South war but a war showing the pointlessness of the Youth's courage in helping to capture, near the end of the picture, a fragment of wall. To bring this out, Huston said, he had written some additional scenes for the picture, including one in which soldiers from another regiment told the Youth that he had not fought in the major battle but only in a diversionary action. "I think it will be very good, kid," Huston said.

"O.K., pal," Rosson said, grinning. "Just tell me what you want."

The man in charge of touching off explosions during the filming of the battle scenes was studying a large map; it showed the location of explosives buried on the field of battle. With his help, Huston and Reggie Callow were instructing the Union cavalry to charge where the explosions couldn't injure them.

"It looks like the Civil War," Reinhardt said. He was wearing a pith helmet and a shirt open at the collar, and he stood next to one of the cameras, his fists pressed to his sides.

"You mean the War Between the States," said Band. "The studio says you can't call it the Civil War in pictures."

Reinhardt went over to Audie Murphy and told him that this battle would look completely realistic. Murphy listened, shifting his bayonet from hand to hand, and then, in one of his rare talkative moments, said that the psychology in all wars was the same—that he believed the psychology of a raw recruit in the Civil War was the same as that of a young man in the World Wars.

"You think the German was a good soldier?" Reinhardt asked.

"We had respect for the Germans," Murphy said. "There was none of this blowing-smoke-rings-in-their-faces stuff. It was a mistake to underestimate the German soldier."

"Yes," Reinhardt said, laughing. "You know, there are three kinds of intelligence—the intelligence of man, the intelligence of the animal, and the intelligence of the military. In that order."

Murphy kept on shifting his bayonet from hand to hand.

"Ready for the big battle, Gottfried?" Katz asked cheerfully. Reinhardt smiled and nodded.

A group of stunt men on horseback were all ready to make a Union cavalry charge across the battlefield. One of them, a young man named Terry Wilson, was riding a restless, snorting horse. A group of extras who were soldiers in the Union Army surrounded Wilson as he quieted his horse and told them that he was going to lead the charge. It would be the first of many services, which he called "taking bumps," that he would perform for Huston, including wrecking caissons, falling off horses, being dragged across battlefields by horses, making horses fall as though shot, and being blown up in the air by what would appear to be exploding shells. Wilson, an ex-Marine, and the other stunt men were rugged, and disdainful of the actor-soldiers, many of whom carried suntan lotion in their knapsacks. Wilson said that stunt men were willing to knock themselves out for a man like John Huston. "He's all guy, you know," he said to the extras. "A guy's guy."

"You get more dough in this war than in the Army," one of the extras said.

"This war stuff doesn't pay so well," Wilson said. "I'll get four hundred dollars for wrecking a caisson and a hundred and fifty for getting blown up. A hundred and fifty for falling from a horse. Seventy-five for rearing a horse. Maybe four hundred and fifty dollars to fall with a horse. If I break my neck, I get thirty dollars a week compensation. I don't do it for laughs, but I'll give Mr. Huston anything he wants."

An elderly man with a full gray beard, who was working as an extra, muttered that Wilson ought to watch himself. "I fought in every war there was in history since the Philistines," he said. "And I'm telling you this one looks the most dangerous. I was a weary foot soldier in the American Revolution. I fought the Philistines in 'Samson and Delilah.' I was in the First World War in 'Sergeant York.' I was with Errol Flynn in the suppression of the Irish Rebellion in 'The Private Lives of Elizabeth and Essex.' I was in all the Napoleonic Wars and the Spanish-American War and the Second World War. I even fought the Civil War once before, in 'Gone with the Wind.' I've been in all the wars, and I speak from experience—this war is going to be the roughest. You haven't seen anything yet."

"If Mr. Huston wants it that way, it'll be all right with me," Wilson said.

"Quiet!" Callow bellowed over a public-address system. "Everybody quiet. This applies to top brass and everybody."

"Forward march!" Katz said to nobody in particular.

"The man from the Pentagon is trying to speed up operations," Band said.

"Well, now!" Huston said, looking dazed and happy. He took off his cap and tossed it on the ground. Then he grasped the microphone and asked all the soldiers to be careful as they proceeded downhill; if anybody slipped, he said, he must be sure to protect the men in front from his bayonet. Then he called, "Action!" There was a good deal of yelling and confusion. The Union cavalry charged down the hill. The explosives went off on the battlefield. The smoke-makers sent smoke drifting over the scene. The line of Union foot soldiers, with Murphy up front, his lips pressed grimly together, started moving downhill toward the battle. After about five minutes, Huston called "Cut!" He laughed, and said it had all looked just wonderful.

The next day, an M-G-M publicity man came out to the ranch to get material on "The Red Badge of Courage." After surveying the wreckage on the field of battle, he said, "This is wonderful art. Too bad we can't use it. Battle stills don't sell tickets. Two things sell tickets. One, stars. Two, stories. No stars, no stories here. Can't sell Huston. Directors don't sell tickets, except De Mille. We'll think of something."

Huston received from Margaret Booth, whose opinion was respected by every producer and director on the lot, an interoffice communication that read:

Dear Mr. Huston:
 I haven't had a chance to tell you how wonderful I feel the dailies [rushes] are. Yesterday the scene between Audie

Murphy and Royal Dano, where they come down the hill after John Dierkes' death, was simply wonderful. Also, the scene of the Army walking down the hill was very fine; in fact, I could go on naming one after another that I felt was great. I hope to get out to the location soon.

Margaret Booth

A few days later, Reinhardt told me he was going to see the first cut of the picture—a piecing together on film of all the scenes shot so far. He did not want Huston to know it was ready yet, he explained, because he wanted to see it with Margaret Booth and Benny Lewis, the cutter assigned by Miss Booth to the picture, before Huston saw it. I accompanied Reinhardt to a projection room in the basement of the Irving Thalberg Building, where we were joined by Lewis and Miss Booth. The cut began with the men drilling on the field at Chico. Miss Booth immediately asked why there was only one shot of the men marching.

"Huston said just one shot and a closeup as brief as we can make it," Lewis said.

"Malarkey," said Miss Booth. "The marching is supposed to be funny, but it isn't funny now. You don't know what kind of marching this is."

"Then let's build it up," said Lewis. "We'll put more of it in."

"More of it back and forth; then it will be funny," Miss Booth said impatiently.

"I could put in a piece where the fat fellow walks by," said Lewis.

Reinhardt spoke for the first time. "Put it in," he said.

At the conclusion of the showing, Miss Booth criticized the scene that showed a group of veteran soldiers laughing at raw recruits; she said she didn't know what it meant. Reinhardt cleared his throat and explained that it wasn't plain because the long shot was a dolly shot and the closeups were not. "John shot it wrong. He forgot to dolly," he said.

"Reshoot it," said Miss Booth, and continued, "That shot of the men digging—that's very dull to me. Cut it right down to the bone, Benny."

"The old man with the lines in his face, turning around and looking over his shoulder?" said Lewis.

"What's he supposed to be looking at?" Miss Booth asked.

"John likes that," said Reinhardt.

"What's he looking at?" Miss Booth asked again.

"At the producer," said Lewis.

"He's a stockholder," said Reinhardt.

"I have news for you," said Lewis. "He's looking at Mr. Mayer. Well, his looking days are over."

"I don't get it, Gottfried," said Miss Booth. "All this individual digging."

"John likes these faces," said Reinhardt.

Miss Booth snorted. "Cut it!" she said, standing up. "I've got to go. Don't put anything back, Benny."

When she had left, Reinhardt said to Lewis, "For the time being, you can keep the shot of the old man turning around toward the camera. John is especially fond of that." He stood up, and, smiling sadly, he said to me, "Let's go up to my office." As we went upstairs, he said, "This is how we make pictures. This will be recut thirty times. The digging scene will eventually come out. But we must go at it slowly. We cannot shock John by doing it all at once."

Seated behind his desk, Reinhardt leaned back in his chair. "Actually, every director should make the rough cut—the film as assembled from start to finish for the first time—himself," he said, and bit the end off a cigar. "But it's almost a physical impossibility. Once the director is through, you can usually do what you want with a picture." He sighed and lit the cigar. "When John sees the first cut, he may holler like hell," he said. "He may ask Benny Lewis to put it all back. But then he'll come around to the way Margaret Booth wants it. There's so much about pictures that has nothing to do with art." He sighed again, and went on, "To me, there are three terrible moments in making a picture. First, the rough cut. Second, the first preview. Third, knowing the picture has opened in New York. For John, the rough cut will be the most painful. I will say to him, 'This is the best picture you have ever made.' He will say to me, 'This is the best picture you have ever made.' John is like a race horse. You must keep him in a good mood all the time. John is a charmer, you know, but he is really very forlorn, a very lonely man. He is out of touch with human emotions." He chewed on his cigar for a while. Then he said, "I wish I had made John reshoot the dead man in the road. It doesn't make the point at all. I felt it when I saw the first rushes. No matter how enthusiastic we are about the script, the cast, and the director, the impact of the first rushes usually tells you whether the picture will be good or not. Once the first impact is gone, it is easy and customary to delude yourself. Subsequent rushes will seem good. Performances will seem extraordinary. Scenes will be effective. The tension, the pressure, the sense of self-preservation, the all-powerful urge of wishful thinking will help bury the first impression, and create hope—even confidence." He smiled cynically and picked up a memorandum he had written to Schary about Tim Durant—a friend and riding companion of Huston's who, though not a professional actor, was playing the part of the General in "The Red Badge of Courage"—saying that Huston had thought it would be a nice gesture, since Durant was playing the General at a nominal salary, for M-G-M to give him a present of a hunting coat, to be made by the wardrobe department. On the memorandum, Schary had made a notation O.K.ing the idea and instructing Reinhardt to order the coat. Reinhardt shook his head absently at the memorandum. "It was different when I worked for Ernst Lubitsch," he said. "Lubitsch was a producer and director who did everything himself. The cutting. Every frame. And he was brutal with himself." Reinhardt looked mournful, like a man who didn't know how to go about being brutal with himself.

Margareth Booth, Reinhardt went on, was very helpful to him. She had been Irving Thalberg's cutter, and she had known Reinhardt ever since he came to M-G-M in 1933. "Margaret really saves me," he said. "She won't work this closely on a picture with all the producers. She feels like a mother to me."

Several times each week, Reinhardt went out to Huston's ranch to see how the picture was progressing. He arrived one day as Huston was preparing to shoot, as part of the first battle, a Confederate bayonet charge—the specific part of the battle that would cause the Youth to run away. "Realism!" Reinhardt said to me as he watched Huston. "How L. B. Mayer hates this!"

"It looks great," Albert Band said.

"Yes," Reinhardt said. "You know, Mayer thinks that John's whole point of view is corroded. He thinks John represents stark realism, which he hates. He thinks I am an intellectual European and want to make pictures that won't go in Kalamazoo, Michigan. Mayer told me that I was making a big mistake with this picture. He begged me not to make this picture." Reinhardt looked confidently around the set.

Huston, in dungarees and a torn blue shirt, was telling Rosson that he wanted a lot of smoke, to obliterate the charging enemy just as they reached the ditch along which the Youth and his comrades were deployed. He explained that the audience was not to see what happened after that. "The Rebs come down at us with bayonets and then it's all blotted out by the smoke. Got it, Reggie?" he said to Callow.

"Yes, sir!" said Callow, and instructed the enemy to come down with bayonets, and then walked on quickly to talk to the smoke men.

"They either want you or they don't want you in this business," Reinhardt went on, still watching Huston. He paused, as if he had just had a new thought. "Me they don't want, but they got to have." He laughed and, taking a white silk handkerchief from his trouser pocket, wiped his face. "They are very cruel in this business when they decide they do not want you," he said. "All you have to do is watch the faces of your underlings. Suddenly your words don't mean anything any more to your underlings and you find yourself standing in a corner saying to yourself, 'What happened to me?' Why don't I buy a house out here, like everybody else? Because deep down I know I don't want to be tied here. I don't want to stay here. I will never buy a house in Hollywood."

Abruptly, Reinhardt walked over and joined Huston at the camera, which was in a ditch behind the Youth and his comrades, to watch the filming of the charge. It was a fierce and frightening attack. The gray-clad soldiers started running across the wreckage-strewn field toward the camera, their bayonets pointed forward, and they leaped toward the Youth just as the smoke machine sent up a thick, impenetrable cloud. "*I* would run from this," Reinhardt said.

"So would I," said Huston. He called "Cut!" and strode away from the camera, his face blackened by smoke and his shirt and trousers stained with sweat and grime.

A visitor had just arrived on location—Sam Spiegel, Huston's partner in Horizon Pictures. As Huston emerged from the smoke of battle, Spiegel went up and slapped him on the back. "How is the Yankee general?" he asked. Huston gave him a smile.

Spiegel was immaculate in brown suède shoes, orange-and-green Argyle socks, tan gabardine slacks, and a brown-and-white checked sports shirt. He was carrying a bright-yellow cashmere jacket and he was smoking a pipe. "Gottfried!" he cried. "How is the commander of the forces?" He took the pipe from his mouth. "How is the war, Gottfried?"

Reinhardt said that things were all right.

"Nice, very nice, Gottfried," Spiegel said, looking around at everyone except the man he was addressing. "How many feet have you shot, Gottfried?"

"About four thousand," said Reinhardt. "We're getting wonderful stuff. Terrific!"

"Bill!" Spiegel called. "Bill Mauldin!"

Mauldin, lolling in the ditch, turned and waved.

"How do you like being an actor, Bill?" Spiegel called.

"Hell, Sam, it's O.K.," said Mauldin.

"You remember the party you came to at my house, Billy?" said Spiegel.

"Sure thing, Sam!" Mauldin called. "Helluva party!"

Spiegel put his head back and murmured a low, satisfied "Ah-h-h." Then he stared sadly at Huston, who was throwing a bayonet at a cigarette stub on the ground. "So, Gottfried," Spiegel said, keeping his eyes on Huston. "The picture is all right, then?"

"It will be a great picture," Reinhardt said.

"Nice," said Spiegel. "I get him next. For 'The African Queen.' I like to get him when he is feeling good."

Howard Strickling, studio publicity director of M-G-M, put out a mimeographed booklet outlining a promotion campaign for "The Red Badge of Courage." "It has BIGNESS. It has GREATNESS! First, last, and always, it is ENTERTAINMENT in the grand tradition!" the foreword stated. The booklet gave the gist of articles that were to be written by publicity-staff people for fan magazines, including "The Audie I Know," by Bill Mauldin, and "I Know Bill Mauldin," by Audie Murphy. Civil War stories, it was asserted in another section, had long made popular movies; "Gone with the Wind" had grossed millions of dollars and "The Birth of a Nation" had been the greatest grosser of all time.

"The Red Badge of Courage" might be a great picture, Strickling told me, and, on the other hand, you couldn't be sure. "We'll know when Mr. Mayer sees it," he said. "Dore is good. He's the nearest thing to another Irving Thalberg the studio ever had. He's idealistic, but that will be knocked out of him in time. The realist at the studio is Mr. Mayer. He always shows what he feels. When he goes to a preview, if he hurries out without talking to anybody after he sees the picture, you know there's trouble. If he stays and chats, you know everything's O.K."

One afternoon late in September, Reinhardt was in a projection room in the Thalberg Building, working with Benny Lewis on the cutting of the picture. Reinhardt's shirt collar was unbuttoned and his necktie was hanging loose. He paced up and down the room, puffing on a cigar; he was worrying about a scene that showed Dierkes, the Tall Soldier, running up to the top of a hill to die.

"We've got to delay him," Lewis was saying. "My God! A wounded man getting up the hill so fast! S.C. will grab him for the track team."

"Start him up the hill," Reinhardt said, pacing. "Then cut to Audie and the Tattered Man chasing him. Then cut back to Dierkes. That will delay it." He stopped beside a telephone and asked to be connected with his office. "I don't want to be disturbed," he told his secretary. He hung up and turned to Lewis. "I've got to have the stuff by tomorrow morning," he said. "Bill Rodgers and Si Seadler are here from New York, and I must show them what I have. How much can we have by tomorrow morning?"

All the shots filmed at Chico, Benny Lewis said, plus some scenes showing battles and the death of Dierkes—about thirty-five hundred feet, or forty minutes, in all.

"I want it," Reinhardt said. The two visitors, he told me later, were important figures in the New York office of Loew's, the company that produces and distributes M-G-M pictures. Rodgers was general manager in charge of sales and Seadler was Eastern advertising manager. Both were key assistants of Schenck. "They can make or break a picture," Reinhardt said, and resumed his nervous pacing.

The next morning, at the studio, there was a showing of "The Red Badge of Courage" that was attended by Rodgers and Seadler. Reinhardt introduced them to me. Nobody talked as the lights dimmed in the projection room, and nobody talked during the showing. The only sound during the brief intervals of quiet on the sound track came from Reinhardt; he was breathing heavily. As soon as the showing ended and the lights went on, he stood up and faced his guests.

"Impressive," said Seadler, a wiry man with a constant look of worried amiability.

"Mmm," said Rodgers. He was a dignified, courteous, white-haired man with eyes as cool as those of a box-office man in a theatre.

"Those death scenes are absolutely superb," Seadler said.

Reinhardt said, "Don't you think we ought to exploit Audie Murphy to the fullest?"

"Can we get his cooperation?" Rodgers asked.

"We're getting his cooperation," Reinhardt said. "And the Defense Department will be very, very grateful for whatever we do."

"They'd cooperate to the fullest," said Seadler.

"We should get this picture out in a hurry," Reinhardt said. "Take advantage of the current war situation. We must sell this picture. New York must sell this picture. This should be one of M-G-M's greatest pictures. Like 'Gone with the Wind.' "

"There's no way of knowing," said Seadler.

Reinhardt said, "What about using drawings by Bill Mauldin for promotion? 'Up Front with Bill Mauldin in the Civil War.' "

"Mauldin's cartoons are too grim," Seadler said. "For this picture, you should concentrate on the beauty of the photography, and at the same time get over the power of the big battles."

"Let's try everything," Reinhardt said. "We must bring the New York office strongly behind this picture. There's no Gable or anything in this picture. We must sell this picture as an important picture, in the great tradition. Like 'Mutiny on the Bounty.' Like 'The Good Earth.' "

"When Mr. Schenck sees the picture in New York, we'll know how to sell it," Seadler said.

"If this picture isn't sold, then all the money will be down the drain," Reinhardt said.

Rodgers spoke up, courteously and slowly; he appeared to be considering the subject with detachment. "We're compelled by law today to sell each picture alone," he said. "No picture of ours has ever gone out without being tested. We don't market them until they have been tried out. But you can be sure that it will be sold. Its greatness depends on how it is received by the public. But you can be sure that we are geared to do our part."

Reinhardt seemed eager to take his cue from Rodgers. He said, "This is an artistic picture, but, frankly, I'm not interested in that. I want to see this picture make money." He seemed to be getting lost in his own salesmanship. "I want to see this picture make millions."

Rodgers smiled faintly. "You can be assured that when we receive it, we'll get after it," he said.

Seadler said, "If the picture is good, I'll say so. I'm the kind of a guy in the company who will speak my piece. Even to Mr. Schenck."

"After you're through, you may think you have a great picture, but then the responsibility is ours," Rodgers said.

"All I'm interested in is that the picture makes ten million dollars," Reinhardt said.

Seadler said, "We'll know how things stand when Mr. Schenck sees it in New York."

The assembled film of most of what had been shot of "The Red Badge of Courage"—pieced together by the cutters under Reinhardt's supervision—was shown a few nights later to Huston, Reinhardt, and Huston's aides, including Rosson, Colonel Davison, Marton, Callow, Katz, and Band. After the showing, Huston and the others looked pleased, and somewhat stirred. Everybody smiled at everybody else.

"Well, now, kid," Huston said to Rosson, putting a hand on the cameraman's shoulder.

"I don't mind saying that the photography looks great, pal," Rosson said, grinning.

"Doesn't it look just swell, kid?" said Huston.

Everyone went up to Reinhardt's office and sat down. Reinhardt's expression was solemn. "I'll make a short speech," he said. "There will be no accolades. People thought this picture would not turn out the way we thought it would turn out. The mood has changed. The big shots from New York have come here, and they have seen the stuff and liked it."

Now everybody's expression was solemn.

"We are doing a remarkable job," Reinhardt continued. "We are working with two hundred extras when we should have two thousand. Last night, someone saw the stuff at Dore Schary's house and asked how much would the picture cost. He was told one and a half million. He said, 'It already looks like three million.' That is the way our picture looks."

Everybody grew even more solemn.

Reinhardt put a cigar in his mouth. Everybody waited for him to speak again. He lit the cigar and blew the smoke out, then said, "If now we bring in the picture three or four days early, everyone will be not only an artist but a hero."

The artists and potential heroes looked at each other.

Reminding Reinhardt that the schedule called for only twelve more days of shooting, Callow said, "We can't bring it in in nine, Mr. Reinhardt."

"Then bring it in in *ten*," said Reinhardt.

Huston said they hadn't saved any time with the leapfrog system, because they hadn't been able to put it into effect. "We didn't have what we were supposed to have—substitute actors to stand in and do what the real actors were going to do," he said. Callow said he hated to disagree, but the fact of the matter was that they had been held up by the smoke-makers, who hadn't been able to get the smoke on the battlefield at the right time and in the right way. "We had bad luck with the wind," he said. Huston repeated that the trouble was lack of men. "If what we're *interested* in is days," he added. Callow said that the leapfrog system wouldn't have worked, no matter how many men they had, because basically it was unsound—the only person who could know what kind of scenes Huston wanted was Huston himself. Then everybody started to talk at once. Reinhardt looked bewildered.

When there was a momentary lull in the talk, Reinhardt said quickly, "If you can't bring it in in ten days, bring it in in eleven. One day early. That's all I ask."

A couple of days later, a long line of Union troops walked slowly across Huston's battlefield in a scene showing the Youth's regiment beginning a charge toward the enemy. They held their rifles low, bayonets fixed and pointed forward. The camera, on a dolly track, moved along with the line. Huston walked beside the camera on the other side of the dolly track and studied the line of soldiers as they started to walk faster and faster and finally broke into a run. Explosions went off at predetermined positions on the field, and soldiers in the line—chosen by Callow to have the honor of dying in action—clutched their midriffs, dropped their rifles, threw up their arms, and fell. Huston called "Cut!" and, with satisfaction, said that the scene looked just great. He took some closeups of the feet of the soldiers in the various stages between the slow walk and the run, and then, as he was getting ready to take closeups of falling men, he suddenly looked surprised and told Rosson to hold things a minute. "I have an idea, Hal," he said, in the amazed tone he sometimes uses. "It might be something, kid." He tossed his head in a conspiratorial gesture at one of the extras, a skinny young man with a long, thin face and a weak chin, who was wearing steel-rimmed spectacles. Huston squatted on the ground with the extra, in what appeared to be deep, concentrated consideration of a problem. Then he nodded briskly. "All right, amigo," he said. "Let's see you do it."

The young man grinned bashfully; then he took a few steps forward, carrying his rifle, threw up his hands, dropping his rifle, and fell to the ground.

"That's the idea, amigo," Huston said, and chortled. He held another brief conference with the young man, and again the young man grinned bashfully.

This time the young man knelt and handed his spectacles to Huston, who placed them on the ground before him. The young man blinked his eyes, groped for the spectacles, put them on, and then collapsed, as though in death.

Huston chortled again. "Very good," he said. "Very good." He put a brown cigarette in his mouth, offered one to the young man, and then called to Rosson. "I've got an extra little bit here, Hal," he said cheerfully. He lighted the extra's cigarette and then his own, and proceeded to work with Rosson on setting up the camera to take the scene of a soldier who falls and puts on his lost spectacles before rolling over in death.

The next day, Huston worked on a new scene he had written to point up the irony of the Youth's heroic action in the general scheme of the battle. This scene would take place just before the final battle, in which the Youth and his comrades capture the wall. Huston directed Tim Durant, as the General (who was wearing, in addition to the uniform provided by M-G-M, the sword that had belonged to Huston's great-grandfather), in a scene requiring him to ride his white horse along the line of raw recruits preparing to go into battle, stopping before each company and inviting the troops to have supper with him after they had won the battle, then pausing to chat with some ragged veterans of battle and, instead of offering them the spurious invitation, offering them a chaw of his tobacco. Durant spoke in a thin, almost nagging voice. As he was departing, one of the veterans called, "Having supper with us tonight, General?" The General rode away, followed by friendly guffaws from the veterans. Huston grew more and more exuberant as he went on to direct Durant in a closeup—the General taking off his hat in prayer and muttering, "Thy will be done, Sir."

"Very good, Tim," Huston said, laughing, and called "Cut!"

"I now become one of the immortals of Beverly Hills," Durant said.

"Ho! Ho! Ho!" Huston said.

Benny Burt, another friend of Huston's, had been given a part in the picture as a soldier in the Youth's regiment. He was a scrawny little man, with large, melancholy eyes. He talked out of the side of his mouth in a staccato manner, and he was not completely happy about his role. He had played a stool pigeon in Huston's "The Asphalt Jungle," and he had played small parts in a number of pictures since then, including "Cry Danger," "M," "The Enforcer," "The Lemon Drop Kid," "Convicted," and "Chain Gang." He had hoped for something bigger in "The Red Badge of Courage," but he was just an anonymous soldier. In his two weeks' work, he had lost several pounds, bringing his weight down to a hundred and eight. "I want to sink my teeth in one good part and I'll set this town on fire," he said.

Burt had been waiting for his opportunity since 1933, when he came to Hollywood. Before that, he had worked in vaudeville and burlesque in a Gus Edwards act called "Snuffy the Cab Man." "I was in burlesque when it was burlesque," he told me. "I'm not one of these Johnny-come-latelies. I do seven different dialects, including a pretty fair Chinaman. My Greek character would kill you. I used to kill Al Capone and all his boys with my Greek dialect when I worked for Capone's Royal Frolics, in Chicago. Every six weeks I wanted to quit, so they gave me a raise every time. Capone and his boys taught me how to bet the horses. They should drop dead what they did to me. If it wasn't for the horses, though, I never would have met *him*," he said, jerking a thumb at Huston, who was fussing over the camera. "It was at the race track. I'm at the track, and I'm with three hoodlums from Chicago. I'm at the hundred-dollar window betting thirty-five hundred for those guys. He"—again he jerked his thumb at Huston—"is behind me, and he says to me, 'I always see you here.' So I tell him to get this horse. He did and the horse won. So he says, 'Here's a hundred-dollar ticket for you.' I say, 'You owe me nuttin'.' So he says, 'Then come have a drink with me.' So we had a couple of drinks. Then he says, 'What you doin' for dinner?' He wants me to have dinner with him. From then on I'm with him morning, noon, and night. I was with him the night his dad died. I told him, 'John, don't you worry, I'll take care of you.' All my life, nobody ever gave me nuttin', but from then on we were like brothers. I did everything for him. I drove him here, there. I let him hypnotize me. I took care of his clothes. His suits cost three hundred and fifty dollars apiece. He has fifty pairs of shoes at fifty-five dollars a pair. It burned me up when Cholly Knickerbocker called him one of the worst-dressed men. I was with him on Thanksgiving and I was with him on Christmas. I was his family."

Burt scratched his whiskered chin and put a brown cigarette in his mouth. Huston used to listen to his advice about betting on horses, he told me sadly, but now he didn't any more. "All I do around here is swallow two tons of dirt in them battles," he said.

Band, puffing on a long cigar, came over and told Burt that, one by one, the supporting actors who were soldiers were dying in the picture and that he was in charge of deciding which ones might live. "Do you know Crawford? I just killed him off," he said. "One more off the payroll."

"Albert, don't kill me," said Burt.

"I'll just have you get wounded," said Band.

"Don't do nuttin' to me. Just let me keep on fightin'," said Burt. His face brightened. "Hey, Albert!" he continued. "You shoulda seen me when I worked in Slapsie Maxie's. I used to come on and yell 'Hey, Maxie! Jane Russell's out in front!' and he'd yell back 'She always was!' "

Band puffed importantly on his cigar, and then said that he might just have Burt shot in the leg.

"Don't do nuttin' to me," said Burt.

Huston stro'led over, an unlit cigarette dangling from a corner of his mouth. Burt whipped out a match. "Thank you, Benny," Huston said.

"How you doin', boss?" Burt asked. "Everythin' goin' all right?"

"Why, yes, thank you very much, Benny," said Huston.

"You gonna rest up Bargain Lass?" Burt asked, referring to one of the four horses in Huston's racing stable.

"Uh-huh," said Huston, his mind obviously on something else. "Well, now, Benny, I need a closeup for the next shot. You might be good for it. You might be very good for it, Benny."

Burt could not contain his delight. "Sure, sure," he said.

Huston laughed and told him to be on the alert for a call.

Sporadically, Huston received communications from Dore Schary, cheering him on. "There's been a little illness at the studio and some people have been absent," Schary wrote as the filming of the picture approached its end. "I've been working so darned hard that on weekends I've had to kind of stay close to home, which accounts for my inability to get up and see you and thank you and everybody personally for a film that I think is going to work together into a very important movie."

Two days later, Huston heard from Schary again. "The material continues to look wonderful," he wrote. "However, I have two slight concerns: (1) I think in some of the shots the dust is so heavy that we lose some of the effectiveness. It is, of course, very likely that in the cutting you plan to eliminate some of this and use the clearer sections. (2) I think that the laughing of the regulars is a little overdone when our new regiment walks past them after the fight. There doesn't seem to be enough provocation or motivation for this, and I am afraid that it sets up a general ambivalence that may hurt us, and, rather than creating interest, will very likely create confusion. The material with the General going past the men and the dinner invitations is wonderful—very rich, real, and human. Again, my best—and stay with it. Fondest, D.S."

.   .   .

Huston was going to play a bit part in the picture, as he did in many of his pictures. He had a three-day growth of beard on his face, and he put on the tattered costume of a veteran Union soldier and stood in the line of jeering veterans for a retake of the scene Schary had objected to. He delivered his line—"Hang your clothes on a hickory limb and don't go near the battle!"—in a callous manner, showing contempt for the Youth and the other raw recruits. Playing the bit galvanized him into tremendous activity. He went about his work still wearing the costume. As the day neared its end, the air became cold, and he put on the bedraggled coat of a Confederate officer, and sat on the running board of a sound truck and listened carefully, through earphones, to the recording of Confederate and Union soldiers calling to each other across what would eventually appear to be a river. Without any lessening of energy, he invited Reinhardt and his crew up to his ranchhouse for a drink, and there showed them a present the leading members of the cast had given him. It was a saddle, to which was affixed a silver plate engraved, "To John Huston with affection from his damn Yankees." He put his arms around it and said it was just about the greatest saddle he had ever seen. The forward pitch was beautiful, like the fenders on a Rolls-Royce. "It follows the shape of the horse," he said, running a caressing hand over it. "This is as beautiful underneath as it is on top. It's abstract sculpture, that's what it is."

Reinhardt adjusted the beret he was wearing, and yawned.

"No saddle has ever compared with it," Huston said to him.

"Beautiful!" Reinhardt said, suddenly enthusiastic, and then urged him to change his clothes, so they could drive to the studio in Culver City. "We must talk about the music for the picture," he said.

"I've thought about that, Gottfried," Huston said. He spoke about the death scenes. "The music should have the feeling of death," he said. "The way it is when you're going under anesthesia. Circular. Coming closer and closer and closer."

"Great," Reinhardt said. "That will be great."

.   .   .

For the next two days, "The Red Badge of Courage" company worked at the studio, on a set representing the Youth's camp. They did some scenes of the camp at nighttime. In another part of the studio, a lot known as Joe Cohn Park, Huston did a retake of the shot of the dead officer the Youth comes upon in the woods. The new shot, he said, was more satisfying—just as gruesome but not as stagy as the one he had taken in Chico.

Schary had been seeing the rushes of "The Red Badge of Courage" every night. "I'm really crazy about the picture," he said to Reinhardt. "It's got a great feeling about it. Audie is swell. Much better than I thought he would be. It's going to be a great picture. It won't be brought in early, but it'll be a great picture."

On the last day of shooting their picture—they had gone three days over the allotment—Reinhardt and Huston sat in the latter's office and talked as if they had trouble thinking of things to say.

"God, it feels kind of funny, doesn't it?" Reinhardt said.

Huston was sketching nightmare faces on a pad, and he frowned as he sketched. "To be finished," he said, not lifting his eyes from the paper.

"Jesus!" said Reinhardt.

"Did you see the last shot in the picture, where they march away from the battlefield?" Huston asked.

"Yes," said Reinhardt.

"That ought to run and run and run," Huston said, sketching.

"Yes," said Reinhardt. "And you even got Audie to smile once."

There was a long silence. Huston crumpled the sheet he had been sketching on, and threw it across the room.

"It's funny," Reinhardt said. "I feel funny. Now we deliver the picture into the hands of the octopus."

"I'm going away for a couple of days' rest," said Huston.

Reinhardt wanted to know where he was going. Up north, with Terry Wilson, the stunt man, Huston said. They were going to shoot ducks.

"I shouldn't say this," Reinhardt said, and he knocked wood three times. "But we've got something solid."

Huston laughed. "This is like seeing your sweetheart off," he said. "You've taken her to the airport. Her plane has taken off. You stand there. We'll never make 'The Red Badge of Courage' again."

Reinhardt said, "I think we've got something great. Very seldom have great novels become great pictures."

" 'David Copperfield' came the closest," Huston said.

Reinhardt said, "If 'Red Badge' turns out to be great, it will give you and me terrific inhibitions about what we do next."

Huston said he knew what he was going to do. He was going to direct and collaborate on the screenplay for "The African Queen" for his own company, and he wanted the picture to make money. "I don't have any inhibitions about making a pile of dough, Gottfried," he added, and laughed.

The company assembled in Joe Cohn Park and shot what they thought would be the last scene—a night scene showing the Cheery Soldier coming upon the Youth lying unconscious in a field. The Cheery Soldier was sprung on the company as a surprise; he was the well-known actor Andy Devine. (Because of the shortness of the part, Devine did not want to be given a screen credit.) With a good deal of bounce and zest, Huston urged on Devine, who carried a lantern (lit by a system of wiring wrapped around Devine under his uniform) in one hand and supported Murphy with the other, as he guided the Youth back through the woods to his regiment.

"Anyway—dyin's only dyin'. S'posin' you don't hear th' birds sing tomorrow—or see the sun come out from behind a cloud. It'll happen jest th' same!" the Cheery Soldier said to the Youth.

"Dyin's only dyin'," Huston said in a singsong to Devine. "Pep it up, kid. Make it fast and funny."

"Dyin's only dyin'," Devine began, immediately catching Huston's rhythm. It was a fast and cheery scene.

After it had been taken, Callow brought a microphone over to Huston, and everyone gathered around. Callow said that, as the loudest voice in the company, he had been chosen to present Huston with a token of appreciation from the crew. The token was a pair of binoculars.

"Oh, God, isn't this something!" Huston said. "My God, these are just marvellous." Many of the crew looked almost tearful. Huston said he knew how hard they had worked for him. "This has been the easiest picture for me to direct, entirely thanks to you, and despite all the hardship I'd be willing to start all over again tomorrow," he said.

"I feel so sad," Reinhardt said to Huston.

"I never had a crew like this," Huston said.

"I feel so sad," said Reinhardt. He looked almost tearful, too.

Huston said, "I once told you we would never make this picture."

"And I said, 'It depends on us,'" said Reinhardt. "I'll never forget it."

Huston and Reinhardt shook hands and said they would get together in a few days, when Huston returned from his duck shooting.

Reinhardt had written a long letter about promoting the picture to Howard Dietz, vice-president in charge of advertising, publicity, and exploitation for Loew's, in New York. Dietz had written back that it was dangerous to ballyhoo a picture without stars far in advance. Now Dietz was making his bi-monthly visit to the studio, and Reinhardt had persuaded him to come along to the Beverly Hills Hotel for a drink with Huston, who had just come back from his shooting trip. Dietz and Reinhardt waited for Huston in the hotel bar. A bland man with a bored air, Dietz had collaborated on several Broadway musicals before he became a publicity director. He had worked for Samuel Goldwyn before M-G-M was founded, and it was he who devised the trademark of the lion and, with the advent of talking pictures, suggested endowing it with the celebrated roar. His boredom seemed to increase as Reinhardt tried to steer the conversation toward the promotion of "The Red Badge of Courage."

"We have terrific stuff in the picture," Reinhardt said. "We must sell it as one of M-G-M's great pictures."

Wearily, Dietz lifted his eyebrows.

"Wait till you talk to John," Reinhardt said, looking anxiously in the direction of the door. "I want you to talk to John."

Dietz sighed, and said he wished he were back home, playing bridge. "Why don't people out here play bridge?" he asked.

"You don't like it here?" Reinhardt said.

"I don't like it because I have to live in a hotel and I don't like hotels," Dietz said.

At this point, Huston and his wife walked in. Huston shook hands with Dietz and told him he had been shooting ducks.

"My icebox is packed with wild ducks," Mrs. Huston said.

"I hate chicken, but I must love the taste of wild duck," Huston said.

Dietz gave a bored half smile.

"I've been telling Howard about the picture, John," said Reinhardt.

"Oh, how are things going with it?" Huston asked offhandedly.

"We have terrific—" Reinhardt began.

Huston did not seem to hear him. He was greeting Sam Spiegel, who had just come into the bar. Spiegel said that it was a great surprise to find everybody right there. "Maybe you can tell me when you will start to write 'The African Queen,'" he said to Huston. "So, how about dinner tomorrow night to talk about it?"

Huston nodded vaguely.

"What are we going to do about all the ducks, John?" Mrs. Huston asked in alarm.

"You just clean the ducks, honey, and hang on to them," Huston said, carefully enunciating each syllable. Suddenly, against an out-of-focus bar background, Huston, his beautiful wife, and the unanswered question about the ducks turned into a Huston scene that was full of mysterious, even sinister possibilities.

Thirty-eight days had been devoted to shooting "The Red Badge of Courage"—four more than the number allotted. Of the estimated total cost of $1,434,789, $1,362,426 had already been spent, and the latest estimated cost of the movie was $1,548,755. The first rough cut of "The Red Badge of Courage" was ready to be shown to Huston. Its seven thousand feet of film would take one hour and eighteen minutes to run off. The closeup of the old man with the lined face had been cut out, but when Huston, accompanied by Reinhardt and me, saw the film, he did not give any indication that he had even noticed it. The closeup of Huston as a ragged veteran had also been eliminated, but he said nothing about it. He made a few suggestions to Reinhardt for trimming one scene and for varying a long scene of the Youth's regiment on the march with closeups of soldiers and horses, but he said that for the most part it was a remarkable job of cutting. He seemed satisfied and ready to drop the picture as his concern, but Reinhardt held him to it. The picture was too short, Reinhardt said, and the story was not clear. "I wrote out my thoughts about this," he added, handing Huston a typewritten memorandum, single-spaced and three and a half pages long.

Huston looked at it impatiently.

"This is very serious, John," Reinhardt said, with the air of a man who takes pleasure in the seriousness of things. "Please read it."

Huston read:

> Aside from its spectacular appeal, the subconscious satisfaction of reliving a glorious and vital chapter of American history, and the nobility, beauty, and deeply moving tragedy of its scenes, THE RED BADGE OF COURAGE must meet one basic requirement to become a success, artistic as well as commercial: the story of the Youth must be convincing. Its development must be organic, consistent, and unbroken. The Youth must inspire measureless sympathy; we must feel for him, go with him all the time. We must understand him, "root" for him, and, finally, admire him.
>
> While I think the first-mentioned requirements have been admirably fulfilled by the film—and I mean "film," for now the footage must speak for itself, all good intentions, all arguments about faithfulness to Stephen Crane, all promises of the script, all preconceived notions that might easily be read into the film, must now be brutally disregarded as irrelevant—

while I believe we have a spectacular, stirring, pure, and beautiful, and at times deeply moving picture, I submit this question to all who are helping to make THE RED BADGE OF COURAGE, and I submit it at the eleventh hour: have we done right by the Youth? For if we have failed to do that, we will have failed altogether.

What is the story of the Youth? (Let us not delude ourselves, however attractive the wrapping may be. The content is what matters. The picture must have a *story*.) One day, on a drill field on a Civil War front, we meet a young fellow. Unlike his comrades, he is in desperate fear of battle . . .

The memo went on to trace the sequence of the picture and declared that there was nothing in it to indicate why the Youth suddenly stops being a coward and becomes a hero. "A beat is missing," the memo ended. "The Youth's story becomes somewhat lost. The line is broken. Such a beat would also bring the picture to its proper length."

"You're right, Gottfried," Huston said when he finished.

Reinhardt looked pleased. He said he had run into Mayer a couple of hours before and had told him that "The Red Badge of Courage" had turned out to be a great picture.

"What did he say, Gottfried?" Huston asked patiently.

"He said only one thing—'Does it have a *story*?'" said Reinhardt.

The two men stayed at the studio late that night, working out scenes that they hoped would give the picture a story.

The following evening, Huston and Reinhardt showed their picture to Dore Schary at Schary's house. A couple of hours earlier, Reinhardt went to a party Mike Romanoff was giving to celebrate the laying of the cornerstone of his new restaurant. Albert Band drove him and me from the studio to the party in Reinhardt's car. "I am so worried about Mocha," Reinhardt said, on the way. Mrs. Reinhardt was in New York, and there was no one at home to feed their French poodle. "Poor Mocha," Reinhardt said.

"Let's go on to the party," Band said. "Mocha will be all right."

"Mocha will go hungry while you stuff yourself at the party," said Reinhardt.

"Mocha will be all *right*," Band said peevishly.

"Albert," Reinhardt said reproachfully, "someday you will be head of the studio, but right now I think someone should go home and feed Mocha. *Then* he will be all right."

The site of the party was a large lot in Beverly Hills a few blocks from the old Romanoff's. A canopy had been set up, and under it were tables covered with food and drink. A crowd was already in an advanced stage of celebrating the new cornerstone when we arrived.

"Everybody is here," Band said, looking over the party. "Clark Gable. Everybody." He was about to join the party when Reinhardt told him that first he had to go feed Mocha.

"And stand over Mocha while he eats," Reinhardt said as Band started off. "Mocha is very nervous."

Band left, and Romanoff asked Reinhardt why he was late. "You missed the ceremonies," he said haughtily. "You missed Ethel Barrymore's address." He touched his fingers to his lips in a gesture of acclaim. "She was better than Franklin D. Roosevelt."

"All that mortar and pestle," a lady standing nearby was saying. "Like it was for the cornerstone of a museum."

"No place else in the world will you find all this," a gentleman with her said, sweeping his arm at the party. "We've got everything in Hollywood. Where else will you find Picassos in the bathroom?"

Reinhardt, watching Ronald Colman and Clark Gable laughing and talking to Louella Parsons, took a Martini from a passing tray. "What are they laughing at?" he asked a writer named Charles Lederer, who was standing by.

"Don't ask questions. Laugh," Lederer said.

Reinhardt laughed.

Band returned to the party, Huston showed up, and the three of us drove off with Reinhardt to Schary's house. We found Schary in his living room, wearing gray slacks, a navy-blue blazer, a baby-blue sports shirt, and loafers, and looking relaxed and happy. With him were Mrs. Schary and Benny Lewis.

"Hello, baby," Schary said, grinning at Huston.

Huston gave Schary an affectionate slap on the back. "How are you, kid?" he said. Everybody sat down.

"Where ya been, doll?" Schary asked Huston.

Huston said he had been hunting, and started talking about ducks, but already the wall panel was sliding up, disclosing a white screen, and he fell silent.

The changes suggested by Huston at the previous showing had been made. Now it was Schary's turn to offer suggestions. "Benny, make a note about that scene," he said as the soldiers began drilling on the screen.

"Yes, sir," said Lewis.

"Make a note about the river crossing," Schary said.

Lewis made a note.

"Catch the guy saying 'Oh, no!' after the digging. It's too modern," Schary said.

When Tim Durant had his horse do a circus dance and shouted "Yippee" several times, Reinhardt gave a loud laugh.

"Got to do better with those yippee's," Schary said.

"We have some new yippee's we haven't put in yet, Dore," Huston told him.

The scene of the Cheery Soldier finding the Youth in the woods was too dark, Schary said, and the men all agreed that it would be best to reshoot it.

The lights went on. The panel returned and the white screen disappeared. There was a momentary silence.

"Sweetie, that line 'gone coon,'" Schary said to Huston. "We had a line just like it in 'Crossfire.' About being busier than a coon. We got two cards at the preview with objections. I don't think we ought to take a chance on this one."

"Possum," Mrs. Schary said. "There's a good little animal."

Schary immediately pointed at Band. "Say 'possum,' say 'coon,'" he commanded.

Band said quickly, "Possum, coon. Possum, coon. Pos—"

"'Goose,'" said Huston.

" 'Gone goose,' " Schary said. "That's it."

Schary then said that there was no fighting in the picture after the Youth's regiment met the enemy at the wall. Huston said he wanted to avoid hand-to-hand fighting, and anything else that would come under the heading of "North vs. South."

Schary said, "The main thing is I feel a lack of climax and culmination in the charge. You don't feel that grabbing and lifting up. What we had in 'Battleground,' for instance."

"Well," Huston said, "we've got one more criticism, and it's more serious than this." He stood up and, putting his hands in his pockets, said that the complaint was that the picture didn't show what the Youth's state of mind was after he ran away from the battle and before he returned and distinguished himself. "It's an emotional thing, rather than a logical thing," Huston said. "If there could be a quiet scene after the boy returns to camp. The Lieutenant with his back to a tree sleeping. Another writing a letter. And the Youth restless in his sleep. A kind of stillness. To show that the boy is not as he was before."

"The more we show of the Youth in camp, before he becomes a hero, the more of a story we have," Reinhardt said.

Schary said, "Dissolve to the boy lying there wide-awake and wide-eyed. Then dawn comes, and a bugle call."

Reinhardt and Huston agreed with Schary that such a scene would give the picture more of a story, and Huston said he would dictate it the next day.

The death scenes of Dano and Dierkes were great, Schary said —great scenes.

"It's good battle stuff, isn't it?" Huston said.

"Gorgeous," said Schary. "Gorgeous shots."

There was a pause, and Mrs. Schary told Huston that she had almost finished a painting and wished he would look at it. Huston said he'd love to. Schary suggested a change in the sequence of some minor scenes at the end of the film. Huston said that the suggestions were excellent, just swell, then turned back to Mrs. Schary. "Show me your painting, honey," he said.

"Dore," Reinhardt said as Huston and Mrs. Schary left the room, "you think anybody will come to see this picture?"

Schary said yes.

Reinhardt asked him how he liked Audie Murphy.

Murphy was very good, Schary replied. "And Mauldin is good," he said. "He looks like Howard Hughes."

Reinhardt sighed with relief.

When Mrs. Schary and Huston came back, she told Reinhardt that she loved "The Red Badge of Courage," and to Huston she said, "You've got a good picture."

"Thank you, honey," Huston said, with dramatic earnestness.

"The picture has a great feeling of the period," Schary said as we were about to go. "It has real validity."

"It will be a great picture," Reinhardt said.

"Good night, sweeties," said Schary.

As we drove away, Reinhardt said, "Every night he does this. My God, the junk he must look at!"

The next morning, Reinhardt found an advertisement in a motion-picture trade paper for "The Red Badge of Courage." It was illustrated with a photograph showing Audie Murphy chatting across a fence with the farm girl whose pig was stolen in the picture. In this photograph, the farm girl was looking worshipfully at Murphy across the fence. There was no such scene in the picture. The promotion of "The Red Badge of Courage" had begun.

Huston had his final session with Reinhardt and his key crewmen in a projection room, where they viewed the revised cut of the picture, including the retakes and the additional scenes in the Youth's camp that had been taken and that Reinhardt and Huston hoped would give the picture more of a story. The showing lasted an hour and twenty-eight minutes—ten minutes longer than the version they had decided was too short. Huston said that the picture looked padded. He was for clarity and direct, brief statement, and wanted no more film than was absolutely necessary. Reinhardt and Huston rearranged the sequence of several scenes and shortened some shots, and by such legerdemain they were able to move the Youth around on the battlefield so that he fought in the battle on film in a more satisfying manner than he had fought in the battle on the ground. Now Benny Lewis, working under the combined direction of Reinhardt and Margaret Booth, began to piece together the shots so as to imprint the Youth's revised movements on the film for what they thought was forever.

M-G-M had given Huston permission to suspend his contract while he made an independent picture, and he moved his belongings from his corner office in the Thalberg Building to a small cottage in the California Studios, in Hollywood, where Horizon Pictures and his partner in it, Sam Spiegel, had their headquarters.

When Huston left, he left his picture, and his four-thousand-dollar-a-week salary, behind. He would now be getting twenty-five hundred dollars a week at Horizon, on his job of converting C. S. Forester's novel "The African Queen" into a screenplay. He left Albert Band behind at M-G-M, too. Before he went, he promised to arrange to give Band credit for adapting "The Red Badge of Courage" to rough screenplay form, and he told Band that he would talk with Dore Schary about giving him a new job. At Horizon, Huston seemed to have forgotten all about Schary, about Albert Band, about Gottfried Reinhardt, Audie Murphy, Stephen Crane, and "The Red Badge of Courage." Reinhardt was philosophic about Huston's exit from the scene after they had been together constantly for ten months. "You see a lot of your colleagues when you make a picture," Reinhardt said. "You see them, be they friends or enemies, and then the picture is finished and you don't see anything of them. Neither closeness nor distance affects the basic relationship." However, Reinhardt's work on "The Red Badge of Courage" would not be over until the picture was ready for release, and his work continually reminded him of John Huston. Also, he said, he was disturbed by the uncertainty about the future of Albert Band. Band missed Huston. He did not know what he was supposed to be doing for M-G-M, and he sat in his office reading. Like Reinhardt, he was on the first floor of the Thalberg Building, but, unlike Reinhardt, he had only a small office, with a battered leather chair, a worn carpet, a desk, a typewriter, and an old couch. His name was not engraved on a brass plate on his door; it was typed on a white card placed in a slot, from which it could easily be removed. There were several photographs of Huston on the walls, and from time to time Band stared at them glumly. Finally, Reinhardt took the matter of Band's career into his own hands. He sent Dore Schary a memorandum saying that Band had rendered a most valuable service to "The Red Badge of Courage," not only during the production and the cutting but also during the preparation of the script. Reinhardt wrote, "I believe that, if given a chance, he would prove to be a great asset to the Studio as a writer, as well as, perhaps, one day, a director. In any event, I should like to put in a good word for him and ask you to keep him on the payroll and give him an assignment." Schary responded by offering Band to Reinhardt, and Band now became Reinhardt's assistant.

A Sunday-night party at David Selznick's is a kind of institution among motion-picture notables, and Huston occasionally dropped in on one. The parties were held in an elaborate Beverly Hills house that once belonged to John Gilbert. Late in the festivities one night when Huston was there, Selznick, who has been an independent producer for many years, drew him aside. "So you finished the picture," he said. "I'm really surprised."

"Yeah," Huston said, looking uncomfortable.

"I'm surprised they made it," said Selznick. "I'm really surprised."

"They made it," Huston said. "Dore was for it all the time."

"I'm really surprised," said Selznick. "How much did it cost? One five?"

"About that, David," Huston said.

"I'm really surprised," said Selznick.

They talked for a while about Schary's support of the making of the picture and Mayer's opposition to it. "I'd like to know what L.B. thinks of your picture," Selznick said to Huston.

"I wouldn't," Huston said.

Bronislau Kaper, who, Reinhardt told me, was a serious and talented musician, was now composing the musical score for "The Red Badge of Courage," and members of the sound department were adding sound effects to the film track. Production No. 1512 was the sixty-fifth picture Kaper had written music for in sixteen years of working for Metro-Goldwyn-Mayer. He is a voluble man, in his late forties, who was born in Poland and, as a young man, had a career as a composer in Germany and France. In the early thirties, L. B. Mayer heard him play some of his compositions in Paris and signed him to an M-G-M contract. He numbers among his talents the ability to beat two-four time with one hand while beating three-eight time with the other, and the ability to make remarks that will get laughs. While composing for "The Red Badge of Courage," he seemed to be constantly working hard at making remarks that would get laughs, depending for his wit on a mild and oblique insult. He always smiled whenever he delivered one, and, for some reason, the recipient usually smiled back. Kaper seems eternally cheerful, but he has a persistent look of dissatisfaction, together with a tremendous enthusiasm for composing music for pictures.

"Every picture is sick," Kaper told me. "That is my premise. We must take the picture and find out what it needs to make it well and healthy." He had seen "The Red Badge of Courage" three times. He knew every foot of it, he said, and what the picture needed would have to be supplied by the music—a strengthening of the continuity, and a definite viewpoint toward the major characters—and he gave me a brief lecture on how he planned to do all this. "After the Youth's regiment wins the first battle, the soldiers act happy," he said. "But I come along, and I tell the audience, with sad music, what is so good about this? I make a little ridiculous the whole idea of one American killing another American. Sometimes I bring phony emotions into the picture to wake the audience up. Other times, on a closeup, I stop the music. Some of the scenes are too punchy. I must bring them down. The music provides the sustained mood that will give the picture continuity and smoothness. The important contribution of the music is to tell the story of the boy. It must be told musically. This is a boy who is a coward, and then he becomes a hero. Why? The music will tell it. The boy sees two men dying. The two death scenes are the most overwhelming ever seen in pictures. This does something to the boy. The power of the death scenes eliminates the boy, so you've got to play the effect of the deaths on the boy. Which is the most important thing in the picture. I play the Tall Soldier's death by letting his breathing be the soloist. The music is the background to the breathing. When he dies, there is a sudden silence. No music. No comment. I give the audience a chance to make its own comment. The second death, as the Tattered Man wanders down the hill to die, with the Youth following him, I play with two instruments only. A trumpet, for the military death, and a harmonica—a gay tune—to show the irony of it. In the letter-writing scene, I said to John Huston, 'It is important not to get sentimental. The Youth is writing a letter home.' 'The boy is afraid,' John said, 'and it is funny.' I said, 'I don't know how to score him as funny.' John said, 'He shouldn't be treated tragically. He is a little ridiculous.' Then he said, 'Banjo!' A stroke of genius! We have a funny sound coming from outside while the Youth sits in his tent and writes. A funny sound to a sad situation. In this way, we give a story to the picture. It is musically interesting when the boy runs away from the battle. I play the fears inside the boy. The music is spasmodic. Like a heartbeat. The entire prologue of the picture, a short scene showing the Youth on sentry duty, will be silent. No music can be as loud as silence."

In the meantime, Reinhardt was working with a writer named Jan Lustig and with Albert Band on the story for a picture called "The Burning Secret." During conferences with Lustig and Band on the general plan for the screenplay, Reinhardt digressed frequently to talk about other matters. One day, he told them that his mother, Else Heims, at the age of seventy-two, was starring in a play in Berlin. He then talked to them about their work and told them not to worry about problems like length when they were writing. "You can always cut later," he said. He told them he had taken up golf, because he wanted to have something he could talk about, the way other people talked about tennis or horses. He spoke of Hollywood, and said that he would never buy a house there, because deep down he had the feeling that he did not want to stay there. He said that Hollywood people were unsure of themselves as soon as they got away from Hollywood. "As Sam Hoffenstein used to say, we are the croupiers in a crooked gambling house," he said. He talked about what was wrong with the motion-picture business. "Dividends are still being paid," he told them, "but the assets are whether Gable is a star. Whether we can cook up a good story."

Reinhardt gave a sad sigh and went on to talk about "The Burning Secret." One of the problems they had to work out, he said, was whether to include an implication of adultery and, if so, how to do it and still leave plenty of room for doubt in the minds of the audience. Another was whether the eleven-year-old boy hero should be shown wearing a Hopalong Cassidy suit. While Reinhardt was deep in this problem, his secretary came in and handed him an interoffice communication from Dore Schary:

Dear Gottfried:

I hate to burden you with bad news just before I go away for a holiday, but our film supply is to be cut exactly 50%. In view of this, we must establish a rule that there is to be only one print of each take during any of your pictures in production and that any additional prints must be O.K.'d by Joe Cohn. We must make every effort to cut down the amount of film used on tests and also wherever possible cut down on the number of tests. Costume tests will be made by the new method of slides.

Will you please advise your directors of this circumstance, and during the shooting of pictures an effort must be made to make certain of values in a scene before shooting it. In other words, we will have to dispense with the "Let's try one just to see what happens" point of view.

I'm sorry, Gottfried, I couldn't get to see you before I left but I've been literally swamped. I'm anxious to see the preview of RED BADGE OF COURAGE and that will be the first thing to look at when I get back.

My best,

D.S.

Reinhardt put the communication down and turned back to Band and Lustig, and with what appeared to be considerable effort he again took up the problems of adultery and the Hopalong Cassidy suit.

One day in the middle of December, Huston and James Agee, the novelist and former *Time* writer, who had been hired to collaborate with Huston on the script for "The African Queen," were working in the Horizon cottage, trying to finish the script in time for Huston's and Spiegel's departure for Africa, where the picture was to be filmed. In the front room of the cottage was a false fireplace containing a gas log. Huston's Academy Award statuettes stood on the mantel. Agee was saying, as Huston paced in small circles, that the trip the river captain, Humphrey Bogart, and the missionary's sister, Katharine Hepburn, would make together down the river on the captain's boat in "The African Queen" could symbolize the act of love.

"Oh, Christ, Jim," Huston said. "Tell me something I can understand. This isn't like a novel. This is a screenplay. You've got to demonstrate everything, Jim. People on the screen are gods and goddesses. We know all about them. Their habits. Their caprices. But we can't touch them. They're not real. They stand for something, rather than being something. They're symbols. You can't have symbolism within symbolism, Jim." He paced the floor and said he was going crazy. "I really hate the city," he said. "I've got to get out to the country and get on a horse. I get all mixed up in the city. You know where I'd like to be this very minute, Jim?" He spread his long arms along the mantel of the fireplace. "I'd like to be in Mexico. God!" He gave a stifled laugh, and said he guessed one of the best periods of his entire life had been spent, in his eighteenth year, in the Mexican cavalry. "What a time that was!" he said. "Always going places in Packards. You'd go the rounds of the cafés. Then you'd go to somebody's finca. Then you'd play the next thing to Russian roulette. You'd cock a pistol and throw it up and hit the ceiling with it. It was great. Just great. I was their top jumping rider. God, those were wonderful days!"

Spiegel put his head in at the door. Huston stared at him for a moment without saying anything. Then he pretended to be shocked. "Christ, Sam'l, for a minute there you looked just like an act Dad used to do in vaudeville," he said in a menacing tone. Spiegel came into the room and looked from Huston to Agee with a hesitant smile. "I was six when I first saw Dad do this act!" Huston went on, in his special tone of amazement at his own words. "Dad played a house painter, come to paint this lady's house. There was a picture of her husband inside the front door. The husband's face would begin to make faces, and then this big head would shove through the door with electric lights for eyes. And I'd roar. And Dad would sing, 'I Haven't Got the Do-Re-Mi.' It was just wonderful. Ho! Ho! Ho!"

"So," said Spiegel. "How are things on the script?"

Huston said things were fine. "Only trouble is, Sam, we just demolished two weeks' work. Threw out every bit of it," he added lightly.

Spiegel swallowed hard. "When?" he asked.

"Just now," Huston said, with a forced grin.

"My ulcers are being formed," Spiegel said, and gave Agee an appealing look.

Agee seemed bewildered.

"We leave in four weeks," Spiegel said to Huston. "We must have the script before we leave."

"Don't worry, Sam'l," Huston said, in the reassuring tone he had used in talking with Reinhardt about the script for "The Red Badge of Courage."

Spiegel said, "Beneath this façade of worry is worry. Did you get anything done today?"

"Don't worry," said Huston. "There's nothing to worry about."

"I like to know what I'm worrying about," said Spiegel. "Now it's that I worry and I don't know why."

"John," Agee said, "when are you going to do the retakes for David Selznick?"

Spiegel wet his lips. "You expect to do retakes for Selznick?"

Huston nodded. "David is in a jam," he said.

"You can't. You have no time," Spiegel said. "Why? Is he offering you a fortune?"

"I'm doing it for nothing," Huston said.

Spiegel shook his head. "You can't do it," he said.

"When a pal of mine is in a jam, I do what I can to help," Huston said.

"You can't do it," said Spiegel.

"Like hell I can't," Huston said.

"No," Spiegel said.

Huston gave a choked laugh. "Your ulcers, Sam'l," he said softly.

Humphrey Bogart, who had made a number of pictures with Huston, was enthusiastic about making another. He and his wife, Lauren Bacall, were getting ready to go to Africa. At the same time, Bogart was finishing "Sirocco" for his own company, Santana, a chore he did not especially care for. "Too many business worries," he told me one day in his living room, while his wife, with the aid of a writer named Richard Brooks and Mrs. Brooks, trimmed a Christmas tree. "The role is a cinch. The role doesn't bother me. I've been doing the role for years. I've worn that trench coat of mine in half the pictures I've been in. What I don't like is business worries. I like to work with John. The monster is stimulating. Offbeat kind of mind. Off center. He's brilliant and unpredictable. Never dull. When I work with John, I think about acting, I don't worry about business. With Santana, I'm bowed down with business worries."

"You and me both, Bogie," said Brooks.

"You know what my director, Curt Bernhardt, said to me today?" Bogart said to Brooks. "He was shooting the ending of a Bette Davis picture over at R.K.O. He said to me, 'When we made the picture, we couldn't decide on an ending. It had an unhappy honest ending, but it was not honest. The dishonest happy ending was honest. The ending now—it's not dishonest and not honest. It'll be something new.' At least they've got an ending. Santana has had eleven writers on 'Sirocco,' and none of them goons has come across with an ending yet."

"This you call a worry?" Brooks said. "Everybody I know is trying to lick an ending."

"Humphrey," Mrs. Bogart said, "how about giving us a hand with this tree?"

"I like to wait till the end," Bogart said. "Then I throw the snow on it."

"I have news for you," Mrs. Bogart said. "There's no snow this year."

"What's the matter? No guts?" Bogart asked.

"Don't pay any attention to him," Mrs. Bogart said to Mrs. Brooks.

"My shoulders are heavy with business troubles," Bogart said. "I've got to talk to the monster and get some comfort." He picked up the telephone and called Huston. A moment later, his face glowed. "Hello, you son of a bitch," he said. "When we going to Africa?"

In January, 1951, Huston and Agee went to stay at a ranch near Santa Barbara, to continue their work on the script of "The African Queen." Reinhardt was worrying again about "The Red Badge of Courage," and he went up to Santa Barbara for a weekend to see Huston. When he returned, he was downhearted. Huston had been very busy. He had had to go foxhunting, he had had to see David Selznick, and he had had to work on the script with Agee. He did not seem interested in talking to Reinhardt about "The Red Badge of Courage."

"We do not have a great picture," Reinhardt said to me when he came back. "There is no story, because we do not show what the Youth is thinking. It is not in the script. John said he would put it on the screen. It is not on the screen. One day in my office, John and I acted out the scene where Audie grabs the flag and leads the charge. It was great. John was Audie, and he was crying. I was the Loud Soldier, and I was loud. The next morning, I went right up to see L.B. He usually does the acting. This time, I did the acting. I acted the scene out for him. Then I asked him, 'Isn't it great?' He said yes, it was great. But we still don't have it. Audie does not cry. The Loud Soldier is not loud. It isn't on the screen."

. . . .

Dore Schary was vacationing in Florida when the trade papers carried lead stories reporting that his contract with Metro-Goldwyn-Mayer had been supplemented by an option to buy a hundred thousand shares of Loew's stock within a period of six years at the then current market value, which gave Schary a chance of making substantial capital gains if the stock went up. The papers also reported that Nicholas Schenck and William Rodgers were with Schary in Miami Beach, where they were to attend a special showing of "Go for Broke," a picture personally produced by Schary. There was no mention of L. B. Mayer in any of the reports.

While looking around for new pictures to do, Reinhardt often said that he missed working with Huston. He wired Schary in Florida suggesting that he and Huston do a picture together about Colonel Paul W. Tibbets, Jr., who dropped the atomic bomb on Hiroshima. "WERE IT NOT FOR NUCLEAR INGREDIENTS SHOULD CALL IT DYNAMITE," he wired. "IDEAL VEHICLE FOR HUSTON. SCRIPT COULD BE READY UPON HIS RETURN FROM SPIEGEL ADVENTURE WHICH SHOULD MAKE HIM EVEN MORE EXPERT IN DANGEROUS LIVING. URGE YOU TO CONSIDER THIS MOST SERIOUSLY AND TO MAKE COMMAND DECISION. HOPE YOU GRASP HEAVY IMPLICATION. HEARTIEST CONGRATULATIONS ON NEW CONTRACT. FINANCIAL SECURITY OF BOSS ALWAYS SOURCE OF PEACE IN EMPLOYEES."

Schary's reply was a memo saying, "I will discuss the TIBBETS story with you on my return. Everybody wants to do the story, so if we do close the deal I will not make any decisions until my arrival home. Meanwhile, get RED BADGE OF COURAGE ready for what I hope will be a wonderful preview."

Metro's promotion department got up an idea for a trailer advertising "The Red Badge of Courage": when the title appeared, the "Red" would fade out and "White and Blue" would fade in.

Bronislau Kaper played the score for "The Red Badge of Courage" on the piano for Reinhardt, and afterward Reinhardt told me that the picture might turn out to be great, after all. "The music says what Crane says in the novel," he said. "That was what was missing—what goes on inside the boy. I called John and sang practically the whole score to him over the telephone. He was delighted." Reinhardt looked delighted, too, and said he was going to talk to Schary about the possibility of M-G-M's issuing the score in an album called "The Red Badge of Courage Suite." He asked me to go along with him to watch the recording of the score for the picture.

The music was recorded on a large sound stage, off which was a glass-enclosed monitor room. Reinhardt and Kaper and I sat in the room with a man called the mixer, Mike McLaughlin, whose job it was to regulate the volume of each section of the orchestra and blend the sounds correctly. The studio's fifty-piece orchestra sat facing the monitor room. (The orchestra included some of the finest musicians in the world, Reinhardt said, and M-G-M paid its musicians better than most symphony orchestras. The first violinist's salary was $25,000 a year, and all the others had a year's contract guaranteeing a minimum of $15,000.) The conductor wore earphones, through which he could hear the dialogue of the picture, which was projected on a screen in back of the orchestra. A wide vertical line, called the cue line, moved across the screen, superimposed on the picture, to indicate to the conductor exactly when the music was to start or stop.

The main musical theme was a triad, three notes of the tonic scale in C major—G, C, and E—to express the Youth's fear. "The triad is great," Kaper said. "It is simple and tragic."

"We're going to have a big fight with Dore," said Reinhardt. "He likes music in pictures to be conventional, discreet, and unobtrusive. We come right out and say it."

"Dore should like this theme," Kaper said. "There is destiny in the theme. It is anticipation of something bad that becomes something beautiful."

One of the first sections of the score to be recorded was the accompaniment for the scene in which the Youth and the Loud Soldier, overhearing the General giving orders to attack, rush off to tell their comrades. Most of the instruments played a simple two-note theme for the attack, with a steady, exciting pulsation from the violins and short calls from the woodwinds.

"Not enough trumpet, Mac," Kaper said to the mixer. McLaughlin turned a dial and brought up the sound of trumpets.

"As soon as the audience *hears* the music, it's no good," Reinhardt said to Kaper. "We have to be careful."

As Kaper had worked out the plan for the score, the picture would open with the M-G-M lion's roar, accompanied by the sound of drums, which would be dissolved in gunfire, and then there would be the silent prologue, showing the Youth on sentry duty; that would be followed by a harmonica playing the familiar gay folk tune called "Kingdom Coming" for the main title—as the name of the picture and all the credits combined are called. Just as Kaper finished explaining this, the words "Produced by Gottfried Reinhardt" came on the screen without music. "Directed by John Huston" was accompanied by piccolos. "Music by Bronislau Kaper" had trumpets. Reinhardt said jokingly that if Kaper had trumpets, the least *he* should have under his name was strings. Kaper conferred with the conductor about putting strings under Reinhardt. Margaret Booth came into the monitor room at that moment, and Reinhardt told her that the music for the main title was wonderful. The orchestra started rehearsing the music for the letter-writing scene.

"I've been seeing so many pictures," said Miss Booth. "I just finished cutting 'Show Boat.' I cut two thousand feet out of it."

Kaper said he did not like the way the orchestra was playing.

"I think you're overdramatizing this little piece of music," Miss Booth said to him, and left.

"She walks in right in the middle of the recording!" Kaper cried. "This is impossible! It must stop!"

"Margaret likes me," Reinhardt said. "She wants to see that everything goes all right with my picture."

Reinhardt and I went back to his office, where we found Band waiting.

"Albert, fix me a drink," Reinhardt said.

Band went into the next room and returned in a moment with a highball.

Reinhardt sighed and sat down behind his desk. Doubts about the chances of the picture's being a hit were again assailing him. "I should have listened to Mayer," he said. "He begged me not to do it. He was like a father to me. He said, 'This is *thoughts*. How are you going to show the boy's *thoughts?*' I promised him we would show them. He told me about John's picture 'The Asphalt Jungle.' 'Pavement,' he called it. He said, 'I loved the picture, but nobody is going in.'" Reinhardt sighed again. "I never should have made this picture," he said. "I did it because I love the book and because I love John. And I thought that John would be able to show what goes on inside the boy. If we had narration for the picture—maybe with that we could show what goes on inside. But John kept saying, 'No narration.' Billy Wilder in 'Sunset Boulevard' had the nerve; after the man is dead, he has him do the narration. Joe Mankiewicz uses narration. Narration is good enough for them but not for John."

He sipped his drink in gloomy silence. Then he said that in the past he had always been able to sense impending catastrophe. "When I was making 'The Great Sinner,'" he said, "I had a wonderful cast—Gregory Peck, Ava Gardner, Melvyn Douglas, Ethel Barrymore, Frank Morgan, Agnes Moorehead, Walter Huston. L. B. Mayer visited my set. Anything I wanted, I got. Then, one day, I looked at the picture. And I tied a terrific drunk on. 'The characters are not alive,' I said. I had wanted John to direct the picture. The studio wanted him. He agreed to do it and then Sam Spiegel pre-empted him. I got someone else. So both John and I made bad pictures. *Before* the reviews, even, people would not go to the theatre. It was a catastrophe. I felt it coming. I feel it coming now."

Twenty days after the date Sam Spiegel had set for his and Huston's departure for England, where they were going to stop over en route to Africa, Huston was still in Santa Barbara working on the script for "The African Queen." Reinhardt telephoned him there from his office. "Stranger!" Reinhardt said. "You never call me any more! You missed the recording. It was wonderful. It has the purity, the honesty, the tragedy, and the nobility of the novel.

I am really crazy about it. I expect not too good a reaction from Dore, but you'll be just insane about it. In the first battle, in the lull in the fighting, they're carrying in the hurt Rebs. Very slowly the music starts. Very strange and eerie it is, and then we cut to the bird singing. It is just glorious. I am just crazy about it. Wait. I'll put Albert on."

Band took the telephone. "John," he said, "you're going to faint when you hear the music."

"Sing him the tune!" Reinhardt commanded.

Band sang "Kingdom Coming" over the telephone, and then Reinhardt took over again. "The title is just marvellous," he said, and laughed. "Piccolos under your name, strings under mine. You will go out of your mind."

Dubbing for sound is the process whereby all sound for a picture is put on a single sound track and synchronized with the picture film. "It is really simple," Reinhardt told me. "We combine the sound tracks made while we shot the picture with all the sound tracks we made here—the additional spoken lines, the gunfire effects, close shellbursts, far shellbursts, birds singing, murmuring voices, dragging feet, wind, water, crickets, music. We have three music tracks, including the orchestra, the trumpet calls, and the drum rolls. We run all the tracks through together and put them on a tape recording. This saves sound film. If anything is wrong, we can correct it before the sound on the tape is recorded on film for the final sound track. For the preview, we will have two tracks, one for the picture and one for sound. If the picture is O.K.'d by Mayer, Schary, and the other executives, we make a composite called Movietone. That is what is used in the theatres. Hollywood's technical superiority is one of the things that make American pictures more popular all over the world than European ones. The sound men look at a picture as though they were looking at an automobile engine. Chichi does not impress them at all. They are all, somehow, scientists."

"The Red Badge of Courage" was dubbed for sound in a dark, close projection room that had what is known as a dubbing console at the rear of the room. Three men were seated at the controls. They were called Bob, Jimmy, and Sparky, and they all looked as though chichi would not impress them. They dubbed one reel of film at a time. For guidance, in addition to the picture itself and the counsel of Reinhardt, Kaper, and Band, the dubbers had charts showing at what points in the footage of each reel they were to dub in such effects as "soldiers yelling," "wounded men shuffling along the road," "bodies thumping in falls," and "horses milling." Reinhardt would hear too much caisson-rolling and not enough music, or Band would hear too much of the Youth's flight from battle and not enough artillery, or Kaper would hear gunfire overwhelming his drums. When Reinhardt said he did not hear enough birds, Sparky and Jimmy and Bob pushed buttons and turned dials on their console or phoned the sound library for more birdcalls. The sound men recorded and re-recorded and re-re-recorded until each one of the critics heard what he wanted to hear.

The process took five days. Reinhardt and Band and Kaper sat with Sparky and Jimmy and Bob hour after hour in the room, seeing the reels over and over, and working for perfection of sound —one more shellburst here, one less rifleshot there, the substitution of a bugle call recorded on Huston's ranch for a stock bugle call from the sound library. One of the most difficult reels to dub had four dialogue tracks, three music tracks, and ten sound-effect tracks, which included, for one scene, a set of sounds labelled "chickens, calm" and a set labelled "chickens, excited." They worked for a couple of hours on this particular scene. Band finally suggested eliminating the calm chickens, and then the sound was just right. When the dubbing was complete, Reinhardt thanked Jimmy, Sparky, and Bob, and told them they had done a wonderful job. Automatically, the sound men told Reinhardt he had a wonderful picture.

"The sound department is like granite," Reinhardt said to me. "The music department is hysterical, the sound department never."

The first showing of "The Red Badge of Courage" to an outside audience was given in a large projection room at the studio.

Huston came down from Santa Barbara for the big night. Reinhardt had invited the cast and crew of the picture, along with Sam Spiegel; William Wyler, the director, a close friend of both Huston and Reinhardt; an M-G-M producer named Sidney Franklin; Paul Kohner, Huston's agent; and Pablo, Huston's fifteen-year-old adopted son. Schary, who had returned from Miami Beach, couldn't come, because he was home with a cold. The official preview of the picture was to be two nights later. Reinhardt told Huston that he had talked to Schary on the telephone, and that Schary had asked him how the picture was. "I told him that Bronny Kaper made the actors *act*," Reinhardt said. "When are you leaving, John?" Huston said he was leaving right after the preview. It was too bad, because he hadn't had the time to do the retakes he'd promised Selznick, he said, but then Selznick had persuaded him to forget the whole thing, and besides Huston had already given Selznick—and Arthur Fellows, an employee of Selznick's and a friend of Huston's—some help on the cutting of the picture.

Reinhardt and Huston turned up at the projection room a few minutes early.

"Is anybody here?" Reinhardt asked a projectionist, shakily.

"Did anybody come?" Huston asked.

"Pablo is here," Reinhardt said.

"Well!" Huston said, with his peculiar way of making the word expand.

Reinhardt and Huston looked at each arrival with the solemnity of people watching for relatives at a funeral. Mrs. Spiegel. Mrs. Huston. Mrs. Reinhardt. Audie Murphy. Tim Durant. John Dierkes. Reggie Callow. Hal Rosson. Paul Kohner. Andrew Marton. Lee Katz. Bronislau Kaper. Benny Lewis. Albert Band. Reinhardt sat down at the rear of the room. Huston sat up front. Reinhardt called him back. "I want all the family together," he said.

The lights dimmed. The showing began with a FitzPatrick travelogue about Holland, in Technicolor.

"I didn't think the picture was in color," Huston said, and forced a laugh.

The audience shuffled its feet, whispered, and looked around. William Wyler arrived late and sat next to Huston. "Is this it?" Wyler said.

"I didn't know it was in color," Huston said to him, and laughed nervously again.

Drums sounded and the M-G-M lion roared. Immediately, there was an awful silence in the room. "The Red Badge of Courage" started, with the prologue showing the Youth on sentry duty on the screen. Huston watched the picture with his mouth open. Reinhardt laughed unconvincingly at the first amusing scene and stared at his neighbors, as if to encourage them to laugh. He stopped in surprise when he saw that they were already laughing.

The audience appeared to be moved by the scenes of Dierkes, the Tall Soldier, running up to the hilltop to die and Dano, the Tattered Man, wandering downhill to his death. "Jesus, Johnny!" Wyler said to Huston as the Tattered Man died on the screen. "Jesus!"

When the lights went up, the audience sat very still for a moment. Then Kohner turned around to Huston and broke the silence. "Damn good, John," he said.

"Wonderful, Johnny," said Wyler.

"My congratulations, John," Band said.

"Johnny, wonderful, wonderful," said Mrs. Kohner.

"Well!" Huston said.

"It's a gem," Sidney Franklin said to Reinhardt.

"Gottfried, I wish I had brought my jelly beans!" Mrs. Reinhardt said. "I am starving."

Spiegel looked at Huston, obviously impressed.

"Terrific, Gottfried. Terrific, John," said Kohner.

"Well!" Mrs. Huston said, looking very happy.

"Boy, Dad!" said Pablo Huston.

There was a sudden surge of excitement in the room. Everybody was shaking hands with everybody else.

"He's the guy!" Huston said, his arm around Bronislau Kaper. "He wrote the music. I just made the picture."

"A beautiful score," Spiegel said. "I discovered Bronny. I brought him to Hollywood."

"I put my heart into it," Kaper said. "I worked harder on this score than on any other ever. I wrote my heart out for this score."

"Jesus!" Wyler said to Reinhardt. "That fella who goes down the hill and dies."

"Royal Dano," Reinhardt said proudly. "He is magnificent."

"Terrific dolly shot," Wyler said.

"Four hundred and fifty feet," said Reinhardt.

"Makes you realize that a war eighty-five years ago was tougher than a war today," said Wyler.

"We've got incredible stuff," Reinhardt said.

"It was the bloodiest war," said Wyler. "No Red Cross. Nothing."

"Incredible. The two sides murdered each other. We've got incredible stuff," said Reinhardt. "How is your new picture, Willie?"

Wyler shrugged. "It's all a gamble," he said. "The only way is to lose big or win big. You can have the biggest success or the biggest flop in the world—initially, it's the same gamble."

Mrs. Kohner came over and said, "Isn't it wonderful?"

"Great," said Wyler.

Murphy looked bewildered. "Seems I didn't do all that," he said softly.

"You sure looked good," Dierkes told him.

Everybody was now telling everybody else that it was a great picture. Huston hugged Reinhardt and said, "It's the best picture I ever made."

"You've got a picture there," Spiegel said, and pursed his lips.

Wyler and Spiegel wandered out together. "The worst that can happen, it will break even," Wyler was saying. "How much did it cost?"

"A million five, Willie," said Spiegel, with satisfaction. "So, it's M-G-M's money."

"M-G-M can afford to make this picture for prestige," Wyler said. "If they get the American Legion behind it—basically, it's that kind of story."

"The music was great," Spiegel said.

"M-G-M has nothing to lose making this," Wyler said thoughtfully.

Reinhardt joined them and stood beaming with delight as they told him again that he had made a great picture. He lowered his head modestly. "John embraced me and said it is the best picture he ever made," he said. "John is in the clouds."

4   What's Wrong with Mocha's Opinion?

ONE AFTERNOON IN FEBRUARY, 1951, six months after Metro-Goldwyn-Mayer put "The Red Badge of Courage" into production, Huston and Reinhardt set out together for its first preview. From the beginning, the picture had stirred up an extraordinary amount of debate at M-G-M. Reinhardt and Huston wanted to make what Reinhardt, over and over again, referred to as "a great picture," and the debate was about whether it would, in fact, turn out to be a great picture, and, if it did, whether it would also make money. Everybody involved in producing the film felt that what happened at the preview would probably answer the question. The New York office, in the person of Schenck, Loew's president, stood by waiting to hear the results; with Schenck were other top executives, including William F. Rodgers, Loew's general manager in charge of sales, who five months before had said to Reinhardt, "Its greatness depends on how it is received by the public." In Hollywood, Mayer, Loew's second in command, who at first had opposed producing the picture but had finally, for reasons of his own, given in, and had been watching the picture's progress closely ever since, was still watching. In Hollywood, too, Schary, who, possibly with Schenck's support, had backed Huston and Reinhardt from the first, and had insisted ever since that he had confidence in the picture's commercial as well as its artistic prospects, was still insisting. The latest estimate that

Loew's executives had on the cost of "The Red Badge of Courage" —Production No. 1512—now stood at $1,548,755, or about $50,-000 over the maximum that Huston and Reinhardt had promised Dore Schary the picture would cost.

Before the preview, Reinhardt and Huston were going to stop off at Schary's home to show him the picture there, because he had a cold and couldn't get to the theatre. I drove with Reinhardt to Santa Monica, where we were to pick up Huston. Reinhardt was wearing a blue beret, and he was smoking a long cigar. On the way, he said that the studio publicity department had shown the picture to Hedda Hopper and that she had telephoned him to say it was the best war picture she had ever seen. "She is absolutely giddy," said Reinhardt. "Tonight, Mayer will be at the preview. Afterward, he might talk to us. He might not. You can never tell. People say, 'Did you see L.B.'s face?' And they think they have a flop. The next morning they say, 'It's O.K. He liked the picture.'" Reinhardt drove recklessly. "Everybody says we have a brilliant picture," he said as we sped along. "John is in seventh heaven."

We met Huston in the cocktail lounge of a hotel overlooking the Pacific Ocean. His exuberance matched Reinhardt's. He immediately said, "Hopper's man, Spec McClure, called me. Hedda says it's the greatest war picture ever made." He and Reinhardt exchanged significant looks, and both burst out laughing.

"We have a great picture," Reinhardt said. He turned to the waiter and said, "Martinis."

"Well," Huston said, and, tilting back in his chair, he put a brown cigarette in the corner of his mouth and slowly looked around the cocktail lounge. It was early in the afternoon, and we were the only patrons there. A cleaning woman was swabbing the floor near the entrance with a mop.

"When are you leaving for Africa?" Reinhardt asked as the waiter brought the drinks.

"In two days, Gottfried," Huston said, lighting his cigarette and, over the flame, intently watching the cleaning woman mop the floor.

"You finished the script for 'The African Queen'?" Reinhardt asked.

"Almost, Gottfried," Huston said absently. "I'll do the last of it on the plane going over."

Reinhardt took a long sip of his drink. "We will have to do the retakes for 'The Red Badge of Courage' in Africa," he said, and laughed with considerable satisfaction.

"Yeah," Huston said.

"When I think of all we went through," Reinhardt said.

"Christ, Gottfried, wasn't it worth it?" Huston said.

Reinhardt gave a nod of happy agreement. "Now, if anything goes wrong tonight, we will have to do everything over in Africa," he said, laughing again.

"Yeah, we'll have to do it all over in Africa," Huston said. "Ho! Ho! Ho!"

Reinhardt choked on his laughter. He stood up, and as he was paying for the drinks, Huston put on a Burberry and matching cap. He pulled the cap down over his eyes and strode quickly over to the cleaning woman who was mopping the floor. He bowed to her and took the mop from her hands. Then he put his arms around the mop, and, hugging it, he did a rakish waltz around the deserted cocktail lounge. Reinhardt beamed at him, and Huston, laughing quietly, danced back to the cleaning woman, returned her mop, and then danced out of the lounge alone to the street. "Cut!" cried Reinhardt.

As we drove toward Schary's house, Huston and Reinhardt talked about the private showing they had held two nights before for a couple of dozen of their friends and colleagues in the motion-picture industry, including William Wyler, Paul Kohner, and Sam Spiegel. They discussed the enthusiastic response "The Red Badge of Courage" had got at the showing.

"You know, Gottfried," said Huston, "I never had such a reaction to a picture before. I never heard Sam and Paul talk that way about a picture. And Willie Wyler called me and said it's one of the greatest pictures he's ever seen. This is Willie's picture. I never made a picture before that Willie didn't have some criticism to make of it. He kept grabbing my arm that night and saying, 'Jesus, this is wonderful!'" Huston laughed. "Willie said that the

Tattered Man's death scene was the most amazing he ever watched."

"We have a great picture," Reinhardt said.

"Well, boys," Dore Schary said when he received us, "I've got bad news for you. Hopper likes the picture."

"Christ, kid!" Huston said. He and Reinhardt both laughed.

"You're happy, huh?" Schary said.

"Christ!" said Huston.

"You're leaving for Africa," Schary said.

"Yeah," Huston said.

"I'll show you a couple of things when you get back," Schary said.

"Christ, kid," Huston said. "I've never had a reaction like this to a picture. Willie Wyler says it's the greatest picture he's ever seen."

"You had Willie there?" Schary said.

"Yeah, and—" Huston paused, as though his mind had gone blank. "Who else was there, Gottfried?"

"You look sort of gay in that cap," Schary said, not giving Reinhardt a chance to answer.

"Well, I'm kind of a sport," Huston said, taking off his cap and coat.

Schary ushered us into the living room. Huston said, "Dore, before you see any of this, I just want to tell you it's the best picture I ever made. I never, never had such a reaction before."

"Let's run it and we'll talk later," said Schary.

"You want to close the blind?" Reinhardt asked. The sun was streaming in.

"Pull it down, Gottfried," Schary said, and Reinhardt pulled down the blind.

The wide panel in the wall at one end of the room slid up, exposing the white screen, and the M-G-M lion appeared on the screen, and its roar dissolved in the sound of gunfire. The prologue of the picture started, showing the Youth on sentry duty near a river. Two of Schary's children bounded into the room and sat down facing the screen.

Schary got up and led them out of the room. "I told you to stay out. I want you to stay out," he said.

Nobody said anything during the showing, and except for some subdued laughter from Huston and Reinhardt at an early comic scene in the movie there was no sound in the room at all but what came from the sound track. At the end of the picture, the lights came on. Schary turned slowly to Reinhardt and Huston and said, "I think you ought to reprise these guys at the end."

"The faces," Huston said, nodding emphatically.

"Yeah," said Schary. "By the way, I'm glad to see you dubbed in 'gone goose' for 'gone coon.'" He was apparently taking his time about giving his opinion. After another long pause, he said, "Well, it's a wonderful picture."

Huston leaped to his feet and went over to Schary. Reinhardt shakily held a match to his cigar, which had gone out.

"I have two suggestions," Schary said as the heads of his children peered around the door. "I think some of the picture will be swallowed by the music. If it were my picture, I would yank the music out of the scene where the boy writes the letter. Close the door, kids!" The heads vanished. "Each time the music has the sense of warmth and nostalgia, it creates a mood that is helpful to the picture," Schary went on. "As soon as the music gets highly inventive, it hurts the picture. I think it'll hurt your picture, John. This picture is gonna stand up for years to come. It's a great, great picture."

Reinhardt and Huston did not interrupt. They were tense, and they were giving Schary their full attention.

"A great picture," Schary repeated. He glanced at some notes he had made. "The only scene I don't like—I still don't understand it, it destroys the mood—is the scene where the recruits are marchin' past the veterans and the veterans are laughin' at the guys." He had lapsed into an even more homespun and chatty manner than usual. "That irony at the end, when the guys think they're winnin' a battle and then it turns out they're not—that's accurate and real. I don't accept it in the other scene. It confuses me. I have to reorient myself. I think that scene should come out. I think it hurts you."

Huston started walking in small circles. "Uh-huh," he said. "Uh-huh. I'm just trying to orient the thought, Dore."

Reinhardt said nothing. He seemed to be making an effort to keep his face blank.

After a while, Huston said haltingly, "The only value the scene has, it's an interruption of that slam-bang of battle."

"That's not a valid argument," Schary said. "The mood of battle is sustained. You don't have to break it."

"You're right," Huston said. "It doesn't need to be there."

Schary looked pleased. "It just confuses you," he said. "The scene always bothered me."

Huston said, "You think it's an error, Dore, to take the view that the sole purpose of the scene is to give you a lift?"

"You don't need the scene," said Schary. "Boys, I think this picture is a great document. It's gonna be in the files. It's gonna be in the history books. It's a great picture."

"Then it comes off," Huston said.

"It must be sold as a great battle story," Schary said. "If we make it too special, you know—a great novel and all that—we'll drive away the kids who come to see a war story."

"The danger is it might be slapped into the big theatres for short runs," Reinhardt said.

"It won't be," said Schary.

"It ought to go to a big theatre that will give it time to build to a long run," said Reinhardt.

"You mean, Gottfried, like the Astor?" Huston asked.

"Yes. Show that the makers of the picture have faith in the picture," Reinhardt answered.

Huston said that reprising the faces at the end of the picture was a great idea.

"Just goes to prove the value of reading your mail," Schary said warmly. "A letter comes from a fella, he says, 'I run a theatre. Why don't you put the name of the picture at the end? All it ever says at the end is "The End." This is a great idea and it costs you nothing.' So I'm puttin' in this new thing at the studio." Schary seemed to be in especially high spirits. "I think this is the best picture you ever made, John."

"So do I," said Huston, laughing.

"So glad we made it," Schary said, and chuckled.

"Yeah, we finally made it," Huston said.

"It's a great picture, and it'll get great notices," said Schary. "I told you what your notices would be on 'The Asphalt Jungle,' didn't I?"

"You did," said Huston. There was a moment of silence.

"You fellas call me right after the preview," said Schary.

"Jesus, I'd love to see this be a big success," Huston said. "You know why, Dore. After everything we've been through with L.B. on this picture."

"Don't worry about it, kiddy," Schary said, grinning.

"Dore, you like the picture?" Reinhardt asked.

"I told you—this picture is gonna be remembered," Schary said. "It's a great picture."

"It ought to run in a theatre like the Astor or the Music Hall," Reinhardt said.

"Not the Music Hall," Schary said. "It should go into a house where people will come to enjoy seeing it, not a place where it will be the object of concern about whether it will gross this much or that much."

"The thing is it's got to have time to grow," Huston said. "I'd go to towns where 'Asphalt' had just opened and the managers would tell me business was picking up, but they couldn't take the chance of keeping it on for five more days."

Schary said that this was the kind of picture that should have special showings, to special groups, who would promote it. Also, it should have a special, and dignified, kind of publicity campaign. "Too bad you're leaving," he said to Huston. "You could handle some special showings yourself."

Huston said it was imperative that he be in England in four days, on his way to Africa.

"I could send the picture to New York with you," Schary said.

"I'll be in New York only one day—Sunday," Huston said.

"Too bad," said Schary. "The press will go crazy about this picture. This is a magnificent picture. It has intelligence and it has art. It fulfills the purpose of the cinema as a medium of entertainment and education. Nothing is wrong except that one scene. And a few tiny places where you go out too quick or hold too long." His telephone rang. The call was from Benny Thau, one of the company's vice-presidents. "I feel pretty good, Benny," Schary said. "No, I can't be at the preview. I don't know whether you'll like it or not, but you're gonna see one of the greatest pictures ever made."

When Schary had hung up, Huston said, "Can he afford not to like it now?"

Schary chuckled.

"I saw L.B. today," Reinhardt said slowly. "Mayer said to me, 'Maybe the picture is a good picture, but it can't possibly be a success at the box office.' I told him, 'I don't know if it is commercial, but it is a great picture.'"

Schary said dryly, "You played that scene wrong, Gottfried. If I had been playing that scene, I would have said, 'If I were starting all over again, I would now enter upon the making of this picture with greater confidence than ever before, with complete and unmitigated confidence.'"

"Too many people say that," Reinhardt said in a low voice.

"L.B. thinks a picture's no good if you don't say it," Huston said.

"I don't agree with you on the music," Reinhardt said suddenly to Schary.

Huston and Schary looked startled. Schary said, "I have no conviction. It's just my personal reaction."

"Audie is twice as good with the music under him, I tell you," said Reinhardt.

Schary replied coolly, "I think all music in pictures has to be cliché to be effective. Let's not debate it. I'll prove it to you. In Marine pictures, you play 'Halls of Montezuma.' In Navy pictures, you play 'Anchors Aweigh.' In this picture, the music that's effective is the sentimental-cliché music. It's a fact. Let's not debate it."

Schary quickly asked Huston whether he intended to sell his father's country house in the San Bernardino Mountains, and told him he'd be interested in it if Huston ever set a price on it.

"So you're going to have your Berchtesgaden," said Reinhardt.

Schary did not seem to hear him. "I'm getting to the point

where I want a place of my own. A *place*," he said. "With *things* on it." He stood up, and congratulated Huston and Reinhardt again. "Call me after the preview, kiddies," he said.

The preview was at the Picwood Theatre, a fifteen-minute drive from Schary's house. M-G-M often previewed pictures there. It was a modern, comfortable theatre, and on preview nights the lights on the marquee always read, "MAJOR STUDIO PREVIEW TO-NIGHT." The purpose of a preview—usually called a sneak preview —is supposedly to spring a picture on an audience without warning, in order to get an uninfluenced reaction. Many previews are advertised on marquees, in newspapers, and by word of mouth, but even these are known in the trade as sneak previews, or sneaks.

The marquee of the Picwood said "HARVEY" as well as "MAJOR STUDIO PREVIEW TONIGHT."

"I hate previews," Reinhardt said to me as he and Huston and I got out of the car. "The smelly house. Popcorn. Babies crying. Ugh! I hate it."

Bronislau Kaper buttonholed Reinhardt in the lobby. "Tell me. What did he say? Tell me everything." Reinhardt led him aside to tell him what Schary had said.

Johnny Green, head of M-G-M's music department, and Margaret Booth came up to Huston and asked him what Schary had said.

"Who's got a nickel?" Huston said. "Albert! Get me some popcorn." Albert Band, who was now working as Reinhardt's assistant, made his way through the crowd to a gleaming popcorn machine, as streamlined as the Picwood Theatre itself.

A man asked Huston whether he had ever heard Tallulah Bankhead's radio show. "If I could find the right thing in the picture, I might get a spot for it on Tallulah's show," he said.

One of the company's vice-presidents, L. K. Sidney, came over to Huston, took a handful of his popcorn, and said, "Good luck, John."

A short man with a cherubic face came over to Huston and pumped his hand. "Remember me? Swifty," he said.

"How are you, Swifty?" said Huston.

"I know you're thinking of other important matters tonight, but this I gotta tell you," said Swifty.

"Of course, Swifty," Huston said, looking very interested.

"The latest about Jack Warner!" Swifty announced. "One of Jack's producers suggests he do a picture about Mexico. So Jack says, 'I don't like Mexican pictures. All the actors in them look too goddamn Mexican.'" Swifty let out a wild guffaw.

"A great story, Swifty," Huston said.

"I knew you'd appreciate it," said Swifty.

Huston tossed pieces of popcorn into his mouth. "Eddie Mannix!" he said, moving to greet a square-faced, hulking man who looked like a football coach—another of M-G-M's vice-presidents.

"Good luck, fella," said Mannix.

Mrs. Huston arrived breathlessly, having driven in from Malibu Beach with Pablo.

Mrs. Reinhardt turned up and said that she had reluctantly left her French poodle, Mocha, at home. "Gottfried!" she cried. "Mocha wanted to come to the preview."

"Silvia, please!" Reinhardt said.

"What's wrong with *Mocha's* opinion?" Mrs. Reinhardt asked.

"L. B. Mayer is here," someone said to Huston. "He just scooted inside."

"How are you? Glad to see you," Huston was saying, shaking hands with still another M-G-M vice-president, as Reinhardt took a stand at Huston's side.

I went in and sat down in the rear. When "The Red Badge of Courage" flashed on the screen, there was a gasp from the audience and a scattering of applause. As the showing went along, some of the preview-goers laughed at the right times, and some laughed at the wrong times, and some did not laugh at all. When John Dierkes, in the part of the Tall Soldier, and Royal Dano, in the part of the Tattered Man, played their death scenes, which had been much admired before, some people laughed and some murmured in horror. The audience at the private showing had been deeply and unanimously moved by the death scenes. There was no unanimity in the audience now. Several elderly ladies walked out. Now and then, there were irrelevant calls from the balcony; one masculine voice, obviously in the process of changing, called out, "Hooray for Red Skelton!" Two or three babies cried. Men posted at the exits counted all departures. I could not see where Huston and Reinhardt were sitting. Across the aisle from me I could see L. B. Mayer, white-haired and bespectacled, sitting with his arms folded, looking fiercely blank-faced. Several M-G-M people nearby were watching him instead of the movie. During a particularly violent battle scene, Mayer turned to a lady sitting on his right and said, "That's Huston for you." There was a slight stir in his vicinity, but Mayer said nothing more.

In the lobby, the Picwood manager, assisted by several M-G-M men, stood ready to hand out what are known as preview cards—questionnaires for the audience to fill out. The first question was: "How would you rate this picture?" Five alternatives were offered: "Outstanding," "Excellent," "Very Good," "Good," and "Fair." Other questions were: "Whom did you like best in the picture?" "Which scenes did you like most?" "Which scenes, if any, did you dislike?" "Would you recommend this picture to your friends?" Below the questions, there was this additional request:

> We don't need to know your name, but we would like to know the following facts about you:
> (A) Male
>   Female
> (B) Please check your age group:
>   Between 12 and 17
>   Between 18 and 30
>   Between 31 and 45
>   Over 45

When the showing ended, the preview-goers milled about in the lobby, filling out the cards under the resentful surveillance of the men who had made the movie. Mayer walked out of the theatre and stood at the curb out front, looking as though he would like to have somebody talk to him. Reinhardt and Huston went into the manager's office, off the lobby, and sat down to await the ver-

dict. Johnny Green, Margaret Booth, Bronislau Kaper, and Albert
Band alternately watched the people filling out cards and Mayer.
Most of the other executives had already departed. Benny Thau
joined Mayer at the curb. Mayer got into his town-and-country
Chrysler, and his chauffeur drove him off. Benny Thau got into a
black limousine, and his chauffeur drove him off. Band went into
the manager's office. Huston and Reinhardt sat looking glumly at
each other.

"Did Mayer talk to anybody?" Reinhardt asked.

Band reported that Mayer had talked to Benny Thau.

The manager came in and handed Reinhardt and Huston a
batch of preview cards he had collected from the audience. Reinhardt read through them rapidly. Huston read some of the comments aloud. " 'This would be a wonderful picture on television,' " he read. " 'With all the money in Hollywood. why can't
you make some good pictures?' "

" 'Fair.' 'Fair.' 'Good.' 'Fair,' " Band read. "Here's one with
'Fair' crossed out and 'Stinks' substituted."

"Here's an 'Excellent,' " Huston said.

"No 'Outstanding's yet," said Reinhardt. He was perspiring, and
he looked grim. "Here's a 'Lousy,' " he said.

"The audience hated the picture," Band said.

Huston seemed dazed. "Call Dore, Gottfried," he said.

Reinhardt dialled the number. After getting Schary, he said,
"Dore," in a low, shaking voice, and after listening for a moment
he said, "You *know*? . . . Who told you? . . . Well, then you
know. . . . Well, a lot of people walked out. . . . Well, a new
batch of cards is coming in. . . . We've counted twenty-two 'Outstanding's so far, fourteen 'Excellent's, thirty 'Very Good's, fourteen 'Good's, and forty-three 'Fair's. . . . Well, Margaret Booth
said the reaction was terrible. . . . No, I didn't talk to L.B. I
didn't talk to Mannix. . . . Well, I think we should take it out
again tomorrow, with a serious picture. Not with 'Harvey.' Maybe
with 'The Steel Helmet.' . . . He is right here."

Reinhardt handed the telephone to Huston, who said, "Well.
. . . Well, Jesus Christ. Dore, I had the feeling they'd rather be
anywhere than in this theatre. Must have been a dozen people

walked out on the scenes I think are the best—the two death scenes. Wait till you see the cards. They're extraordinary. They're either raves or they say it's the worst picture they've ever seen. They just hate it. It's extraordinary."

An M-G-M man put his head in at the door. "Thirty-two walkouts," he said. The capacity of the Picwood was sixteen hundred, and it had been filled at the start of the showing.

The manager said sympathetically to Reinhardt, "How much did it cost? A million five?"

After Huston hung up, he said to Reinhardt, "Christ, Gottfried! I never saw one like this before, did you?"

"You can't force an audience to like a picture," Reinhardt said bleakly. "God! Tomorrow morning at the studio! How I hate to walk in there! They'll all be my enemies."

"Well, good night, Gottfried," Huston said. He was driving home with Mrs. Huston and Pablo.

Reinhardt walked to his car with his wife and me. "It's a cruel business," he said. "It isn't worth it. Almost a whole year." He looked at his half-smoked cigar with distaste. "M-G-M doesn't know what to do with a picture like this." He put the cigar in his mouth. "Did you see John? John was demolished tonight."

The next morning, Reinhardt telephoned me, sounding serious and tense, and said that the studio was going to have another preview that night, in Pasadena. He had not slept a wink all night, he said. He had not heard from Schary. He had not heard from Mayer. He had called Huston, who was going to meet him at the studio to go to the Pasadena preview, and he invited me to go along with them.

When I arrived at the Thalberg Building, Reinhardt was in conference with a writer about a possible new picture. I waited in the room at the rear of his office. Preview cards were scattered about the room. The "Good"'s, "Very Good"'s, "Excellent"'s, and "Outstanding"'s occupied the armchairs. ("Huston is to be congratulated. To those who can take grim reality, it's in the class of 'All Quiet on the Western Front.'") Everything below "Good" was spread out on a couch. ("The worst I have ever seen. The Tall Sol-

dier's death scene is tripe." "Very poor. I fell asleep. Most monot-
onous picture I have ever seen." "Audie Murphy is too good of an
actor to be stuck in such a stinker as this.") Albert Band came in
and said that Reinhardt wanted to put narration—passages from
the Crane novel—into the picture and to add a scene at the beginning that would show the Stephen Crane novel being opened
and its pages being turned, so that the audience would know the
picture was based on a great book. "Gottfried wants to move the
prologue, that wonderful scene with the Youth on sentry duty at
the river, and put it in later on," Band said indignantly. "I don't
approve."

In Reinhardt's inner office, a while later, Huston sat rocking back
and forth in a chair across the desk from Reinhardt. Band was pacing up and down behind him.

"Mayer has written it off," Reinhardt said. "Dore will back it.
It's a good thing this is not a cheap picture. If it were, they would
forget it entirely."

"Did you speak to L.B.?" Huston asked.

"He wouldn't talk to me," said Reinhardt. "Margaret Booth
told me to call him. I said, 'Why should I? He should call me.' But
then I called him. He didn't call me back. L.B. told Dore, 'There
are flops and there are successes. There are good pictures and bad
pictures. Let's go on making pictures.' "

Huston gave a low, muffled laugh.

"I always felt you must put over this picture the shadow of
Stephen Crane," Reinhardt went on. "We must come right out
and say, 'Here is a great American novel about the Civil War.'
With your blessing, John, I would like to try a preview where we
have narration. And at the end the narrator will say"—he picked
up a copy of the novel, opened it, and read—" 'So it came to pass
that as he trudged from the place of blood and wrath his soul
changed. He came from hot plowshares to prospects of clover tran-
quilly, and it was as if hot plowshares were not. He had rid himself
of the red sickness of battle. He had been an animal blistered and
sweating in the heat and pain of war. He turned now with a
lover's thirst to images of tranquil skies, fresh meadows, cool

brooks—an existence of soft and eternal peace.'" He clapped the book shut. "Spencer Tracy should do it," he said.

"How many passages?" Huston asked wearily.

Band, who had talked the matter over with Reinhardt, said five passages.

Reinhardt said, "John, you have to tell people what the picture is. We should start the narration at the beginning, before the scene at the river. That scene is puzzling. You pay for clever openings. We must tell them, 'Here is a masterpiece.' You've got to tell it to them."

Huston got to his feet and began pacing around the office.

"It might make the difference between life and death," Reinhardt said.

"It might very well," Huston said, without conviction. "Let's try it, by all means."

"The people must know this is a classic," Reinhardt said.

The second preview was held at the Pasadena Theatre, in Pasadena. It was a Friday night, and a long line of teen-agers in bobby socks and blue jeans stood at the box office. The feature attraction was a picture starring Ginger Rogers. The scene of the veterans jeering at the recruits, which Schary had disliked, had been cut for this showing. It was the only change that had been made so far. The audience showed absolutely no appreciation of the improvement. Emerging from the darkened temple, they joyfully got to work on the preview cards. The character several of them liked the best was, they wrote, "the pig," and one, in apparent reference to the farm girl whose pig was stolen, wrote "the sister." Which scenes did they like most? Answer: "Where the guy went crazy." Reinhardt hovered anxiously around the audience as it gave him its considered opinion of his picture. "Look, they're grinning," he said, staring hopelessly at a pack of youngsters in blue jeans giggling over their preview cards. "Take a good look at your movie audience."

"Well," Huston said.

"Terrible," Reinhardt said, leafing through a batch of the cards. "Worse than last night."

"Christ!" Huston said. "Listen, Gottfried. I want to tell you a story about Dad. The morning after he opened in 'Othello,' in New York, I went around to see him at his hotel. The reviews were just terrible. Through the door, I heard Dad laughing, 'Ho! Ho! Ho!' I went in, and there stood Dad, the tears running down his face, and he was laughing, 'Ho! Ho! Ho!' "

"I'm in a humorous mood," Reinhardt said.

"That's apparent," said Huston. "Is Norman Corwin in town? We ought to get him to do the narration."

"Spencer Tracy," said Reinhardt.

Too down-to-earth, Huston said. The narration should be read as if it were poetry, he said, and suggested Gregory Peck.

"Spencer Tracy should do it," Reinhardt said.

"Get 'the sister' to do it," said Albert Band, and started to laugh. Huston and Reinhardt silenced him with their glances.

"Albert," Huston said, "someday you will be head of the studio." He spoke mechanically, sounding flat and sad, and there was nothing at all of the former theatrical emphasis in his manner. He seemed tired. He walked away from Reinhardt and then turned around and faced him silently, his face drained of all expression.

"We'd better call Dore," Reinhardt said.

On the way back to town, Reinhardt had some violent things to say about the audience, about all movie audiences. He denounced bobby-soxers. He denounced everybody under the age of twenty-one. He denounced reviewers of motion pictures and said that they were responsible for all this. Then he subsided and was quiet for a long while. When he spoke again, he sounded puzzled. "It never happened to me like this before," he said.

The next day, Huston left Hollywood. He telephoned me in the morning to say goodbye. He did not say anything at all about "The Red Badge of Courage." "Well, now I'm off to Africa, kid," he said. "We're going to have a lot of fun making 'The African Queen.' " There was nothing in his tone to indicate he believed it.

At noon, about the time Huston's plane was taking off, Reinhardt, standing outside the M-G-M barbershop at the studio, was confronted by L. B. Mayer. Some producers and several directors and actors were standing nearby, watching the two men. Mayer shook a finger in Reinhardt's face. "You don't want to make money!" Mayer said. "You want to be an artist! Would you work as an artist for one hundred dollars a week? You want to make money. Why don't you want the studio to make money? Are you willing to starve for your art? You want to be the artist, but you want other people to starve for your art!"

Reinhardt reported the details of the scene to his wife. "Mayer hated the picture," he said. "I knew it would be like this. It was terrible, going to the studio. They are all now my enemies."

His wife suggested that the two of them go out of town for a day's rest. Reinhardt welcomed the idea. He telephoned Albert Band, who had taken care of Mocha in the past, and asked him if he would keep an eye on Mocha. Band refused. Reinhardt took the refusal stoically.

Reinhardt felt it was now up to him to figure out changes that might be made in "The Red Badge of Courage" that would bring the reactions of audiences closer to what might be considered favorable. "In the projection room, this picture is great," he said, pacing fitfully in his office after his day's rest, while Band lounged in an armchair, taking notes on a memo pad. "In the theatre, the audience is looking for a story and there is no story. The Breen Office loved the picture. They O.K.'d the whole thing. I keep trying to tell the studio they must sell the picture. Suddenly, nobody on the lot understands Stephen Crane. And John is gallivanting in Europe and Africa." He sat down behind his desk and took a cigar from a large mahogany box. "I wish I were rid of the red sickness of battle." He cut off the end of the cigar with a small gold knife. "I'd like to go far away."

"To Africa?" Band asked, with a short laugh.

"Albert, you are the most insensitive sensitive man I have ever known," Reinhardt said morosely.

Band batted his eyes. "The audience hated Tim Durant's high-pitched voice for the General," he said.

"John loves Tim's voice," Reinhardt said. "John thinks it is wonderful to have a general who does not boom."

Reinhardt and I left his office for the commissary, to have lunch. "John doesn't care any more about the picture," he said as we walked along. "John doesn't care about anything, and I am left here to listen to Louis B. Mayer." When we arrived at the commissary, Reinhardt ordered the M-G-M special cold plate, Fresh Shrimp à la Louie, and ate it in gloomy silence.

A couple of days later, Reinhardt wrote a memorandum to Schary:

Dear Dore:

I know you are busy, and as it is hard to reach you, I shall make a written report.

(1) We are dubbing the General's voice. I have interviewed several actors and found a very good one.

(2) We will have a less confusing opening. We start with a dignified period cover of the novel, underlining the classical value and illustrating the style and subject matter of the piece. As we leaf through the pages the credits appear. The last page we show brings what was previously the foreword. Narration fades in as if it were being read from the book and, as the printed words dissolve to the drilling, the rest of the foreword is spoken, setting the pattern for the rest of the film.

(3) The sentry scene, in this case, comes, I believe very effectively, after the letter scene. He [the Youth] is already scared, we know him already a little when he has his first contact with the enemy.

(4) We take out the dead soldier in the woods. I think, without the slightest sacrifice, we can thereby eliminate excessive grimness.

(5) At various moments in the picture, we will hear Stephen Crane's words sketching, in short and poignant and beautiful sentences, the psychological development of the Youth. (I have always maintained that what makes the book

outstanding are the *thoughts* and *feelings* of the Youth, not his actions. How can they possibly be dramatized? John thought they would be inherent in the scenes, in the expressions of the Youth's face.)

(6) I have tried out the passages in question with the film and am convinced that this technique, legitimate as it is when filming a great novel, will do wonders to the picture. It will not make some of the people who basically dislike the picture like it. But it will immensely clarify it for those who are now confused. It will prepare them for what is coming and tell them what it is about; namely, the INNER evolution of a man. It will also demand the necessary respect from the average audience, so that we can at least expect a true and more dignified reaction. I, personally, believe that, in addition, it will make the picture actually *better* and more dramatic.

(7) Especially the last passage of the book read over the last shot—"So it came to pass that as he trudged from the place of blood and wrath his soul changed. He had been to touch the great death and found that, after all, it was but the great death. Scars faded as flowers and the Youth saw that the world was a world for him. He had rid himself of the red sickness of battle. He turned with a lover's thirst to images of tranquil skies, fresh meadows, cool brooks—an existence of soft and eternal peace"—should make our end one of real beauty and filled with emotion.

(8) As you will have heard, the Breen Office approved the picture in toto and LOVED it. Could we perhaps release it exclusively to them? Seriously, I was quite baffled by the violent reactions pro and con; the accolades of the Wylers, Scharys, Hoppers, and numerous unsolicited admirers on the lot and, on the other hand, the brutal reception by so large a part of the audience, especially those terrible kids at the last preview. However, taking a leaf from our hero, I have since regained, yes, increased my courage. Have you?

(9) I have several ideas as to the presentation and selling of "Red Badge." Would you, and perhaps Howard [Dietz],

like to discuss them with me? (One is to run, prior to the release, tantalizing pictures of our actors in the papers without mentioning their names—only the names of the characters.)

(10) Incidentally, we are going ahead with your idea of reprising pictures of the cast at the end.

(11) Second veterans' scene has been cut out.

(12) I am at your disposal.

At Dore Schary's invitation, I dropped into his office in the Thalberg Building at eleven-thirty one morning a week or so after the Pasadena preview. Schary's name, on the plate nailed to his door, was engraved in letters twice the size of Reinhardt's. Hanging on the wall in the outer reception room was a bronze plaque reading:

> There is hardly anything in the world that some man cannot make a little worse and sell a little cheaper, and the people who consider price only are this man's lawful prey. —RUSKIN

I found Schary's two woman secretaries and his executive assistant, Walter Reilly, in the secretaries' room, busily discussing how busy their boss was.

"He got in early, before me, and cleaned up his desk," one of the secretaries was saying.

"At four o'clock, he has Garbo," the other secretary said. Her telephone rang. "Will let you know. Will call you," she said. "It's murder today."

"Wow! Some day!" said Reilly. "And tomorrow San Francisco."

Through an open door, I could see Reinhardt sitting, alone and dejected, in an adjoining conference room, at the head of a long table, staring at a bright-red leather couch. He had at last succeeded in getting a fifteen-minute appointment with Schary to talk about his memorandum. When he left Schary, he was going to work on the problem of dubbing in narration for "The Red Badge of Courage." He had not obtained Spencer Tracy as narrator, and was trying out various actors he thought had a narrator's kind of voice.

The door to Schary's office swung open and Schary came out,

his face composed and smooth, and his eyes innocent behind rimless spectacles. "Gottfried!" he called.

Reinhardt followed Schary into the office and closed the door.

"Wow!" Reilly said again, looking at a secretary's calendar. "How's he going to get through in time to go home and pack?"

"You going to San Francisco with him?" one of the secretaries asked.

Reilly nodded. "Got to get him there first thing in the morning," he said. Turning to me, he added, "He's speaking to the Drama Festival at the College of the Pacific, at Stockton. You want to read his speech?" He handed me a mimeographed copy. Hollywood, Schary was going to say, was the intellectual whipping boy for all the other communities—"maybe because we are more critical of what we love most." I read on:

> I might say that there appears to be a slight change going on, and we in the motion-picture industry look on this change with a little bit of hope and, at the same time, with enormous sympathy for the medium which is about to inherit the abuse that normally and consistently is pinned upon us. That medium is television. Television, because of its time strictures and enormous demands, is beginning to deflect some of the criticism from the motion-picture industry. Some of us look upon this with mixed feelings. We listen to the critics belabor TV. Every once in a while, of course, we pick up a small stone and toss it ourselves, just to keep the pot boiling. . . . There have been florid, fluent, and flatulent explanations about the art of the cinema and its differences in Germany, France, Italy, England, and America. I have studied these differences, I have noted them, I am aware of them, I respect them, but I still maintain that the American motion-picture industry, which is best identified by its generic term "Hollywood," has accomplished more, has entertained, enlightened, and informed more people over a longer period of time, than any other motion-picture community in the world.

Schary went on to say that movies were criticized for their senti-mentality, but that he thought sentimentality was a good thing, because it was the answer to cynicism. He would tell the students, "Keep your sentimentality fresh, abundant, sweet-smelling. To do so is to believe in humanity." He concluded his speech by saying, "Sentimentality should be worn boldly, like Cyrano's white plume, and if anyone detects a trace of that plume in my hatband, I am not ashamed but proud."

Reinhardt came out of Schary's office and, with a sad, tired smile, said to me, "Dore is giving careful study to everything I wrote him. Now Dore wants to see what happens with the nar-ration."

In his inner office, Schary told me, "I like a busy room. I don't like a bare room. I concentrate better in a busy room." His room was busy, not only with visitors, secretaries, and assistants but with hundreds of small, medium-size, and large gadgets. From where he sat, he looked out on several lions, made of iron, paper, or plastic; autographed baseballs; a bowling trophy won by a team known as the Schary Hunky-Dorys; an ancient typewriter in a glass case; an antique lamp with a red glass shade; lead soldiers, in the uniforms of various ages and nations; and a large china pitcher embossed with a portrait of George Washington and the words "Peace, Plenty, and Independence." On a shelf at his side, near his head, was a photograph of his mother. On his walls were paintings by his wife, including one of the Schary family in their back yard.

Schary sat at an L-shaped table with a glass top. "I like air underneath," he said. "I concentrate better with air underneath." He was pleased at having been given an option on a hundred thou-sand shares of Loew's, Inc., stock at the current market value of $16.50 a share. He explained to me that if within the next six years he bought the stock and its value went up to twenty-one dol-lars, for example, he could sell it and make a profit of a half-mil-lion dollars.

"Mayer used to own a lot of stock, but he's sold most of it. He's still my boss, though. Mayer and Mr. Schenck are my bosses," Schary said. He went on to say that he liked his job and got along fine with his top boss, Mr. Schenck, and that he enjoyed tussling with the problems that came along and working them out. "I love problems," he said. "I love the problems inherent in show business. I love the risks, the excitement in the work, and all the people who are problems. The only thing I miss is the time to study. I love to read a lot. In about ten years, I want to get out of the industry. I've been in show business for eighteen years, and when I retire, I want to write books about it and teach and lecture. I love to teach the youngsters who are just coming up in show business."

For the time being, Schary said, he was content to just go along in charge of production at Metro-Goldwyn-Mayer. He knew where he stood with Mr. Schenck. Mr. Schenck, in New York, decided on general policy—the number of pictures to make each year, and which ones, and at what cost. "The how he leaves completely to me," Schary said. "Of course, I'm in close touch with him all the time. There's not a thing that goes on in this studio that he doesn't know about. He knows the place inside out." Exactly what Mayer did at the studio was not so clearly defined. "He calls me and tells me what he thinks of the pictures," Schary said. Mayer had told him that "The Red Badge of Courage" was grim and had no story and would not make money.

"I still think 'The Red Badge of Courage' is a beautiful picture," Schary said confidently. "It's ahead of its time and behind its time." He paused, then continued, "To me, the picture is a moving, completely honest, perfect translation of the book. It's imaginative and it has good performances. It's a wonderful picture. A normal business risk. Of course"—he unwrapped a stick of chewing gum—"Mayer says, 'If they're so goddam artistic, why don't they spend their own money?'" Schary chuckled tolerantly and put the chewing gum in his mouth. "And there is some validity to what he says. So you have to find reasonable ground to stand on. There are big gambles worth taking, but you can't go crazy. The discipline of art is important."

Schary said he was tired of listening to people rant and rave about the limitations put on the creative artist in the movie business. There were limitations, he agreed, but they were not peculiar to the industry. "It's the age-old problem of any individualist," he said. "When it comes to subjecting the artist to pressure, the history of art shows that art flourishes under pressure. Titian's art flourished under pressure. The pressures in our business or in radio or in television only serve to create better programs. Art in motion pictures improves whenever the heat is on. During the war years, when anything went, pictures were worse. With the heat on us now, better pictures are being made and more individuals are asserting themselves. Pressure is not necessarily a bad thing. It enables us to compete on a much higher level."

Reinhardt was on a sound stage with a young actor, working on a test recording of the narration that was expected to make audiences aware that "The Red Badge of Courage" was a classic.

" 'He now wished he was dead,' " the actor said into a microphone.

" 'He now wished he was dead. He now wished he was dead,' " Reinhardt said. His eyes looked bloodshot.

" 'He now wished he was dead,' " the actor said.

"Right. 'He now wished he was dead,' " Reinhardt said passionately. Then he sighed heavily. "You know, my father didn't want me to go into this business," he said to me. "My father always said, 'Only on the stage is it good. Everything behind the stage, in back of the scenes, and everything that goes on before, all of it is no good.' "

The actor said, "Mr. Reinhardt, how's this? 'He wished that he, too, had a wound, a red badge of courage. He now thought that he wished he was dead.' "

"All right," Reinhardt said listlessly. "God, I wish I was dead!" He gave a cynical laugh.

A week later, Schary had a new lamp on his desk. Its base was a three-foot brass figure of a bearded, helmeted Viking. Schary had found the figure in a small shop in Los Angeles. "The boys on the lot made the lamp for me," he said. "I love it. When I left R.K.O., I wanted to form an independent company, and I planned to use the Viking as my symbol. It stands for everything I like—courage and initiative and everything." He gave the Viking a look of approbation and then he told me that "The Red Badge of Courage" was going to be all right now that narration was being added. He had not yet decided definitely on who would do the narration. "The voice of the narrator must be warm, intimate, and dignified," he said. "I may have to do it myself."

Schary said he might make some other changes. "I want to get more of the text of the book into the picture," he said. "I want to tell the audience the narration is from the book. A lot of people don't know this is a book. I want to be blunt with them. Put them in a more receptive mood. I want to tell them they're gonna see a *classic, a great novel.*" Apparently he now agreed with what Reinhardt had said in his memorandum, and had forgotten the idea he had when he saw the picture with Huston and Reinhardt, of selling the picture as a great battle story instead of making it special— a great novel and all that, which would drive away the kids who would come to see a war story.

I asked Schary about an item I had come across in the New York *Times* saying that the picture would be released in small art theatres, rather than big theatres. "Another unfounded rumor," he said. "Your first impulse with these rumors is you want to run them down. I was reading Sandburg's life of Lincoln the other night. The part where Lincoln said you can't run down all rumors. So I suddenly decided the hell with it. Everything is so close in this town you're bound to get rumors no matter what you do. Lincoln would have said, 'The hell with it.'"

"Chaplin never got it. Garbo never got it. Lubitsch never got it," Reinhardt was saying. "Luise Rainer got it twice." He was referring to the annual Motion Picture Academy Award. Clad in a dinner jacket, he was driving to the R.K.O. Pantages Theatre, where the presentations for pictures released in 1950 were to be made. A large sticker, bearing a picture of the statuette, was pasted on the windshield of his car, to get it past police lines. His wife and I were with him. "The best ones never got it," Reinhardt said.

The stage of the Pantages Theatre was dominated by a giant copy of the statuette, and rows of smaller copies were arrayed on each side of it. This time, Joseph L. Mankiewicz got it, Darryl

Zanuck got it, and L. B. Mayer got it—Mayer in a "special presentation" honoring him as the founding father of the Academy and the inaugurator of the star system. He received a big hand. "This is truly an experience," he said, holding his statuette to his chest. "This fills me with humility and great responsibility in the years to come."

M-G-M gave a party at the Beverly Hills Hotel after everybody who was going to get it had got it. Huston had been one of the nominees, for his direction of "The Asphalt Jungle," but Mankiewicz had beaten him, with "All About Eve." Almost all the top executives, stars, producers, and directors of M-G-M had accepted invitations for what they had hoped would be more of a celebration. At the party, Schary stayed on one side of the room and Mayer stayed on the other. Both had a good deal to say about who had got it and who had not got it, and they both concluded that things weren't too bad, because Paramount had done worse.

It was the privilege of Arthur Freed, producer of most of M-G-M's successful musicals, to use L. B. Mayer's private dining room at the M-G-M studio with or without Mayer. The day after the presentation of the Academy Awards, he invited me to lunch there. The room opened off the main dining room, where most of the M-G-M people lunch at small tables with paper doilies bearing the figure of a lion. Mayer's room had one table, a round one with a white tablecloth, on which places were set for six. Among the room's appointments were mirrors, fluorescent lights, a telephone, and a menu headed "Mr. Mayer's Dining Room," from which Freed ordered M-G-M Special Chicken Broth and Fresh Crab Legs à la Louie. Freed had not attended the presentation ceremony; he had listened to the speeches over the radio. "I'm glad L.B. got it," he said. "He's a great picture-maker."

Freed is a stocky, unsmiling man of fifty-six who has worked for M-G-M for twenty-three years. He said that Mayer had started the producer system in Hollywood when he made Irving Thalberg his first producer, and that Thalberg, a brilliant man, had had sense enough never to put his name on the screen. "Irving always said credit is great when it's given to you, not when you take it,"

Freed explained. Mayer had chosen Thalberg because he had recognized his capabilities. "L.B. always believes in getting somebody smarter than himself," said Freed. "The average fellow wants somebody not as smart. L.B. thinks in terms of an attraction. He is known as an extravagant man. That's what built this studio— his extravagance. He isn't cut out for the small picture. He has a great inspirational quality at this studio. I've spent twenty years with Louie Mayer at the studio and I used to have dinner with him every night, and I have a real understanding with him on a real basis. He's the only man who never got panicky in a crisis, of which this business faced many, and the only executive who thought always in big terms. Every musical I made, there wasn't one I didn't find Louie Mayer a help in. He's nuts about my latest musical, 'Show Boat.' He came to the preview and cried."

Freed exudes an extraordinary kind of confidence in his musicals, and he usually carries with him reports showing the receipts of his current releases. The reports indicate that Freed's pictures are making money. A successful songwriter before becoming a producer, Freed wrote the lyrics for "Pagan Love Song," "Singin' in the Rain," "Broadway Melody," and "You Are My Lucky Star," among others, and he had since incorporated most of the songs into musicals, some of which he named after the songs. The first musical he produced was "Babes in Arms," in 1939, starring Mickey Rooney and Judy Garland, which netted the studio more money than any musical in the past ten years. "It was the biggest money-maker M-G-M had that year," Freed went on. "Everybody said I was nuts when I said that Judy would be a star. Everybody said I was nuts when I picked Gene Kelly. I gave Gene his first break. I brought him out here. I'm not interested in the Arrow Collar type. I'm interested in *talent*. Same with Judy. As a kid, she had talent. I gave Judy her first break. I ran 'Babes in Arms' the other day, and I swear I had *real* tears in my eyes. I bought 'Annie Get Your Gun' for Judy. Just because I thought she would like it. When she left the picture, it cost the studio a million dollars to get somebody else. Not that money matters. L.B. was so concerned he himself said he personally would foot her doctor bills. He didn't have to. The studio paid. The studio cared about what happened to Judy. After all, we practically brought her up. She meant something to us. After all, musicals have been the backbone of M-G-M for years."

The biggest money-making star at M-G-M, Freed told me, was Esther Williams, and he told me why. "She's not only good-looking, she's cheerful," he said. "You can sell cheerfulness. You can't sell futility. Take John Huston. A great talent. I'd like to make a picture with him myself. He makes a picture, 'Treasure of Sierra Madre,' and it's a success with the critics but it'll take years to get its cost back from the public. Why? It's futile. Even the gold disappears in the end. It's not television that is our competition. No more than night baseball. Television can't run the movies out of business. Fundamentally, a picture is not complete unless an audience is out there. Without an audience, you don't know where the laughs are. This is show business. You need laughs. You need cheerfulness. That's the whole reason for show business in the first place."

A waitress brought the chicken broth and Freed bent his head to it. After he finished it, he said, "L.B. knows how to bring up the stars. L.B. is a great baseball man. He has always believed in that second team coming up. He learned it from watching Connie Mack build up the minor leagues in baseball. One thing about L.B. He never makes any pretension about pictures as anything but entertainment. If a writer complains about his stuff being changed, he always says, 'The Number One book of the ages was written by a committee, and it was called the Bible.'"

After lunch, we went to Freed's office. Vincente Minnelli, the director, was there waiting for him. Freed asked his secretary to let him know when L.B. was free. He then started a discussion with Minnelli of plans to make a musical based on "Huckleberry Finn." Freed said that he wanted to make "Huckleberry Finn" the kind of picture that Mark Twain would love. "I want to find a new kid to play Huck," he said. "I want to find a real kid. You find a real kid, they're real like Lassie or Rin-Tin-Tin. Say, Vince, I meant to tell you the latest about Joe Pasternak. He's talking about this new girl he's got and he says, 'You should hear her sing. She's a female Lena Horne.'"

The dictograph buzzed, and Freed switched it on. "You there?" a voice said.

"Yeah. How ya fixed, L.B.?" Freed said. "Yeah. Right away." He switched off the machine and asked me to go along to Mayer's office with him.

"I'm leaving," Minnelli said.

"Yeah, so long," Freed said, and hustled me upstairs.

Freed and I came to a door that was guarded by a dapper young man with a small mustache, who whispered to us to go right in. Mayer, seated at his cream-colored desk, was talking into one of his four cream-colored telephones, thanking someone for congratulating him on getting the Academy Award. On a couch sat the actor George Murphy, who nodded to us.

"I'd rather be loved than get ten million dollars," Mayer was saying emotionally.

Freed motioned me to a cream-colored leather chair, and he sat down in another.

When Mayer had finished with his call, Freed stood up, took a paper from a pocket, and showed Mayer the receipts on his latest musical.

"Great! I knew. I knew before it opened!" Mayer said, sweeping Freed back into his chair. He turned to Murphy. "Did you go to the Republican dinner last night?" he asked.

"I couldn't," Murphy said. "I was with you."

"That's right," Mayer said. There was a soft buzz, and he picked up his telephone. "Thanks," he said. "I couldn't hear anything. I couldn't see anything. My eyes were blinded with tears. They're giving me a recording of the whole ceremony, so I can know what I said and what happened. So I can hear it." He hung up and turned to Freed. " 'Show Boat'!" he said. "I saw 'Show Boat' and the tears were in my eyes. I'm not ashamed of tears. I cried. I'll see it thirteen times. Thirteen times! Tears! Emotion!"

"It's great entertainment," Freed said. "It's show business."

Mayer stared across the top of Freed's head.

"There's a singer in the picture," he went on. "Black. He has one song. He"—Mayer jabbed a finger in Freed's direction—"got the man to come all the way from Australia to sing this one song.

The way he sings, it goes straight to the heart." Suddenly, Mayer lowered his voice to a basso profundo and began a shattering rendition of "Ol' Man River." Tears came to his eyes. He stopped in the middle of a line. "It's worth more than a million dollars," he said. "Talent!" Again he jabbed a finger at Freed. "He found the singer. All the way from Australia."

"There's no business like show business, all right," Freed said.

"It takes work to find talent. These days, all the smart alecks know is cocktail parties," Mayer said.

"I hate parties," Freed said. "I go to a party, I always get sat next to somebody I have to talk to. Some people in this town, they'll book eleven parties a week if they can."

"Money!" Mayer went on, as though he had not heard Freed. "Do I personally need any more money? I have a job at the studio. Do I stay here for money?" He paused.

Freed said quickly, "If you make seventy-five thousand dollars a year, you can say, 'I make more money than a Supreme Court Justice.' That's all money is good for any more. You can't keep it any more."

"I need money the way you need a headache," Mayer said. "I want to give the public entertainment, and, thank God, it pays off. Clean, American entertainment. Opera! Mr. Schenck tells me they don't like opera. We make a picture, 'The Great Caruso.' Look at the receipts! My wife broke down and cried when she saw the picture. But Mr. Schenck says they don't like opera!" He glared at Freed.

Murphy cleared his throat. He stood up and asked if it was all right to leave.

"Hold yourself in readiness!" Mayer said.

"Yes, sir!" said Murphy, and left.

"Sentimental," Mayer went on. "Yes! Sentiment is the heart of America. I like Grandma Moses. I have her paintings in every room of my house. I'm not ashamed of it. This is America. I know. I used to chase turkeys myself on a farm. Her pictures are life."

The dapper young man came tiptoeing in. "Mr. Zimbalist is waiting," he whispered, and tiptoed out.

This elicited no sign from Mayer. He was talking about people he thought were trying to harm the motion-picture business, the allies of the people who wanted to make pictures showing mothers being socked on the jaw; namely, the movie critics, who praised all kinds of sordid pictures made in foreign countries, and discounted the heart-warming pictures made in Hollywood. "As soon as it says the picture was made in Italy, some eighty-dollar-a-week critic writes a big rave review calling it art," Mayer said. "Art. 'The Red Badge of Courage'? All that violence? No story? Dore Schary wanted it. Is it good entertainment? I didn't think so. Maybe I'm wrong. But I don't think I'm wrong. I know what the audience wants. Andy Hardy. Sentimentality! What's wrong with it? Love! Good old-fashioned romance!" He put his hand on his chest and looked at the ceiling. "Is it bad? It entertains. It brings the audience to the box office. No! These critics. They're too tony for you and I. They don't like it. I'll tell you a story. A girl used to knock our movies. Not a bad-looking girl. A little heavy back here. All of a sudden, the girl disappears. Then I hear she went to Warner's, writing scripts for a thousand dollars a week. I'm on the golf links. I see Howard Strickling running across the green. You know Howard." Mayer huffed and puffed to demonstrate how Strickling ran across the green. " 'Why are you running?' I ask Howard. He tells me the girl tried to commit suicide. I go with him, just as I am, in my golf clothes. In the hospital, the doctors are pushing her, trying to make her walk. 'Walk! Walk!' She don't want to walk." Mayer got up and acted out the part of the girl. "Suddenly, she sees me, and she gives a cry! 'Oh!' And she walks. And this is what she says: 'Oh, Mr. Mayer, I am so ashamed of myself. When I think of how I used to knock the movies, I am ashamed.' "

That was the end of Mayer's story. Freed looked puzzled.

"You knock the movies, you're knocking your best friend," Mayer said.

5   Looks Like We're Still in Business

SUDDENLY, late in the spring of 1951, the big word around the M-G-M studio was "narration." Having reached the conclusion that his friends and colleagues had loved "The Red Badge of Courage" because they understood it, and that the public (or at least that very odd sampling of the public that comprises preview-goers) had hated the picture because the public was unable to understand it, Reinhardt, with Huston's and Schary's consent, had begun to dub in narration. Only Mayer didn't think that narration ("Jabber, jabber, jabber. Who wants to listen?") or anything else would help. "We are using the words of Stephen Crane himself to tell the audience what is happening," Reinhardt said to his wife one night, "and the picture will start with an introduction that tells the audience that they are going to see a great classic. Dore is writing the introduction himself. L.B. says to me the picture is no good because there is no story. I tell him we are adding narration to the picture, but he says narration won't help what isn't there. L.B. is a dangerous man. If you're his enemy, he destroys you. If you're his friend, he eats you. John is gone and now I have to face L.B. alone. I don't know why it is; every time I go to lunch, I have to run into L.B. Today, on my way to lunch, he came at me like a battleship: 'Mr. Reinhardt!' Then he told me the same things all over again. 'Why don't you want to make a hit? Why don't you want to make money for the studio?' Today I said to him, 'When John Huston comes to me and says he wants to make a picture, I am honored. You hired him. I didn't.' He didn't hear me. He talks about the picture as though it were refrigerators."

"Gottfried!" Mrs. Reinhardt said. "I think everybody is demented."

"You know, I like Dore," Reinhardt went on. "Dore still speaks well of the picture. He backed the picture in the beginning and he does not change because of the previews. Dore is a lucky man and a nice man. Dore says to me, 'The jury is still out.'" Reinhardt laughed. "Dore is really lucky. He is on the telephone every day now with Nick Schenck. Dore is a nice man. Nick Schenck thinks the picture might be a bust. But Dore doesn't want it to happen."

"Gottfried!" Mrs. Reinhardt said. "Now I know everybody is demented."

The next morning, Reinhardt made his daily visit to the studio barbershop, to be shaved. The chief barber, whose name is Mano, lathered Reinhardt's face and whispered the latest gossip in his ear. At the studio, Mano had the reputation of being an M-G-M authority, having served as L. B. Mayer's barber for ten years and having seen every M-G-M picture produced in that period. "Did you see the list of the ten worst pictures of the year?" he asked Reinhardt.

Reinhardt shook his head.

"Dore's personally produced picture is on it," Mano said. "'The Next Voice You Hear . . .' Best. Worst. So many lists. How's your picture?"

"Great," Reinhardt mumbled.

"L.B. cried at the preview of 'The Great Caruso,'" Mano whispered, shaving Reinhardt's chin. "Six hundred tears they counted."

A man sitting in the next chair—Edgar J. Mannix, one of the M-G-M vice-presidents—looked over at Mano and said, "You mean six million dollars."

Reinhardt closed his eyes and sighed.

"L.B. and Dore," Mano whispered soothingly. "It's going to be a knock-down, drag-out fight."

A week later, another picture personally produced by Dore Schary, "Go for Broke!," which was based on the activities of the Japanese-American troops in the European campaigns of the last war, was having what is called an invitational première at the

Egyptian Theatre, in Hollywood. I attended it with the Reinhardts. On the way to the theatre, Mrs. Reinhardt kept up a steady
chatter about her French poodle, Mocha, and Mocha's resistance
to taking pills for his hay fever, but Reinhardt acted as though
his mind were on some faraway subject. Mrs. Reinhardt asked
him several times what was the matter, and each time he replied
that nothing was the matter.

Schary's picture got a big hand. As the Reinhardts and I were
driving home, a limousine carrying Schary and his family drew up
alongside us. Schary, looking elated, rolled down a window and
shouted, "Did you have a good time?"

"Wonderful!" Reinhardt shouted back, and let the Schary car
cut in ahead of him in the heavy traffic.

Ten days after the opening of "Go for Broke!," I joined Mayer
as he sat in his private dining room at the studio talking about the
picture to Arthur Freed, the M-G-M producer of musicals. Mayer
had not approved of "Go for Broke!" "I don't like Japs!" Mayer
said. "I remember Pearl Harbor!" He looked grim. Picking up his
private menu, he said he wanted some lamb chops, and Freed
said, "Likewise." Freed remarked that lamb chops were easy to
digest. Mayer told Freed about a friend of his who had dropped
dead that morning. Heart attack. No warning.

When his chops arrived, Mayer fell to with what seemed to be
a hearty appetite. When he had finished, he pushed his plate
away. "Dore wants to make pictures about Japs," he said. "All
right. I'm through trying to tell him." Mayer said that he'd had
plenty of disagreements with other M-G-M production heads
working under him—especially Irving Thalberg and David Selznick—but they'd always admitted in the end that he was right.
"Do you know how many times Irving would have seen 'Quo
Vadis'?" he said. "He'd have worn out the prints! Or David. That
boy could have been one of the outstanding men of our time.
Why, he even wrote poetry, and it was beautiful. I told him, 'You
have an opportunity to be the greatest and you're just frittering it
away.' He didn't listen."

The waitress brought Mayer's dessert—a bowl of fresh strawberries. "I'll tell you Irving's words to me," he went on, mashing up the strawberries. "He was with Laemmle. Making three hundred and fifty dollars a week. Laemmle didn't like him—a young fella, getting all the attention. I hired him for five hundred dollars a week, and then I asked him, 'Why did you leave Laemmle?' He said, 'I watched you in New York when you were a distributor of pictures. You were different. I would rather be first violin under your direction than conductor of the orchestra.' Those were Irving's words to me. After six months, I wanted to make him a partner. Irving knew the business, and what he didn't know he was willing to learn through work. And he listened to me. Stars. Garbo. I was over in Europe making 'Ben Hur.' They tell me about this girl and the man—"

"Mauritz Stiller," Freed said.

" 'Tell him I want him and I want the girl,' I said. Her arms were like that," Mayer continued, spreading the fingers of his hands around an imaginary watermelon. "She had legs! Fat! But the face! I make a deal. Four hundred a week for her, and a thousand for him to bring her over. I told her American men don't like fat girls. 'Ja, ja, ja, ja.' That's all she could say. When she got here, she had taken off tremendous weight. 'Ja, ja, ja, ja.' " Mayer fluttered his lashes like Garbo. "No professional I ever handled was as honorable as her. I offered her a hundred and fifty thousand dollars once to hold her in case we made a picture. 'Suppose I took the money,' " Mayer said, again pretending to be Garbo, " 'and then the studio did not do the picture.' Imagine! A few weeks ago, Benny Thau brought her in my office. She wanted to do a story that would never be a hit in this country. In Europe, yes. Here, no. She always said, 'I want to play opposite an artist.' Gable? No, she didn't want Gable. But, you know, I never got mad with her. Turning down a hundred and fifty thousand dollars! Can you question a woman like that?"

"Talk of art grows and the audience diminishes," Freed said.

"I'll never forget the way Irving used to swing his watch when he was thinking," Mayer said. "He was in my office, telling me a story. I say, 'A man as able as you, you've got an inferiority complex.' He goes ahead and tells his story, and I don't like it. I say, 'Irving, I don't like it.' He starts acting out the story. It's 'Red Headed Woman.' For Jean Harlow. I say, 'Irving, you're going to jail. Tell the truth. It's a wonderful thing to tell the truth. Jean Harlow, she's a platinum blonde—that's the truth.' Irving says the hair won't show. That was Irving and I working together. He'd get mad. He'd come back. Then he'd start again. He'd always come back. That I like. Stand up!" he cried abruptly, looking at me and standing up. "I stand up for you. Why? I stand up for a lady." He sat down. "Nowadays, there's no manners. He's making pictures about the Japs. Last week, who went to see the picture? All the Japs! This week, the bottom fell out of his box office."

Sam Spiegel flew in to Hollywood from London for a few days to take care of some business matters. He telephoned me to say that he had left Huston, sick in bed with the flu, twenty-four hours before in a hotel in London, where Huston had gone on his way to Africa. "I have never seen John so depressed. He is so shocked and disappointed because of the bad reaction to 'The Red Badge of Courage,'" Spiegel said. "I have never been so rushed. I just had my smallpox for Africa. In New York, I get the tetanus. The typhus I'll get when I go back to London. I have a million things to do. I can't be bothered worrying about M-G-M's pictures; otherwise I would call Dore and tell him not to touch John's picture. Too bad. I guess the picture is a bust."

"You know, I really like Dore Schary," Reinhardt said as we drove from the Reinhardts' house, in the hills above Sunset Boulevard, to a theatre in the town of Pacific Palisades for the third preview of "The Red Badge of Courage." The picture was being shown for the first time with narration, with a booming voice dubbed in for Tim Durant's thin, high-pitched one, with the scene of the dead officer in the woods cut, and with some other slight changes that Reinhardt thought would increase the audience's understanding of what the picture was about. "Dore is one of the few sympathetic executives I know," Reinhardt went on. "He called me today and he said, 'Don't worry. Don't be disturbed. I am coming with a baseball bat, and anybody who doesn't like the picture I will hit over the head.' "

All the leading M-G-M executives attended this preview, with the exception of L. B. Mayer, whose absence was puzzling to some people. The picture in its new form opened with a shot of the cover of the Stephen Crane novel. James Whitmore, the actor, had been chosen for the role of the narrator, and as the book was opened, Whitmore was heard delivering the introduction written by Dore Schary, in which it was explained that the picture was based on a classic written in 1894 and it was pointed out emphatically that the novel had been "accepted by critics and public alike as a classic story of war." "Stephen Crane wrote this book when he was a boy of twenty-two. Its publication made him a man," Whitmore said. A portrait of Stephen Crane was flashed on the screen. The introduction explained, further, that Stephen Crane's book had a story. "His story is of a boy [the Youth] who, frightened, went into a battle and came out of it a man with courage," Whitmore said, in Schary's words (Huston's idea of the theme of the movie, which was simply that courage is as unreasoning as cowardice, was not alluded to in the introduction), and then Whitmore said that the remainder of the narration was taken from the classic itself.

The third preview audience was no more and no less respectful than the first two had been. People did not seem impressed by the fact that they were seeing a classic. Many people laughed at the tragic scenes, exactly as people in the other audiences had laughed; just as many others seemed shaken or moved by the same scenes. A shot of a crazed soldier marching in a line of wounded and singing "John Brown's Body" while keeping time with a tree branch for a baton had been received at the previous showings with some laughter as well as horror. This audience laughed or acted horrified, too. The death scenes of the Tall Soldier, played by John Dierkes, and the Tattered Man, played by Royal Dano, had been hooted and jeered at by the audiences at the earlier previews, and they were similarly received now. Some young patrons had giggled and elderly patrons had walked out on an especially noisy scene showing the Youth, in his flight from battle, coming upon an artillery battery, and some young patrons giggled and elderly patrons walked out on the scene now. On the other hand, some patrons previously had given the movie their quiet attention, and there were patrons now who did the same.

After the showing, the executives and Reinhardt gathered around Schary in the lobby. He seemed to have a new attitude toward the picture. There was no baseball bat in his hand. He looked angry.

"Gottfried, the way this picture plays now, it's got no story," Schary said.

Reinhardt glanced quickly at Margaret Booth, at Johnny Green, and at Bronislau Kaper, who nodded in agreement as Schary said that he thought the pattern of the battle scenes was wrong. He suggested changing the order of certain scenes and eliminating others.

Reinhardt looked puzzled and hurt and was silent.

"We make these changes, we'll bring the picture into its proper focus," Schary said.

Reinhardt looked surprised, and still said nothing.

Schary said that he wanted to cut out the death scene of the Tattered Man. Huston and Reinhardt had often said that it was not only the best scene in "The Red Badge of Courage" but the best scene of its kind ever made, and that it brought out some of the essence of the novel.

Reinhardt seemed too distraught to reply.

"The construction of the sequence in which the troops are withdrawn is bad," Schary went on in an indignant tone. "You can't have 'em going back and forth, back and forth. You've got to get the audience worked up, and then you've got to deliver. Like you do with a dame. The way you have it now, Gottfried, you get the dame interested and then the guy leaves her."

Reinhardt stared at him mutely.

"Get 'em ready and charge!" Schary said, raising a clenched fist. "Charge, Gottfried! Build to a climax, and *bam!*"

"Yes! Yes!" Johnny Green said.

"Maybe what we need is more of the kind of effect we had in 'Go for Broke!' " Schary said.

"Yes, make it add up," Margaret Booth said.

"The Tattered Man makes the audience seasick," said Schary.

"Correct!" said Bronislau Kaper, who six months before had called the scene "overwhelming" and had been so proud of the combination of sharp trumpet (for the military effect) and gay harmonica (for the ironic effect) he had worked out for the scene.

"He's absolutely right!" said Margaret Booth, who had sent Huston a memo eight months before saying that the scene was "simply wonderful."

"They'll cheer!" Schary said.

Reinhardt's face turned red. He stared at Schary in silence and then said slowly, "No, Dore. I don't see it that way."

"Get 'em ready, Gottfried, and it'll be a good picture," Schary said. "It'll play like a doll." He did not seem to have noticed Reinhardt's objection. "They'll cheer." He clapped a hand on Reinhardt's shoulder. "I'm leaving. See ya at the factory, kid." He walked off.

Albert Band came up to Reinhardt. "Best preview cards so far," he said. "We got several 'Outstanding's.' "

"Now, on top of everything, I have a fight with Dore," Reinhardt said as I walked with him and Mrs. Reinhardt to their car. "I told John till I was blue in the face we should have only one battle. John is lost in the jungles of Africa and I have to fight with Dore."

On our way back to the Reinhardts' house, Reinhardt kept on complaining that now he would have to argue with Schary, particularly about saving the Tattered Man's death scene.

"I must tell you, Gottfried," said Mrs. Reinhardt, "you are the only man I know who will make himself a martyr. For what? For a scene that *irritates* everybody? I tell you, everybody hates that scene."

"They loved it until now," said Reinhardt. "The greatest thing in the picture."

"Gottfried! Look!" Mrs. Reinhardt cried suddenly as Reinhardt slowed the car for a traffic light on Wilshire Boulevard. She pointed out the window. Louis B. Mayer was walking, with great energy, along the street; he was taking his nightly constitutional.

Reinhardt gave a sigh and nodded his head knowingly. "He wasn't there tonight," he said. "I was so happy to think I no longer had to fight with him. Now I find out I have to fight anyway. I have to fight with Dore."

"Gottfried, you are so cryptic!" Mrs. Reinhardt said.

"All right," Reinhardt said grimly as he drove past Mayer. "Mayer is leaving the studio. Eddie Mannix told me the day of the 'Go for Broke!' preview. L. B. Mayer is leaving M-G-M."

The next day, Reinhardt found several preview cards on the desk in his office. They ranged from one marked by a "Male— Over 45" that said, "It all stinks. Talk, talk, and bum-bum boring," to one marked by "Female—31-45" that said, "I will tell everyone I know not to miss it. Pictures of quality, poetically conceived and executed with originality, are rare. This is one of the greatest ever made." Reinhardt sent the cards to Schary, along with a memo:

Dear Dore:

These cards came in today and I happened to find them on my desk. I wish you would read them. Not that they make a special point, or one we don't know ourselves—not that they can teach us much (in fact, one of them attacks something we know has helped the picture enormously, if only because it killed every single bad laugh—the narration)—but I do think they bear out what I was trying to articulate this morning: those who don't like the picture will never like it. I doubt that with the material at hand we can make them. Those who like it—well, they just like it. They may object to this or that detail, but they will like the quality. And that is the only thing we've got to sell and that is the only reason why you and I wanted to make the picture.

Gottfried

A couple of days later, Schary personally took over the supervision of changing "The Red Badge of Courage." I found him sitting at his table in his office, with his sleeves rolled up. "While the narration helped, the big trick was setting up an outside voice saying, 'Look, this is a classic,'" he told me. (The big trick had been achieved by his introduction.) "It set up the proper frame of reference. It identified the picture, and now the first third of the picture plays like a doll. Now"—he put his feet up on a stack of M-G-M manuscripts on his desk—"the trick is to make the points of the story clear without disturbing the integrity of the picture. I'm reconciled to one thing. There's a group of people who, no matter what we do, won't like the picture, so we've got to play to those who will. This is what I'm gonna do with the picture: The way Gottfried and John had the picture, the regiment begins to charge and then withdraws and then charges again. The audience anticipates a climax that does not come, because the regiment does not go through with the first charge. I'm gonna take the two charges and make them one. That'll help the audience. The audience feels the picture is diminishing. 'Is the Youth gonna have the courage to charge again?' is too subtle a concept for the audience. They want that mental relief. They want the satisfaction. Then, when the charge comes, we'll stay with it. And the audience goes along! And *bam!*" Schary pounded a fist into the palm of his other hand.

"I've been giving a lot of thought to 'Red Badge,'" Schary continued. "I'm gonna see the picture with the changes tonight. I'm doing an experiment. I'm cutting out the Tattered Man's death scene. I think it won't work, but I want to look at it that way. One thing keeps circulating in my head. The audience loses sympathy for the boy when he runs away from this hurt and bleeding man. I wrote to Gottfried about it. He sent me some of the preview cards and I told him you have to approach these things with firm conviction but with an open mind, with passion and yet reasonableness, with experience and yet the desire to be bold and new. I told him there was no easy way to make pictures. They all pull at your guts and at your mind. I told Gottfried to keep his heart brave, and that I wouldn't hurt his picture ever."

Schary was silent for a moment, and then went on, "The trouble with this job is if you're a fella who never wavers, they say you're an obstinate son of a bitch. If you change your mind, then they say, 'You can talk him into anything.' I know that there's a lot of criticism of me—of how I want to like people and how I want them to like me. If I'm honest, I have to say it's something deeper, but it is also a weakness." Schary paused, as though embarrassed at admitting a weakness. "I don't want to hurt anybody, and I don't like to be hurt myself. You try desperately to work out a relationship with people. Whatever way you do it, it doesn't seem to matter one way or the other. Zanuck doesn't care about whether he's gonna hurt someone. But it doesn't help him. It wouldn't make my job any easier if I did it his way."

As I was leaving Schary's office, I met Albert Band, who was going in. He said he had an appointment with Schary to talk about an original story he had written. "I prefer direct contact with Dore to going through Gottfried," he said.

"I don't understand it," Reinhardt said to his wife at their house that evening. He was going over to Schary's to see what had been done to his picture. "This morning, I told Dore I understand his problem but he must not get panicky. He's going ahead without me. I don't understand. So many of them *loved* the picture. John isn't here, and it's terribly unfair. It puts me in a bad position."

Reinhardt said he had to be at Schary's house at a quarter to ten, and left. Mrs. Reinhardt asked me to stay with her while he was gone, and as we sat around, with Mocha lying at her feet munching contentedly on pistachio nuts, she talked at some length about problems of life in southern California, including dresses ("Nobody in this entire city knows how to fit the bosom"); coats ("You don't have to go to I. Magnin or to Teitelbaum for a mink coat any more. They are selling them now in the Thrifty Drugstores"); hairdressers ("They never give you anything to read. Every time I pick up a movie magazine, all I find is 'The Happy Home Life of June Allyson'"); the history of the cinema ("I wish Gottfried were Baby LeRoy. Baby LeRoy retired at the age of four and a half with four million dollars in the bank"); and literature ("Gottfried's latest writer has been out here for ten weeks on a fifteen-hundred-dollar-a-week, week-to-week basis. Now he tells Gottfried, 'I need more time. I've got to live with the characters awhile. I don't hear the drums yet.' He is like a writer I know who is doing a screenplay for Sam Goldwyn and says, 'Sam Goldwyn is to pictures what Aristotle was to the drama' ").

Three hours passed before Reinhardt came back. "I need a stiff drink," he said. He poured a stiff drink and drank it at one gulp. He poured another and sat down. He shook his head sadly. "Love's labor's lost," he said. "Love's labor's lost. They took out the cavalry charge, which Margaret Booth calls the roughriders. They took out the wounded man singing 'John Brown's Body,' and another wounded man who complains about generals. They took out the veterans, and Dore turned to me and said, 'Do you miss it? I don't miss it at all.' They took out the Tattered Man's death scene. Again Dore turned to me and asked did I miss it. It reminds me of my good friend Bernie Hyman, who wanted to put Mozart in 'The Great Waltz.' I said, 'You cannot put Mozart in a picture about Strauss.' He said, 'Who's gonna stop me?' Same thing. I don't know what to say when Dore says, 'Do you miss it?' Sure I miss it, but how can you argue about it with Dore?"

They had changed the battle scenes around, he said, to fit Dore's pattern of battle. "Dore doesn't see the difference," Reinhardt said. "It's silly to work on finesse. Nobody appreciates it. Because some people in the audience laughed, they took out the artillery scene John wrote to show what Crane meant when the Youth is running away from the battle and sees the artillerymen still fighting and calls them fools. They took out the key scenes that built the picture up to the feeling Crane had in the novel. I'd like to know what John would have said. It is grotesque. The narration put the audience in the right mood for the picture, and it kept them in the right mood. But suddenly Dore wants to change the picture. It is now like a different picture." He spoke in a low monotone, with a good deal of puzzlement. "I am stymied," he said. "I don't know how to combat it. I don't understand any of them. They loved the picture. And now this is what they are doing to it."

.   .   .

John Huston's wife was living at Malibu Beach with their year-old son, awaiting the birth of their second child. When I went over to see her, she told me she had not heard too much from Huston since he had gone abroad to make "The African Queen," but in that week she had received two letters. She sat on the beach, in the balmy sunshine, reading about her husband's adventures in the Belgian Congo:

> Last year there were some man-eating lions about and they seized the natives out of their huts and dined on them. Every morning and evening we go after elephant. I'd like to get one with really big tusks. In fact, we've got him all picked out. But so far something has always happened so that I couldn't get a shot. Stalking elephant is most exciting. They don't see at all well and if one stays down wind of them one can get very close. Yesterday morning we were after them in some forest and we weren't more than six or eight yards away from them finally. Just a little wall of vines between us and them. I tell you it gave me a very funny feeling.

The second letter started:

> To begin with, I didn't get my elephant. Never saw the big tusker again. . . . The company, including Katie and Bogie, will arrive tonight. They've been in Stanleyville for several days. Naturally, I haven't seen any of them yet. Sam is with them. I'm anxious to get him here, what with mosquitoes and leopards and snakes and all.

On June 23, 1951, the local newspapers carried front-page stories announcing that L. B. Mayer was quitting M-G-M, the studio he had helped establish twenty-six years before. One story said, "The sixty-five-year-old production chief, one of the giants of the film industry, started more rumors brewing by adding that he is not retiring. 'I am going to remain in motion-picture production, God willing,' he said. 'I am going to be more active than at any time during the last fifteen years. It will be at a studio and under conditions where I shall have the right to make the right kind of pictures—decent, wholesome pictures for Americans and for people throughout the world who want and need this type of entertainment.'" Another story pointed out that Mayer had been dissatisfied with M-G-M policies since the appointment of Dore Schary as chief of production three years before; that he had been in disagreement for a long time with Nicholas M. Schenck, president of Loew's; and that for seven consecutive years he had received the highest salary in the United States.

Now that the news was official, people in the industry seemed rather shocked by it. Many who had formerly spoken harshly of Mayer now spoke sympathetically.

"After all those years on the throne!" an M-G-M vice-president said to Reinhardt. "What's going to happen to him now in this lousy, fake town?"

Reinhardt gave a short, cynical laugh. "I am rather proud that I have never, during my eighteen-year relationship with M-G-M, kowtowed to L.B.," he said. "I marvelled at him. I was amused by him. I was afraid of him, and sometimes I hated him. I never flattered him. I never flattered myself that he liked me. And I never believed that Mayer would really leave the studio."

The two men reminisced about Mayer's heyday. The vice-president knew a man in New York who had once mentioned the size of Mayer's salary to Schenck. Schenck, who, though president of the company, took a smaller salary himself, had waved a disparaging hand and said, "Oh, Louie likes that sort of thing."

Two days after the news about Mayer was out, "The Red Badge of Courage" was previewed again, at the Encino Theatre, in Encino. Nobody looked for Mayer this time. When I arrived, I found Dore Schary beaming at a placard that announced the next attraction, "Go for Broke!" "It's gonna play here all next week," he said.

Before "The Red Badge of Courage" started, a newsreel came on.

"The picture looks better already," Mrs. Reinhardt said in a loud voice.

Reinhardt laughed uneasily.

The Tattered Man's death scene had definitely been cut out, and most of the other changes that Reinhardt had seen at Schary's house had now been made permanent. The battle sequences added up to an entirely different war from the one that had been fought and photographed at Huston's ranch in the San Fernando Valley. The elimination of scenes accounted for part of the difference. The old man with the lined face who was digging was gone, the ragged veterans gibing at the recruits both before and after a battle were gone. Many small touches—brief glimpses of the men at war—had been trimmed, including a closeup of a wounded man berating an officer for "small wounds and big talk." The last shot in the picture—of the Youth's regiment marching away from the battlefield—which Huston had wanted to run long, had been cut to run short. (Reinhardt had succeeded in getting Schary to restore the wounded man singing "John Brown's Body" and part of the scene of the Youth shouting at the artillerymen.) The revision had some odd results. Audie Murphy, who played the Youth, started to lead a charge with his head wrapped in a bandanna, rushed forward without the bandanna, and then knelt to fire with the bandanna again around his head.

The audience reaction seemed to be friendlier, although there still were walkouts and laughter at tragic scenes. Schary emerged from the theatre, and as Reinhardt came over to him, Schary grinned and said confidently that the picture was now a doll. "Everything is better now, sweetie," he said to Reinhardt. "The audience understands this boy now."

"The Tattered Man scene was the greatest in the picture," Reinhardt said.

"The picture was better without it," said Lawrence Weingarten, an M-G-M executive. "Now Dierkes stands out as a single vignette," he said.

"If you would just put back the Tattered Man—" Reinhardt began.

"You're wrong, Gottfried," said Schary. He turned to Weingarten. "Did you miss the scene?" he asked.

"Not a bit," said Weingarten.

"It's one of the greatest scenes," said Reinhardt.

"Did you miss it?" Schary asked Kaper.

"No!" Kaper said. "No! No!"

"You haven't disturbed your picture at all, Gottfried," said Schary.

Reinhardt drew a deep breath. "Missing it or not missing it is not the point," he said.

"You're wrong," said Schary.

Schary left, and Reinhardt began to read some preview cards Albert Band had put in his hands.

"Not a bad preview," Band said.

" 'A war picture about the Civil War is ridiculous at this time,' " Reinhardt read aloud. He shrugged and gave the cards back to Band. "The funny thing is that tonight John would have sided with Dore."

"John doesn't care," Kaper said. "Call me Metro-Goldwyn-Kaper, but I tell you the purpose of a motion picture is to be successful."

"This picture will not make money," said Reinhardt. "I knew it the day I saw the first rushes."

"I knew it when I first read the script," Mrs. Reinhardt said.

"She hated it," said Reinhardt. "She wouldn't talk to me when I told her I was going to make it." He looked blankly at his wife, at Kaper, at Band, and at me. "So now I do not have a great picture and it will be a flop."

Two days later, Reinhardt told me that he had made a study of the latest preview cards. The percentage of members of the audience who said they would recommend the picture to their friends was much higher. "That is the important thing," he said. "I had a very serious talk with Dore. He will accept the responsibility for the picture as it is now, and he will write this to John. He is going to release the picture as it now is. He said he would be a bad executive if he let the picture out any other way." Reinhardt did not sound happy, but he sounded happier than he had two nights before.

Huston was now concerned with other things. To his wife, he wrote:

> We're in a place called Biondo that's on the Ruiki River about thirty miles from Pontiaville and the Lualaba. But what a long thirty miles it is. Once a week provisions are brought in and the exposed film is taken out. There hasn't been very much rain (for the Congo) and the river has fallen several feet so that now it's just barely navigable. . . .

At about the time Huston was writing this, Reinhardt, who had not heard anything at all from him since the first preview of their picture, sat down alone at home one evening after dinner and typed out a letter to him by the one-finger method:

Mr. John Huston
Darkest Africa
Dear John:
    This is not an official letter. This is not the producer writing the director, but rather the Tall Soldier addressing the Youth. For despite the physical incongruities implied in this statement, that is exactly how I feel: like the Tall Soldier, having "in his ignorance" held the line, now giving up his soul, telling the Youth who ran away what happened. "Laws, what a circus!"
    Lacking all signs of life from you, I find it difficult to carry the analogy much further. I am too unfamiliar with your present circumstances, although I presume that on a Spiegel location you will have had a brush with a Tattered Man, a very short one, to be sure, for the Tattered Man turned out to be one of the first casualties, in more ways than one, and is one of the main reasons for this accusatory confession.

However, whatever these transitory episodes, one development is inevitable, one happening is sure to be in store for
you: you will one day return to your regiment, and that will
be painful. True, your desertion will not have been noticed.
People will say you have been fighting somewhere "on the
right." And you will say we have seen nothing of the real
fighting. But it will be painful just the same. For, no matter
what anybody says, you will find your regiment decimated.
Irretrievable casualties will stare in your face, and the sur-
vivors are bruised and battered and bitter.

The Tall Soldier will be gone, or at least his soul. The real
adversary of all of us, Louis, the Captain—he will be gone.
The minor executives, the Lieutenants, will be, as usual,
asleep. But in Dore you will find again your Friend. For that
he is.

He did have *his* moments of wavering, and serious moments, too. When, in the heat of battle, he parted with his
watch, when he cut out the death of the Tattered Man,
when he wanted to cut out "John Brown's Body" (or shall
I say: "John's Body"?), a surgical operation which I was
able to prevent him from performing, when he shortened
the last shot of the picture, when he eliminated the first veterans as well. Maybe, deep in his heart, sometimes he, too,
felt tempted to run away. And the only reason he stuck it
out in the end was that he was more afraid of the Captain
than of the public. Be that as it may, he did stick it out. And
he *is* a Friend. And, whatever his mistakes (and who knows,
maybe they aren't even mistakes; maybe he is right?), if this
war of ours should by a miracle, in spite of all the confusion,
the intramural disagreements, the unpopularity of the cause,
the abundance in casualties, be crowned by victory, he will
in his way be as responsible for it as the Tall Soldier or even
the Youth.

But even if you should disagree with him completely, your
position will be a weak one. Just as the Youth's triumph,
when he returns the watch to the Friend, is a hollow one, no
arguments of yours can retroactively make up for your ab-

sence. Right or wrong, the decisions in battle must be made by those who take part in the fighting. As you know, it doesn't matter how beautiful the strategy may be. The test of battle is what counts. So, all that remains for you upon your return is to "get mad" and, even if somewhat belatedly, to become a hero, and to fight bigger and better battles, make better, if not necessarily bigger, pictures, and stay with them.

This, in short, is what happened: after you left us, there was a long lull in the fighting. The picture was taken off the release schedule and all decisions were postponed until, as we discussed doing the day before your departure, we had another preview with narration. Only four weeks ago did we have this preview. The reason for this delay was that we couldn't get into the dubbing rooms. A lot of other products had to be rushed through first. Unfortunately, it leaked out what kind of an audience reaction we had had at the first two previews and there were some damaging items in the press to that effect. Especially, a New York *Times* story did word of mouth a good deal of harm. Professional circles in New York and locally were whispering that M-G-M had a dud on their hands and didn't know what to do with it. Some went so far as to assert that "The Red Badge" was so bad it couldn't be released. There were those who conceded that the picture may very well be an artistic achievement but would surely be a commercial disaster. There was very little I could do to stem this tide of unfavorable and often vicious comment, especially as some of it unquestionably emanated from the studio itself. The New York *Times* man, for instance, told me that his information came directly from one of our executives. Naturally, the whole Mayer situation, which thank God has since come to its dénouement, did not help matters any.

Reinhardt told Huston about the picture's new opening, which involved the shots of the book and the portrait of Crane, about Schary's introduction, and about the narration, which "seemed to succeed in keeping the audience concentrated on the Youth's inner development." "Fewer people walked out," he said, "and while I did not kid myself and still felt that a large part of the audience did not care for the picture at all, I was quite satisfied with our effort. I felt we had a very distinguished, immensely beautiful, and, to those who appreciated it, a very moving and even great picture." He then said that Schary, seeing the picture for the first time with an audience, had become worried:

> Dore had secretly higher hopes for the picture box-office-wise than I. I was long resigned to the limited appeal I believed we could count on. And all I tried to do was to put the picture in its best possible shape to further this appeal, recognizing fully its limitations. Dore was not quite in the same mood. He wanted to conquer the resistance of the audience, which he clearly—and we both—felt. I, frankly, believed that was futile. And dangerous to boot. Because I seriously questioned our ability to win the hearts of those who objected to the picture basically; those who hated it. On the other hand, we might easily, in trying to win them, lose those who were already our friends, those who loved the very things the others hated. Actually, there wasn't much of a fight. I was in a very bad position to fight. Dore had behaved wonderfully all along in the face of violent opposition, bordering on sabotage. I had to be—and am—very grateful to him for that. In acting so courageously, he assumed a definite and heavy responsibility for the picture. How could I deny him the privilege to salvage a million-and-three-quarter-dollar investment?

It took Reinhardt several more hours to outline the changes that had been made in the picture. And then he wrote:

> Well, John, I felt very bad. Except for the time when I finally gave in to you on Audie, I hadn't been that miserable. You see, I had been able to fight all studio opposition, because I always had the deep conviction that I was helping

make a work of art. Not these two times. The fact that I could have never won my fight without Dore's blessing made this last situation only more difficult and painful. I never harbored much hope for a commercial success. I know you did. I reminded Dore of his letter to Mayer where he explained that this kind of picture should be made by a studio like M-G-M regardless of commercial considerations. It was to be a "classic." Mayer and all the other executives loathed the idea. To go ahead with the project under the circumstances was a fateful decision for a producer. More than for a director. A producer is not supposed to divorce his judgment from commercial considerations. Even the head of a studio can sometimes with impunity think in purely artistic terms. He makes forty pictures a year. The producer makes one or two. If those are flops—that's his product. He is a flop. He may be an "artist" but a flop. I knew and weighed all that. I didn't care. I was delighted to make this picture with you. Up to these two moments, when I suddenly saw before me the spectre of the unartistic flop.

I sincerely hope that all this is terribly exaggerated. In any event, my dwelling on it seems highly superfluous. The fourth and last preview with these changes (all except the cavalry charge, which I made Dore put back before) went unquestionably much better. The cards too for the first time showed an astonishing improvement. Only thirty per cent would not recommend the picture this time. The picture had lost some of its complexities and colors. It was now a straighter, simpler picture. The consensus was, "You can follow it now. You can understand it now." Whether that is desirable I shall leave to posterity's judgment. Anyway, Dore was happy. He felt—and, in a way, was—vindicated. He was sure. Everybody agreed with him. Weingarten, Kaper, the cutters, the assembled studio personnel, even Silvia. It was a very fine picture. Everybody tells me it is.

But I would have to lie if I said it was the picture that I had hoped for (even in my "limited" way) or that I wanted to make. I cannot speak for you, of course. For you are not

here. But I tried to. In fact, I did. I did try especially to per-
suade Dore to put back the Tattered Man scene. He was ada-
mant. And, I admit, there is a lot of sense in what he says.
And I believe that the audience, or a large part of it, agrees
with him. Certainly very few will miss the death of the Tattered Man, since they haven't seen it. But I have seen it.

I would never have made this picture without you, John. I
wanted it to be a John Huston picture. For it to be anything
else now seems to me senseless. I told Dore that. Dore thinks
it still *is*. Maybe he is right. Everybody tells me so. Maybe I
have a special idea of a John Huston picture. Maybe even
more special than John Huston has.

Dore told me that he would write you, that he accepts the
whole responsibility for the present cuts, that he knows he is
right, that this is one of those times when an executive has
to step in and make the final decision—if he wants to be an
executive.

I sincerely hope that he is right. I pray that he is right. I
know that I have done everything I could to make this what
it should be. I pray that the discrepancy between what it
should be and what it is is not too great. I wish nobody ill. I
believe in sincerity and friendship and talent. Yet I realize
that these three priceless qualities can be easily defeated by
geography and power. I bow smilingly and, as I said before,
without ill will. And with humility. Because I can be terribly
wrong.

Good luck, John.

Yours always,
Gottfried Reinhardt

Huston's reply, a cable from darkest Africa, was briefer. He said,
"DEAR GOTTFRIED. JUST GOT YOUR LETTER. KNOW YOU FOUGHT
GOOD FIGHT. HOPE YOU NOT TOO BLOODY MY ACCOUNT. LET'S MAKE
NEXT ONE REINHARDT NOT A HUSTON PICTURE. JOHN." Reinhardt read
the cable, then went upstairs to Schary's office to ask the man who
now had the authority of vice-president in charge of production

and of the studio to give him an assignment, in addition to the two he had as a producer, as a director of a motion picture.

Schary was talking to me one afternoon a week later about the future of motion pictures. His photograph had appeared in the Los Angeles papers that morning, along with the news that he had been chosen judge for the Downtown Business Men's Association talent show, open to boys and girls between the ages of five and eighteen. In the photograph, he had a slight, bemused smile, and his eyes were good-natured. He looked exactly the same now. People in the motion-picture industry, he told me, had to be constantly prepared for change. "People who make predictions about change are those who are afraid of it or don't know about it," he said. "You say, 'Let's try this,' or 'Let's try that.' You watch and see what happens. The pontifical statements about change in our industry amuse me. A certain progression of changes was inevitable in this business even before the advent of TV. Of course, with TV there's a certain kind of picture we won't be making. We'll say, 'Let TV make it.' We'll make fewer pictures and bigger ones— bigger in the sense that we will aim higher." He cited "Quo Vadis" as an example of the kind of picture that TV would never be able to make, an eight-and-a-half-million-dollar picture dealing with the history of Christianity. "They sat here with 'Quo Vadis' for years," he added, "but I activated it. They'd still be stalling around with it if I hadn't been here."

Schary was inclined to be gracious about his predecessor, L. B. Mayer. He had heard that Mayer had not liked "Go for Broke!," but he thought that Mayer had a right to his opinion. "Mayer was surrounded by enormous prestige and enormous power," he said. "He undoubtedly left this studio with bitterness. Why? What do people tell me? Good things about myself, not bad things. What did they use to tell him? Good things, not bad things. He had no way of knowing. I have to be careful now not to be put in the same position Mayer was in. I understand Mayer. He's an old man. He's rich. He's healthy. Let him enjoy himself now. I don't know what the hell he got mad about. He could have been so happy here.

Mayer once said to me, 'Wouldn't it be better if you had men with years of experience to sit down with you and help you make decisions? Wouldn't you like it better?' I said no. This job has to be a one-man operation. There has to be one boss. He listened to everybody and he came up with a piece of junk. Before I arrived at the studio, he made the basic decisions. The committee would tell him stories. They had a story board and two storytellers to help him pick the stories. That was the first thing I felt was all wrong. I wanted the authority to pick the stories. I said I would discuss controversial stories with him and we would come to a decision. I got the authority. And the only difference of opinion I ever had with him was on 'The Red Badge of Courage.' And that was settled amicably. After we decided to make the picture, he said, 'We're in this now and we're in it together.' Maybe the reason he got mad was because he had a disagreement with Nick Schenck six months ago. Mayer was annoyed with Schenck because Schenck did not tell him the details of the deal in which I was given the option to buy a hundred thousand shares of Loew's stock. The deal was a New York decision. Maybe Schenck didn't want to tell anybody."

It was Mayer who, in 1948, had invited Schary to come over to M-G-M. Schary was head of production at R.K.O., which Howard Hughes had bought a few months earlier. Hughes had told Schary he did not want to make "Battleground," a picture Schary had been preparing to produce himself. "That's why I left," Schary said. "Hughes didn't think the picture was a commercial picture. I came over here and bought the story from R.K.O. for a hundred thousand dollars. And we made it. The rest is history. It cost a million six, took forty-five days to shoot, and will probably clear a profit of three million." When Schary left R.K.O., Mayer immediately sent word to him that he'd like to see him. "I went to see him at his house, and he told me he'd like me to come and run production at M-G-M. I said I wanted him to know that if he thought of me as the executive who would get out the scripts, I wasn't interested. I said if I took the job, I wanted to be head of production. He said then that he planned to leave the studio and retire in one year, two years, or, at the most, three years. We signed a three-year deal. And we agreed on what I said I meant by 'head of production.' I would pick the stories, I said, and be responsible for the cast, for who directs, and for who produces. I said, 'If that's what you mean, fine.' I said, 'I'd be challenged by the idea, if you want me to do the job.' And that's the way we signed it."

Schary grinned and leaned forward. "Let me tell you about Nick Schenck," he said. "Schenck is a man near seventy. He's a wonderful fella. He's shrewd. Smart. Hard. You always know exactly how you stand with him. Because he tells you. You know exactly what he's thinking. Because he tells you. He says, 'You fellas make the pictures!' He only wants to be consulted on high policy. From there on in, you know exactly where you stand. He's a great businessman."

Schary was to take the train to New York the next day for a conference with Schenck.

Things were going to be different from now on, Reinhardt told me on September 3, 1951, the day he started his first job as a director. His picture, "Invitation," was about a wealthy girl (Dorothy McGuire) who has only a year to live and whose wealthy father (Louis Calhern) hires a handsome, penniless young man (Van Johnson) to marry her. "I have stars and I have a story in this picture," Reinhardt said. "I will try to make this picture a little gem."

In addition to stars and a story, Reinhardt had expressions of good wishes from his wife (a solid-gold watchchain charm engraved "Forti Nihil Difficile") and from his brother Wolfgang (a gold forty-franc coin their father, Max Reinhardt, had carried as a good-luck piece), a memo from Margaret Booth ("I know you are going to have a wonderful picture and needless to say you will be a fine director, so all my best wishes and thoughts are with you. With love"), and a letter from Schary ("My every good wish today on the start of INVITATION. You're a versatile fellow, and I'm sure we'll have a good picture with this one. Good luck and my best wishes").

Reinhardt felt so pleased about the picture he was going to direct that he began to feel more pleased about the picture he had recently produced. "The Red Badge of Courage" was now ready to be released. Schary told Reinhardt that he would order "the boys in New York" to give the movie the special promotion a classic film derived from a literary classic deserved. "It is up to New York from here on," Reinhardt said to me. For the past year, he said, he had been trying to make a picture that was both an artistic and a commercial success; now he was going to simplify matters. "I will give them just what the doctor ordered," he said. He had a new job, a new outlook, and a new contract with M-G-M. To celebrate, he bought a new Cadillac convertible. "Money is good for bribing yourself through the inconveniences of life," he said. Reinhardt rapidly gained the reputation of being pleasant to work with, patient, quiet, modest, and a good director, and several people on the set eventually paid him one of the highest compliments the industry knows. "Gottfried is a real person," they said.

Band tagged after Reinhardt around the lot, and the slightly rebellious manner he had developed right after the disastrous first preview of "The Red Badge of Courage" faded completely away. Now, when he was asked to look after Mocha, he was extremely solicitous of Mocha's ailments, and he listened with a respectful manner whenever Reinhardt was talking.

After a week of shooting, Reinhardt had a visitor on the set—his friend Joe Cohn, M-G-M vice-president and head of the Production Office. Cohn is a cheerful, white-haired man with white rings around the pupils of his eyes, which give him a birdlike look. He had told Mayer that the studio shouldn't make "The Red Badge of Courage." "How you doing, Gottfried?" he asked. "How's the picture? On schedule?"

"We'll bring this one in early," Reinhardt said.

Cohn said he had heard that "The Red Badge of Courage" would open in New York in a few weeks.

"The Astor?" Reinhardt asked quickly.

"I have news for you," Cohn said cheerily. "The Trans-Lux, a little place on Lexington Avenue in the Fifties. Don't worry, Gottfried. It'll get brilliant reviews, and it won't make a nickel."

.   .   .

Four days before "The Red Badge of Courage" opened in New York, for its first regular run—at the Fifty-second Street Trans-Lux, a house with a seating capacity of five hundred and seventy-eight, only half that of the Astor—the first advertisement appeared in the New York newspapers: "M-G-M, the company that released 'Gone with the Wind,' presents a new drama of the War Between the States—Stephen Crane's immortal classic, 'The Red Badge of Courage.'" The ad announced "A John Huston Production," "Screenplay by John Huston," "Adaptation by Albert Band," "Directed by John Huston" (letters three times as large as those in the other credits), and "Produced by Gottfried Reinhardt" (letters the same size as Albert Band's).

The day after the opening, I saw Reinhardt at the studio, and he said he had not had time to read the reviews. Two days after the opening, he ran into Eddie Mannix at lunch. Mannix told him that the first day's business had been weak.

A week later, Reinhardt showed me the reviews that had been relayed to him from the New York office. The *Tribune* said:

> Stephen Crane's "The Red Badge of Courage" has been transformed by John Huston into a striking screen close-up of a young man's introduction to battle. With war hero Audie Murphy as a raw recruit in Union blue, this seventy-minute vignette is a study of one man's emotional adjustment to an environment chokingly filled with powder smoke and animal terror. The dialogue is sparing but acute, and the camera work is a procession of visual effects detailing most vividly the progress of a Civil War battle. Except for a redundant narration that clutters up the sound track from time to time explaining facts already clear in the images, there are no concessions made to movie conventions in this film.

The *Times* critic wrote, "Now, thanks to Metro and John Huston, 'The Red Badge of Courage' has been transferred to the screen with almost literal fidelity." He felt, however, that the picture could not convey the reactions of Crane's hero to war, for Crane had conveyed them "in almost stream-of-consciousness descriptions, which is a technique that works best with words." He continued:

> This is a technical problem Mr. Huston has not been able to lick, even with his sensitive direction, in view of his sticking to the book. Audie Murphy, who plays the Young Soldier, does as well as anyone could expect as a virtual photographer's model upon whom the camera is mostly turned.

The *Mirror*'s reviewer called the picture "a brilliant emotional drama, a memorable war saga," added that "the carnage between the states forms a grim backdrop for the personal story of a young raw recruit," and wound up by saying that the picture "comes aptly as the industry celebrates its silver jubilee. It's a wonderful example of modern film art." The *Daily News* critic gave the picture a three-star rating. The *Morning Telegraph* called it "fine" and "thought-provoking," and said it "has been brought to the screen by the brilliant John Huston as an offbeat motion picture, not to be compared or contrasted with anything else you've seen lately, a strange and strangely exciting work that stands unique in the recent history of the movies." The reviewer went on to say that the picture "may not fit very neatly into the idea that motion pictures represent entertainment for the whole family, but it comes very close to a true work of art for all that."

The *World-Telegram & Sun* reviewer said, "John Huston has written and directed a stirring film in an understanding and close reproduction of the novel."

"If someone other than John Huston had made Stephen Crane's 'The Red Badge of Courage,' there would have been little cause for disappointment," the *Post* critic began, and then praised Huston, saying that he "studies his men in intimate close-up, he lays out his battles in long vistas with climaxes mounting as attackers climb the screen like the Teutonic knights coming across the ice of Lake Peipus in Eisenstein's 'Alexander Nevsky.'" He continued:

The picture does not become a fully realized experience, nor is it deeply moving. It is as if, somewhere between shooting and final version, the light of inspiration had died, Huston got tired of it, or became discouraged, or decided that it wasn't going to come off. Perhaps the story itself stood revealed, too late, as a thin and old one, and there wasn't enough time to go back and do it over. So they cut losses and cut footage, thereby reducing a large failure to the proportions of a modest, almost ordinary picture. . . . Mr. Huston's product is that of a splendid director who had lost interest, who was no longer striving for that final touch of perfection, who had missed the cumulative passion and commentary on human beings that mark his best pictures.

Time said that Huston had avoided "the customary Hollywood clichés of battle" and that "both the camera and the spoken commentary (taken word for word from Crane's novel) are filled with human understanding as they follow Murphy's wanderings through the rear areas." *Newsweek* said that " 'The Red Badge of Courage' bids fair to become one of the classic American motion pictures," and the *Saturday Review of Literature* remarked that "if Stephen Crane's 'The Red Badge of Courage' is considered a classic of American nineteenth-century literature, John Huston's adaptation of it for the screen may well become a classic of American twentieth-century film-making. Adhering to Crane's characters, his structure, and his theme, Huston has discovered for all time how to make a printed page come alive on the screen."

Not one of the reviews made any mention at all of Gottfried Reinhardt, Dore Schary, Louis B. Mayer, or Nicholas M. Schenck.

A couple of days later, Reinhardt received a cable from Huston: "REVIEWS RECEIVED. THINK EXCELLENT ON WHOLE ONLY THEY DON'T KNOW HOW MUCH OF WHAT IS GOOD IN FILM YOU ARE RESPONSIBLE FOR. BUT I DO. JOHN."

By the time "The Red Badge of Courage" was in its second week at the Trans-Lux, I was back in New York. I dropped in at the theatre late one afternoon and found the manager standing in front of the box office gossiping with the cashier. The marquee said, "JOHN HUSTON'S THE RED BADGE OF COURAGE. A MAJOR ACHIEVEMENT—N.Y. TIMES. MASTERFUL—CUE." I asked the manager how business was. "Not socko," he said.

Schary came to New York the next week, and I went over to the Sherry-Netherland to see him. Walter Reilly, Schary's executive assistant, invited me into the sitting room of Schary's suite. "The boss'll be right with you," he said. "We just got back from Washington. He saw the President."

Schary, when he appeared, looked full of health and energy. "Just got back from Washington," he said, giving me a cordial handshake. "Saw the President. Had a fifteen-minute appointment. He stretched it to twenty-five. Nice guy, the President. Boy, I'll be glad to get on a train and get the hell out of New York. I never liked living in the East anyway. The pressures! I'm running around all the time. How's my schedule, kiddy?" he asked Reilly.

Elizabeth Taylor would be up to see him in twenty minutes, Reilly said, and the next day there would be Winthrop Rockefeller, who wanted to talk about making a short subject.

"You ever met a Rockefeller?" Schary asked me.

I said no.

"Hah! Some people lead such a sheltered life," said Schary. "My, but I keep busy! Reviewing the studio policies with the New York boys can exhaust a fella. Today I had an all-day session with Nick Schenck. At the end of an all-day session, he looks as though he just got out of a shower, and you're punchy. The way his mind works! He asks for a complete picture of a situation and asks what you think, and you tell him, and then he makes his decision, and that's it." Schary said he had also been working with Howard Dietz on the advertising campaign for "Quo Vadis." It was going to open simultaneously at the Astor and the Capitol in a week. "If you make a picture with enough vitality, you do very well with it," he said.

"The Red Badge of Courage" had vitality now, he said, but it was too early to tell how it would do. "Great notices," he said. "That picture is a credit to the studio. By the way, Reinhardt is gonna be a hell of a director. I saw his picture 'Invitation.' It's a good little picture. Reinhardt is a great raconteur. Like John, he knows how to tell a story. He is gonna be a very stylish director, a very terrific director."

Schary said he had been having a hell of a lot of fun working with Schenck. "I'm very crazy about that man," he said. "You know exactly where you stand with him. A very reasonable man. He thinks fast. He's agile. He doesn't waste a lot of time going around through Dixie. He's the most respected man in the whole picture business. He's smart and he's shrewd. He has tact and he has wisdom. He's got wonderful balance. There's not a thing going on at the studio he doesn't know about. He knows how to manage the business."

There was a buzz. Reilly admitted Elizabeth Taylor and her agent, Jules Goldstone.

Schary asked Miss Taylor if she wanted a drink. She asked for a gin-and-tonic.

"Take sherry," said Goldstone.

"Gin-and-tonic," said Miss Taylor.

"Give the girl anything she wants!" Schary said exuberantly.

Reinhardt received a letter from John Huston:

Dear Gottfried:

A fine thing! What gets me is the sneaky, underhand way you went about it. I can see now that you had it all planned out way back there: "When Huston's deep in the African forest, stricken with malaria, his consciousness dimmed by bites of the tsetse and his limbs swollen with elephantiasis— then I shall become a director." No doubt your hands tremble as you are holding this letter. I, Huston, have returned. I am among the living, and I know well how to deal with your treachery. I shall strike without warning. Silvia may find you sprawled on your wide veranda, transfixed by one of those same arrows from a pygmy's blowgun. Or it may happen in your office, late of an evening, when you and Albert are working over your next script. The cleaning women will discover the two of you at your desk, inclined a little forward, grinning at each other as though in delight at having finished a perfectly splendid scene. I take it for granted that Albert will be sitting in the big chair behind the desk; he is the producer now, of course. Now that the cat's out of the bag, you might tell me some of the details. As a matter of fact, I heard about it only day before yesterday. I don't know the name of the picture or who's in it or anything, except that your leading lady thinks you're the best director she ever had. I expect I'll be in New York in a week or two. Your letter, if one is forthcoming, may not reach me before I leave. I'll call you in any case.

                                                    The Monster

Huston arrived in New York from London just as Reinhardt arrived to work on a screenplay with a writer here. Neither Huston nor Reinhardt went to the Trans-Lux, where "The Red Badge of Courage" was in its sixth, and last, week. Huston didn't want to see the picture in its final form. He looked tired—even more tired than he had looked nine months before, at the preview of "The Red Badge of Courage" in Pasadena, where I had last seen him. The creases between his eyes and at the sides of his mouth looked deeper. His tweed cap seemed too small for him, and so did his suit. Its peg-top trousers were the latest thing in England, he told me. "Dore wrote me a letter," he said, and took the letter from a pocket and handed it to me.

Dear John:

    I don't know if you have seen the finished print of RED BADGE OF COURAGE but we did have to make some cuts and we did have to bring clarification by the use of narration that helped us enormously and brought the audience reaction from a majority negative response to a big majority positive response. I don't think we sacrificed any of the integrity that you poured into the movie and I hope you like it. The final important thing is that the picture has been accepted by critics as the classic that we thought it would be, and maybe over the long pull we'll get most of the money back.

If I had to do it all over again I would still let you make it. I hope things are well with you.

My fondest always,
Dore

"I lied to Dore," he told me, in a mildly conspiratorial tone. "I called Dore up and said I had seen the picture. I told him I approved of everything he had done."

Huston planned to spend ten days in New York promoting "The African Queen" and making various arrangements for his next picture, "Moulin Rouge," based on a recent novel, of the same name, about Toulouse-Lautrec. This would be another independent picture. Schary had agreed to release him from his contractual obligation to make another picture for M-G-M right away, so he was able to go ahead with plans for "Moulin Rouge." Huston had a lot to say about "The African Queen," and its possibilities of success. He thought it would be a big commercial hit. "I may yet become the Last Tycoon," he said. He looked as if he wanted to laugh, but he didn't.

I went with Huston and his wife, who had in the meantime had her second child, to see Reinhardt and his wife, who were staying at the Plaza.

As we got out of the elevator at the Reinhardts' floor, Huston glanced at a small man wearing a derby who was talking to a crumpled old lady in a wheelchair. The small man was talking in a low, hoarse monotone, and at Huston's glance the man looked over at us sideways, full of mysterious promise. Huston glanced at him again and seemed to lose interest. The small man wearing the derby suddenly lost his promise. There was no Huston scene. Huston led us quickly to the Reinhardts' suite and knocked on the door. Reinhardt opened it.

"Well, Gottfried," said Huston.

"Hello, John," Reinhardt said, sounding cordial but ill at ease. The two men shook hands, then looked uncomfortably at each other. Reinhardt took a white silk handkerchief from his pocket and mopped his brow with it.

"Well!" said Huston to Mrs. Reinhardt. "Well!" The word sounded as small as it was.

Reinhardt put a cigar in his mouth and nervously held a lighter to it.

Mrs. Reinhardt and Mrs. Huston said hello to each other.

"It's been a long time," said Reinhardt.

"Yeah," said Huston.

"Not since the Pasadena preview," Reinhardt said.

"Yeah," said Huston.

Mrs. Reinhardt gave a shriek of mock laughter.

"Sit down," Reinhardt said to Huston, and everybody sat down.

"Well, how is everything, Gottfried?" Huston asked.

Reinhardt said that everything was all right. "Did you see the picture?" he asked.

"No, Gottfried," said Huston. "How is the picture, Gottfried?"

"The reviews were wonderful," Reinhardt began.

"I know, Gottfried," said Huston. "I saw the reviews."

"After you left, we had a lot of trouble—" Reinhardt began.

"I know," Huston said. "I got your letter, Gottfried."

"You read it?" said Reinhardt.

"Of course, Gottfried," said Huston.

"I fought, but there was nothing I could do," said Reinhardt. "You were not here."

"What are you doing now, Gottfried?" Huston asked. "You're a director!" He laughed as though it took a great effort to laugh.

Reinhardt said that he had just finished directing a picture and was making plans to start on another.

"That's wonderful, Gottfried," Huston said.

"What are you doing now?" Reinhardt asked.

Huston said that he was doing some promotion work on "The African Queen" and thought the picture would be a hit. "I hope it makes a pot of dough," he said, and added a faint "Ho! Ho! Ho!"

"You think 'The African Queen' will be a commercial success?" Reinhardt asked.

"I hope so, Gottfried," said Huston. "You know, there's a strange irony in what happened to 'Red Badge.' Even though a lot of people in the business think otherwise, my other pictures did all right at the box office. 'The Maltese Falcon' was a very great success. I believe it grossed over four million bucks. Another one was 'In This Our Life.' 'Across the Pacific' was also very successful, and 'Key Largo' was a very great success. 'Treasure of Sierra Madre' was a very expensive picture—two million eight, I think it cost— and even though it didn't make an immediate and resounding bang at the box office, it did very well, and by this time it should be showing a profit. 'The Asphalt Jungle' made money, and 'We Were Strangers,' although it wasn't successful, didn't actually lose money. The only picture I ever made that seems as though it's going to be marked down simply as a box-office failure is 'The Red Badge of Courage.' And I thought that was the best picture I ever made."

There was a heavy silence.

"Hell, let's go to '21,' " said Huston.

"Like old times," Reinhardt said. "I went to '21' my first evening in America. I adored it. I had dinner at Dinty Moore's. Then I was taken to see 'Of Thee I Sing.' Then I went to '21.' I adored it. And I adored America."

"You adored it!" Huston said dimly. "You adored it, huh, Gottfried?" His tone had a hint of amazement in it.

There was a flicker in Reinhardt's eyes. He took the cigar out of his mouth and shook gently as he laughed.

"Let's go to '21,' " Huston said impatiently.

About a month later, after Huston had returned to Europe and Reinhardt to California, Sam Spiegel brought a print of "The African Queen" from London to New York. United Artists was going to release it. He looked affluent, well groomed, and at peace. "I fly to the Coast tonight," he said. "Then I fly back to New York. I will be here forty-eight hours, and then I must fly back to London. I must be in a dozen places at once. We are going to have a big hit on our hands. The picture will make a lot of money."

That week, Huston wrote me from the château in Chantilly that he and his family were occupying to say that he was planning to bring a horse over from Ireland and train him on the steeplechase course in Chantilly, and if all went well, he planned to ride the horse himself at some of the race meetings the next year. "Have you heard that 'The African Queen' is the greatest success England has had in years and years?" Huston wrote. "Indications are that it will also be very big in America. In England, however, its future is assured. With my percentage, I stand to make a lot of money. . . . I'm going to have it all in twenty-dollar bills with a rubber band around it."

When "The African Queen" opened in New York a few weeks later, it was received enthusiastically by both the critics and the public. Among the critics, there were only two dissenters—the reviewer for the *Post*, who said that the picture had some aspects of a Tarzan movie and that "Huston has put out two considerably less than perfect pictures in a row," and the reviewer for the *Times*, who said that the picture had been made to insure popularity, and that "with this extravagant excursion into realms of adventure and romance of a sort that, to our recollection, Mr. Huston has heretofore eschewed, the brilliant director has put himself in a position where he can be charged with compromise."

A couple of months after that, United Artists announced that "The African Queen" was the biggest hit it had had in five years.

In certain circles, "The Red Badge of Courage" continued to receive tributes of one kind and another. Reinhardt had not succeeded in getting M-G-M to bring out a record album of the score, but the studio did send the original manuscript of the music to Syracuse University, which Stephen Crane attended briefly in 1891. In the Stephen Crane Collection of the university, the score, together with photographs of the cast in costume, is now on file. Lester G. Wells, curator of the university's special collections, saw the movie seven times when it played in Syracuse; then he asked for the original of the score, and M-G-M agreed to lend it to the collection.

The picture was not nominated for any of the Motion Picture Academy awards, but the *Film Daily* included it in its list of the five best-directed pictures of the year. It was named second-best picture of the year by the National Board of Review. ("A Place in the Sun" was first.) The Motion Picture Academy nominated Huston for an Oscar for his direction of "The African Queen," and Bogart was nominated for one for his acting in the picture. Bogart won his Oscar, but the prize for direction went to George Stevens, for "A Place in the Sun." (" 'A Place in the Sun' is only a reasonably good picture," Stevens said to another director. "The industry doesn't want good pictures. It wants the norm.") The picture the Academy named the best of the year was Arthur Freed's musical "An American in Paris." The Irving Thalberg Award, the honor bestowed by the Academy upon the person who is considered to have done most for the movie industry in the past year, was won by Arthur Freed. Darryl Zanuck, who reminded the industry members gathered for the occasion that he had won the Thalberg Award three times, presented it to Freed, describing him as "a creative producer" and declaring, "His pictures have been perfect examples of creative art."

In Paris, Huston was worrying about the business end of producing "Moulin Rouge," as well as writing and directing it. "I am trying to learn all the things Sam Spiegel was born knowing," he wrote me. "I find it pretty hard going. As a bona-fide producer, I don't dare admit to being ignorant of what 'off the top' means. But I damn well am. I was a couple of days trying to figure out what three and a half per cent of seventy per cent amounted to before giving it up. Now I just try to look wise. I'm afraid it won't be very long before I give that up, too."

At Metro-Goldwyn-Mayer, it was announced that the studio would be known thenceforward simply as M-G-M, since Goldwyn and Mayer were no longer there. Louis B. Mayer announced that he would produce pictures independently, and set about buying film properties; he started off by outbidding Metro for the film rights to the musical "Paint Your Wagon," for which he paid $225,000. Around that time, Loew's, Inc., paid Mayer $2,750,000 in return for a release from the company's agreement to pay him ten per cent of the net receipts of every picture made between April 7, 1924, and the day he left the company.

Mayer's cream-colored office at the studio was taken over by Joseph L. Mankiewicz, who had left Twentieth Century-Fox and Darryl Zanuck, because, he said, he was determined to make a drastic change in the conventional pattern most movie-makers conformed to. Mankiewicz moved from Fox and Zanuck to M-G-M and Dore Schary, to work on a film as a director and writer.

M-G-M announced that the studio would make forty pictures in the coming year and that eighteen of them would be musicals. Arthur Freed announced that he would produce half a dozen of the musicals himself, including one to be made in France and another in Scotland. Audie Murphy became greatly in demand as a leading man for Western melodramas. John Dierkes was cast as a Western bad man in the movie "Shane," produced and directed by George Stevens. Royal Dano, whose characterization of the Tattered Man had drawn high praise from everybody who had helped to make "The Red Badge of Courage," as well as from many others who had seen the early version—in which his death scene was included—did not immediately find any other acting jobs in Hollywood. He returned to his home in New York to do some television work, then appeared in a picture called "Flame of Araby," then obtained a small part as a Georgia cracker in a Broadway musical called "Three Wishes for Jamie." When Reinhardt temporarily dropped his activities as a producer and became a full-time director, Albert Band was reassigned from his job as Reinhardt's assistant to a job as assistant to a producer named Armand Deutsch, with whom he set to work on a movie called "The Girl Who Had Everything." Deutsch was so impressed by Band's abilities that he petitioned Dore Schary for a raise for him, and it was granted.

Reinhardt devoted himself to directing a movie trilogy entitled "The Story of Three Loves," on which Lee Katz, unit production manager for "The Red Badge of Courage," was again unit production manager. Reinhardt had finished one part of the trilogy, starring James Mason and Moira Shearer, and he wrote me that Schary and all the other executives at the studio loved it. "I have to admit it myself; it's really pretty good," he said. A stray kitten turned up at the Reinhardts' house and was adopted as a playmate for

Mocha. It was christened Lee Katz. Mrs. Reinhardt was working very hard, too. She was preparing to move. Reinhardt had decided that he might be in Hollywood to stay, after all, and this time, instead of renting a house, as he had always done before, he had bought one. The new house had a large garden and a swimming pool, and although he felt a bit more tied down, he told me, it was really terrific, and that was why he had finally, after eighteen years with M-G-M, bought a house.

The total cost of making "The Red Badge of Courage"—Production No. 1512—turned out to be $1,642,017.33. The picture received only slight attention in Nicholas M. Schenck's annual report to the stockholders of Loew's, Inc., for the fiscal year ending August 31, 1951. In this document, the cost of producing and releasing the movie was merely included in the $26,243,848.61 item "Film Productions Completed—Not Released." (The report also showed that the net income of Loew's, Inc., for the year was $7,806,571.83, that dividends of $1.50 a share were paid on the 5,142,579 shares of stock outstanding, and that Loew's directors and officers were paid $2,789,079, of which $277,764 was paid to Schenck and $300,000 to Mayer.) At the annual stockholders' meeting, however, the movie was mentioned by several of the stockholders, as well as by the chairman of the meeting, J. Robert Rubin, a tall, gaunt man with pince-nez and a quiet, gracious manner, who is a vice-president of Loew's and counsel for the firm. (Mr. Rubin's compensation for 1951, according to the report, was $224,439.) The meeting began at ten o'clock on the morning of April 29, 1952, in a projection room on the eighteenth floor of the Loew's State Theatre Building, at 1540 Broadway, at Forty-fifth Street. It was attended by a hundred and fifty stockholders (out of a total of 37,991), who represented three hundred thousand shares of stock. (Four million shares of stock were represented by the management, as holders of proxies for that number.) The first mention of "The Red Badge of Courage" was made by the chairman, during one of his attempts to entertain the stockholders while ballots for the election of a board of directors were being passed out. He took a slip of paper out of his pocket, and, reading from it, informed the stockholders that Esther Williams, who is under contract to M-G-M, had recently been voted one of the year's most popular stars by the magazine *Modern Screen*. Then he took out another slip of paper and read, in a drone, "Ladies and gentlemen, I'd like to call your attention to the fact that M-G-M pictures have received great honors. Each month, *Coronet* magazine chooses three favorite pictures to recommend, and during the past twelve months we have had ten of our pictures chosen for recommendation by *Coronet* magazine. I'm sure you'll agree that that is a pretty fine record." Rubin raised his eyes and, removing his pince-nez, gazed at the stockholders. Their attention seemed to be fixed on their ballots. He cleared his throat, put his pince-nez back on, and read off the names of the ten pictures. "The Red Badge of Courage" was one of them.

A stockholder named Greenstock stood up and asked whether "The Red Badge of Courage" had made money.

"No, 'The Red Badge of Courage' did not make any money," Rubin said.

"Why didn't 'The Red Badge of Courage' make any money?" Greenstock asked.

"Well, it was a beautiful picture, but that wasn't enough," Rubin said. "It didn't come to a climax, the way a picture is supposed to do. The picture didn't appeal to the public. Mr. Schary was very keen about the picture. It played here in a special house and everything, and the *Times* put it in as one of the best pictures of the year. But the public didn't go for it." Rubin removed his pince-nez.

"I want to say something," a stockholder named Mrs. Wentig remarked. "In reference to 'The Red Badge of Courage,' I want to say of course we're interested in dividends, in profits, but it's a tribute to the company that they had the courage to put out a picture that did not make money."

Rubin gave her a gracious nod. "It was good for our prestige," he said.

"It set good standards for the movie industry," Mrs. Wentig said, raising her voice. "I say do more of it, and I'm glad you made the picture even if it didn't make money. Make more movies like that!"

"Well, thank you," said Rubin, looking dismayed.

At the conclusion of the meeting, the stockholders were shown "Singin' in the Rain," a new Arthur Freed musical, and then they descended to the restaurant, in the basement, for the company's annual free lunch. Rubin moved among the stockholders, giving each one a kindly nod. He escorted an elderly, gray-haired lady to a chair and brought her a tongue sandwich. "It's very good," he said. "I could eat one myself. Did you like the meeting?"

"Where is Mr. Schenck?" the lady asked. "Why doesn't he come to the meeting?"

"He leaves this sort of thing to us," Rubin said. "You don't want him to neglect important and pressing business matters, do you?"

"Not if he's fixing to increase our dividends," said the lady.

At a nearby table, Charles C. Moskowitz, vice-president and treasurer of Loew's, Inc. (his compensation was $188,176 for the year), was talking with Eugene W. Leake, chairman of the Retirement Plan Committee of Loew's. Moskowitz is a bald, chunky man with a gray mustache, who wears glasses with heavy tortoiseshell rims, and usually has a white carnation in his lapel. He handed Leake a cigar. "Smoke a good one, Judge," he said.

Leake, a white-haired man with a small head and a pink face, put down a half-smoked cigar and lit the good one.

"The meeting went all right, Judge," said Moskowitz. "The only thing they're worried about is 'The Red Badge of Courage.' They've got worries."

"Heh-heh-heh," said Leake.

"Moskowitz!" a stockholder called. "When are we going to hear about the profits from our foreign interests?"

"Forget it, Judge," Moskowitz said, waving his cigar at the stockholder.

Leake laughed.

"My gosh, I just realized!" Moskowitz said to Leake. "I haven't seen a picture since yesterday. Can you imagine that, Judge?"

"It's not easy to imagine," said Leake.

"I try to see every picture that's made. If not at the office, then at home," Moskowitz said. "I know every picture that's being made at the studio in Culver City at this very minute. Isn't that right, Judge?"

"That's right," said Leake.

"I can tell you who is directing every one of our pictures at this very minute, who is producing, and the names of the leading characters," Moskowitz said. "Mr. Schenck can do the same, only more so. I had Eddie Mannix on the phone last night for an hour. Today, I'll talk to Dore Schary. I know the business inside out. I've worked for Loew's forty years. I started as a bookkeeper. I thought the work was going to be steady, Judge." He beamed at Leake.

Leake laughed again.

"I worked for Nick Schenck when he was spending days and nights going from theatre to theatre doing everything himself, even being the cashier in the box office—in the days when our theatres had vaudeville," Moskowitz went on. "There's not a man in the business who's more respected for his capabilities than Mr. Schenck. Put him in a room where *anything* is being talked about and he'll learn it. There's no branch of this business he doesn't know."

"He keeps tabs on every little thing," Leake said. "The minute a picture is released, there he is on the telephone, the reviews in his hand."

"Brilliant!" said Moskowitz. "The minute he sees a picture, he knows whether it will go. Brilliant!"

Almost two years before, I had become interested in "The Red Badge of Courage," and I had been following its progress step by step ever since, to learn what I could about the American motion-picture industry. Now, three thousand miles from Hollywood, in an office building at Forty-fifth and Broadway, I began to feel that I was getting closer than I ever had before to the heart of the matter. Reinhardt's and Huston's struggle to make a great picture,

Mayer's opposition, Schary's support, the sideline operations of a dozen vice-presidents, the labor and craftsmanship of the cast and technical crew, the efforts of Huston's aides to help him get his concept of the Stephen Crane novel on film, the long series of artistic problems and compromises, the reactions of the preview audiences—all these seemed to compose themselves into some sort of design, but a few pieces were still missing. I felt that somewhere in the offices upstairs I might find them.

The accounting and executive offices of Loew's are on the seventh floor. Moskowitz had two ways he used for getting to his private office—a carpeted corridor leading directly to it, and a roundabout route through a vast, pillared room. After lunch, Moskowitz took Leake and me through the big room. It contained a hundred and twenty-five desks, many of them occupied by clerks or accountants operating machines to tabulate admissions at Loew's theatres and returns on Loew's pictures. To make himself heard, Moskowitz had to raise his voice.

"Looks like we're still in business. Right, Judge?" he said to Leake.

"Heh-heh-heh," said Leake. "Looks that way, all right."

Moskowitz waved his cigar in greeting to the backs of the clerks and accountants, and walked on.

The walls of Moskowitz's outer office were covered with photographs of M-G-M stars, all of them autographed ("To Charles Moskowitz, from a very devoted member of the M-G-M family. My best wishes—Robert Taylor." "To Charles Moskowitz—I sincerely hope I shall be able to repay in the future the faith you have in me today. Gratefully, Mario Lanza"). There were photographs of Lionel Barrymore, Walter Pidgeon, Van Johnson, Gene Kelly, Esther Williams, and Lassie (this one autographed with a paw print). There was also a photograph of Dore Schary ("For Charlie, with my fond good wishes, Dore").

Moskowitz looked at the pictures proudly and told Leake that he'd be seeing all the stars in a few weeks, at the studio. "Mr. Schenck is going out to see things at first hand," he said. "And where Mr. Schenck goes, Moskowitz goes close behind."

. . .

Four floors below, I found Howard Dietz, advertising-and-exploitation head of Loew's, who told me there was no point in throwing good money after bad to promote a picture that was clearly a bust. "Schenck thinks the picture is doomed to be a box-office failure," he said. "As a commercial property, it's no good. The country isn't interested in the picture. It turned it down. I didn't like the picture. Schenck wasn't enthusiastic. But that isn't the point. Anything that makes money we're for." He smiled wearily, looking as bored as he had looked when he sat in the bar of the Beverly Hills Hotel, a year and a half before, listening to Reinhardt's plea for a good promotion campaign for "The Red Badge of Courage." "The phony talk I've had to listen to about this picture!" he said. " 'It's a classic.' 'Art.' Nonsense. A novel is a novel. A poem is a poem. And a movie is a movie. Take the Wordsworth poem 'I wandered lonely as a cloud' and make a movie about it. What can you show visually? 'I wandered lonely as a cloud That floats on high o'er vales and hills When all at once I saw a crowd, A host of golden daffodils.' We might have a cloud, some vales and hills, and then a batch of daffodils." He laughed. "You can't do it. What stops you is the equity that goes with the classic. It's borrowed imagination. You know, I'm not of the school that believes that popular entertainment need be art. And neither is Schenck. He's a showman. That's our business."

A few doors down, I found Si Seadler, Loew's Eastern advertising manager, in his office working on plans to escort a hundred motion-picture-theatre exhibitors from all over the country on a three-day visit to the studio to see all the M-G-M movies awaiting release. (A few days later, the trade papers carried a reprint of a message from Dore Schary to the exhibitors. "We believe that the sunshine of showmanship can dispel gray clouds of pessimism," he wrote in the course of offering a hearty hello on behalf of Mr. Nicholas Schenck, the executive staff, and the five thousand employees of M-G-M.) Seadler's telephone kept ringing, and his look of worried amiability increased as he alternated between the phone and giving instructions to a young man whose face reflected Seadler's worry but not his amiability.

"I've got a mob of people all asking whether 'Seeing Is Believing' is the official name of the junket and how much it's all gonna cost," the young man said.

" 'Seeing Is Believing' is official, but check with Howard Dietz —it's Howard's idea," Seadler said. "The cost is a hundred thousand dollars. Be sure to tell everybody we think it's worth it. It's Howard's idea."

The telephone rang. "The minute you called me, I took care of it," he said. "You're as big as Charlie. Bigger. Don't worry." He hung up. "From the Coast," he told me, with distaste. "Everybody fighting with everybody. Human beings in conflict. That's the way it is with creative people. Thank God this is a business office. Any problem or conflict comes up here, Mr. Schenck says, 'My boy—' and gives us the word." Seadler waved his hand. "No more conflict."

"I like the way he calls everybody 'My boy,' " said the young man.

"A great executive," said Seadler.

"Will Mr. Schenck get out to the studio in time to play host to the exhibitors?" the young man asked.

Seadler shook his head. "Dore Schary will do it," he said. "Mr. Schenck is the president. Dore works for him."

Seadler told me he had given Schenck his opinion of "The Red Badge of Courage" before it was released, as he had promised Reinhardt he would a year and a half before, when he saw some scenes from the then unfinished film. "Mr. Schenck saw the picture, and he knew right away it wouldn't go over with the public, and I agreed with him," he said. "It doesn't pay to be so faithful to a book, the way John Huston did it. As a great novel, 'The Red Badge of Courage' is a great novel. As a movie, it's too fragmentary. There's no story. The country wasn't interested in the picture, as Howard says. A novel is a novel, as Howard says, and a movie is a movie. The picture was beautiful, but it was just a vignette. As soon as Mr. Schenck saw the picture, we knew it was a flop. Let's just say it was a flop *d'estime.* I guess that's the way Mr. Schenck would put it."

On the tenth floor, Arthur M. Loew, president of Loew's International Corporation, which is a subsidiary of Loew's, Inc., chatted with me about what he called the pattern of economics of the industry. His office had recently been redecorated, along with all the other offices on the floor, in a style that included streamlined potted plants, African sculpture, desks that were jagged boards attached to walls, and an air-conditioning system that distributed a chemical to prevent people from catching cold. Loew, the son of Marcus Loew, one of the founders of the company, is a wiry, restless man in his early fifties; in addition to supervising the international distribution of pictures owned by Loew's, Inc., he has supervised the production of one movie, "The Search," and personally produced another, "Teresa," both of which made out very well with movie critics and movie audiences. He started in foreign distribution in 1920, and he is in charge of a hundred and thirty sales offices, in thirty-eight countries. Every day, he checks on the receipts of forty theatres owned and operated by Loew's outside the United States and Canada. (A Supreme Court decision twenty-three months earlier had upheld a lower court's order for the divorcement of motion-picture production from motion-picture exhibition, and Loew's, like other picture corporations, was now working out the separation.) As Loew talked, he played with a button that controlled a sliding cork wall at one end of his office.

"We have a pretty definite knowledge in this office of what the public wants, and we know one thing—pictures that are liked in this country are liked abroad," Loew said. "We operate in a pattern of economics brought on by public taste." He pushed the button, and the cork wall slowly receded. "The mechanism operating that wall costs only three hundred and seventy-five dollars," Loew said as the adjoining room came into view. It had a modernistic conference table rimmed by modernistic chairs. "That's where we confer about foreign sales," he said.

Internationally, he added, "The Red Badge of Courage" had not done well at the box office, and, here and there, Loew's was trying to book it as the lower half of a double bill that featured a musical starring Esther Williams, M-G-M's biggest money-making star. At the moment, "The Red Badge of Courage" was playing as the lower half of such a bill in nine theatres in Australia. "It's a problem picture," Loew said. "It gets poor public response. Nothing glamorous always hurts a picture. In England, we put the picture in a theatre in London where it played only on Sunday afternoons. The critics saw it and liked it, so we've put it in a small house for the regular run. But it's not making any money. No point in wasting promotion on a picture that won't go." Loew pushed the button, and the cork wall slid back into place.

"Nick Schenck was afraid of 'The Red Badge of Courage,' " Loew went on. "In the beginning, when Dore joined the company —I was glad to see him get the job—Schenck gave him free rein. He even let Dore make a few pictures Schenck really didn't want to make. But now Schenck is pulling back on the reins."

On the sixth floor of the Loew Building, J. Robert Rubin, sitting at his desk, was looking over the papers neatly stacked on it. It was a long, dark desk in a long, businesslike room that had on the walls autographed photographs of half a dozen prominent Republicans, dead and alive. "I didn't imagine there would be any controversy about a movie at the meeting," he said to me softly. "All they usually want to know about is dividends. Well, this is the one day of the year when we like to make the stockholders feel the company is theirs. It's better to have them friendly than unfriendly. My, hasn't 'The Red Badge of Courage' created a fuss, though! Mr. Mayer was against making it to begin with, but Mr. Schary was very keen about it. Funny thing is Mr. Schary still likes the picture, even if it didn't make any money." He gave a thin laugh. "Can't have much of that sort of thing," he said. "We're not in business for our health. We're a business. Just think of our board of directors! There's not only Mr. Schenck, Mr. Moskowitz, Mr. Leake, and myself but Mr. George A. Brownell, Mr. F. Joseph Holleran, Mr. William A. Parker, Mr. William F. Rodgers, Mr. Joseph R. Vogel, and Mr. Henry Rogers Winthrop. We have to make money or we go out of business."

Rubin, who is a native of Syracuse, and a graduate of the Syracuse University law school, had been in the motion-picture business since 1915. He had helped a friend organize a picture company called New York Alco, and when the company failed, after a year, a new company, called Metro Pictures Corporation, was founded in its place, with Louis B. Mayer as one of the owners. Loew's bought out Metro in 1920. In 1918, Rubin and Mayer had founded the Louis B. Mayer Pictures Corporation and made movies for Metro. Irving Thalberg joined them about two years later. Rubin handled many of the legal entanglements involved in the transactions, including the purchase by Metro, in 1924, of the Goldwyn studio, in Culver City, and, that same year, the purchase of the Louis B. Mayer Pictures Corporation by Metro-Goldwyn.

"Mr. Mayer, Mr. Thalberg, and I made quite a trio," Rubin said. "Thalberg was a genius. He had a conception of pictures no one has been able to duplicate. Mr. Mayer built up the studio to what we have today. He knew how to build an organization, and how to run it. It was always exciting to work with him. He was dynamic. He would dramatize everything. I used to say, 'Louie, you're the best actor on the lot.' He'd say, 'I only show what I feel.' Mr. Mayer always liked good pictures. Clean pictures. I don't care too much what kind of pictures we make. When a picture is liked in this office, it is liked everywhere. What Mr. Schenck is in favor of, we are for. All of us here like the kind of pictures that do well at the box office."

A dictograph in Rubin's half-open desk drawer clicked.

"You trying to get me?" Rubin said into the machine.

"Come into my office. I want to show you some reviews," the voice from the drawer said.

"Right away," said Rubin. "I'm with Mr. Schenck," he said to his secretary.

As I arrived in Nicholas M. Schenck's office, a little later, he was talking with Howard Dietz about the reviews of the new M-G-M Technicolor movie "Scaramouche," which had just opened at the Music Hall. "I would have bet a hundred to one that 'Scaramouche' would get the finest notices," Schenck said. "I can't understand it. It opens at the Music Hall, and Mr. Tribune knocks it. Three stars in the *News*. I would have given odds it would get four stars."

"There are no rules in this business," Dietz said flatly.

"I still think that 'Scaramouche' is a very good picture, my boy," Schenck said seriously, and he raised his right index finger at Dietz in a gesture of kindly warning. "And I think the audiences will think so, too."

Schenck spoke decisively, confidently, and with a strong air of knowledgeability about his business. He is a compactly built, energetic man in his late sixties, with graying hair brushed back and parted on the left. He has a quietly direct manner and a benevolent air. The day I saw him, he was deeply tanned, and he was wearing a double-breasted gray suit, a white shirt with blue stripes, a small-figured dark-blue necktie, and tortoise-shell glasses. He sat behind a large, highly polished mahogany desk, on which were framed photographs of his three daughters as children, all with long curls; a carafe and two glasses; an ashtray; a brown leather folder; and four yellow pencils with sharp points. At his feet was a brass spittoon. His office was small and modest. It had a green carpet; a fireplace, on the mantel of which stood a black iron statuette of the M-G-M lion; a couch covered with brown fabric; four worn chairs; and Italian walnut panelling. The panels had been bought from the mansion of Senator William A. Clark, on Fifth Avenue. Schenck had gone to work for Loew's in 1907, and he had been in the same office for thirty years. When he shifted from executive vice-president to president of Loew's, after the death of Marcus Loew, in 1927, he refused to leave the office.

Schenck lit a cigarette and cocked his head slightly at Dietz, who took a cigarette, too. "I like 'Scaramouche,'" Schenck said. "I like entertainment. Clean, wholesome entertainment. Romance and love. I love dramatic, romantic stories. But I can't go only by my own taste. I don't like slapstick. Audiences like slapstick. What are you going to do? The audience is the final judge."

"I wish I knew who first said that popular entertainment had to be art," Dietz said blandly.

Schenck shrugged. He had been working hard, he said, study-

ing the budgets of various pictures, considering their casting problems, and seeing, on an average, four films during the week and
three over the weekend at his home in Sands Point. "You have
to see other people's pictures as well as your own," he said. "Any
picture that becomes good or important, I see it. You have to
know about everybody's taste. Everybody must work and we all
have a job to do."

"It's no secret around here that you work hard," Dietz said.

Schenck smiled broadly and, unbuttoning his coat, patted his
ribs. "I weigh a hundred and forty-one in the morning, a hundred and forty-three at night," he said.

"I don't know whether it's your work or your golf that does it,"
Dietz said.

Schenck's smile broadened, and he buttoned his coat. "You're
right, my boy, there are no rules," he said, raising his right hand
again. "It all comes from the brain. You can't get into the other
fellow's brain. You decide what pictures will be made. You decide
who will be in the cast. You decide what it will cost. The budget
means a lot to me. Unfortunately, stories don't grow on trees, so
you have to compromise on what you are going to make. You
can't take too many chances where you are paying terrific overhead and terrific weekly salaries."

"There are no rules for choosing what you're going to make,"
Dietz said. "You know what to choose only by growing up in the
fabric of the business."

Schenck said that he did not read the scripts of all the movies
M-G-M was planning to make, but he did read an outline of each
script or idea for a script. When he read the outline for "The Red
Badge of Courage," he said, he felt that the studio was taking a
big chance. At the time, Schary was in New York, and was not
feeling well. "I went right over to Dore's hotel to talk to him," he
said. "Dore had been having differences with Louie about the picture. They had not been getting along too well before that, even.
I found Dore sick, and sicker over the trouble with Louie. Right
from the hotel, I called Louie, and had him talk to Dore. I arranged for Dore and Louie to talk it over when Dore got back
home. But Louie remained opposed to making the picture, and on

other things he wasn't seeing eye to eye with me. Eventually, I had to support Dore."

Schenck lit another cigarette. "Dore is young," he said. "He has not had his job very long. I felt I must encourage him or else he would feel stifled. It would have been so easy for me to say no to him. Instead, I said yes. I figured I would write it off to experience. You can buy almost anything, but you can't buy experience." He smiled in a wise, fatherly manner.

" 'The Red Badge of Courage' was not a whole motion picture," Dietz said. "It was a fragment. It wasn't a good picture."

"Before I saw it, I had heard it was very bad," Schenck said. "But it was better than I had been led to expect. I would call it a fairly good picture. Only, it was above the heads of our audiences. For me, it was good entertainment. But not for our audiences. I felt immediately we would have to take a loss on it, and we have. When I saw the picture was not doing any business, we stopped spending money on promoting it."

"Yes, I decided that," Dietz said to Schenck. "You know, I don't always have to go to you about what money I'm going to spend. We tried a concentrated campaign on the picture in a couple of spots and it didn't go."

"The public didn't take to the picture," Schenck said. "The next picture John Huston made—and this time he was making it for his own company—he made a commercial picture, a tremendous hit."

"Don't forget he made the picture with stars," said Dietz.

"The best performances I have ever seen them give," said Schenck.

" 'Red Badge' had no stars and no story," said Dietz. "It wasn't any good."

"They did the best they could with it," said Schenck. "Unfortunately, that sort of thing costs money. If you don't spend money, you never learn." He laughed knowingly. "After the picture was made, Louie didn't want to release it," he said. "Louie said that as long as he was head of the studio, the picture would never be released. He refused to release it, but I changed that."

Schenck puffed quickly on his cigarette. "How else was I going to teach Dore?" he said. "I supported Dore. I let him make the picture. I knew that the best way to help him was to let him make a mistake. Now he will know better. A young man has to learn by making mistakes. I don't think he'll want to make a picture like that again." Schenck picked up one of his yellow pencils and jotted something down on a memo pad. Then he buzzed for his secretary and asked her to get Mr. Schary on the telephone at Culver City. After a couple of minutes, he picked up the phone and said, "Hello, my boy. How are you doing?"

—1952